A GENEALOGY

OF THE

Leavenworth Family

IN THE

UNITED STATES,

WITH

Historical Introduction, Etc.,

BY

ELIAS WARNER LEAVENWORTH, L. L. D.,

OF

SYRACUSE, N. Y.

BEING A REVISION AND EXTENSION OF THE GENEALOGICAL TREE COMPILED BY WILLIAM AND ELIAS W. LEAVENWORTH, THEN OF GREAT BARRINGTON, MASS., IN 1827.

"One generation passeth away, and another generation cometh; but the earth abideth forever."

"Honor thy father and thy mother, that thy days may be long upon the land which the LORD thy God giveth thee."

SYRACUSE, N. Y.:
S. G. HITCHCOCK & CO., 4 WEST FAYETTE STREET,
1873.

PREFACE.

HOW THIS BOOK CAME TO BE WRITTEN, AND ITS HISTORY.

Fifty years since—in the fall of 1823, Gideon Leavenworth, the son of Thomas, and great grand son of Thomas, of Woodbury, the common progenitor, probably, of all the Leavenworths on this continent, made a visit at the residence of his nephew, Dr. David Leavenworth, in the village of Great Barrington, Mass. Gideon L. was then residing at New Marlborough, Mass., and the author was at home from College, spending his fall vacation. I had never before had the pleasure to meet him. It was soon apparent that the old gentleman was an intelligent, kind hearted and genial person, and quite fully informed in regard to the various members of the family. Indeed his tastes ran very strongly in that direction, and before the expiration of his visit, the author and his brother, the late William L., of Allentown, New Jersey. had obtained from him a very general genealogy of the family, beginning with his grand father, Dr. Thomas, or as he was indifferently called, Deacon Thomas, of Stratford, Ripton Parish, Connecticut, (now town of Huntington,) and extending down to the time of such visit. And in those cases where his knowledge was defective, he furnished the addresses of members of the family, who could supply the deficiencies. The stock of information thus obtained was subsequently somewhat enlarged and perfected by correspondence with various members of the family—which at that time was mainly confined to the States of Connecticut, Massachusetts, Vermont and New York. This work was principally done previous to the year 1828, but was allowed to remain unimproved until the year 1840. In that year it was embodied in the form of a Genealogical Tree. The brother of the author caused it to be lithographed, and some fifty impressions, more or less, were struck from the plate, when, unfortunately, it was broken and rendered useless. The few copies thus obtained were given away to the members of the family who had most interested themselves in procuring the facts which were embraced in them, and the whole of them were soon disposed of.

The information contained in this Tree was obtained entirely from the said

Gideon, and from the correspondence with other members of the family. There was no examination of Grave Stones, none of Church, Town, Probate or other records. It was such a work as two young men—the one in College, and the other engaged in mercantile and manufacturing business—might be expected to produce in their leisure hours. And yet it embraced nearly all the male members of the family down to the last generation of that day.

The Tree contained some serious errors, but more omissions. Gideon supposed his grandfather, Thomas, to have been one of three original immigrants, who came over about 1690, Thomas, Edmund and David, whereas, Thomas, of Woodbury, and his wife Grace, and his brother John, were the original immigrants; they possibly brought with them the two sons of Thomas, Thomas and John, though it is more probable that they were born here. But there is one gross error in the Tree which cannot be charged to Gideon. It is the making of Edmund, instead of Dr. Thomas, the grand father of Gideon, for, as Gideon was born some years previous to the death of his grand father, Dr. Thomas, and in his early life lived in Woodbury and Waterbury, he must have been well informed in regard to him. This was doubtless an error of our own, in writing down the facts or in copying them. He was also mistaken in regard to the time of the immigration to this country, which he supposed to have been about 1690, but which was probably after 1664, and certainly some years before 1683, in which year Thomas, of Woodbury, our first common ancestor, died. There were also other minor errors and omissions.

A desire to correct the errors of said Tree, to supply its deficiencies, and to bring the genealogy of the entire family down to more recent times, often flitted through my mind, and seemed, in advance, to involve the expenditure of but little labor and time. But the pressure of a multitude of public and private duties, ever devolving upon me, deferred the undertaking until the year 1864; when, not doubting that I had before me the labor of a few months, or perhaps, of a year, I embarked in this ten year enterprise.

After writing a large number of letters, and ascertaining many new and important facts, finding the work growing on my hands and far from being finished, and my time yearly more and more engrossed by other duties, I caused a circular to be printed in the year 1865, a copy of which will be found in the Appendix, marked, Letter A. Many hundreds of these were issued during the next five years, and yet the work was not complete. New families were discovered yearly, and the facts in relation to the old families were by no means exhausted.

Finding my work so far from its completion, so much labor still remaining to be done; finding so many neglecting even to answer my letters, so many others answering only to promise for the future, then never performing; finding others destitute of all family pride and interest in the subject, and others still, quite impatient because the work was so long delayed, and having made great progress in the work and obtained some interesting facts in regard to the family, I caused another circular to be printed in the year 1870, and have been issuing it constantly, from that time to the present. This was written to endeavor to awaken a deeper interest in the family generally, and to encourage those who were impatient at the long delay, and to communicate some facts to those who took an interest in my undertaking. A copy of this circular will also be found in the Appendix, Letter B.

The work is now far from being complete. It never can be made *perfect* by any amount of time, labor or expense. Very many facts are gone beyond recovery, buried with the years before the flood ; other facts can only be had by personal visitation, and perhaps not even then, and others still by an examination of Church, Town, County and Probate records, and the head stones and monuments of our ancestors. All of this has been largely done, and the genealogy and general history of the family is, perhaps, as nearly complete as is usual in similar works, or at least, as could be hoped for from one whose labors never end, and whose time is always too short for his duties.

Unfortunately the Parish records of the Congregational Church in Ripton, (of which the second Thomas was a deacon and one of the founders,) during the long ministry of its first pastor, Mr. Mills, are lost and nothing remains prior to 1773, except a few scattered entries of names of orignal members of the church, and some notes of church and society meetings. This I learn from the Rev. B. L. Swan, late of Stratford.

This would, beyond doubt, have furnished a large number of interesting facts, now forever lost, unless it may yet be found in the hands of some of his descendants.

But there are many isolated facts which might yet be gathered up, and no doubt there are many errors, which will be discovered, in branches of the family where I have depended entirely upon the information of others, and perhaps other errors. These errors always exist and always will in works of this kind. They arise from a very great variety of causes, largely from defects of memory and information, from mistakes in the original entries where the facts are preserved, from mistakes in copying such entries, and more often still from the impossibility of correctly reading many words, and far more, figures. Hundreds of such have been corrected and yet many more will no doubt be still found. But is it too much to hope, that in long years to come, when all of us who are now upon the stage shall have been summoned home by our Heavenly Father, the leisure, the industry, the perseverance and care of some future scion of the blood, will revise this imperfect work, correct all its errors, enlarge its bounds, perfect its plan, and enlighten other generations yet unborn with a more perfect history of the pious and worthy ancestors from whom they have descended ?

This work can possess very little interest for any persons except the descendants of our common progenitors ; and it is for them that I have particularly designed it. It embraces all that I know or have been able to learn of the family. It contains, perhaps, more of biography than genealogies usually do, but far, *far* less than it would have done had it been in my power to obtain the necessary statistics of our ancestors, or had my own knowledge enabled me to write them. For, as the book has been written mainly for the members of the family, I think it highly desirable that they should be made as fully acquainted as possible with their ancestors and one another. But unfortunately my own acquaintance with the members of the family extends but slightly beyond my own immediate relatives—my uncles and my cousins, and I have no *personal* acquaintance with a dozen families beyond that narrow circle. Having spent all the active part of my life in Central New York, far from the homes of the great body of the family, and having known little of leisure at any period, I have had no time or opportunity to cultivate the acquaintance of its various members; nor have I, during the ten years in which I have been engaged on the work, been able to make but few visits for the purpose of gleaning new facts and extending my acquaintance.

Not doubting, however, that during the fifty years in which I have given more or less attention to the genealogy of the family, I have become possessed of more information in regard to it than is possessed by any other one of its name, I have felt it to be a duty which I owed its members, to embody, arrange, impart and preserve this knowledge and information. I have been far more solicitous in regard to the preservation of the facts, than in regard to the phraseology in which they are clothed. It will, I trust, be borne in mind that the work has been written and arranged only in the fragments of time which could be obtained while all the time occupying various positions of grave responsibility, and involving labor and care abundantly sufficient for the most robust health, and the most untiring industry. I think I have never devoted an entire day to the work except when sometimes I could sieze upon a passing holiday, or at others, as now, find a day or two when too unwell for business, but able to sit in my room at home and write. I trust, therefore, that my readers will not look for classical elegance, nor criticise too closely the phraseology made use of or the order in which the facts in regard to each member of the family may be found. No *very* uniform arrangement will be discovered. While commencing the work with a systematic plan, I have very often been compelled to depart from it in consequence of obtaining new facts year after year relating to the same person, and inserting them out of their regular order. In very many instances when the facts have become complicated and perhaps confused, I have re-written the entire sketch of a member; but more frequently, for want of time, I have inserted the additional facts in such order only as was most convenient.

Without further explanation or apology, I commit the work into the hands of those for whom it was written. I regret its imperfections, and I am, without doubt, far more conscious of them than any of those who may hereafter look at them with a critical eye. Whoever shall in the future undertake to correct them, publishing another edition, and bringing the genealogy down to his time, will be the most ready to excuse all and every omission and other imperfection.

I regret that I have been unable to obtain engravings of some of the prominent members of the family, and particularly of the older members, now in their graves; but in their day, photography was unknown, and portrait painting in the country, almost equally so. Their features are lost in their graves, and their memories are fast passing into forgetfulness, feebly preserved to a slight extent by this labor of love and duty.

But if this work shall be the means of diffusing among the different branches of the family a more perfect knowledge of their kindred, if it shall acquaint them more perfectly with the virtues of their ancestors, and more particularly if it shall stimulate the young men of the present generation and those who are to follow them, to imitate their good examples and to strive for still higher attainments in learning, virtue, and goodness, I shall be satisfied with my labors, be compensated for the time spent in them, and feel an increased pleasure and pride in being the member of a family which has borne itself honorably during the two hundred years of its existence this side of the Atlantic, and which has done and is still doing something for its own honor and for the good of the world.

The history of Woodbury, by Wm. Cothren, Esq., now in two volumes, and the history of Waterbury by Dr. Henry Bronson, which are model works of the kind, have been of much service to me, and I have not hesitated to draw upon them for any facts and sketches which would give interest to this volume ; and to those of my readers who do not already possess them, I take pleasure in recommending them as worthy of their perusal, and of a permanent place in their libraries.

But I must not forget before taking leave of the reader, to return my most sincere thanks to all those persons, both gentlemen and ladies, who have aided me in this protracted and almost interminable labor. They are especially due to the Hon. Green Kendrick, and the Hon. F. J. Kingsbury, of Waterbury, to the Hon. Truman Smith, of Stamford, and the Rev. B. W. Swan, late of Stratford, who kindly furnished me with all that appears relating to the family on the parish and town records of Stratford, and the probate records at Fairfield down to 1759. To Mr. Kingsbury I am particularly indebted for sketches of various members of the family which are acknowledged in the body of the work.

I am also greatly indebted to Wm. Cothren, Esq., of Woodbury, who has just now finished the second volume of his invaluable and most elaborate history of that town, for a very careful and exhaustive examinaton of the town records of Woodbury down to 1729 ; of the probate records of Woodbury district from its organization in 1719 till the year 1871 ; of the grave yards at Bantam, in Litchfield and the old yard near "Ruccum" in Roxbury, and the new grave yard there ; the north burial ground in Woodbury, and of those at Ripton and the White Mills in the town Huntington, and for all the valuable facts which could be derived from them.

John H. Leavenworth, Esq., of Roxbury, Dr. D. C. Leavenworth, of New Haven, Lorenzo W. Leavenworth, Esq., of Bridgeport, and Eli Leavenworth, Esq., of Stepney, have obliged me greatly by their contributions ; and I am also under special obligations to Charles J. Hoadley, Esq., Librarian of the

State Library at Hartford, for his kind and prompt attention to every request for information.

I have also received material aid from Miss Mary Ann Leavenworth of Westport, the late Mrs. Green Kendrick, of Waterbury, the late Mrs. Pierre Mundry, of Bridgeport, daughter of LeGrand Leavenworth, Mrs. Eliza A. Wheeler, of Southford, daughter of Calvin Leavenworth, and especially from Mrs. Jane R. Shelton, of Huntington, who has been indefatigable in searching out every kind of information in relation to the family, and particularly relating to her great grand father, Edmund Leavenworth, the son of Deacon Thomas, of Ripton, and in relation to his descendants.

All the parties above referred to, reside in the State of Connecticut.

I have also received material aid from Mrs. Robert L. Wilson, of Hinesburgh, Vt., daughter of the late General Nathan Leavenworth, of that town, and from Henry Clay Leavenworth, of Charlotte, Vt., and especially from Abel Edwin Leavenworth, of New Haven, Vt., formerly of Hinesburgh, and from the Hon. George C. Cahoon, of Wheelock, in the same State.

Many thanks are due to Treat M. Leavenworth, of Galway, N. Y., and to his son Edwin, of Amsterdam, and not less to the late Ebenezer Leavenworth, Gloversville, Mrs. Charlotte L. Brown, of Honeoye Falls, daughter of the late John Peck Leavenworth, of Rush, N. Y., to Horace Leavenworth, of East Genoa, N. Y., and to Mrs. Mary Boughton, of Nassau, N. Y., daughter of David Leavenworth, deceased, of that place,

The late Hon. Zebulon Leavenworth, of Leavenworth, Ind., Ebenezer Leavenworth, of Dongola, Ill., the late John W. Leavenworth, of St. Louis, Mo., and his brother Mark, late of the same city, Mrs. Sally M. Langdon, of Solon, Iowa, daughter of Jehiel Leavenworth, Isaac H. Leavenworth, of East Saginaw, Michigan, and particularly Edmund Leavenworth, of Ann Arbor, in the same State, Alson E. Leavenworth, of Chicago, and his mother Sally Leavenworth, widow of the late Judge Alson Leavenworth, of Cattaraugus, Cattaraugus County, N. Y., the late Rev. Abner J. Leavenworth, of Petersburgh, Va., and the Hon. Mark Leavenworth, of San Jose, Cal., have all kindly assisted me in various ways during my protracted labors.

To the multitude of others who have furnished me with the facts in regard to their own families, who are too numerous to be mentioned here, I feel my obligations and I return my thanks ; and to each and all of the above I would say, that I both hope and expect that when the work shall finally reach their hands, they will find it a satisfactory return for all their labor and kindness, even with all its errors and other imperfections.

Thankful to a kind Providence which has permitted me to reach the end of these labors—thankful that He has spared my life till it has now reached its seventieth year—that he has given me health and strength for the last ten years to devote to this interesting object—thankful for the extensive acquaintance which I have been enabled, mostly however, by correspondence, to make with so many of my relations scattered over the union, and warned by impaired health and the flight of years, of the approaching close of the specified period allotted to man, I bring my imperfect labor to a final end, with many thanks for your kind attention to my numerous and often my persistent requests, and with the kindest wishes for your welfare both in the world that now is and in that which shall be hereafter.

Dated at Clifton Springs, where I am detained by one of the warnings which a kind Father sends down to remind us of our mortality, this 31st day of May, 1873.

E. W. LEAVENWORTH, of Syracuse, N. Y.

NOTE.—After all the attention which I have been able to devote to this subject, there are still a few names which cannot be connected with any of the families herein, and as there is no doubt of their descent from Thomas Leavenworth, of Woodbury, they will be found in the appendix, (Letter C.)

2. In the course of the investigations growing out of this work, the books mentioned in the appendix, Letter G, have been examined in quest of facts illustrating the family, and giving its history. The other examinations therein mentioned have also been made.

INTRODUCTION.

INTRODUCTION.

HISTORY OF THE FAMILY.

OF ENGLISH DESCENT.

There can be no doubt that the family of which the genealogy will be found in this volume, came to this country from England, between the year 1660 and 1680, and probably between 1664 and 1675. No data have been discovered by which the precise year can be determined.

Hinman's catalogue of early names etc., Hartford, 1852-56, does not reach down lower than the letter *(c)*, except for Hinman.

The volumes published by the New Haven Historical Society, containing the records of the colony from the settlement in 1638 only down to 1665, the year when the New Haven and Connecticutt colonies were united.

It is by no means certain that the name now exists in England, nor does it seem probable that it was ever very common there.

I have had the directories of most of the large cities of England carefully searched for the name at two different times without success, and have had extensive inquiries made for it in different parts of the Island with the same result.

In the hope of finding the name at some earlier day, I have caused careful searches to be made of the indices to the wills at Drs. Commons, of the Chancery proceedings for the north, and of the indices for wills at York for one hundred years. The same in Surrey, Westminster, and Middlesex ; at the church of St. Clare, and at other churches in Southwark, and have caused postal cards to be sent to all the old parish churches in London, where all the Leavenworths yet found in England had their residences. These efforts have not been crowned with all the success which might have been anticipated and desired, but they were not without important results. It appears upon a tax roll in the parish of St. Clare, Southwark, London, that Thomas and Edward Leavenworth were each assessed for a hearth tax in that parish, in the year 1664. There was also found at the Faculty Office, London, the marriage license of Peter Leavenworth and Sarah Wood, dated June 11th, 1729. These are the only traces of the name in England which all these inquiries and searches have brought to light, It appears, however, in Russell's life of Sir Gerald Massey, in his Lives of eccentric personages, at page 96, that one Sir Lewis Leavenworth, was living in London about the year 1750, (but the year is not closely defined), but of whom I have learned nothing beyond what is stated by Russell.

This is abundant proof that the family was in England, and was there before or about the time of the emigration of the first Thomas Leavenworth to this country.

Indeed it is quite probable that the Thomas Leavenworth, of Southwark, in 1664, and the Thomas Leavenworth of Woodbury, who died there in 1683, the common ancestor of the family, are one and the same person. For in confirmation of this supposition it may be remarked that on the 11th day of June, 1684, after the death of her husband, Grace Leavenworth, the widow of the said Thomas, executed two several bonds with great formality, under her hand and each attested by her coat of arms, the one to George Musgrave of London, and witnessed by Lawr. Hammond, Fran Burroughs, John Leavenworth and Benjamin Bullivant; the other to Mary Gawthorn of London, and witnessed by the same persons, except the said John Leavenworth. These bonds are now in the State Library, at Hartford. From these bonds it is quite evident that the said Thomas, had dealings with and relations of some kind to people in London, which might naturally grow out of his former residence there, and which would not be probable upon any other supposition.

I come, therefore, not only to the conclusion above, but also to the commonly received opinion that the said Thomas came over soon after the restoration of Charles the second, a period when many dissenters and republicans found it both convenient and safe to leave their country to escape the dangers and persecution of those unhappy times.

WHERE THEY LANDED.

Tradition has been quite uniform in saying that he landed at New Haven, and settled soon after at Woodbury. Unfortunately the two volumes of the records of the New Haven colony only come down to the year 1665, and all the records since that time are lost. Had they been preserved, they would probably show the date of the arrival of Thomas and his brother John. But the town of Woodbury was not settled till after 1670, nor was it constituted a town, till 1674.

FINANCIAL CONDITION.

What his condition as to property was at that time does not appear, but it is abundantly evident that he became a very large land owner before his death in 1683. For it appears by entries in an old account book of Joseph Boothe, of

Stratford, a relative of Wm. A. Boothe, of New York, that Thomas Leavenworth, a son of the first Thomas, was living in Stratford, and dealing with the said Boothe from 1695 till 1702. He must, therefore, have left Woodbury when but twenty-two years of age, and before he could himself have acquired any considerable amount of property: and if he had acquired any before leaving Woodbury, it would probably not have been real estate. But it appears most abundantly by the first half dozen volumes of Woodbury town records, that early in life, and soon after 1700, he was the owner of many pieces of land or farms in the town of Woodbury which he would not have bought, living in Stratford, but which he must have derived by inheritance from his father and his Uncle John. He became however, also the owner of all the lands which his brother John received from his father Thomas, and his Uncle John. (Book 20, p. 130, date, Sept. 11, 1705.)

He deeded lands in Woodbury, to nearly all his children, (see book 3, p. 170, date, Apr. 9. 1725; book 4, p. 164 and 165, in Dec., 1733; book 5, p. 139, Oct. 10, 1735; book 6, p. 50, May 16, 1739; book 7, p. 85, Dec. 4, 1744; and several pieces to some of them.

He deeded lands at Good Hill, (book 4, p. 164–165; book 5, p. 39; at Transylvania, Aug., 1707, and also at Ruccum). Good Hill is in the west part of the town of Woodbury. Grassey Hill lies south of it. Ruccum lies southwest of Good Hill, in Roxbury; and from the early settlement of the country has been a Leavenworth neigborhood.

In addition to the above, it may be noticed that, by his will, Dr. Thomas, in addition to his lands in Stratford, left other lands still, in Woodbury, to his widow, and several of his sons.

All of these lands he no doubt received from his father, and his Uncle John, except so far as he acquired some from his brother John by the deed of Sept. 11, 1705; and these lands were such only as his brother John had received from his father, and Uncle.

It is quite probable, therefore, that the first Thomas brought with him from England the means of establishing himself comfortably here, on his arrival.

It might seem singular that there is no record of a single deed in the town records of Woodbury, to the first Thomas L., or to his brother John; and it would be quite inexplicable but for the fact that the *first* volume of the Acts of the proprietor's, and also of the records of the town of Woodbury, are lost; and the town was created in 1674, nine years previous to the death of said Thomas, a period, most of which was embraced no doubt in said first volume of town records and proprietors' acts. That Thomas and John were *original* proprietors of the town, appears at page 64, of volume first, of Cothrens' Woodbury.

It should be noticed, also, that a deed from Grace Leavenworth to her sons, Thomas and John, dated May 26, 1687, is recorded in book 1, page 45, of the Woodbury records. This shows that the early deeds, previous to the death of her husband in 1683, must have been recorded in the lost volume.

The conveyances for the land which Thomas and John acquired as original proprietors, were no doubt recorded in the volume of the acts of the proprietors, now lost.

COAT OF ARMS.

From the fact that the bonds above referred to were attested by the coat of arms of the said Grace Leavenworth, it would seem that they were persons of some position and standing, in England. The existence of this coat of arms was known to some of the older members of the family, particularly to Miss Mary Ann Leavenworth, of Westport, and Mrs. David Shelton, of Huntington, the grand-daughters of the second Edmund Leavenworth, who had often seen it painted on the walls or wainscoting over the mantel in the homes of Edmund and Gideon Leavenworth, about two miles above Birmingham. The home of Edmund was taken down a generation since. That of Gideon has passed into other hands, and the arms have been obliterated by a coat of paint. They were supposed, therefore, to be lost forever, the impressions attached to the said two bonds having been stolen from the state library, between 1842 and 1856; but, fortunately, in 1870, Lorenzo W. Leavenworth, Esq., of Bridgeport, in the course of his inquiries and investigations in relation to the family, found in the hands of an old lady of eighty years, Mrs. Fanny Thompson, of Bridgeport, a descendant of Edmund Leavenworth, a very ancient copper plate, upon which was engraved a coat of arms. It was evidently executed for the benefit of Capt. Gideon Leavenworth, who was so unwise as to have the motto left out and in its place to substitue his own name. This plate was uneven, battered and worn. I caused it to be engraved anew, and sent one of the impressions to Mrs. Shelton, and one to Miss Leavenworth, who each recognized it as identical with those in the homes of Capt. Gideon and his father Edmund, on the bank of the Hoosatonic, above Birmingham. There was a blunder made, however, in the execution of this old plate, which was doubtless made from an impression. The animals—lions—are made to look the wrong way, for in heraldry, they are never drawn looking to the right. The crest, for the same reason was wrongly posed; for these reasons, I have caused the plate to be re-engraved and these errors corrected, and omitting the name of Capt. Gideon, have substituted a motto in the room of that which has been lost.

Whether this is the same coat of arms with that of Sir Lewis Leavenworth, I have not been able to ascertain.

RESIDENCE OF THE FIRST THOMAS.

The exact spot where the first Thomas L. settled, is undoubtedly at the north end of Good Hill. It was for a long time a matter of serious doubt; but it appears by a deed, dated the 23d day of March, 1729, 3d vol., p. 18, of Woodbury records, that Dr. Thomas had land added to his *homestead* at the north end of Good Hill. Now, as Dr. Thomas never lived in Woodbury after 1695, nor after he was twenty-two years of age, nor after his marriage, he never had any homestead there except that which he enjoyed under his father's roof. The north end of Good Hill was then the home of the first Thomas Leavenworth; and Mr. Cothren who has carefully examined this record and who is famaliar with the locality, says that this is the modern John Leavenworth's place, as he fully believes. That Thomas L., the son, lived in Woodbury until 1795, appears in book 2 of W. records, page 132.

GENERAL CHARACTER.

Of the character of the family, there is little to be said that cannot with equal truth be said of most of the good and early families of New England. They brought with them the pure and rigid principles, and the stern and unyielding spirit which had characterized the Puritans of England for a century previous, which survived the inhuman persecutions of the bloody Mary and the tyranny of the stubborn and bigoted Elizabeth, and her blind and stupid successors, and which found their congenial home among the Puritans of New England. I find therefore, that Dr. Thomas was received into the communion of the Stratford Church, on the 6th day of February, 1697-8, having "owned the covenant" on the 11th day of the previous January, and in his 24th year. He was one of the first members and founders of the Ripton Church, and his wife also joined with him, together with his children, James, Ebenezer, Mark, Mary and Hannah then or soon after. It appears also by the Parish records of the Huntington Church, that he was one of the deacons in 1726 and probably from the beginning. His son Ebenezer was " collector of Parish rates " in 1727 ; and his son James was a Parish officer in 1736. His son Mark who was educated at Yale, was 58 years the minister at Waterbury ; and the younger sons, David, Thomas and Zebulon, who settled in Woodbury, became members of the church there. Such was the religious character of Dr. Thomas and his family ; and that character so early and so strongly impressed upon the family, has been largely handed down through the successive generations to the present time. The family has furnished about the usual proportion of clergymen, lawyers and physicians, of merchants and manufacturers, while the bulk of the family have followed the occupation of their first ancestors, and devoted their lives to agriculture.

The family are not distinguished by remarkable wit, brilliancy of genius, but they possess in a high degree the more solid, practical and valuable traits of character. They are not wanting in enterprise, energy, public spirit, and that strong vigorous common sense which is the great lever which moves the world ; and a large number of them have been the early pioneers in various parts of the country.

The third Thomas was before the Revolution one of the early pioneers in the valley of Wyoming, and was driven out with his family houseless and homeless by Col. John Butler and his tory and Indian allies. Col. Jesse, the son of the Rev. Mark, was not only one of the patentees of the towns of Danville and Peacham, in Caledonia County, Vt., but was one of the very first and most enterprising of the early settlers in Danville, going there in 1783, building mills, etc., and often representing the town in the legislature. Gen. Nathan L., the son of Nathan and grandson of Dr. David, of Woodbury, was with his father a pioneer in Hinesburgh,Vt., while Dorman and Abel the sons of the third Thomas, were also pioneers in the adjoining town of Charlotte, where they were afterwards joined by their brother the fourth Thomas. Their descendants still remain in these two towns, and have spread into adjoining parts of the state. For more than forty years Gen. Nathan was a prominent man in Vermont, having represented the town of Hinesburgh more than twenty years, and having held the office of Senator, Presidential Elector and member of the Governor's Council.

Lemuel L., the son of John; was one of the earliest settlers at Whitesboro, having moved there with his large family the next year after judge White in 1785, and he was followed by his half-brother Amos, who came with his large family in 1794, and settled on the north bank of the Mohawk, in the town of Deerfield, now the town of Marcy; and his son Ralph as early as 1818 crossed the Mississippi and settled permanently at St. Genevieve. And another son of the third Thomas, with his family settled at New Canaan, Col., Co., in 1796, and this son John was one of the early settlers of Genoa, in the county of Cayuga, where he spent his life and died in 1851. Seth M., and Zebulon, the grandsons of the first Zebulon were the owners and founders of the village of Leavenworth, on the Ohio, the capital of Crawford Co., Ind., to which they gave their name. There they settled in the year 1819, at the mouth of the Big Blue, having purchased the land from the Government. Zebulon died there in the year 1872, and his surviving sons still remain there. Gen. Henry L., the grandson of Mark, having won distinguished laurels in the battles of Chippeway and Niagara in the war 1812, was some years after placed in command of the troops on the western frontiers, and built Cantonment Leavenworth on the Missouri, and gave his name to the most important town on that celebrated River.

This account might be much farther extended by allusions to those who in more modern times have settled in the still newer western states, and to those who at an early day crossed the mountains and cast their lots upon the coast of the distant Pacific. But the above will suffice to present a general idea of the character of the family for energy and enterprise.

The careful reader will not fail also to notice, that in all our national contests, from the old French war of 1760 down to the great rebellion, the family has ever been active and patriotic, ready if need be to lay down their lives for the country.

The Rev. Mark L., of Waterbury was a chaplain in the French war, and his son Jesse probably took a part in it.

In the war of the revolution it will be seen that not only the first Edmund but also his sons Gideon and Eli, and David, the son of John of Woodbury, and Col. Jesse were captains and were active and efficient; while Abijah, another son of Edmund was a Lieutenant and lost his life, and nearly every member of the family, of suitable age, was engaged first or last in the contest.

In the war of 1812, which was far from being popular especially in New England, Gen. Henry commanded a Regiment at the contested and bloody battles of Chippeway and Niagara, was in the hottest of the fight, and won a reputation of which his family may well be proud.

In the rebellion, Col. Jesse Henry of Milwaukee, and Abel Edwin of Vermont, held important commands and were actively engaged, and Dr. Melinus and several others laid down their lives, while a greater number still went through the war.

Like most other families, the great mass of its members have fortunately occupied the middle ranks of life—the golden mean—secure from the multiplied temptations and dangers of great wealth and of pinching poverty. This is the class from which the vast majority of the valuable men of the country have sprung in the past and will spring in the future. And I take special pleasure in saying here, that in all my investigations into the history of the members of the family I have never found one individual who was ever arrested or punished for a crime. While some of the members have not always been exempt from the weakness of our nature, the general good character of the family has been remarkably preserved.

DERIVATION OF THE NAME.

In regard to the derivation of the name there is a variety of opinions and nothing is *clearly* decided.

In Domesday book (time of Wm. 1st,) vol. 4th, edition published by the Records commission at page 232 occurs the name of "Leuenot," and at page 206 of the same vol., also occurs the name of "Leouenot."

A volume of the English records commission entitled "Placita de quo warranto—temp Edw., 1st, 2nd and 3rd (folio) at page 284, mention is made of the name of "Levenoth" in Hertfordshire, incidentally in giving a boundary (time of Edward 1st.)

On the 27th of June 1627, administration on the estates of "Constance Levenoth, spinster," "Christian Levenoth, spinster," and "Robert Levenoth, bachelor," was granted to "Christian Levenoth" their mother, all of Gitinge poure, in the county of Gloucester.

In Arthurs etymological dictionary of family and christian names page 180, I find the following derivation of the name: "Leavenworth—local (Welch) Llyvngwerth—the smooth, level farm, castle or court on the Worth or place on the river Leven."

The Rev. Isaac Taylor in his "Words and Places," pages 121 and 122 says: "Worth" is a place warded or protected and has a meaning nearly the same as *ton* or *garth*. It is probably an enclosed homestead for the churls subordinate to the tun. Anglo Saxon "Weorthing," English "Worth."

A "ton" or "tun" was a place surrounded by a hedge or rudely fortified by pallisades, page 120.

Hence arises the terminations of the names of so many persons and places with "worth" and "ton."

From Llevn—smooth—we get the name of Lock Leven and Three Rivers called Leven in Scotland, besides others of the same name in Gloucestershire, Yorkshire, Cornwall, Cumberland, Lancashire, page 215.

Others on the contrary have thought that the name may not have been indigenous to England, but brought from Germany and Anglicized from the German family name of "Lowenwerth," which may be possible, but if so it was probably at a very early day.

The name may have been formed from some one of the early names mentioned above; "Levenoth" might easily have grown out of "Leuenot," and Leavenworth out of "Levenoth"; but it will be observed that Peter Leavenworth was living in London in 1629, while a family of Levenoth's were living in Gloucestershire in 1627. Some members of a family may however change their names while others do not, and the derivation from the name of Leuenot, in the time of William 1st, mentioned in Domesday book, is by no means improbable; such changes have been in the past, and still are of the most common occurrence; but it seems to me quite as probable that the etymology given above from Arthur's Dictionary is the correct one.

THE SPELLING.

But whatever may have been the derivation of the name, the spelling of it from the earliest known period, down to the present day, by every member of the family has been uniformly the same. The names of Peter L., found in the Faculty office London, of Thomas and Edward found in the church of St Clare and of Sir Lewis Leavenworth, are all spelled in the same manner as it is spelled to day. And again while the name is incorrectly spelled in the body of the wills of Thomas, James and Mary Leavenworth, in each instance with an s and in the bonds of said Grace having an "ing" the signature of Grace L., to each of the said two bonds, that of John L., her son, as a witness to one of them and that of her other son Dr. Thomas in the 3rd volume of the town records of Stratford, page 27, is in each instance spelled in the same manner as now. It is therefore quite evident that the name has undergone no change from 1629 to this time, though often spelled in public documents, records, books and the papers of the day in a very great variety of ways, often omitting the a, or adding an s, or both, or inserting an "*ing*" in place of the "*en*."

PRESENT DISTRIBUTION OF THE FAMILY.

Before closing these remarks, it may not be inappropriate, perhaps, to allude to the present distribution of the family. It has *two* progenitors in common. So far as appears, John the brother of the first Thomas was probably never married. There is no intimation of such an event, and as he gave all his property equally to his two nephews, Thomas and John, and no allusiion is made to a wife, it leaves such a conclusion quite probable; but it seems from page 162 of Cothren's Woodbury, vol. 1st, that Thomas and John L. were *householders* in 1682; but if said John was ever married, it is evident that he had no children, and probably his wife died before him.

John the brother of Dr. Thomas was perhaps married, but there is no entry of his marriage or death in the records either of Woodbury or Stratford, and in the first named town he resided till he moved to Stratford, and in the last till 1718, and probably later. There is an entry in the Stratford records of the baptism of Ebenezer, the son of John, in June, 1706 ; but as his brother Thomas' son, Ebenezer, was born Apr. 7, 1706, and as no mention is ever again made of Ebenezer the son of *John*, may there not be an error in the Stratford record ? There is at least no evidence yet discovered of any other descendant from John the brother of Dr. Thomas, unless the John L. who is mentioned in the appendix, letter (c) was his descendant, which is not impossible ; and I have a slight suspicion that he never married.

All the members of the family excepting perhaps the descendants of said John last mentioned, are descended from seven of the eight sons of Dr. Thomas, (Ebenezer having died unmarried), and from his three daughters, Sarah, Mary and Hannah.

I have always been accustomed to look to each of the name, (regarding in this connexion only the male members) as being descended from one of these brothers. To me they seem to stand out quite separate and distinct. The descendants of some of the brothers have been numerous ; of others there have been comparatively few. They have lived largely in groups, and while the male descendants of some have long since disappeared from their native homes in Connecticut, they have become numerous in other parts of the Union. Others have remained largely in Connecticut ; but with the exception of John, none of the brothers have a majority of their male descendants in that state at the present time.

The different male members descended from the seven brothers are now distributed substantially as follows, taking them as near as may be in the order of their birth :

1. Those of James are residing in the town of Monroe, Ct., and in the counties of Saratoga, Montgomery and Fulton, in the state of New York. They consist of less than a dozen members in both states.

2. Those of David divide themselves naturally into two branches. Those of his son Nathan, since the death of Gen. Nathan and of his son Henry consist only of Nathan of Hinesburgh, and on his death will become extinct. Those of Dr. David's son, Ebenezer, divide into two entirely distinct families ; those of the Rev. Ebenezer and who are few in number and reside in Illinois ; and those of David, of Nassau, who are far more numerous than those of any other great grandson of Dr. Thomas, and reside principally in the county of Rensselaer, N. Y., where the said David lived and died, and in the southern counties of Steuben and Chemung.

3. The descendants of John, of Woodbury, constitute a majority of all the Leavenworths now in Connecticutt, and reside largely in Roxbury, but also at New Haven and Norfolk. They are also widely diffused in other states.

Those of John's son David, through his grand-sons Gideon and Morse are mainly in Connecticut; those through his grand-son David are in New York, Michigan, etc.

Those of John's son John are in Connecticut, New York and California.

Those of his son Lemuel, were in the state of New York, and are extinct.

Those of his son Elihu reside in Connecticut at New Haven and Bridgeport, and in the states of Michigan and Illinois.

Those of his son Amos, at St. Genevieve and St. Louis, in Missouri.

4. The line of Zebulon has been the least prolific of the seven sons, and its numbers, which are in all less than a dozen, reside at the towns of Leavenworth and Mt. Vernon, in Indiana, and at St. Louis, Mo.

5. The Rev. Mark L., had five sons who grew to manhood and from them have sprung, perhaps, more of the eminent men of the family than from either of Dr. Thomas sons, which was owing no doubt to their superior education ; but this branch of the family seems in imminent danger of extinction. There are none now remaining except Elisha of Waterbury, son of Dr. Frederick who has no son and is now unmarried, Frederick P., of Shreveport, La., grand-son of Dr. Frederick who has no son but three daughters, Mark Jesse of Andover, N. H., and his son Mark Henry his youngest child now 12 years of age, all descendants of Col. Jesse, and Edward L., of New York and Staten Island, grandson of Elisha, now upwards of forty years of age and unmarried.

6. The descendants of Thomas are somewhat numerous. Those of his son Asa are at Genoa, Wolcott, New Canaan and Syracuse in the state of New York, and at St. Catharines in Canada.

His son Gideon has but one grandson Franklin, and he with his sons Woodard, Enos and Franklin reside at Wilksbarre in Pennsylvania.

Those of his son Abel are at New Haven and Bristol, and Charlotte in Vermont, and at Sandy Creek, N. Y.

Those of his son Thomas by his first wife are in Connecticut, Michigan and Iowa, and those by his second are in Franklin Co., N. Y.

Those of his son Samuel are in Connecticut and at Allegan, Grand Rapids and Ann Arbor, Michigan.

Those of his son Dorman are at Charlotte, Vt.

7. The descendants of Capt. Edmund, the youngest son of Dr. Thomas, are limited to Mark Eli of Newtown, Ct., and his brother Gideon, and Mark Elis' son Eli, both of Rochester, N. Y., and their sons.

If therefore I am correct in the above facts, it appears that Dr. David and Zebulon of Woodbury, have now no male descendants in Connecticut ; the Rev. Mark has but one, Elisha of Waterbury ; Capt. Edmund has but one, Mark

Eli of Newtown ; James has but three Eli, Andrew and George of Munroe and Bethel, and of the six sons of Thomas four of them have none, Samual has but one, Thomas has some six or eight, and all the residue are descended from John.

Much more might be written upon the subject of the family, but the patience of most readers will perhaps have been already exhausted. Those who desire a more intimate and perfect acquantance will find it in the following pages. I commit it to their hands with a thankful heart that my life has been spared to finish it, so far as it is finished, and that my labors are drawing to a close.

E. W. LEAVENWORTH.

Syracuse, June 7th, 1873.

NOTE.—The original town of Stratford was twelve miles square or thereabouts, fronting on the sound and bounded on the East by the Hoosatonic River. It was early divided into the Parishes of Ripton, New Stratford, North Stratford and Stratfield.

In 1789 the Parishes of Ripton and New Stratford were incorporated into a town by the name of Huntington.

In 1798 the Parish of North Stratford, was taken from Stratford and incorporated as a town by the name of Trumbull.

In 1821 the Parish of Stratfield, was incorporated by the name of Bridgeport.

And in 1823 New Stratford was taken from Huntington, and incorporated by the name of Munroe.

The town of Woodbury was incorporated in 1674 ; a settlement having been made there about two years earlier under the name of Pomperaug.

It was bounded n. by Bantam, (Litchfield) e. by Mattatuck, (Waterbury) s. by the Pootatuck (Housatonic) River, w. by Weantinogue, (Mew Milford.)

It comprised the present towns of Woodbury, Washington, Bethlem, Southbury, Roxbury and a small part of Middlebury.

Washington was incorporated in 1779, containing the societies of Judea and New Preston. Southbury, in 1787 ; Roxbury, 1801 ; Middlebury, 1807.

The above towns are in Litchfield Co., except Southbury and Middlebury, which are in New Haven Co.

Watertown was taken from Waterbury and made a town in 1780. Up to 1795 it included most of Plymouth, (Northbury). From 1739 to 1780, Watertown was a parish by the name of Westbury,

SPECIAL NOTICE.

SPECIAL NOTICE.

FOR THE MEMBERS OF THE FAMILY ONLY.

The writing of this Genealogy has necessarily involved a very careful study of the family in all its details. While there is much that is gratifying in its history, there are other things, if I mistake not, especially in its present condition, much to be regretted. We all feel a just pride in its past history in the high character and valuable services of many of its members, and in the frugality, energy, integrity, enterprise, public spirit and general good conduct which have characterized it.

But I very much fear that its standard of character has not been elevated during the past fifty years. While the country has moved on with prodigious strides in wealth, improvement and the general education of the people, have we moved forward with the advancing tide, or have we stood still? I will not be too confident, nor too emphatic on this point, but let us for a moment look at it, and examine briefly the past history of the family.

About fifty years since Gen. Henry was enjoying the laurels won at Chippeway and Niagara, and was at the head of the army in the valley of the Mississippi, while his half-brothers Mark and Frederick were active leading citizens at Waterbury, and pioneers in the manufacturing enterprises of that wealthy and prosperous town.

Seth M. L., had recently graduated at Williams College, and he and his brother Zebulon were busily engaged in laying the foundations of the town of Leavenworth on the Ohio, where for a generation more they were the most prominent and wealthy citizens of the village, and were well known throughout all that part of the state.

Gen. Nathan L., of Hinesburgh, was one of the most highly honored citizens of Vermont, filling important public positions for more than forty years, and his first cousin the Rev. Ebenezer I. L., who had then been recently graduated at Williams, was a most devoted and useful clergyman of the Presbyterian church in central New York.

David and Isaac L., grandsons of the 3rd Thomas, were the principal merchants at Great Barrington, Mass., and among the most spirited, enterprising and respected citizens of that beautiful town.

The descendants of John in Woodbury and Roxbury, and of James in Montgomery and Saratoga counties, and of Thomas both in Connecticut and Vermont, were among the substantial and highly respected citizens of their respective towns, while isolated members like John Peck L., at Rush, Lemuel, at Whitesboro, John, at Genoa, Isaac, at New Haven, and many others in various places were equally valued and respected citizens.

But how is it now? Can we enumerate as large a number of valuable men at the present day? My personal knowledge is not sufficient to enable me to speak with great confidence on this point; nor do I desire to do so. It might not be in perfect taste. With many fears in regard to the answer to be given, I will submit the question to the fuller knowledge and perhaps the better judgment of many members of the family.

But I am impressed with a strong conviction that the reply must be in the negative, and that we have not improved, (if we have not deteriorated) in the last half century, for the want of a sufficiently high appreciation of the value of knowledge and mental discipline. A thorough education is an almost indispensable requisite to any valuable success in life, and to the accomplishment of any great good. It is an investment which its possessor can never lose. It is an unfailing source of pride and perennial enjoyment, the foundation for extended ufuselness, the means through which an honorable support may be secured, and which brings out into the fullest development all the latent powers and energies of the man.

The great want of our country at the present day, the one from which every interest, public and private, and our National reputation, both at home and abroad, are suffering the most serious injuries, is the want of a high sense of honor and unbending integrity in our citizens. The great interests of the country are not suffering from the want of industry or enterprise; not for the want of education or ability, but they are suffering most seriously in every department of business of whatever character, and in every branch of our Government, State and National, from the deplorable want of common honesty. From the distinguished gentlemen—whose wisdom or folly—govern this great country in our National Legislature, at Washington, down to the petty thieves who fatten on the plunder of our cities—there is a succession of knaves who seek the offices of the country, that they may be enriched by the sale of themselves and the robbery of the people.

And yet if a life of seventy years actively spent in a great variety of public and private stations, has indelibly stamped upon my mind one truth more deeply than another, it is this, that there is no trait of character more valuable to a person in any condition or business in life, none which more certainly insures success in any profession or occupation, none which more dignifies and enobles its possessor, none which gives him more respect or a wider influence with his fellow men, than a high character for unbending integrity; and without this great sheet-anchor, all natural abilities, however great; all acquirements, however extensive or profound, are comparatively vain and useless. They can give no success in life which is worthy of the name, none which can give satisfaction to its possessor. While I would not belittle the *crime* of dishonesty, I am ever more impressed by its *folly* than its *criminality*, by the *weakness* and *stupidity* which permits a person to sacrifice all that is dear and valuable in life to an *ignis fatuus* which only lures to deceive, rather than by the *degradation* of character which the *knavery* necessarily implies.

Impressed with these views, anxious for the improvement and honor of the family, desirous to stimulate the energies and ambition of those who are to follow me, and to do all in my power to aid those among them who think the acquisition of knowledge and the cultivation of the mind are paramount objects in life, I have resolved by my will, to establish three scholarships for the gratuitous education of any young men of the name of Leavenworth, to establish one at Yale College in New Haven, one at Hamilton College at Clinton, Oneida County, N. Y., and one at the University of Michigan at Ann Arbor. I have thus located them that one of them may be convenient for nearly every member of the family, and I intend that each shall be sufficient to defray the *necessary* expenses of a *prudent* young man during the four years of his college course.

I insert this notice here, that it may catch the eye of *every member of the family*, and I ardently hope that when the scholarships are established, there may in all future time be a young man ready to fill each vacancy as soon as it may arise at either of the institutions, and that each person who enters upon one of these scholarships may have elevated views of the value of life, of its duties, privileges and responsibilities, may diligently improve his opportunities, fit himself for the highest usefulness among his follow men, and do honor to the name of Leavenworth.

E. W. LEAVENWORTH.

SYRACUSE, JUNE 20, 1873.

N. B.—My will after my death will no doubt be found recorded in the office of the Surrogate of this County—Onondaga, N. Y., at Syracuse, and will show fully the rights of the members of the family in these scholarships.

I pray that no person who shall ever receive the advantages of one of these scholarships, may ever so misapprehend the wisdom of his Creator or the constitution of the world in which we live, as to believe for a moment that his interests *in this life* can ever be advanced by a single act inconsistent with the highest personal honor and integrity.

It is for the education of men of this character that these scholarships will be established. It is my hope and prayer that they may be potent means, not only in elevating the position and character of the family, but that they may from year to year, through all time, send out into the active duties of life men who will not only be diligent in business, but who will live for the good of mankind and the honor of their Creator.

CORRECTIONS, OMISSIONS, ETC.

CORRECTIONS, OMISSIONS, Etc.

Those into whose hands this work may fall, will confer a very great favor by advising the author of any errors or omissions which they may discover. That there are many scattered through its pages he has no doubt.

He would also be very happy to receive a genealogical statement of the descendants of daughters as well as sons down to the present time.

Blank ruled sheets will be found in many of the volumes, inserted expressly for the purpose of being used in noting all corrections, omissions, etc., for permanent preservation.

It is not impossible, should his life be spared many years, that he may, hereafter, publish a second edition, enlarged and corrected.

And if not, all corrections and additions will be carefully preserved, and with the letters and other papers, engravings, etc., will be carefully packed and boxed, and deposited in some safe place at Syracuse—perhaps in the vault of the Syracuse Savings Bank—for future inspection and use, should they ever be wanted by any future historian of the family.

SYRACUSE, June 20, 1873.

Residence of E. W. LEAVENWORTH,

Syracuse, N. Y.

Erected 1842.3.

GENEALOGY.

GENEALOGY.

---

1. THOMAS LEAVENWORTH.

Born in England.

Married Grace ——, who died as supposed in 1715. They emigrated to America, as learned only from tradition, after 1664. He died at Woodbury, August, 3, 1683.

An inventory of his personal estate was taken August, 20th, 1683, amounting to £225.2.1. This appears by the Probate records of Fairfield District, also that he left two sons and one daughter. Names not given, that of the daughter never ascertained.

CHILDREN.

3. THOMAS, b. 1673, d. Aug. 4, 1754, at Ripton.
4. JOHN, b. —— d. after 1718.
5. DAU. b. —— d. ——

His wife Grace survived him and remained at Woodbury, for a time, perhaps permanently. On the 11th day of June, 1684, she executed two bonds, one to George Musgrave, of London, in the presence of Law'r Hammond, Fran Burroughs, John Leavenworth and Benjamin Bullivant—the other to Mary Gawthorn, of London, widow, in the presence of the same parties, except the said John Leavenworth.

These bonds are among the papers on file in the State Library of Connecticut, at Hartford. Connecticut Archives, Private controversies, 11 document, 152.

From fac similies of her signature kindly sent to me by Charles J. Hoadley, Esq., State Librarian, it is evident that she was at the time of the execution of said bonds, quite advanced in life, or very infirm, doubtless the former.

Speaking of these bonds, in a letter to the author, under date of August 17th, 1864, Mr. Hoadly remarks, "There was a seal "attached to her name on both bonds, with a coat of arms, but "both these seals were stolen from the documents since 1842 "and before 1856. Upon one of the bonds, (both of which seem "to have been executed in Boston,) the name of John Leaven-"worth appears as a witness, I send you a fac simile of both the "autographs."

She was living, probably at Woodbury, in February, 1686, and owned land in Hasky Meadow, about a mile from Woodbury village. And on the 26th day of May, 1687, she deeded lands in Woodbury, to her two sons, Thomas and John, and on the 28th day of May, 1687, she also deeded other lands to Henry Deering, of Boston, Mass., Book 1 of Woodbury Records, p. 45 Etc.

(See copy of the letter Appendix D., and of the letter of John Ward Dean, Secretary of the New England Historical and Genealogical Society in relation to the witnesses to the Execution of the Bond mentioned below.)

The first Thomas L, was a farmer, and settled, no doubt, on Good Hill, in the west part of the present town of Woodbury, not far from the line of Roxbury, and there and in that vicinity, the family have remained from that day till the present, and are now quite numerous there. In 1733-4, his son Dr. Thomas. had a controversy with Benjamin Hurd, in regard to the line of these lands. Book 3d, p. 25 of Woodbury Records.

A tradition in the family, is, that he landed at New Haven.

No doubt, he came from England. In Russells Lives of Excentric Personages, page 96 in the life of Sir Gerald Massey, reference is made to Sir Lewis Leavenworth, as living in London, and to a ball given by him about the middle of the last century.

From Miss Harriet E. Bainbridge, of London, I learn that she finds the names of Edward and Thomas Leavenworth, in the parish of St. Clare, Southwark, in 1664. This is about the time the first Thomas is supposed to have arrived at New Haven. She also finds in the Faculty office, London, the marriage license of Peter Leavenworth and Sarah Wood, in 1729.

The execution of the bonds above mentioned, shows that there were business transactions between Thomas L. and persons in London, which would not probably have existed, had he not been formerly a resident there.

Little is known of the first Thomas. His head stone does not seem to be found in the cemeteries at Woodbury. But he was evidently a prosperous man in his affairs, judging from the property he left, and brought up his children in habits of industry and frugality. But unfortunately, few facts are preserved from which to form definite opinions in regard to his character, save as the characters of children shed light upon those of their parents.

2. John Leavenworth.

Brother of the first Thomas, no doubt came from England with him. Born in England.

Married (probably not.) Died in 1702, at Stratford, but settled first in Woodbury.

An inventory of his estate was taken October, 12th, 1702, and letters of administration were granted to his "cousin" Thomas L. of Stratford, no doubt his *nephew*, as nephews were then often called "cousins." The letters were granted November 7th, 1702, and his property was equally divided between his two nephews, Thomas and John.

The deed from John L., (son of Thomas,) to his brother Dr. Thomas, of lands in Woodbury, dated September, 11th, 1705, shows that the above mentioned John was his uncle, and brother of the 1st Thomas. See Book No. 20, p. 130, of Woodbury Records.

John L. bought land in Woodbury, in 1692—Book No. 2, p. 130, but whether it was the brother or son of the first Thomas, does not appear. Probably it was the brother of the 1st Thomas, as John the son of Dr. Thomas, was probably too young at that time to be dealing in lands.

From page 65 of volume 1 Cothren's Woodbury, it seems that he was one of the original proprietors of Woodbury, and on page 163 of the same volume, it appears that he was a *householder*.

But it does not appear otherwise that he was married, and on his death he gave his property to his nephews, Thomas and John, sons of his brother Thomas. But his wife might have died before him and childless.

There is a very interesting article in the 25th volume of the New England Historical and Genealogical Register, giving a full and minute account of "House of the olden time." It was an ancient house built early in the last century, on Summer street, in Boston, directly opposite to Trinity Church, and which was still standing and in good preservation up to or near the time of the great fire in 1872, when I suppose it must have been destroyed. But it may have been torn down as the ground is now October 1873, built up in stores.

In the "Book of possessions," (a book which though on a small scale, resembles Doomsday book—and was ordered by the General Court about sixteen years after the settlement of Boston,) the premises in question are described as the garden of Gamaliel Wayte, who had however a lot on the south side of Mill street, in 1642, and probably lived there. But in 1694 his son John Wayte, lived on the lot and sold it to John Leavenworth. He mortgaged it the same year to Simeon Stoddard, who eventually became the owner, and sold the property in 1727 to Leonard Vassall, who was born in Jamaica, in 1678. Then the said Vassall erected the house in question, about 1730. Vassall also built at Quincy, (then Braintree,) a little earlier, the house now owned and occupied by Charles Francis Adams. The principal apartments were finished with arras, tapestry and wainscot, as was used then in the best houses of the day.

As the bonds mentioned in No. one were executed in Boston, John Leavenworth must have been there in 1684, and doubtless he was there again in 1694, when this property was purchased by him. The description of said house as given in the Register, shows that it must have been one of the finest residences then existing in or about Boston.

It is a very remarkable fact that the original boundaries of said lot as given in said "Book of Possessions," have never been enlarged or diminished down to the present time.

Whether John Leavenworth ever personally occupied the said premises does not appear, I had supposed that his residence was always at Woodbury or Stratford.

Children of Thomas, of Woodbury.

3. Dr. Thomas Leavenworth.[2]—THOMAS.[1]

Born 1673, perhaps at Woodbury, possibly in England.

Married Mary Jenkins, about 1698, at Stratford? She was a daughter of David Jenkins, by his wife Grace, born in 1680, and died at Ripton, in June, 1768, aged 89. Ripton Parish was then a part of Stratford, now town of Huntington. He died at Ripton, August 4th, 1754, aged 77, and was buried at Ripton Center, and also his wife.

1695, June 10, John Judson, of Woodbury, buys house and lands of Thomas L., and sells to him property in Stratford, where he lived that year and onward probably, till 1721. Till 1795, he lived in W. Woodbury Records 2d Book, p. 132. Same date he bought lands in Stratford, and also in 1702–3.

1697–8 was received into communion with the Stratford Church, having on the 11th of January, of that year "owned the covenant."

1702, he obtained land in Woodbury, from John L., his brother—Book 1, p. 58.

1716, December, 16, had bought land of Edward Burroughs.

1717, January 30, sold land to his brother John.

1717, March 18. received land near Robert Wheelers.

1719, February, 25, signs a petition for a Bridge at Ripton.

1721, Sold his homestead in Stratford.

1724, Dr. Thomas L., and his wife became original members of the Church at Ripton, and at the same time or afterwards, James and his wife, Ebenezer, Mark, Sarah, Mary and Hannah, his children, join.

1726. Mention is made of him as *Deacon* Thomas, and as one of the Society's Committee.

1727. He is the Society's Committee and Collector of rates.

1728. December 31, order to lay out to Dr. Thomas L., 1 1-2 acres of six mile division lands.

1731. He was interested in a copper-mine, in Woodbury.

1734. May 5th, received a bequest from his son Ebenezer, in the distribution of his estate, March 1734–5. He also had a controversy this year, with Robert Wheeler, respecting some lands at Ripton.

1748. July 6, made his will.

1754. June 12, his widow, Mary, offers his will for probate.

1754. July 15th, his will proved.

See copy of same in Appendix Letter E.

Dr. Thomas was a man of position, influence, energy and wealth. He was one of the founders of the first Church, at Ripton, a Deacon, Society's Committee, etc., etc. He had a proper appreciation of the value of learning and educated his son Mark at Yale, where he was graduated in 1737. His son David was educated a physician, and practiced at Woodbury, where he died.

He left a large property for those times, and the place where he resided, and as much of his real estate was in Woodbury, where he had not resided long, if at all, after becoming of age, he probably inherited it from his father Thomas, and also other lands, which he had disposed of previous to his death.

He evidently gave to his children all the advantages, usually enjoyed at that period, as all of them became active, useful and prominent men in after life, in the places where they resided.

His will is recorded in the Probate Court of Fairfield District, in Book 1754 to 1757, pages 41 to 44.

CHILDREN.

6. James, b. September, 1, 1699, d. after August 1, 1759.
7. David, b. October 12, 1701, d. April 10, 1755.
8. Ebenezer, b. April 7, 1706, d. in 1734.
9. John, b. November 3, 1708, d. in 1783.
10. Zebulon, b. about 1710, d. May 2, 1778.
11. Mark, b. about 1711, d. August 20, 1797.
12. Thomas, b. —— d. after 1795?
13. Mary, b. about 1717, was alive in 1748, and d. at the age of 96.
14. Hannah, b. about 1719, was alive in 1763.
15. Sarah, b. October 6, 1722, according to the Stratford records. but really b. November 6, 1721. She was baptized in 1722. Was alive in 1748.
16. Edmund, b. 1725, died July 17, 1785.

Dr. Thomas resided at Stratford, as early as 1695, and probably moved to Ripton, about 1721.

He deeded to his children from time to time, after 1730, large tracts of land in the town of Woodbury, mostly on Good Hill. They were no doubt, inherited from his father, who resided on Good Hill, and probably near the residence of the late John Leavenworth. See Book 6, p. 50. Book 7, p. 85 of Woodbury Records. The Records of Woodbury, for twenty years after 1725, abound in these Deeds.

The will of his widow, Mary L., bears date May, 11, 1758. She beqeuaths legacies to her son James, to her two Grandsons, sons of Dr. David, deceased, Nathan and Ebenezer, also to her sons, John, Zebulon, Mark, Thomas and Edmund, and to her daughters Mary Perry, Hannah Moss, and Sarah Perry.

This will was recorded July 4th, 1768, and will be found in Book of Fairfield District Probate Records, dated 1769 to 1774, pages 29 and 30.

Dr. Thomas L., by an instrument in writing, dated 1714–15, agrees to maintain David Jenkins, who was his father-in-law. Rev. Mr. Swan suggests that David Jenkins may have married Grace L., after her husband's death. I see no evidence of it, though it is not improbable. The reason above is sufficient for the agreement. Grace Jenkins died in 1715.

The residence of Dr. Thomas, was directly on the banks of the Hoosatonic, about two miles above the present village of Birmingham, and a short distance below the site of "Leavenworth's Bridge." Here he had a large farm fronting on the river, for more than a mile.

His son Capt. Edmond built his house directly above his father's, and quite near, and lived and died there. The farm passed to Edmund by his father's will.

Edmund's son Gideon built his house, directly above his father's, twenty rods more or less intervening.

Not a vestige of Dr. Thomas' dwelling now (1872,) remains. The cellar of Capt. Edmund's remains, and a guard wall along the bank of the river. The house built by Gideon, remains in good condition, and is large and quite commodious. It also stands near the bank of the Hoosatonic, and directly on the bank of a small stream coming down from the west, on which they had a saw mill, and where the timber was much of it prepared for the Bridge.

There was a ship or boat yard on the river, between the dwellings of Capt. Edmund and his son Gideon, where they built such vessels as navigated the river, down to a time within the memory of those now living.

This property has remained in the family for one hundred and fifty years and more, and is now owned by the present Mrs. David Shelton, of Huntington, the Great-grand daughter of Dr. Thomas, from whom, being now childless, it must pass into other hands.

No doubt, in 1721, before Birmingham or Shelton were even dreamed of, Dr. Thomas may have imagined that a town would naturally grow up on the river, and the small stream which there enters the Hoosatonic, may have determined his location.

Leavenworth's Bridge, which was a Toll Bridge, was built originally, by Capt. Edmund L., and his son Gideon, and by the latter was subsequently rebuilt. The west end of the bridge rested on his farm. It was built about 1768-9.

I have been full and minute in my account of Dr. Thomas and wife, for the reason that he is the common progenitor of the whole family, now in the United States.

The head stones to the graves of himself and wife, still remain in good condition in the old cemetery, near the Ripton Church, of which he was one of the founders.

4. John Leavenworth.[2]—(THOMAS[1st])

Born ——— ——— propably in Woodbury, possibly in England. He lived for a time in Woodbury. Settled in Stratford, as a blacksmith. Died after 1718. He sold land in Stratford in 1705 and 1715. In 1705-6, he bought the house, lot, shop, etc., of Abram Kimberly. This ground is now covered by the Summer residence of Wm. A. Booth, Esq., of Stratford and New York. Kimberly was a blacksmith.

CHILDREN.

EBENEZER, baptized June 1706, at Stratford. According to the Stratford records, this Ebenezer was son of John, but may not this have been Ebenezer, the son of his brother Thomas, born April 7th, 1706? There is no information of the birth, marriage or death of John, the son of the 1st Thomas.

He or his uncle John, probably the latter, bought land in Woodbury, in 1692. Book 2d, p. 132.

On the 11th of September, 1705, he sold to his brother Thomas, both then residing at Stratford, all his interest in lands in Woodbury, derived from his father Thomas or his Uncle John. Book No. 20, p. 130.

He seems to have been a man of character and standing, as it appears by the Colonial Records of Conn., vol. 6, p. 68, that he was a Deputy to the General Assembly, from the town of Stratford, in the year 1718.

Children of Dr. Thomas ,of Stratford, Ripton Parish.

6. James Leavenworth.[3]—THOMAS,[2] THOMAS.[1]

Born September 1st, 1699, at Stratford.

Married Hester Trowbridge, August 23, 1720. She was probably a daughter of James Trowbridge, of New Haven, Ct., by his 2d wife Esther, or Hester Howe, whom he married September, 1692, and had this daughter in 1694. She died at Ripton, in 1780, aged 86. His will is dated August 1st, 1759, but as it was not proved till April 25th, 1763, he probably did not die till that year, though in Bronson's Waterbury it is stated to have been in 1759, (p. 516.) It was between 1759 and 1763.

He and his wife were original members of the Church at Ripton, and he was Collector of Church rates in 1736.

He left a large real estate as appears by his will, a copy of which will be found in the Appendix Letter F., and is recorded in the records of Fairfield District, in a Book dated 1761, to 1763, p. 465, to 468. His personal property was appraised at £435. 7.11,

CHILDREN.

17. MEHITABLE, b. July 28, 1721, d. in 1807, aged 86, m. Josiah Wetmore.
18. TAMER, b. May, 28, 1727. d. after 1759, m. Samuel Hurd.
19, SAMUEL, b. February 21, 1729, d. after 1759.
20. DANIEL, b. March 25, 1731, d. March 3, 1810, aged 79.

21. ANNE, b. April 4, 1733, d. after 1759, m. Edward Lake, of North Stratford.
22. MARY, b. August 13, 1735, d. after 1759, there unmarried.
23. JAMES, b. July 8, 1737, d. May 6, 1806.
24. ESTHER, b. January 27, 1739–40, d. after 1759, then unmarried.
25. EBENEZER, b. September 22, 1743, d. before August 1, 1759.

All born in Stratford. He bought lands at the White Hills, in Ripton Parish, in 1728. See Stratford Records. I think he lived in that part of the town of Stratford, now known as Monroe, and his descendants are still residents there, at and about Stepney, on and near the Hoosatonic R. R. He has also a large descent in the counties of Fulton, Montgomery and Saratoga, N. Y., at Gloversville, Kingsborough, Amsterdam, and Galway, etc., etc.

7. David Leavenworth.[3]—THOMAS,[2] THOMAS.[1]

Born October 12, 1701, at Stratford.

Married SARAH HURD, June 3, 1730. She was a daughter of John Hurd, and was born April 3, 1702, and died before 1736, June 25, 1727, joined the Woodbury Church, and his wife April 7, 1734. He died April 10, 1735, at Woodbury. He was a physician. Cothren or his printer errs ten years in his mariage, which he puts in 1720. He resided at Ripton Parish, in April 1725, as well as his father Deacon Thomas. Third vol. of Woodbury Records, p. 127 and 170. The lands by said deeds conveyed, were received from his father as appears by thc records.

CHILDREN.

26. NATHAN, baptized August 4, 1731, d. August 4, 1731.
27. DAVID, baptized August 4, 1731, d. August 4, 1731.
28. NATHAN, b. November 1, 1732, d. February 16, 1804.
29. EBENEZER, baptized December 29, 1734, d. in 1778 of Small Pox.

His will was proved in Woodbury Probate Court November 8 1735, 2d Probate Book p. 36. He left lands in Ruccum and on Good Hill, where were the early homes of the family, and where many of them still reside.

His two sons received a portion of the estate of their Grandfather Thomas. See his will. He removed from Ripton to Woodbury, between April 1725, and June 1727.

He was no doubt a gentleman of character, education and intelligence, as few better or more valuable men have been raised in the family, than his son and Grandson the two Nathans, of Hinesburg, Vt., his great Grandson, Henry Clay L., of Burlington, and his Grandson the Rev. Ebenezer I. Leavenworth.

8. Ebenezer Leavenworth.[3]—THOMAS,[2] THOMAS.[1]

Born April 7, 1706, at Stratford. Removed to Ripton. Died in 1734, unmarried. He was an original member of the Ripton Church.

He was collector of Parish rates at Ripton, in 1727. In December 1733, Dr. Thomas deeded to him lands at Good Hill. Book 4, p. 165, Woodbury records. He had lands at the White Hills, in Ripton in 1731. See Stratford records.

His will bears date May 25, 1734. After making specific bequests to his father and brother Edmund, he divides the rest equally to his brothers and sisters, giving however, a double share to his brother James, whom he makes his Executor. Date of Book 1716 to 1735, page 272.

9. John Leavenworth.[3]—THOMAS[2] THOMAS[1].

Born Nov. 3, 1708, at Stratford, baptized ——————, in Bridgeport, (then Stratfield,) a parish of St, ——, as there was no pastor in St. ———.

Married (1st.) Deborah Hurd, about 1737? She died January 1, 1746.

Married 2d, Mary Bronson, Jauuary 29, 1747. She was the daughter of Ebenezer B. and Mary Mann, and born July 21, 1719. He died in 1783. He resided at Ripton, in 1733. Book 4, p. 164 of Woodbury Records.

His father deeded to him lands on Good Hill, in 1733, and he received a part of the estates of his brother Ebenezer and his father Thomas. He probably died about 1784–5.

CHILDREN—FIRST WIFE.

30. DAVID, b. about 1737–8.
31. ABIGAIL, b. about 1739.
32. JOHN, baptized July 19, 1741, d. in 1821, in Woodbury.
33. LEMUEL, baptized October 9, 1743, d. April 30, 1825.
34. DEBORAH, baptized May 8, 1745, d. —— —— in Woodbury.

CHILDREN—SECOND WIFE.

35. SYBIL, b. 1747, d. —— ——, m. —— Keeler, of Fairfield.
36. AMOS, baptized August 9, 1753, d. at Deerfield, N. Y., September 2, 1828.
37. AVIS, b. 1754, d. —— ——, m. Simeon Castle, of Roxbury.
38. ELIHU, b. October 5, 1756, d. December 25, 1756.
39. ELISHA, baptized July 3, 1763, d. early, before his father.
40. ELIHU, h. June 10, 1763, d July 1, 1817.

They were all born in Woodbury.

His will was proved at Woodbnry, February 17, 1785, 8th Prob. vol. p. 164. His sons Amos and Elihu were his Exec's.

He had a number of slaves with their families, which he disposed of by his will.

He was during his life one of the leading men of the town of Woodbury.

He lived on Good Hill, near the residence of the late John L., and on or near the very ground where his Grandfather first settled and died. The cellar is still visible.

10. Zebulon Leavenworth.[3]—THOMAS,[2] THOMAS.[1]

Born 1710, in the town of Stratford.

Married ESTHER ——, about 1744. She died in 1793. June 27, 1742, joined the Woodbury Congregational Church. He died May 2, 1778, in Woodbury, Conn. Was a farmer, and probably spent his life there. Bronson in his history of Waterbury, p. 516, states his death as being in 1793. Dr. Thomas deeded lands to him on the north end of Good Hill, October 10, 1735, book 5 p. 39.

CHILDREN.

41. MARY, baptized July 16, 1745, d. 1814.
42. ESTHER, baptized June 21, 1747, d. 1749.
43. ESTHER, baptized May 20, 1750, d.
44. ZEBULON, b. November 14, 1752, d. 1795.

45. EUNICE, b. March 2, 1755, d.
46. ANNA, baptized August 22, 1757, d.
47. HULDAH, baptized May 30, 1759, d.
48. ALICE, baptized August 13, 1761, d.

June 6, 1778, his will was proved at Woodbury, 7th Probate vol., p. 256.

The only male descendants of this son of Dr. Thomas, are the sons and Grandsons of Zebulon and Seth M. L., of Leavenworth, the capital of Crawford Co. Indiana, on the Ohio. They are now (1873,) living at Leavenworth and Mount Vernon, Ind., and St. Louis, Mo.

11. Rev. Mark Leavenworth.[3] (THOMAS,[2] THOMAS.[1])

Born in 1711, at Stratford. Graduated at Yale College, in 1737.

Married (1.) RUTH PECK, February 6, 1739-40, daughter of Jeremiah, and grand daughter of Rev. Jeremiah Peck, first minister of Waterbury. She died Aug. 8, 1750.

Married (2.) SARAH HULL, December 4, 1750, daughter of Jesse Hull, of Derby, and cousin of Gen. William Hull. She died May 7, 1808, aged 82 years.

In March 1760, he was appointed chaplain of the 2d Connecticut Regiment, commanded by Col. Nathan Whiting. He served from March 24th, to November 10th, 1760, and was reappointed in March 1761. He went with the regiment to Canada.

CHILDREN.

49. COL. JESSE, b. November 22, 1741, d. December 12, 1824.
50. MARK, b. May 26, 1752, d. in Paris, 1812.
51. JOSEPH, b. January 19, 1755, d. January 6, 1756.
52. SARAH, b. December, 11, 1756, d. February 23, 1793.
53. WILLIAM, b. February 23, 1759, d. November 24, 1836, at Bridgeport.
54. DR. NATHAN, b. December 11, 1761, d. January 9, 1799.
55. JOSEPH, b. June 15, 1764, d.
56. ELISHA, b. October 21, 1766, d. May 3, 1802.
October 13, 1766 Bronson has it.

All born in Waterbury.

For the following sketch of him I am indebted to his lineal descendant, the Hon. F. J. Kingsbury, of Waterbury.

REV. MARK LEAVENWORTH,

Was born in Stratford, Conn. He is supposed to have fitted

for college, and probably began his preparation for the ministry, with that famous teacher of the young, Rev. Jedediah Mills, (Y.C. 1722,) then minister of Ripton. He was licensed to preach by the New Haven East Association in 1738, having graduated at Yale iu 1737. In 1739, after preaching a few Sunday's on trial, he was unanimously called to succeed Rev. John Southmayd, in the church at Waterbury, Conn. Mr. Southmayd was a man of culture and ability, and not advanced in years, but his health was poor, he was possessed of some means and he desired to be relieved from his charge. He lived seventeen years after this, an honored and influential citizen, and it is a tribute to Mr. Leavenworth's discretion and ability, which will be appreciated by all young clergymen who have had their predecessor in their congregations, that Mr. Southmayd at his death, made Mr. Leavenworth his executor.

Mr. L. had a £500 settlement, and £100 salary, but they prudently took a bond from him that the £500 should be returned if within twenty years he turned churchman, or was guilty of any immorality or heresy which rendered him unfit for his work. At the end of about ten years he was released from this bond.

He was ordained in March, 1740, having made good use of his time in some respects, as he was married the preeeding February to one of his new congregation, Miss Ruth Peck, granddaughter of Rev. Jeremiah Peck, first minister of the town.

This year, 1740, Whitfield first preached in New England, and from this and other causes, arose differences dividing the people into two sharply opposing theological parties. The Whitfield party were called "new lights," among these was Mr. Leavenworth, evidently a progressive man, and as the conservative party were the stronger in Connecticut, this fact doubtless, somewhat affected Mr. L's theological standing and importance in the State for many years.

In 1744 for assisting at the ordination of Rev. Jonathan Lee, of Salisbury, supposed to be thoroughly tainted with the Whitfield heresy, and inclined to the Cambridge platform, Mr. Leavenworth, Rev. Mr. Humphrey's, of Derby, and Rev. Mr. Todd. of Northbury, (Plymouth,) were tried and "suspended from al, associational communion." It is probable, however, that this sentence was soon revoked, or possibly disregarded.

In 1747, Mr. L. refused that part of his salary which was levied upon the church of England inhabitants, showing a strong love of justice and a liberality in advance of his time.

In 1760, in the old French War, he served as chaplain to Col. Whiting's 2d Connecticut Regiment, enduring with spirit the hardships of that campaign. He was on the State Committee for raising troops in the Revolution, and his name heads the list of those in Waterbury, who took the oath of fidelity after the declaration of independence.

He was a member of the Connecticut Society for the promotion of Freedom in 1793. So that age had not impaired his interest in the public weal.

He was a man of sound judgment, strong character, much personal diguity, living in a style of elegant hospitality for those times, a keen wit, and of considerable ability as a preacher. Dr. Bronson in his History of Waterbury, from which much of this article has been obtained, says of him, that "he had a large heart in the right place—was kind to the poor and beloved of all." Two of his printed sermons still exist, one a funeral sermon on the dealh of Daniel Southmayd, Esq., a prominent member of his congregation, preached in 1754. The other the Annual Eleetion sermon preached at Hartford, before the General Assembly, May, 1772. Copies of these are among the collections of the Connecticut Historical Society, at Hartford. They are creditable productions.

Dr. Sam'l. Elton, of Watertown, now some years dead, remembered Mr. L., as he appeared to him, when a boy, at the church at Watertown. He said he was a man of medium height, straight figure, commanding appearance and voice, and a bright dark eye, that he stood up in the pulpit and looked around for a moment on the congregation and then announced his text. "The father's, where are they? and the prophets!—Do they live forever?" He then went on to speak of the changes that had taken place in that congregation within his own memory in a manner that made a deep impression on his youthful hearers.

He laid the corner stone of a new church, which bore his initials "M. L. 1795," and which is still to be seen, though the building has been removed from its original site and converted to secular uses.

He died Aug, 20, 1797, in the 86th year of his age, and the 58th of his ministry, having publicly officiated only a short time before his death. He died and was buried at Waterbury.

12. Thomas Leavenworth.[3]—THOMAS,[2] THOMAS.[1]

Born at Stratford, Ct.

Married (1.) BETTY DAVIS, 17—. She died April 24, 1758. (2.) RHODA OLDS, October 10, 1758. She died at Watertown, May 1, 1794, aged 67. December 7, 1760, he owned the half-way covenant and joined First Congregational Church, Woodbury.

He received July 6, 1748, from his father, one whole right in commonage in Woodbury, and one third of the remainder of said rights in commonage, with £100, (old tenor,) Upon tbe death of his brother Ebenezer, he received March 1734–5 a part of his estate. In 1727, he was Collector of rates at Ripton. He was a tanner and settled in Woodbury, but failed in business, and went to Wyoming, where he again began business, but was driven out by the Indians in 1778, and while still within sight of his home, saw it in flames. A part of their pewter ware was put into a brass kettle and sunk in a well, or buried in the bank of a stream. They returned to Oxford, Ct., and he died, after 1795? at the residence of his son Gideon, in Hamden, and was buried in the neighborhood of Shephard's Brook. He lived in Woodbury in 1752, and before and after.

CHILDREN.

57. ASA, b. 1744, d. November 19, 1828.
58. TRIPHENA, b, July 3, 1746, d. must have died early.
59. GIDEON, b. February 21, 1748, d. June 7, 1833.
60. SAMUEL, b. 1751, d. April 12, 1807.
61. DAVID, b. February 1, 1756, d. young.
62. BETTY; b. October 28, 1760, d.
63. ISAAC, baptized March 7, 1762, d, young.
64. ABEL, baptized February 10, 1765, d. January 25, 1813.
65. THOMAS, baptized December 28, 1766, d. in 1849.
66. DORMAN, b. October 28, 1770, d. May 31, 1861.

Mr. Cothren says, administration was granted on his estate, November 16, 1781, at Woodbury. Administration granted to John L. the 3d, 7th Probate Book page 71. It would seem that this *must be* correct. But Jared L. Pitcher, son of Polly L., who was the daughter of Gideon, Thomas' son writes me that he died near Shephards Brook, in the town of Hamden, seven miles from New Haven, and was buried there, and that he was over 80 years of age, and that his Grandfather Gideon, has often told him about it. This is not in the Woodbury district. My mother informed me that he spent the winter of 1795-6 with his grandson David, at Canaan, N. Y., then returned to his son Gideon's, at Hamden, and soon after died there.

We cannot suppose any error in the *Records*, nor does it seem possible that two independent and perfectly reliable sources of information should be incorrect. Could Cothren refer to another Thomas L ?

When driven out of the Wyoming Valley with his family, they picked their way as best they could, through the woods of Pennsylvania, New Jersey and New York, living mainly on berries, and reached their friends in Connecticut, with only the few clothes they wore.

Dorman the youngest child, he led by the hand, Asa and some of the older children probably never went to Pennsylvania. I think Thomas lived at Waterbury in 1770.

His failure in early life at Woodbury, and the second loss of all his property in the Wyoming Valley, leaving him with a large family of small children was most embarrassing and disheartening, but did not prevent him from so raising and educating his children, as to enable them to attain respectable and independent positions in society.

13. MARY LEAVENWORTH[3], THOMAS[2], THOMAS[1].

Born at Stratford about 1717. She died at Huntington, aged 96 years.

Married about 1740 ? Joshua Perry of Ripton, a brother of Abner Perry, who m. her sister Sarah. Her 5th child ANNA was born May, 11th, 1751. The brothers were farmers living on adjoining farms, and nearly opposite to Derby. She seems by the Parish Records to have been an original member of the church at Ripton in 1724, but the Records perhaps do not distinguish the original from later members.

In the record of the will of Dr. Thomas Leavenworth, his father-in-law, in the Probate office at Fairfield, he is called JOSEPH. This is an error. In the origiual will, still on file there, the name is JOSHUA.

In vol. 1778 to 1781, page 178 and 179 of the Probate Records at Fairfield, is found an inventory of the estate of Joshua Perry, dated February 1st, 1779, amounting to £288,08, and an additional inventory, dated May 14th, 1774 of 100 acres of land in Derby £340. This inventory was proved by Samuel Adams, Executor.

CHILDREN.

1. ISRAEL,
2. JOSHUA, b. about 1755 probably.
3. EBENEZER.
4. DAVID, b. July 19, 1746, at Ripton.
5 ANNA, b. May 11, 1751 at Ripton.
6. ARTHUR.
7. MARY.
8. JAMES, all b. in Huntington—then Ripton.

1. ISRAEL had quite a numerous family—was a farmer, lived some years in Whitesboro, N. Y.

Children.—1 ELI; 2. JAMES; 3. ISRAEL; 4. LEVI; 5. LUCRETIA; 6. MARY; 7. JOSHUA; 8. SARAH.

The first three followed no particular business and did little justice to the name of Perry.

4th. LEVI studied medicine and was for some years a physician at Stockbridge, Mass., then went to Canada.

5th. LUCRETIA married Mr. —— Eddy of Moravia, Cayuga Co., and in 1836, was living there with a family of children.

6th. MARY died when aged 26, at Oswego, while on a visit to her uncle.

7th and 8th. Of JOSHUA and SARAH I am not informed.

2. JOSHUA was graduated at Yale in the class of 1775,—studied theology with his uncle Mark Leavenworth of Waterbury, who often had a large number of young men under him preparing for the ministry. Dr. Brace informs me that sometimes there were fifteen or twenty. Was settled some years at Mount Carmel, near New Haven Conn., married a Miss Strong of Farmington, an accomplished and wealthy lady, became a farmer, had one feeble minded or perhaps idiotic child, who lived about thirty years. JOSHUA died in 1812.

3. EBENEZER an active and energetic farmer died at Oxford Conn., unmarried, early in life.

4. Rev. DAVID PERRY, (son of Joshua Perry and Mary Leavenworth, of Ripton Parish, now Huntington, Stratford, Conn.,) b, July 19, 1746, O. S., graduated at Yale College, in 1772.

Married JERUSHA LORD, of Middletown, Conn., Aug. 20, 1776, (daughter of Ichabod Lord, of Colchester, Conn.) He studied theology with the Rev. Mark Leavenworth, his uncle at Waterbury. He was Pastor of the Congregational church at Harwinton, Conn., ten years, when by reason of troubles which resulted from the agitation of questions relating to the "Half Way Covenant," he left in 1784, and was installed Pastor of the Congregational church in Richmond, Mass., whither he removed in October of that year.

He labored there as a successful minister for thirty-three years. and died of disease of the heart, June 7, 1817. His remains were followed to the grave by his wife and ten cbildren and numerous grand-children.

He was a man of commanding presence, and his figure was one to be remembered as he walked up the aisle of his meeting house on Sunday, with his gun in hand, a practice common with the clergy, upon the frontier of that early day.

She was born at Marlboro, Conn., February 7, 1755, O. S., and died at the residence of her son John B. Perry, in Lee, Mass., July 13, 1832. With a delicate constitution and slender health, she gave birth to eleven children, all but one of whom lived to old age.

With a small salary, much of which was paid in produce, by the aid of this admirable woman, Mr. Perry educated three of their sons in College, and at his death left a handsome patrimony for the support of the family, The farm which he cultivated with the aid of his sons, remained in the possession of the family until 1871.

Their Children.

1. DAVID LORD, b. Connecticut, June 21, 1777, m. ANNA SMITH STRONG, of Hartford, Conn., May 22, 1805, d. at Sharon, Conn., Oct. 25, 1835.
2. FREDERICK, b. Conn., Nov. 21, 1778, m. ZERUJAH SHERRILL, of Richmond, Mass., January 20, 1811.
3. ALFRED, b. Connecticut, April 28, 1780, m. LUCY BENJAMIN, of Williamstown, Mass,, Nov. 1, 1814, d, in Perryton, Ill., Sept. 10, 1838.
4. JOHN BULKLEY. b. Connecticut. Nov, 22. 1781, m. SARAH LORD LESTER, of Jewett City, Connecticut, April 30, 1811, d. in Lee, Mass., December ,24, 1843.
5. JERUSHA LORD, b. Connecticut, Aug., 19, 1783. d. in Richmond, Mass., March 25, 1862.
6. MARY, b. Aug. 4, 1785, d. April 7, 1865.
7. ERASTUS, b. April 17, 1787. m. First—MARY TREADWELL, of Farmington, Connecticut, Sept. 1, 1814, m, Second—CLARINA CRITTENDEN, of Richmond, Mass.. d. in Albany, N Y.
8. ASA, b Oct, 30, 1788, m. PHILURA AYLSWORTH, of Canaan, N. Y., Sept.. 1, 1823.
9. FLORELLA. b, April 4, 1791, d. May 28. 1807.
10. SARAH, b. Aug. 16, 1793, m. to Samuel Gates, of Richmond, January 17, 1822, d. at Saratoga Springs, N. Y., Oct. 20, 1856.
11. DANIEL, b. Dec. 12, 1795, m. CATHARINE AYLSWORTH, of Canaan, N. Y., October 1, 1822, d. in Burlington, Vt., April 4, 1869.

The first five born in Harwinton, Conn., the others in Richmond.

1. Rev. DAVID LORD PERRY, b. in Harwinton, Conn., June 21, 1777, graduate of Williams College in 1798, and was 3 years a tutor there. Ordained in Sharon, Connecticut, June 6, 1804.

Married to ANNE SMITH STRONG, of Hartfotd, Connecticut, May 22, 1805. d. in Sharon, suddenly of apoplexy, Oct. 25, 1835 He was a successful minister in the Congregational chnrch, and greatly beloved and mourned by the people of his charge.

ANNE SMITH STRONG, wife of the Rev. David Lord Perry, (daughter of Rev. Nathan Strong, D. D., of Hartford, Connecticut,) b. Sept. 10, 1778 d in Sharon October 1840. Her father, Dr. Strong, was a man ot superior intellect, full of wit and humor, and of unbounded powers for labor, which he fully used. In harmony with the thoughts of that day, he published a theological work entitled "The doctrine of Eternal Misery, consistent with the infinite benevolance of God,"

Their Children.

1. Rev. JOHN McCURDY STRONG, b. September 7, 1806, d. in Batticotta, Ceylon, March 10, 1838
2. ANNE FLORELLA. b. April 3, 1808, d. in Brattleboro, Vt., May 1867.
3. Rev. DAVID CHARLES, b. January 5, 1810
4. Dr. NATHAN STRONG, b. October 6, 1811, d in Ohio May 1855.
5. CATHARINE LORD, b. June 17, 1813,
6. THEODORE, b. January 28, 1815.
7. JERUSHA LORD, b. June 21, 1817.
8. Dr. EDWARD, b. May 25, 1820.
9. Dr. CORNELIUS, b. June 17. 1822
10. Dr. FREDERICK WILLIAM, b May 7, 1824, d in ---- February 20, 1863.

All born in Sharon.

1st. Rev. JOHN McCURDY STRONG, PERRY, b. in Sharon, September 7, 1806, graduate at Yale, in 1827. Ordained in Mendon, Mass., in 1832.

Married August 12, 1833, HARRIET JOANNA LATHROP, b. 1817, (daughter of Charles and Joanna Lathrop, of Norwich, Connecticut,) went as a missionary to

Ceylon, in 1835, d. of cholera in Batticotta, Ceylon, March 1838, of which also, his wife died about the same time. Their child,

HARRIET JOANNA PERRY, b. in Ceylon, October 1835, resides in New Haven, Connecticut.

3. Rev. DAVID CHARLES PERRY, b. in Sharon, January 5, 1810, graduate at Yale, in 1833, ordained in North Fairfield, Connecticut, December 1838. From 1845 to 1857 he was settled in Barlow, Ohio. In 1857 he was disabled from preaching by being thrown in a rail way car from a tressle, down 60 feet into a ravine. He now resides at Marietta, Ohio.

He married April 26, 1838, MARGARET WILLIAMS, (daughter of William G. and Tryphena Williams, of North Hartford, Connecticut. She d. in Sharon, August 3, 1840. Second. He m. in 1841, POLLY M. FERRY, (daughter of Ebenezer and Charity Ferry, of Danbury, (Bethel,) Connecticut) She d. in 1845. Third. He m. in 1847, SARAH PLATT, (daughter of Ebenezer and Mary Platt, of Danbury, Connecticut.) She d. in 1848. Fourth. He m. in 1850, ESTHER C. WALTON, b. January 24, 1819, (daughter of Nathan and Ruth Way Walton, of Cincinnati, Ohio.)

Children by Second Wife.

1. GEORGE HOWARD PERRY, b. in Fairfield, Connecticut, November 28, 1842, d. in Barlow, Ohio, April 4, 1845
2. CHABLES STRONG PERRY, b. in Fairfield, April 7, 1844, graduate at Marietta, Coll., in 1865. Prof. in Ohio Inst. for Deaf and Dumb, in Columbus, Ohio.

By Fourth Wife.

3. SARAH FRANCES, b. in Barlow, Ohio, Sept. 25, 1855.

5. CATHARINE LORD PERRY, b. in Sharon, June 17, 1813. Married in 1842, Dr Reuben B. Merriman, of Litchfield, Connecticut. He subsequently resided in Niles, Mich. They separated and he went to parts unknown. She now resides in Austin, Texas.

Children.

1. ALICE FLORENCE MERRIMAN, b. in Litchfield, Connecticut, July 1843. Married Col. Benjamin R Townsend, of the coast serviee during the late war, now of Austin, Texas. A Planter. Their child,

CATHARINE TOWNSEND MERRIMAN, b. in Austin, 1867.

1. CATHARINE MERRIMAN b. in Litchfield, in 1845, d. in Lacon, Ill., in 1850.

6 THEODORE PERRY, b. in Sharon, January 28, 1815. Married in Gallipolis, Ohio, April 26, 1841, Elizabeth Heath Cushing, (daughter of Gen. Nathan Stone and Mary Lincoln Cushing, daughter of Gen. Lincoln, of Revolutionary memory.) She died in Lacon, Ill., Sept. 6, 1848. Second. He married Oct 31, 1849 Jane Emaranda Brown Stebbins, b. Oct. 20, 1827, (daughter of Clark Brown and Mary Tobey Stebbins, of Springfield, Mass.) She d. in Lawton, Mich., November 28 1868 From 1838 to 1864, he was in the grain trade at Lacon, and since then in Chicago, residing in Evanston, Ill.

Children by First Wife.

1. EDWARD CUSHING, b. May 22, 1842, d. at Lacon, July 27, 1844.
2. FRANCES LINCOLN, b. August 9, 1844, d. at Lacon, June 21, 1846.
3. THEODORE CUSHING, b. June 24, 1846, d. at Lacon, June 26, 1847.

By Second Wife.

4. IDA STRONG, b. December 14, 1850.
5. MARGARET STEBBINS, b. December 15, 1853.
6. THEODORE CLERC, b. July 13, 1855.
7. JENNY CLARK, b. December 27, 1861.
8. FLORENCE MARY, b. in Chicago, July 3, 1865.
9. FRECERICK WILLIAM, b. in Lawton, Mich., November 26, 1868, d. there December 1, 1868. The first seven b. in Lacon.

JERUSHA LORD PERRY, b. in Sharon, June 21, 1817. Married in 1847, Rev. Francis Joseph Clerc, D. D., son of the late Rev. Laurent Clerc, D. D, professor in the Asylum for the Deaf and Dumb, at Hartford, Connecticut.

He is now Rector of Burlington College, New Jersey.

Children.

ADELE; FRANK; EMILY; EDITH; date not communicated.

8. EDWARD PERRY, M. D., b. in Sharon, May 25, 1820, graduate at Medical College of New York, in 1845. Married January 2, 1848, Emily Craig, daughter of Moses and Rachel Carhart Craig, of Peapack, N J. She was b. there, April 26, 1828. He now resides in Peapack.

Chlldren.

FRANCIS CLERC, b. August 13, 1850, d. in Somerville, N. J., March 9, 1851.

RODIE CRAIG, b. October 20th, 1852, a daughter.

ALFRED FRANCIS, b. August 13, 1858, d. August 7, 1863. All b. in Peapack, where the family now reside.

9. CORNELIUS PERRY, M. D., b, in Sharon, July 17, 1822, graduate of Medical College of New York, in —— Married May, 1848, Lucy M. Swayze, b. in 1830, daughter of Edward H. Swayze, of N. J. He now resides at Wenona Station, Ill.

Children

FANNY; EVELIN; dates not given.

10. FREDERICK WILLIAM PERRY, M. D., b. in Sharon, May 7, 1824, graduated at Yale Medical College, in 1846. Married November 8th, 1849, Caroline, Blakeley Latham, daughter of John and Mary T. Peddell Latham, of Mendham, N. J., b. March 18, 1826. He was a physician of Mendham, N. J., where he died February 11, 1863. He was a man of great energy of character and firmness of will; for several years a coroner in New York. He stepped on a nail which caused mortification and death.

She married second, Thomas Hallock Vance, of Cold Water, Mich.

Children.

1. MARY ANN, b. in Mendham, N. J.. January 23, 1851, now studying law at the University, at Ann Arbor, Mich.
2. CARRIE LATHAM, b. in Mendham, July 2, 1852.

2. FREDERICK PERRY, b. in Harwinton, Connecticut, Nov. 21, 1778. Married January 20, 1811, to Zerujah, daughter of Henry and Lois Chidsay Sherrill, of Richmond, Mass., b. March 16, 1785, d. in Stockbridge, Mass., January 29, 1866

He was b. at Harwinton, Connecticut, November 21, 1778, graduated at Williams College, 1802. He studied theology with his father and the Rev. Dr. Hyde of Lee, but was never licensed. In 1804, he was Principal of the Academy at Williamstown, and in 1805, tutor in the College there. From 1807 to 1811, he was a merchant at Richmond.—then for three years at Lenox, still as a merchant, and in 1815 he settled at Stockbridge.

Mr. Perry has been for many years the oldest living graduate of Williams College. He has ever been noted for wonderful perseverance and industry, and at his present great age of 94 is able to attend to the various details about his premises in Stockbridge, where he now resides.

Children.

1. ELIZA SHERRILL, b. in Lenox, Mass., June 5, 1812.
2. FANNY LOUISE, b. in Lenox, June 27, 1813, d. in Albany, August 29, 1836.
3. SARAH LESTER, b. in Stockbridge, Mass., January 27, 1824, d. in Austerlitz, N. Y., January 2, 1862.

ELIZA SHERRILL, married June 26, 1834, in Stockbridge, Edward McKinstry Teall, b. in Hillsdale, N. Y., January 8, 1808, d. in Albany, April 10, 1849.

Children.

1. SUSAN, b. in Albany, April 27, 1835.

2. LOUISA, b. in Albany, January 17, 1837, d. in New York, June 25, 1860.
3. EDWARD MCKINSTRY, b. in Albany, July 27, 1839.
4. ELIZA, b. in Albany, March 31, 1842, d. in Albany, May 12, 1843.
5. FREDERICK, b, in Albany, March 30, 1844, d. in Stockbridge, Mass., August 28, 1844.
6. SARAH, b. in Albany, June 27, 1845, d. in Albany June 7, 1846.
7. FREDERICK WILLIAM, b. in Albany, December 22, 1847, d. in Albany, May 30, 1848.
8. HENRY DWIGHT, b. in Albany, March 26, 1849.

1. SUSAN TEALL, b. in Albany, April 27, 1835, married George W. Perry, of Bennington, Vermont, b. October 8, 1833. They reside in Chicago.

Children.

3. EDWARD MCKINSTRY TEALL, b. in Albany, July 27, 1839, married June 11, 1862. Katharine Mead of Chicago.

2. FANNY LOUISE PERRY, b. in Lenox, Mass., June 27, 1813, married in Stockbridge, April 29, 1835, to Rev. E. Parsons Ingersoll, of Lee, Mass., b. there in 1804. He became a Professor at Oberlin College; now resides in Kansas. She d. in Albany, August 29 1836.

Their Child.

JAMES BIRNEY INGERSOLL, b. in Oberlin, Ohio, February 27, 1836, d. in Topeka, Kansas, August 16, 1862. Mr. Ingersoll's parents were David and Sarah Parsons Ingersoll of Lee. The latter was grand daughter of the renowned Rev. Jonathan Edwards.

3. SARAH LESTER PERRY, b. in Stockbridge, January 27, 1824, married there November 29, 1842, to Rev. Philander Oliver Powers, son of Oliver and Azuba Corruth Powers, of Phillipston, Mass., missionary in Turkey. He was born in Phillipston, Mass., August 19, 1805, d. in Kessab, Syria, October 2, 1872. She d. in Austerlitz, N, Y., January 2, 1862, soon after their return from the east on a visit.

Children.

HARRIET GOLDING POWERS, b. in Broosa, Asia Minor, April 14, 1845

FREDERICK PERRY POWERS, b. in Trebizond, Asia Minor, June 29, 1849. He is now an editor in Newport, R. I., and a young man of decided promise.

3. ALFRED PERRY, M. D., b. in Harwinton, Connecticut, April 28, 1780, graduate of Williams College, 1803, and of Philadelphia Institute, under Dr. Rush. Married Nov. 1, 1814, LUCY BENJAMIN, (daughter of Nathan and Ruth Seymour Benjamin, of Williamstown, Mass.,) b. in Egremont, October 11, 1792. He d. in Perryton, Ill., Sept. 10, 1838.

He was a successful practitioner of medicine in Stockbridge, for and during eighteen years, deacon in the Congregational Church more than twenty years. He was a man of uncompromising rectitude in every department of life. He removed with his family to the far west in 1838, and soon after died of the fever of the country, leaving Mrs. Perry in that then distant and wild country with a large family of children, without friends at hand, or facilities for comfortable living. She proved herself equal to the emergency, brought up her large family successfully, every member of which has done honor to the name.

Children.

1. LUCY BENJAMIN, b. in Williamstown, Mass., Oct. 3, 1815, d. there February 11, 1842.
2. ALFRED WHITMAN, b. in Stockbridge, Mass., December 19, 1818.
3. DAVID LORD, b. in Stockbridge, Mass., September 30, 1820.
4. JOHN BUCKLEY, b. in Stockbridge, June 16, 1823. Was drowned in a cistern June 29, 1825.
5. MARY, b. in Stockbridge, February 8, 1826.

6. GEORGE BUCKLEY, b. in Stockbridge, July 7, 1828.
7. NATHAN BENJAMIN, b. in Stockbridge, July 31, 1830.
8. CHARLES LESTER, b. in Stockbridge, February 20, 1833.
9. SARAH LOUISE, b. in Stockbridge, Oct. 11, 1836.

1. LUCY BENJAMIN, b. October 3, 1815, m. Prof. John Tatlock, Professor of Mathematics in Williams College, August 16. 1838, b. in Liverpool, Eng., December 4, 1808. She died in Williamstown, February 11, 1842. He now practices law in Pittsfield, Mass., and, being a Congregational clergyman, preaches from time to time.

Child.

1. JOHN TATLOCK, JR., b. in Williamstown, January 1, 1842; d. there March 1, 1842.

2. ALFRED WHITMAN PERRY, b. in Stockbridge, December 19, 1818; m. Mary Boon in Farlow's Grove, Ill., Mar. 31, 1841; b. in Bloomsburgh, Pa., April 8, 1822. Mr. Perry resides in Geneseo, Ill., and is President of the Northwestern Illinois Coal Company.

Children.

FANNIE LOUISE, b. in M. May 9th, 1866, Marshall P. Walcutt, b. Oct. 21, 1858, son of Geo. and Margaret Teine of Walcuttsville, Ind.

Children.

1. ALFRED PERRY, b. July 6, 1867.
2. GEORGE ELTON, b, May 21, 1869; d. June 1, 1869.
3. FRANK BARTON, b. April 9, 1871.

2. CLARA BARTON, b. December 24, 1845.

3. DAVID LORD PERRY, b. in Stockbridge Sept. 30, 1820, m. Harriet Andrews, dau. of Alanson and Sarah H. Gates Andrews, of Ashland, O., August 17, 1852, b. August 2, 1831, at Ashland. Mr. Perry is now a real estate dealer in Chicago.

Children.

1. LUCY BENJAMIN, b. in Geneseo, Ill., May 24, 1853.
2. IDA LOUISE, b. in Geneseo, Ill., June 7, 1856.
3. CHARLES SPAULDING, b. in Geneseo, Ill., March 26, 1859.
4. DAVID LORD, b. in Hinsdale, Ill., January 14, 1868.
5. EVERETA HOWE, b. in Hinsdale, Ill., July 15, 1872.

5. MARY PERRY, b. in Stockbridge, Mass., February 18, 1826; m. Joshua Edward Ford in Williamstown, Mass., September 6, 1847, son of George Washington and Mary Edwards Ford, of Ogdensburg; b. August 3. 1825, and died in Geneseo, Ill., April 3, 1866. They sailed for Syria as missionaries of the American Board, December 28, 1847. where they remained nearly twenty years, in the faithful performance of the work for which they left friends and worldly prosperity. Mr Ford commanded respect and esteem for his ability and character, and in his death was greatly mourned by the friends of missions. Mrs. Ford now resides with her younger children in Geneseo, Ill.

Children.

1. NATHAN b. July 13, 1849.
2. GEORGE ALFRED, b. May 30, 1851.
3. LUCY MARIA, b. April 12, 1853, d. in Syria December 20. 1858.
4. JOHN JACOB, b. February 11, 1855; d. in Syria November 28, 1855
5. CHARLES HENRY, b. October 9, 1856.
6. SARAH, b. September 26, 1859.
7. EDWARD ALBERT, b. December 5, 1863.

The surviving children are all in this country. All born in Syria.

6. GEORGE BUCKLEY PERRY, b. in Stockbridge, Mass., July 7, 1828; m. Maria Louise Tyler, dau. of Duty S. and ——— ———Tyler, of North Adams,

Mass., May 3, 1855. b February 21, 1834. He is now residing in North Adams, in the insurance business, and interested in iron ore beds.

Children.

1. CORNELIA TYLER, b. in North Adams, Mass., October 29, 1856.
2. ALFRED TYLER, b. in Geneseo, Ill., August 19, 1858.
3. ANNIE LOUISE, b. in Geneseo, Ill., April 30, 1860.

7. NATHAN BENJAMIN PERRY, b. in Stockbridge July 31, 1830. M. Minnie Suviah, dau. of Rodman H. and ——————Wells, of North Adams, Mass., December 4, 1856, b. December 4, 1835. Mr. Perry now resides in Albany, and is a member of the firm of Perry & Co., one of the largest manufacturers of stoves in the world. He is a man of quick perceptions, large business capacity, and great industry.

Children.

1. EDWARD RODMAN, b. in Geneseo, Ill., March 27, 1861.
2. FRANK SPAULDING, b. in Geneseo, March 25, 1863.

8. CHARLES LESTER PERRY, b. in Stockbridge, Mass., February 20, 1833. M. Maria Janette Wells, dau. of Ira and Caroline Bosworth Wells, of Rockville, Ct., February 4, 1858, b. October 5, 1837, in Vernon, Ct.; d. in Rockville, Ct., September 20, 1865.

Second, m. Fannie Smith, dau. of James T. and Pamelia Heath Smith, of Little Falls, N. Y., March 17, 1871, b. in Little Falls, N. Y. He resides in Geneseo, and is Secretary of the Northwestern Coal Company.

Children, by first wife.

1. META CAROLINE, b. in Geneseo January 3, 1859.
2. CARL, b. in Geneseo May 28, 1863, d. there November 10, 1864.

9. SARAH LOUISE PERRY, b. in Stockbridge October 11, 1836. M. September 27, 1871, at Geneseo, Ill., Rev. James G. Dougherty, b. September 22, 1838. He is settled over a church in Wyandotte, Kansas.

Child.

LUCY TAFT, b. ——————June 15, 1873.

4 JOHN BUCKLEY PERRY, b in Harwinton, Ct., November 23, 1781. M. in Jewett City, Conn., April 30, 1811, Sarah Lord Lester, b. in 1783, d. in Lee, Mass., November 21, 1836. He died there December 24, 1843.

Mr. Perry was for a long course of years a successful merchant at that place, of the early New England stamp. His wife was a most genial character, bright witty and attractive.

Child.

An infant b. in Lee May 10, 1813. Soon died.

5 & **6**. JERUSHA, d. about 1863. MARY, April 7, 1865, both at Richmond and unmarried.

7. ERASTUS PERRY, b. in Richmond Mass., April 17, 1787, m. September 1, 1814, Mary, dau. of Gov. John and Mrs. Dorotha Pomeroy Treadwell, of Farmington, Conn., b there December 28, 1786, d. there August 10, 1825. He d. in Albany May 3, 1858.

Second, he m. in 1827, Clarissa, dau. of Levi and Mary Crittenden, of Richmond, Mass., b. there May 20, 1785, d. in Somerville, N. Y., 1862.

Children, by first wife.

1. JOHN STRONG, b. December 17, 1815.
2. ROGER HOOKER, b. February, 18, 1818, d. January 26, 1819.
3. SAMUEL HOOKER, b. February, 1820, d. April 14, 1821.
4. MARY, b. May 6, 1822, d. May 9, 1822.
5. MARY 2d, b. July 7, 1825, d. August 6, 1825. All born and died in Farmington.

John S Perry

By second wife.

6 MARY NORTON, b. in Richmond, Mass., December, 1828, and now resides in Albany, N. Y.

1. JOHN STRONG PERRY, b. in Farmington, Ct., December 17, 1815, m. May 11, 1846, Mary Jane, dau. of Josiah and Mary Willard, at Plattsburgh, N. Y., b. In Westminster, Vt., April 19, 1826, d. in Albany June 22, 1864.

Second, he m. in Boston, January 24, 1867, Mary Elizabeth, dau. of Calvin A. and Mary Wyman, of Woburn, Mass., b. October 22, 1833, d in Albany, N. Y., June 30, 1869.

Third, he m. in Brooklyn, N. Y., January 25, 1871, Adeline L., dau. of Jones, of Clyde, N. Y., b. in Marengo, N. Y., June 30, 1825.

Children by first wife.

1. HARRIET WILLARD, b. March 14, 1847, d. in Albany November 6, 1852.
2. FLORENCE, b. July 5, 1849.
3. HENRY WEBB, b. July 14, 1851, d. in Albany July 12, 1852.
4. JOHN TREADWELL, b. in Saratoga Springs May 24, 1853.
5. WILLARD ELMORE, b. January 31, 1856.
6. JESSIE MAY, b. May 21, 1857, d. in Plattsburgh, N. Y., July 20, 1872.
7. EDITH, b. July 21, 1859.
8. GEORGE STERLING, b. June 27, 1862, d. in Albany July 11, 1862.

Child by second wife.

MARY ELIZABETH WYMAN, b. June 10, 1869.

All except John Treadwell born in Albany.

FLORENCE PERRY, b. in Albany July 5, 1849, m. in Albany September 10, 1868, Rev. William Tatlock, of Stamford, Conn., b. in Liverpool, Eng. He is Rector of St. John's Episcopal church in that place, Assistant Secretary of House of Bishops, Indian Commissioner of Protestant Episcopal church, and member of Executive Committee of the Board.

Children.

WILLARD LANGLEY, b. in Stamford June 15, 1869.

HERBERT PERRY, b. in Stamford April 11, 1871.

8. ASA PERRY, b. in Richmond. Mass., October 30, 1788, m. September 1, 1823, Philura Aylsworth, dau. of William Aylsworth, of Canaan, N. Y., b. October 12, 1792, at Canaan Four Corners, N. Y. William Aylsworth was b. at North Kingston, R. I., and his wife, Catharine Haven, was b at Newport, R. I. They now reside in Richmond.

Children.

1. ALBURTUS, b. in Richmond, Mass., June 21, 1824
2. GEORGE, b. in Richmond December 1, 1827; is one of the publishers of the Home Journal, New York.
3. DAVID, b. in Richmond December 3, 1829. Resides at Pensacola, Fla., engaged in the shipping business.
4. EDWARD AYLSWORTH, b. in Richmond March 15, 1830. Is a lawyer, resides at Pensacola; was a Confederate Colonel.
5. CATHARINE HANNAH PIERSON, b. in Richmond, August 27, 1834. She m. H. B. Stevens September 6, 1866, b. in Richmond September 11, 1818. He was the son of Wm. Stevens, b. in Lanesboro, Mass., and Parny Branch, b. in Richmond, where they resided.

ALBURTUS PERRY, b. in Richmond, Mass., June 21, 1824, m. Eliza Grant, dau. of Hon. A. P. Grant, of Oswego, N. Y. He is now (1873) Mayor of the city of Oswego, and a prominent lawyer there.

9. FLORILLA, d. at Richmond at the age of 18.

10. SARAH PERRY, b. in Richmond, Mass., August 16, 1793, m. January 17, 1822, Hon. Samuel Gates, of Richmond, son of Samuel and Elizabeth M. Gates, b. February 11, 1785. D in Saratoga Springs, Oct 30, 1856, childless.

Mr. Gates was a successful merchant, and a large manufacturer of iron. He possessed marked abilities, for which he was called to fill many offices of honor and trust. His political and religious opinions were strong and decided, from which he could not be for a moment swerved.

11. DANIEL PERRY, b. in Richmond, Mass., December 12, 1795. M. Oct. 1, 1822, Catharine Havens Aylsworth, dau. of William A. and Catharine Havens, of Canaan, N. Y. She was born in Canaan Four Corners April 8, 1787, and d. in Chicago February 3, 1872. He died in Burlington, Vt., April 4, 1869, in which place the family had resided about forty years.

Children.

1. An infant not named.
2. JOHN BUCKLEY, b. in Richmond, December 12, 1825, d. in Cambridge, Mass., October 3, 1872.
3. SARAH ELIZABETH, b. in Richmond, September 24, 1828, d· in Burlington, Vt., March 23, 1868.
4. WILLIAM AYLSWORTH, b. in Burlington, Vt., April 1, 1830.
5. GEORGE WHITING, b. in Burlington Vt., October 8, 1833.

[For an account of John Buckley Perry, see No. 234, Rachel Lucretia Leavenworth.]

3. SARAH ELIZABETH PERRY, b. in Richmond, Mass., September 24, 1828, m. September 17, 1856, in Burlington, Vt., Hiram Nelson Ballard, b. in Georgia, Vt., July 4, 1829. She d. in Burlington, Vt., March 23, 1868. He resides at Northport, Mich., will soon remove to Chicago.

Children.

1. ELLA LUCRETIA, b. May 29, 1858 ; d. in Burlington August 4, 1858.
2. CATHARINE PERRY, b. June 9, 1859 ; d. in Burlington, September 21, 1859.
3. SARAH PERRY, b. November 12, 1860.
4. ANNA REID, b. November 8, 1862.
5. MAGGIE TATLOCK, b. February 14, 1865 ; d. at Burlington the same day.
6. HELEN MARIA, b. September 30, 1866. All born in Burlington.

4. WILLIAM AYLSWORTH PERRY, b. in Burlington, Vt., April 1, 1830 ; m. September 14, 1871, Ruth Winters Olinger. Lives now at Park Ridge, Ill.

5. GEORGE WHITING PERRY, b. in Burlington, Vt., October 8, 1833, graduated at the University of Vermont ; m. August 5, 1857, in ——— ——— Susan, dau. of Edward M. and Eliza S. Teall, of Albany, N. Y., b. April 27, 1835.

He was, for a number of years the Principal of the Female Seminary, at Monroe, Mich. ; now a real estate and loan agent at Chicago. John B. and George W. were both distinguished for their scholarship at the University, and became eminent teachers in their manhood.

Children.

1. GEORGE AYLSWORTH, b. in Chicago, May 28, 1858.
2. FREDERICK, b. ——— ———, January 23, 1860 ; d. ——— ———, July 17, 1860.
3. EDWARD TEALL, b. in Monroe, Mich., January 23, 1860
4. CLARENCE HALL, b. in Burlington, Vt., February 23, 1870.

5. ANNA the fifth child of JOSEPH PERRY and HANNAH LEAVENWORTH was born at Ripton Parish, May 11, 1751, and married Capt. Elizur Brace of Harwinton, Nov 24, 1774, and died at Oswego, N. Y., June 30, 1843.

Capt. BRACE was born at Harwinton, Aug. 7, 1752, and died at Oswego, April. 19, 1825.

Children.—1. ELIZUR P ; 2. ANNA ; 3. NANCY ; 4. JOHN C. ; 5. ARTHUR ; 6. STEPHEN ; 7. DAVID ; 8. S. J. MILLS ; 9. ALMIRA ; 10. HORACE ; 11. SAMUEL W.

1. ELIZUR P. was a bright child, but at the age of 12 lost his mind from epilepsy, and at the age of 20 wandered from his home—lay in the woods all night—was badly frozen and soon after died.

2. ANNA was born at Harwinton Dec. 14, 1775, and died there Apr. 1777.

3. NANCY was born at Harwinton May 17, 1778, married Feb. 1, 1798, Dr. Walter Colton of Pompey, Onondaga Co., N. Y., and died instantly March 25, 1843, of heart disease or apoplexy at Monroe, Mich., she was a lady of rare virtues.

DR. COLTON was born at Long Meadow, Mass., was the first practicing physician at Pompey, and he soon rose to eminence in his profession and was appointed one of the Judges of Onondaga County.

After a number of years he removed to Oswego and became for years a leading and valuable citizen of that town. He framed the act of incorporation as a village, and was often at Albany on the business of the town.

In later years he removed to Monroe, Mich., where he died of the cholera, September 27, 1834, aged 61. Their children were 1, CARLOS; 2. CLARINDA; 3, HAMILTON.

1. CARLOS, was born in Pompey July 29, 1800. He was for some time head clerk in the great forwarding house of Alvin Bronson at Oswego. In the war of 1812-15 when the village was attacked by the enemy he was seized and carried on board of the Commodore's ship, and held some weeks in order to extract from him information in regard to Government property. But as he refused to inform though severely threatened, he was sent back under a flag of truce, to the great joy of the citizens, who assembled by hundreds on the shore to receive him. Subsequently he settled at Monroe Mich., and was made Recorder of the City and County Clerk, which offices he filled with great credit for many years. He then removed to Toledo, Ohio, where for some years he was "Treasurer of the Board of Trade," Secretary of the "Mutual Insurance Company of Toledo," which position he still holds at the age of seventy-three, a hard working efficient and trusty officer.

He married Sophia A. Brigham of Upper Canada, Dec. 21, 1833.

Children,—1. WALTER ABRAHAM; 2. ELLEN B.; 3. ANNA S.; 4, HAMILTON C.; 5. ALPHEUS F.

1. WALTER ABRAHAM, b. Dec. 26, 1834, married Miss VanHorne, of New Jersey, in 1869. He is a commission merchant and prominent business man at Toledo, Ohio.

2. ELLEN B, b. Oct 5, 1839, d. Mar. 20, 1840.

3. ANNA SOPHIA, b. July 21, 1842, married H. Daughaday of St. Louis, and has two children.

4. CHARLES HAMILTON, b. July 10, 1844, d. Aug. 10, 1862, at Cumberland, Maryland, of typhoid fever, then 2d Lieut. of Zouaves 84th Ohio Regiment; he was a young man of much promise.

5. ALPHEUS F., is an artist and painter, he spent some time under the bes instructors in Europe, attained a high position and is now settled at Toledo, where he has opened his studio.

2. CLARINDA COLTON was b. in Onondaga, Feb. 1802, and married Jan. — 1821, S. Van Rensselaer Bill. Mr. Bill was a Shipmaster on the western lakes and died in the meridian of life.

Children.—1. MARIA; 2. MARY; 3. VANRENSALAER; 4. CLARINDA; 5. HARRIET.

3. HAMILTON COLTON was b. in Manlius, N. Y., Feb. — 1805, married Sept. 1833, Melinda S. Allen. He settled as a forwarder at Milan, Ohio.

Children.—SHELDON; CARLOS; CHARLOTTE; CAROLINE: CORNELIA; CORDELIA.

1. SHELDON early in the Rebellion entered the army as a Lieut. of volunteers in the 67th Ohio, and in the first hard fought battle at Winchester, Va., fought March 23, 1862, he was all but mortally wounded, and lay hepless upon the field of blood among the dying and the dead, from the afternoon of the con-

flict till the next day He suffered greatly from his wounds, and found little relief until some three or four years after he submitted to a surgical operation and the removal of a ball from his person.

4. JOHN C., the fourth child of Capt. Elizur Brace was born Sept. 13, 1779, at Harwinton, Conn., married Mary Lyon of Salina, Onondaga Co., and died at Oswego Feb. 11, 1844, of paralysis. He was a carpenter and joiner. His wife preceded him by many years.

Children.—NANCY; JOHN.

NANCY married George Clark of Cooperstown. They had a large and prom ising family who are widely scattered. The parents reside in Davidson Co., Tenn.

JOHN married in Rochester, and soon after the death of his father he removed to Georgia and acted as Sec'y., and principal director of a lumbering company, mainly from Onondaga, he is supposed to remain there.

5. ARTHUR born April 3, 1781, in Harwinton, married about 1809 Cynthia Moulton of Floyd, Oneida Co. He died at Sodus, Wayne Co., N. Y., April 18, 1850. He was a skilled blacksmith, and was employed by Mathew McNair of Oswego to iron the Belinda, the first vessel built at that place.

Children.—WILLIAM ; HAMILTON and CLARINDA.

William married —— Kingsbury, of Skaneateles, and had by her two daguhters and a son. The family is in California.

Hamilton married in California, and died childless.

Clarinda came to her death by the hands of her mother, when less than a year old, in a fit of mental derangement, in which condition she finally died.

Arthur then married again —a widow—and had two daughters—supposed to be married and living in Wayne Co., N. Y.

6. STEPHEN—the 6th child of Capt. Elizur Brace, b. October 22d, 1782 at Harwinton, Conn.

Married (1) LOIS RICE, of Oswego He died at Springfield, Ohio, Sept. 12, 1843. He was one of the original members of the First Presbyterian church, at Oswego, and for more than twenty years an active Ruling Elder. He was a practical and scientific farmer, and was very active at an early day in introducing choice varieties of fruit into Oswego county.

Children.—1 GEORGE ; 2. ALMIRA ; 3 LAURA ; 4. JULIUS ; 5 JAMES ; 6. JULIA ; 7 HENRY ; 8. MARY ; 9. HARRIET ; 10. LUCRETIA ; 11. JANE ; 12. LARRAIN ELIZABETH,

GEORGE was a successful Druggist at Rochester, and died unmarried ; age 29.

ALMIRA married Ebenezer Pardee, of Skaneateles, and removed to Medina Co. Ohio, and raised a large family.

Children.—HARRIET ; JAMES ; CATHARINE ; RICHARD ; MARY ; JOSEPH ; EPHRAIM ; ELIZABETH.

Mr. P. was a merchant and banker. In the autumn of 1862, he removed to Rochester, Penn., and died in about three years, and his wife shortly previous ; leaving his family in independent circumstances.

The 3d, 6th, 8th and 9th children of Stephen Brace, Laura, Julia, Mary and Harriet died of consumption at Oswego, before reaching the age of 20 years, and were buried there by the side of their mother, who died of the same disease. In consequence of this mortality, Mr B. removed to Springfield, O., where his eleventh child, Jane, m. A. D. Hayward, and d. the year following, leaving an infant daughter, who is now married to a clergyman there. Lucretia, the tenth child, then m. Mr. Hayward, and had a large and interesting family, some of whom are now settled in zife.

Elizabeth, the last child, was, at three years of age, adopted by her Uncle, the Rev. S. W. Brace of Skaneateles, and m. August 30th, 1854, James H. Sherrill of New Hartford. They removed to Iowa, and lived some years, but now reside at Belle Center, O. in prosperous circumstances. Mr S. is a Ruling Elder of the Presbyterian Church there. They are childless.

7th. D AVI BRACE, the seventh child of Captain Elizur, familiarly known at Salina for half a century as "Dr Brace" b. May 5th, 1784 at Harwinton Ct. m, September 12, 1812, Sally Carman, niece of Deacon Joseph Forman, of Onondaga Hollow. He early settled at Salina, N. Y., when it was only known as "Salt Point." Syracuse was then unknown A Presbyterian church was organized at Salina in 1810, and Dr. B. was elected a Ruling Elder, which position he held for fifty years, until not another original member of the church was left. He was a druggist and grocer, and the "Poor man's friend." He died ten years since, or more.

CHILDREN.

1. AURORA; 2. MARK; 3. SUSAN; 4. JOHN C.; 5. ANNA; 6. EDWARD; 7. SARAH M.; 8. CHARLES; 9. MARY; 10. CAROLINE; 11. EMMA.

AURORA m. May 1, 1833, W. Turner, of Boston, who died at Salina April 25, 1842.

Children.—AURORA H,; ELLEN; SARAH B.; DAVID W., and WILLIAM, who died in infancy.

1. AURORA H. m. September 8, 1870, Rev. S. H. Todd, of the M. E. Church of California, now Presiding Elder of his district, and now resides at Wilber, Douglass Co., Oregon.

2. ELLEN is a fine teacher, and at the head of one of the public schools of Syracuse.

3. SARAH B. m. September 18, 1859, L. B. Reynolds, of Bridgewater, Oneida Co. Now a resident of Galesburg, Ill. Mr. R. is a graduate of Hamilton College, studied law and was admitted, but is now a large farmer. They have three children.

4. DAVID W. is a student at law at Syracuse.

MARK, JOHN C., EDWARD, and SARAH M., children of David Brace, died, the first three in infancy, and the last in childhood.

SUSAN, the third child of Dr. Brace, m. April 10, 1844, J. M. Arntz, of Salina.

Children—CAROLINE, a teacher in one of the public schools, and three sons under age and at school—WILLIAM, ARTHUR and EDWARD.

ARNA, the fifth child of Dr. Brace, remains with the family at Salina, and is unmarried.

CHARLES, the eighth child, m. October 8, 1852, Phila A. Tompkins, of Oswego. He follows the business of his father as druggist and grocer, and is childless.

MARY, the ninth child, m. Aaron Brower, of Palatine, Montgomery county, N. Y., who died July, 1868. They had four children, of whom only two are living—CHARLES B. and DAVID.

CAROLINE, the tenth child, was m. April 28, 1859, to Theophilus Civille, of Coeymans, Albany county.

Children—SARAH A. B., ACTON T., EMMA B.

Mr. C. died very suddenly, March 6, 1868, leaving his family in easy circumstances.

EMMA, the youngest child, is unmarried, and is a teacher in the public schools of Syracuse.

8. SAMUEL J. MILLS BRACE, the eighth child of Capt. Elizur Brace, was born at Harwinton September 10, 1785, and died at Clarkson, Monroe county, about the year 1860. M. Susan Newell, of Hanibal. He lived on the paternal homestead, at Oswego, for many years, and had a family of sons and daughters now in active life.

9. ALMIRA BRACE was b. February 10, 1787, at Harwinton. M. October 24, 1806, Joel Burt, late Collector of the port of Oswego; d. at Oswego February 10, 1848.

Children—1. THOMAS J.; 2. CECELIA; 3. SAMUEL W.; 4. ELECTA V.; 5. EMILY; 6. ANNA P.; 7. ELIZUR B.; 8. HENRY; 9. PHOEBE A.

THOMAS J. m. November 8, 1829, Susan Perry, of Huntington, Ct., and d. October 23, 1833.

SAMUEL W. and ANNA P., still live at Oswego, and are unmarried.

ELECTA d. d. at Oswego April 20, 1836.

ELIZUR B. m. February 7, 1858, Harriet Knowlton, of Oswego, and d. the year following.

PHOEBE A. m. July 30, 1863, W. H. Tompkins. They reside at Oswego, and are childless.

The remaining four children died early in life.

10. HORACE BRACE, the tenth child of Capt. Elizur, was b. April 4, 1788, at Harwinton. M. March 25, 1822, Emma Barnum, of Manlius, who d. September 12, 1852, at Union Mills, La Grange Co., Ind. He d. at Marshall, Mich., of typhoid pneumonia, September 27, 1838. He settled first at Salina, as a merchant. On the opening of the Erie canal, he removed to Albany and formed the first regular transportation company on the Erie canal, under the name of Brace, Joy & Co., consisting of five partners, one at each of the cities of Buffalo, Rochester, Utica, Albany and New York. They were very prosperous until the New York partner became a defaulter.

Mr. B. then removed to Marshall, Mich., and became a large farmer, and President of the Bank of Marshall.

Children.—1. MARGARET E.; 2. SARAH F.; and THOMAS B.

MARGARET was b. ——— 1823, at Salina; m. ——— 1845, Robert Dykes, merchant; now Collector of Internal Revenue, for the Northern District of Ind. They have had nine children, four of whom, only, survive, viz.—

1. ROBERT B., EMMA F., WILLIAM A., and WALTER L.

SARAH F., b. ——— 1826, at Albany, m. ——— the Rev. Rufus Patch. She d. about eighteen months after their marriage.

HORACE B., b. at Orville, Onondaga Co., in 1830, and d. at Marshall, Mich., in 1837.

11. The Rev. SAMUEL WILLIAMS BRACE, the eleventh and last child of Capt. Elizur, was b. May 1, 1790, at Rutland, Vt.

His father and sundry others from Litchfield, Co., Ct., emigrated to Vermont in 1789, but in 1796 he removed to the town of Pompey, Onondaga Co., N. Y. After a few years he removed to the town of Lysander in the same county. There was not then, and never had been, a school of any description in the town. The principal opportunity which Samuel W. enjoyed for attending school, were two winters spent with friends in the town of Manlius; yet he formed the purpose of enjoying the advantages of a life at College. In pursuit of this object, in the winter of 1809, he walked from Oswego, where the family were then living, to Hamilton Academy, Clinton, Oneida Co., (now Hamilton College), a distance of nearly one hundred miles, as the route then was. In this institution, under the instruction and encouragement of its able instructor, Seth, afterwards Professor, Norton, his progress in learning was so creditable that he was soon promoted to the station of assistant teacher. By this means he was able to pay for his tuition, besides paying his other small expenses, being compelled to rely entirely upon himself for support. After two years of diligent study, teaching school in the winters, he entered the Sophomore class at Hamilton. The summer preceding he spent in teaching a classical school at Onondaga Hollow, which was the germ of the present Onondaga Academy, which was founded mainly through the efforts of the Hon. Joshua Forman, and the Rev. D. C. Lansing, then the pastor there.

Saml W. Brace

It was at this place and time that the attention of Mr. Brace was first effectually called to the subject of personal religion.

In the autumn of 1812 he joined his cfass in college, which consisted of six members, and was the first who graduated with a regular commencement, from this rising seminary. Soon after graduating in 1815, Mr. B. entered the Theological Seminary at Andover, where he graduated in 1818, having finished the three year course and been licensed to preach the gospel.

He commenced his ministry at Dracutt, Middlesex Co., Mass., including within the bounds of the congregation the territory of Chelmsford, on which the flourishing city of Lowell is now situated. There he labored six weeks, during a most interesting revival. Declining an invitation to preach as a candidate to a large and wealthy congregation at Londonderry, N. H., he repaired to Bridgewater, Oneida Co., and spent seven months in the midst of a revival which reached almost the entire population. He declined an urgent and unanimous call to settle at B., and accepted a call to supply the desk of the Rev., afterwards Dr., Axtelle, at Geneva, N. Y., during his absence on account of ill health. His introduction to the place was through the influence of the Rev. Henry Dwight, previously the model pastor of the first church of Utica, but then, by loss of health, President of the Bank of Geneva. Here a powerful revival followed the labors of Mr. B., and reached the adjoining town of Phelps, when he was called as their pastor and guide, and was ordained and installed by the presbytery of Geneva, in December, 1819. He remained at Phelps four years, and his labors were eminently successful, new members being added to the church at nearly every communion.

In February, 1824, Mr. B. accepted an invitation to labor as associate pastor with the Rev. Mr Aiken, of the First Presbyterian Church atUtica, then a village of about ——— inhabitants. After some months it was judged best to organize another church, which was done, Messrs. Frost, of Whitesboro, Coe, of New Hartford, and Aiken and Brace taking part in the service. It was called "The Bleecker Street Presbyterian Church of Utica." Twenty-seven names were first enrolled on forming the church, but it was greatly enlarged at its first communion. Near the close of the year Mr. B. was duly installed by the Presbytery of Oneida. After a very successful ministry of more than four years, during which time more than 250 persons were added to the church, Mr. B. removed to Skaneateles, and on the unanimous call of the people, was installed as pastor of the church at that place, by the Presbytery of Cayuga. In accepting this call, Mr. B. was obliged to decline a call fromEast Hartford, Ct., which was repeated and declined after the lapse of a year.

Having in 1843 entered upon the sixteenth year of his ministry at S., and impressed the power of Divine truth in eight revivals, he took a dismission from them, and removed to Binghamton. Broome Co., then a village of about —— — inhabitants. Here, on a unanimous call, he became the acting pastor of the Congregational church. After a residence here of about three years, not marked by any remarkable success in his ministry, he resolved to retire from the active duties of the pastoral office, and to preach in vacant churches, as opportunities might offer. In pursuance of this object, he removed again to Utica in August, 1845, and purchased a pleasant home, on Whitcsboro street, in the western part of the city, where he now resides, (September 15, 1873), in the eighty-third year of his age, Until quite recently he has been actively engaged in the duties of the ministry, but is now suffering from a slight shock of paralysis, which, however, does not affect his mental powers, and from which he is gradually recovering, being now able to walk easily, and to travel.

During the twenty-seven years that he has been in Utica without a pastoral charge, he has been the stated supply of the churches at Bridgewater, Paris Hill, Sangerfield, Norwich Corners and Winfield, in all of which, except the last, special success attended his labors. The success of his labors through life has been often remarked, and, as near as can be ascertained, about eighteen special revivals were enjoyed in connection with his personal labors, while he was often called upon to aid his professional brethren under similar circumstances. Many young men, also, by his advice and encouragement, have been led to seek an education and the ministry.

In November, 1819, previous to his ordination at Phelps, Mr. B. married Harriet Kilham, the third daughter of Deacon Gustavus Kilham, of New Hartford, Oneida Co. She had been a pupil of his while teaching a classical school there, and the engagement was then made. They lived in the enjoyment of great happiness for nearly forty years, when she died of disease of the heart.

In July, 1862, Mr. B. was married to Miss Martha B. Fish, of Troy, Pa., with whom he still lives.

In June, 1871, the College of Liberia, (Africa), conferred upon Mr. B. the degree of D. D., the first which it had ever conferred. Mr. B. had long been the warm and active friend of the institution, and had aided it greatly by sending to it valuable books from his own library, as well as from those of his ministerial brethren, and had long acted as the Agent of "The African Colonization Society," without fee or reward.

This aged clergyman was also for many years, the efficient and successful Agent of the "Oneida County Bible Society," with a merely nominal compensation.

14. HANNAH LEAVENWORTH[3], THOMAS[2], THOMAS[1].

Born about 1719 at Stratford.

M. first, Nicholas Moss, of Derby, March 25, 1740. He was born April 28, 1716, and died in a fit November 24, 1759, at Derby.

M. second, Jonathan Dickerman, of Mount Carmel, Ct. Thomas Dickerman came from England in 1635, and settled in Dorchester, Mass., and died in 1651. His son Abram died in 1711.

Abram had a son Isaac, b. 1677, d, 1758. Isaac had a son Jonathan, b. 1719, d. 1792.

Jonathan had five sons,—Enos, b. 1743; Jonathan, b. 1747; Hezekiah, b. 1754; Joel, b. 1757; Amos, b. (near) 1760.

Jonathan Dickerman, the son of Isaac, had three wives. The first wife died in 1760, and her gravestone bears the name, "Rebecca, wife of Lieutenant Jonathan Dickerman." His second wife was Hannah Moss, from Derby. She had no children by Mr. D., and d. October 15, 1780, at Mount Carmel. The third wife's name was Deborah ———. Enos, the son of Jonathan, had a son Enos, b. in 1775, who, at fourteen years of age, went to live with his grandfather, and from his son Elihu, b. in 1802, and now living at North Haven, Ct., I have been able to obtain the above facts, through the indefatigable perseverance of the Rev. Benjamin L. Swan, of Oyster Bay, late of Stratford.

CHILDREN—OF HANNAH L. ETC.

1. NEHEMIAH, b. August 18, 1741, at Derby, where he died January 3, 1762, in the French war, unmarried. He was taken sick near Oswego, returned to Conn., and died there and was buried by the side of his father, at Derby.

2. NICHOLAS, was master of a vessel and was lost at sea.

3. JOSEPH, b. April 22, 1758, and d. in September, 1827. He was a farmer and died at Volney, Oswego Co., N. Y.

At a Probate Court held at New Haven on the first Monday of January, 1760, John Hibbard, Judge, Administration on the estate of Nicholas Moss, is granted to his widow, Hannah Moss, on her giving a bond for £1000, one-third of the estate is given to the widow, a double share to the oldest son, Nehemiah Moss, and a single share to each of the younger sons, Joseph and Nicholas.

In September, 1763, administration of the estate of Nehemiah Moss, was granted to his mother Hannah.

Was not Nicholas Moss a son of the Rev. Joseph Moss, (graduate of Harvard, 1699), b. April, 1679, and ordained at Derby in 1706? The parish records of Derby would probably show, but have never been examined.

October, 1873—the town records show that he was the son of William Moss.

JOSEPH MOSS, third son of Nicholas Moss and Hannah Leavenworth, m. Eunice Smith, dau, of Isaac S., at Derby, about 1775.

CHILDREN.

1. HANNAH, b. August 15, 1776, d. December 12, 1828, at Red Hook, Duchess Co., N. Y.; m. Samuel Somers.

2. LUCY, b, Jan, 30, 1778: m. Capt. Mordecai Prindle, at Derby and d. there.

3. NICHOLAS, b. September 22, 1780, d. August 6, 1855; m. Apoma Wooster, and d. at Palermo, Oswego Co., N. Y., August 6. 1855.

4. JOSEPH, JR., b. January 12, 17 82, d. at Volney, Oswego Co., N. Y., October 7, 1828; m. Betsey Collins.

5. NEHEMIAH, b. August 24, 1784; d. unmarried at Red Hook, N. Y.

6. STEPHEN, b. March 3, 1789, d. aged about 40, at Staten Island, in 1827.

7. ISAAC SMITH, b. July 6, 1791; was drowned in the Oswego river; m. Hannah Hubbard, and lived in Volney.

8. SAMUEL, b. October 20, 1795 or '96; d. September 21 or 22, 1849, at Bridgeport Ct.; m. Sarah Perry.

9. EUNICE, b. June 29, 1798; m. Amos Collins, and d. at Poultney, Vt.; in December, 1847.

10. NANCY, b. February 3, 1801, m. Amos Collins, and lives at Whitehall, N. Y. They were all born at Derby, Ct.

1. HANNAH; the first child of Joseph Moss, m. Samuel Somers, of Volney, Oswego Co., N. Y., who died there in 1826, and had six children—HENRY, SAMUEL WOOSTER, EUNICE, OLIVER, TRACY and JOSEPH, and resided in Volney.

HENRY SOMERS, b. January 19, 1798, m. Mary Kellogg, and had six children, Thomas, Celeste, Emily, Lucy, Henry and Martha.

His son Thomas m. Almira Osgood, and had three children:—Burt, Bertha and Artemas.

His daughter Celeste m. Truman Bachelor, who was a farmer, and is dead. She has two girls, Mary and Addie.

His daughter Emily m. Hoel Lawrence, a pattern maker.

His daughter Lucy m. Archibald Bishop, of New York, a real estate broker.

His son Henry m. for his first wife, Louisa Spafford, and for his second, Josephine Houser.

His daughter Martha m. Abraham Scriber, and has one son Henry.

Samuel Wooster Somers m. Ann Smith, and lives in Abingdon, Mass., and is a farmer; has several children;—1. Martha, m. Jonah Lane; 2. Mary; 3. Lydia, m. George Pratt; 4. George; 5. Charles; 6. Abbie; 7. Maria; 8. Eunice. His sister Eunice m. Calvin Sears, and lived in Indiana. Their children were Earll and Martha. His brother Oliver is unmarried. His brother Tracy, a farmer, m. Miss Perry, and went to Indiana and died there. They had four children.

His brother Joseph m. Mary Knapp in September, 1847; lives in Clay, Onondaga county, N. Y., and has children—Eudora, Artemas, Hattie and Joseph Dean. Eudora m. James Moyer February 1, 1871.

2. LUCY, the second daughter of Joseph Moss, of Derby, m. Capt. Mordecai Prindle, of Derby, Ct., had five children, and d. at Derby.

1. ABRAM, lost at sea when about nineteen years of age.

2. WILLIAM, m. a Miss Smith, of Derby, and had one son, Nelson, now living at Derby, Ct. William was a shoemaker.

3. MORDECAI, d. unmarried.

4. JANETTE, m. Nathan Church, and lived and died at Derby.

5. ELIZA, m. Mr. Durand, and lived and died at Derby.

3. NICHOLAS, the third child of Joseph Moss, of Derby, m. Apoma Wooster, lived at Derby, and then moved to Volney in 1819, then to Palermo, and had six children, who were all born at Derby.

1. NICHOLAS, b. February 11, 1802. He resided at Bethlehem, Ct., and then at Palermo, N. Y., and d. at Volney, N. Y., October 16, 1860. He m. Clemira Lambert, of Bethlehem, March 20, 1822, and had seven children.

1. LOVINA, b. September 16, 1824. She m. William H. Allen, and had one son, George, who m. April 3, 1865, Augusta C. Snyder, and has three children and lives in Conn. *Children*—Hattie M. b. January 8. 1866; George H. b. November 5, 1868; William H., b. Sept. 11, 1870.

2. LAMBERT. b. May 4, 1828, m. Lydia Stearns, and has seven children, and has lost one; lives at Fulton, N. Y.

Children.—1. FRANK A.; FREDERICK A.; ELLE L.; JOHN L., d. April 2, 1871; JULIA C.; ANNA; NOBLE and an infant.

3. NORRY, b. November 23, 1833, m. Benjamin Franklin Lanterman, a machinist, and resided in Chicago; d. in January, 1870, and had four children,—1. Perry Moss; 2. Clara Lamson; 3. Benjamin; 4. Frank, d. Jan. 11, 1870.

4. NEWTON, b. April 16, 1835, m. Minerva Gardner, lives in Michigan, and has two children.

1. GEORGE FRANKLIN, b. December 8, 1870; 2. CLARISSA M., b. Jan. 23, 1873.

5. EMILY, b. August 21, 1837. m. Josiah Wheelock, has one daughter, and lives in Hartford, Ct. Her daughter Emma was b. July 4, 1859.

6. CLARISSA, b. ——— m. May 1, 1861, Charles Whittaker, who is a grocer and lives in Fulton. She has two daughters,—1. Clara Moss, b. March 13, 1863; 2 Hattie L. Holbrook, b. October 8, 1865.

7. SARAH L., b, September 26, 1844, m. William Taylor, a machinist; has one son and lives in Fulton. *Children*—Ernest William, b. July 26, 1872.

2. DANIEL, the second child of Nicholas Moss, and grandson of Joseph, of Derby, b. October 16, 1803, m. rs. Wooster, is a sea captain and has no children.

3. ABRAM T., the third child of said Nicholas, b. March 24, 1806, is a farmer, and m. Sally Ann Ferriss January 28, 1832, and lives in Palermo, Oswego Co., N. Y.

Children—1. FERRISS, b. April 18, 1833, d. July 8, 1837.

2. SARAH ANN, b. August 25, 1843, m. Robinson Young September 22, 1868, and had one child, Lene, b. March 8, 1872.

4. WHITNEY, the fourth child of said Nicholas, b. May 26, 1808, d. May 25, 1842, unmarried.

5. LOVINA, b. August 8, 1810, unmarried.

6. SARAH JANE, b. July 8, 1814, m. July, 1840, A. C. Tucker, of Fulton, a merchant, and had three children,—Arabella, b. September 22, 1842; Apoma, b. June, 1845, and Jennie, b. July 4, 1849. Apoma m. May 7, 1873, Swits Conde, of Oswego, a manufacturer of knit goods. Jennie m. February, 1870, Roy Barnes, of Floyd, N. Y., and has one dau. Maud, b. Oct., 1870.

4. JOSEPH MOSS, JR., fourth child of Joseph of Derby, m. Betsey Collins, and had ten children.

1. NEHEMIAH, b. ——— d. September 14, 1803.

2. SMITH, b. February 12, 1806, m. January 27, 1833, Lucy Chaffee, and died November 12, 1859; had one dau, Mary L., b. October 18, 1839, m. first, Lucien Moss and second, Thomas Clark, of Palermo.

3. CAROLINE, b. ——— m. Hiram Munger in 1827 or '28, and had children—1. Betsey; 2. Lavinia; 3 Emma; 4. Lewis; 5. Daniel; 6. Joseph; 7. Henry; 8. Ellen; 9. Ida.

1. Betsey m. Lorenzo Cole, and had one daughter.
2. Lavinia m. Willis Johnson, a Baptist clergyman—had no children.
3. Emma m. Henry Eager; both d. They had three sons and one dau.
4. Lewis m. Harriet Edick; no children.
5. Daniel died unmarried.
6. Joseph died unmarried.

7. Henry m. Camilla Johnson and had one daughter.
8. Ellen m. George Whitney, and had one son and one daughter.
9. Ida m. Perry Jacobs, no children.

4. WILLIAM, b. ——— m. Sally Hows, September 30, 1835, and had three ch.
1. DENNIS, b. September 30, 1837, a lawyer, m. Hannah King; has one son, William, and lives in Kansas.
2. ANDRUS, b. November 10, 1839, m. September 10, 1863, Lovisa Jones, and resides in Volney; he is a farmer; no children. He and his father spell the name Morse, also his brother.
3. JANE, b. April 17, 1847, m. William Keeler; lives in Kansas and has one dau.

5. JANETTE, b. July 6, 1813, m. Abel Bennett July 4, 1837, and has a son and a daughter, 1. Hannah M.; 2. Robert G.

1. Hannah M. b. October 11, 1838, m. George Bohennan August 6, 1856, and has three children—Wallis G., b. April 12, 1861; Nettie, b. December 1, 1866; Estelle, b. May 18, 1873.
2. Robert G. b. January 29, 1844, m. March 15, 1868, Addie Parker. She d. August 6, 1869, leaving a son Addison, b. August 6, 1869; m. second, March 6, 1870, Augusta Van Buren, and has one child, Lena Augusta, b. August 20, 1873.

6. APPELINE, m. Clinton Burritt, and has one daughter, Elizabeth, who m. ——— Pritchard, and has three children—Lina, Clinton and Eve May.

7. MARIETTE, m. David Baldwin.

8. KING, m. Susan Tefft November 26, 1849, and has three boys,—Herbert George, b August 25, 1850; Joseph Stephen, b. November 20, 1855; Elbert King, b. July 16, 1866. Resided at Fulton, and d. there September 16, 1867.

9. SANFORD, b in 1825, d. October 4, 1842.

10. GEORGE, b. in 1822, and d. October 10, 1838.

5. NEHEMIAH, the fifth child of Joseph of Derby, was b. August 24, 1784, and died unmarried.

6. STEPHEN, the sixth child of Joseph of Derby, was b. March 3, 1789; m. and had one son, William, and d. aged about 40. William lived in Bridgeport and d. at Milford, Ct., in 1864.

Stephen Moss was born in Derby, and was a Sea Captain. He married Sarah Miner, of Nassau, N. P.; d. on the voyage home and was thrown into the Sea, his son William being then ten years of age. His widow died in Philadelphia two years after the death of her husband.

WILLIAM A. MOSS was b. in Derby and m. Sarah Moss of Bridgeport, May 30, 1843, and d. of heart disease at Milford April 19, 1864 and buried in Bridgeport. He was an upholsterer Sarah, his wife, died in Bridgeport, March 6, 1873. They had four children.

1. ADELAIDE, b. February 29, 1844,
2. LOUISE, b. February 12, 1847.
3. EMMA, b May 13, 1853.
4. WILBERT, b. July 10, 1863.

Adelaide m. John Peck, a farmer, son of Cornelius and Mary Ann Peck, at Milford, September 21, 1864, and have five children—Fannie, b. August 31, 1865; Henry C., b. January 2, 1867; John Otis, b. June 25, 1868; Clifford Miner, b. March 2, 1870; William Moss, b February 18, 1872

Louise Moss m. George William Wirtz, October 19, 1868, at Bridgeport, and has two children—Robert, b. July 19, 1870; Adelaide b. September 1, 1873.

Emma and Wilbert, who are not of age, reside at Bridgeport. He is a harness maker.

7. ISAAC SMITH, the seventh child of Joseph of Derby, was b. July 6, 1791, m. Hannah Hubbard, had six children, and resided in Volney: was drowned September 15, 1850.

Children.—1. MARYETTE; 2. SARAH; 3. WILLIAM; 4. JAMES; 5. GILES; 6. NICHOLAS.

There are but three of them living,—1. MARYETTE, m. James Parker and lives in Oswego. She has eight children—1. James, 2, Martha, 3. Sarah Louise, who m. Robert Althoner, 4. Adelaide, m. —— Van Horn, 5. William, d., 6. John, 7. Edward, 8. George. James Parker d. February, 1873.

2. SARAH, m. Peter Speed, and lives in Fulton.

Children.—Giles, Cora and Carrie, twin girls, and Nicholas.

3. WILLIAM, m. Maryette Van Buren and had seven children,—1. JAMES, m. Emma Van Buren; 2. EUNICE, m. Wales Briggs; 3. FLORENCE, m. Joseph Baker; 4. WILLIAM, d.; 5. WILLIAM, d.; 6. MARIETTE; 7. WELLINGTON.

4. JAMES, d. unmarried.
5. GILES, d. unmarried.
6. NICHOLAS, m. Adelia Barrett; no children; lives in Fulton.

8. SAMUEL, the eighth child of Joseph of Derby, b. October 20, 1795 or '96, d. September 21 or 22, 1849. He was a painter. M., first, Lucy Perry, dau. of Abner P., of Huntington, March 6, 1820. She was b. August 28, 1795; d. March 27, 1821. They had one child, LUCY PERRY, b. March 12, 1821, d. in May, 1836.

He m. second, SARAH PERRY, a sister of his first wife, and resided at Bridgeport, Ct. She was b. December 21, 1784; m. April 5, 1822; d. May 25, 1855. He had one dau., SARAH, b. December 7, 1826. She married her cousin, William A. Moss, son of Stephen, who was the brother of Samuel. She had four children and d. in 1873. Samuel Moss and Sarah Perry had, also, two sons who d. in infancy. WILLIAM H., b. September 10, 1823, d. September 22, 1824. SAMUEL W. b. May 12, 1825, d. July 22, 1826. See Sarah Perry, in No. 15, for further facts in regard to Samuel Moss and Sarah Perry.

9. EUNICE, the ninth child of Joseph of Derby, was b. June 29, 1798, and m. in 1813, at Hampton, Vt., Amos Collins. She d. in 1847.

Children.

1. WILLIAM NELSON, m. Joanna Potter, and had eight children,—1. Amos, d. at five years; 2. Isaac, d. November 6, 1868, aged twenty-six; 3. Eunice, d. aged nine years; 4. Burret, d. aged four months: 5. Irving; 6. Horace; 7, Anna; 8. Frederick, d. aged four months. They resided at Palermo, N. Y., and he was a farmer.

2. LEVI SMITH, m. Mary Ann Merwin, of New Haven, Ct., and had three children,—Mary Ann, who m. —— Burgess; Jennie, m. —— Burgess; Frederica.

3. MARY ANN, m. Isaac Potter, resided in Buffalo, N. Y., and had four children—Prince Albert, Eunice, and two others, names unknown.

4. E. B. COLLINS, m. Anna Hotchkiss, and resided in Fulton; a merchant; had four children—1, Lena; 2, Nellie, m. September 28, 1872, Frank Evans, and had Robert Herman; 3, Herman; 4, Bertha. Frank Evans resides at Bloomington, Ill.

5. JOSEPH NORRIS, m. Harriet Rice; resides in New York; a merchant; has two children—Frederick and Ada.

6. LOUISA, m May Lock, and had four children: 1, Herbert, 2, Edward, 3, Frederick; fourth, name unknown; reside at Granville, Vt.

7. LUCIUS, m. Louisa Austin and had two children—Alice and Walter. Resides at Castleton, Vt.; is a hotel keeper

10. NANCY, the tenth child of Joseph of Derby, b. February 3, 1801, m. December 31, 1817, Amos Collins, who was b April 24, 1794, and d. April 24, 1851 They resided near Whitehall, N. Y. They have two children, Orange and Nehemiah. Orange, b. August 12, 1821, m. 1849, Harriet Collins, who was b. in 824, and had six children—Orville E. b. April 18, 1850; Edward A., b. January 23, 1852; Josephine, b. November 29, 1854; Florence, b. June 28, 1856; Ida, b. April 1, 1857; Amos, b. December 6, 1861. Orville, Florence and Ida, married.

NEHEMIAH m. 1851, Maria Benjamin, and had four children. He was born December 17, 1827; she was b. December 3, 1831, and had four children—Marian, b. July 14, 1852; Cyrus, b. April 1, 1854; Alice, b. September 19, 1858; Eunice, b. October 6, 1861.

15. SARAH LEAVENWORTH,[3] THOMAS,[2] THOMAS.[1]

Born November 6, 1721, at Stratford, as stated by Cothren, in his history of Ancient Woodbury. M. ABNER PERRY, of Ripton, and after the marriage of her sister about two years, as is supposed. The Stratford records state her birth as October 6, 1722; but she was baptized in September, 1722. He was b. at Stratford in 1715. She was living at the date of her father's will, July 6, 1748; also of her mother's, May 11, 1758. Whether she was still living at the date of her husband's will, June 22, 1776, does not appear; but, as it contains no reference to her, she probably was not.

Deacon Daniel Bennett and Abner Perry, the son of the Testator, were appointed Executors. The latter presented it for probate January 2, 1792. This will may be found in the old records of the Stratford Probate District, now at Bridgeport. Distribution of the estate was made October 5, 1795. Real estate valued at £283, 7s. 6d. was apportioned to each of the sons.

CHILDREN.

1. GRACE, b. ———, the eldest child.
2. EUNICE, ———
3. ABNER, b. in 1759. The will speaks of him as the eldest son.
4. SAMUEL LEAVENWORTH, b. ————
5. A son, who died in his infancy. All born at Ripton. Grace and Eunice were married at the date of their father's will. The order of the births is not known, farther than is stated above.

ABNER PERRY was the son of Samuel Perry, who was born at Stratford in February, 1681-2, and m. Elizabeth ——— and the grandson of Arthur Perry, who came to Stratford about 1675, and m. Anna, the only daughter of Joshua Judson, about 1676. By her he had,—

1. WILLIAM, b. June, 1677.
2. ANNA, b. January, 1678-9.
3. SAMUEL, b. February, 1681-2.
4. SARAH, b. January, 1682-3.
5. ELIZABETH, b. September, 1684.
6. YELVERTON, b. August, 1686. dismissed to Ripton church, 1722.
7. SETH, b. January, 1687-8.
8. RUTH, b. May, 1690.
9. DANIEL, b. April, 1692.
10. JOSHUA, b. December, 1694. dismissed to Ripton church, 1724.
11. CALEB, b. August, 1696.
12. DEBORAH, b. March, 1697.
13. JOSIAH, b. August, 1699.

The children of Samuel, the third son of Arthur, were,—

1. ELIZABETH, b. August, 1713.
2. ABNER, b. September, 1715.
3. MARY, b. October, 1718.
4. SAMUEL, b. May, 1721.
5. WILLIAM, b. August, 1723.
6. MOSES, b. 1727, d. 1727.
7. JAMES, b. 1728-9.

The Rev. Benjamin L. Swan, late of Stratford, Ct., now of Oyster Bay, N. Y., suggests that Arthur, above can scarcely fail to have been a son of Arthur P., of Boston, 1638-1652, born too near his father's death to be mentioned in his will. But he does not appear to be mentioned in the list of his children, as given by Savage, which are,—

1. ELISHA, b. December 20, 1637, d. soon.
2. SETH, b. Mar. 7, 1639, bap May 13, 1640.
3. JOHN, b. April 26, bap. May 1, 1643.
4. ELIZABETH, b. January 28, 1647.
5. SARAH, bap. Dec. 15, 1647.
6. DEBORAH, d. in 4 days, bap. July 1, 1649.

1. GRACE PERRY, m. Jared Beardsley, of Monroe, and had nine children,—

1. SAMUEL THOMAS,	4 JARED PERRY,	7. POLLY ANN,
2 ELIJAH ABEL,	5. AZIEL BLAY,	8. MARTHA BLAY,
3. ISRAEL ABNER,	6. SALLY BETSEY,	9. GRACE AURELIA.

1. SAMUEL THOMAS BEARDSLEY m. Elizabeth St. John, of Norwalk, and moved to Charlotte, N. Y. His descendants are supposed to be there. He was a clothier, and had ten children. The following are the names of some of them:—Samuel Thomas, Antoinette, Rebecca, Mary Ann, Elizabeth.

2. ELIJAH ABEL BEARDSLEY, d. a bachelor, at Monroe; he was a farmer.

3. ISRAEL ABNER BEARDSLEY m. Esther Toucey, and had a son and daughter He was a farmer and settled in Newtown. The son m. Miss Beach, and is dead; he was a farmer. Flora Jane, the daughter, m. Aaron Sanford, of Reading, Ct. He was high sheriff of the county; has two children, a son and daughter. The daughter, Elizabeth, m. a gentleman from Cincinnati, and has one child. The name of the son is not known.

4. JARED PERRY BEARDSLEY m. ——— and he and his wife are dead; they lived in Monroe. They had three children, Seymour, Mary Ann and Styles. Seymour m. Miss ——— Drew; Mary Ann m. Edward Hurd, and all lived in Monroe.

5. AZIEL BLAY BEARDSLEY m. Flora Toucey, a sister of Esther Toucey. He was a farmer and lived in Newtown; he is dead. They had seven children,—Philo, Emily, Elizabeth, Theodore, Frances, John, and Mary. Philo and Mary are dead. Elizabeth m. a Mr. Dick; he is a hotel keeper at Newtown. The others are all unmarried; they all live in Newtown, Ct.

6. SALLY BETSEY BEARDSLEY, d. unmarried at Trumbull.

7. POLLY ANN BEARDSLEY, m. Styles Beach, of Trumbull, and had three children,—Abel Styles, Walcott, and a daughter Polly, who m. ——— Plumb. They all have children and grandchildren. They are farmers and live in Trumbull. Polly Ann and her husband are dead.

8. MARTHA BLAY BEARDSLEY m. ——— Deming a farmer, of Woodbury, and had no children. She d. in Monroe.

9. GRACE AURELIA BEARDSLEY m. Henry Lewis, a hotel keeper, of Monroe; he is dead. They had one dau., Elizabeth, who m. a Mr. Clark. She is now a widow, lives in Monroe, and is childless.

2. EUNICE PERRY, m. David Merwin, of Milford. They are both dead. They had eleven children:—

1. ISAAC,	4. MERRITT } Twins.	7. NANCY.	10. MEHITABLE.
2. DAVID.	5. MARK, }	8. EUNICE.	11. MARTHA.
3. JOHN PERRY.	6. SARAH.	9. POLLY.	

1. ISAAC MERWIN m. twice and moved to Whitesboro, N. Y., where his descendants are supposed to reside. He had three sons and daughters; one was Alma.

2. DAVID MERWIN, m. Martha Gillett and had ten children,—David, Jared, Albert, John, Mary A., Catharine, Eunice, Elizabeth, Grace, and Louisa. They are all married except Louisa, and have children and grand-children. Albert, John and Grace are dead. Martha m. died about 1830.

   1. David, m. Martha Tibbals, and has two sons:—1, George P., who m. Annie E. Byers. He is a manufacturer of linen collars, cuffs, etc., and lives in New York; has two sons, Robert L., b. about 1864, and George T, b. about 1866

   2. Nathan T., who m. Mattie L. Parsons. He is a Congregational clergyman, settled at Trumbull, Ct., and ha two children,—Florence Loveland, aged eight years, and Nathalie, aged six years.

   2. Jared, m first, Mary Stowe, and had two children, Charles and James. Charles is a resident of New Jersey, and teacher in a high school; he is m. and has two children. James m. Mary Hodge, and has three children

He is a paper manufacturer. Jared m. second, Mary J. Platt and had three children, Sarah, Albert and George. Sarah is m. and lives in Chicago, and has four children. Her husband is a carriage-maker.
3. Albert is married.
4, John m. Martha Camp ; was a farmer and lived in Milford ; d. about 1855 ; had one daughter, Lillie, d.
6. Catharine, m. Silas Pardee. They still live in West Haven and have two daughters—Belle, who m. John Warren, of Hamden, a farmer ; Ida, who m. James Tolls, book-keeper in New Haven Co. Bank.
7. Eunice, m. Henry Myers, who was in the shoe trade. She is living ; he died about 1870.
8. Elizabeth, m. Asa Hoyt and lives in New Haveu ; he is a mason and a master builder. They had eight children, of whom six—Mary, Belle, Charles, Ella, George, and Frederick are still living.
9. Grace m. William Smith and had three children—Ellen, Annie, and Catharine ; William Smith and wife died about 1858.
10, Louisa lives in Milford, unmarried.

3. JOHN P. MERWIN lived in Bridgeport, m. Julia Shelton, of Huntington, and had three children—Harriet, Mary and Merrit. Merrit m. Margaret Spencer, of New York, and had one child, now dead. Harriet m. Iverson H. Knapp and lives in Bridgeport and her sister with her, unmarried ; she has no children.

4. MERRIT MERWIN m. Catharine Peck, of Milford, and had two children—Charles and William ; he died January 20, 1863. William m. Sarah Peck, of Orange, and has two sons, Drummond and Merrit, both unmarried ; Charles is also married and has four children;

5. MARK MERWIN m. twice, had seven children ; m. first, Susan Miles. *Children,*—1, Samuel, b. June 28, 1819 ; 2. Susan Maria, b. January 12, 1821 ; 3. Martha, b. December 24, 1823 ; 4. Nathan Perry, b. March 10, 1825 ; 5. Marcus, b. August 26, 1827 ; 6. Samuel M., b. December 20, 1829. Married, second, Julia Curtiss, May 14, 1837, and had one child, Caroline, b. Oct., 1838.

Susan M. m. Mr. Treat, a farmer, and lives in Orange ; has two sons, unmarried—Frank and George.
Martha m. James Burns, of Milford, and had one daughter, Georgiana.
Nathan P. m. Ann Baldwin, of Milford ; a farmer and has two children—Nellie and Mary.
Marcus m. Elizabeth Platt, of Waterbury, Ct., and has two sons and three daughters,—Eugene, Wallace, Frances, Jenny and Emma.

Mark Merwin is still living at the age of eighty-three years, (1874) ; his second wife d. October, 1868.

6. SARAH m. *Jerry* Baldwin and moved to New Milford. Was a farmer ; both died about 1855. They had a son Merrit and three daughters.

7. NANCY m. Garret Stone, of New Milford, and removed to Pennsylvania ; both dead ; had three daughters, one of whom married a Ball and had a son.

8. EUNICE was never married ; she was drowned about 25 years since.

9. POLLY MERWIN m. Sheldon Platt and moved to New Milford ; both dead ; they had two sons and two daughters ; the sons were Merrit and Orrin, the daughters Martha and Laura. Merrit is a Congregational minister, living in New Jersey ; is m. and has children. Orrin m. a Gaylord ; their children were Charles, Mary, Sarah and Lavina. Martha m. William Canfield ; children, Edward, Frederick, George, and one daughter, living in Bridgeport. Laura married, moved west and died.

10. MEHITABLE m. Samuel Potter, of Orange, Ct. ; no children ; both dead.

11. MARTHA m. Jerry Davis, of Hamden ; no children ; both dead many years since.

3. ABNER PERRY JR., m. Elizabeth Dunham, who was b. October 12, 1762.

She was a sister of the wife of his brother Samuel L., and had six children, one son and five daughters. He died September 7, 1843, aged 84.

CHILDREN.

1. ELIZABETH, b. November 21, 1781.
2. SARAH, b. December 21, 1784
3. ANDREW. b. October 5, 1793.
4. LUCY, b. August 28, 1795.
5. MARY ANN, b. May 12, 1798.
6. SUSAN, b. May 25, 1800.

1. ELIZABETH PERRV m. Harman Clark, of Monroe; they are both dead. They had three children,—Elisha, Treat and Eliza. Elisha m. Alice Lewis, of Bridgeport, and has three children,—Walter, William Henry and Mary Jane. All but Walter are dead. Elisha and Walter are carriage painters, and he and his wife and son live at Bridgeport. Eliza m. Jerry Alling and had one child, Augusta, who d. aged fifteen years. He was a cooper, living in Huntington. They are all dead. Eliza d. of consumption one year after the birth of Augusta. Treat Clark m. Phoebe Dibble, moved to California, settled at SanFrancisco, and has seven children. Four of the children are Serata, Henry, Mary and Nettie. He is a carpenter and joiner. Serata, the eldest daughter was m. at San Francisco about two years since, and is about 22 years of age.

2. SARAH PERRY, m. April 5, 1822, Samuel Moss, d. May 25, 1855, and had three children, two sons who died early, and a daughter Sarah, b. December 7, 1826. They are all dead. Sarah Moss m. her cousin WIlliam Moss, a nephew of her father's, who is also dead. She d. in March, 1873, aged 46. They had one son Wilbert, and three daughters, Adelaide, Louisa and Emma. Adelaide m. John Peck, of Milford, where he was born, and has five children,—Sarah Frances, Henry Cornelius, John Otis, Clifford Minor, and Willie Moss. He is a farmer. Louisa m. William Wirtz, and has a son and daughter,—Emma and Wilbert Moss; are unmarried. (For a full account of Samuel Moss etc., see "Hannah L., No. 14."

3. ANDREW PERRY, b. October 5, 1793, and d. June 15, 1851; a farmer; m. Mary Judson, of Huntington, and had six children—Charles Robert, George Judson, David, John, Harriet A., and Grace Ann. Charles R. settled in Macon Co., Missouri, is a farmer and has eight children. The eldest son, Andrew is about twenty-one years of age, and is a farmer. His eldest daughter is married. Mary and Emiline are two of the daughters. George is also married and has fiue children; he m. Sarah Murphy, of South Britain, Ct.. and lives in Huntington. *Children*—Mary, Charles, George, Franklin and Frederick, aged 9, 7, 5, 3, and 1 years. David m. Aurelia Lane, of Monroe, and has one child, Herbert, aged three years. John m. Miranda Hurd, of Huntington, and has two children, Lucy, aged fiv e years, and Howard, aged two years. He is a manufacturer. The other two sons are farmers. Harriet A. m. Nathan Botsford, of Milford, is now a widow living in Milford. and has four children—Charles, aged nine years, Anna, aged seven, Elnathan, aged five, and Carrie, aged three. Grace Ann is unmarried.

4. LUCY PERRY m. Samuel Morse as his first wife, and had one daughter, Lucy, who d. aged fourteen, at Bridgeport.

5. MARY ANN PERRY, b. at Huntington in 1798, m. Cornelius B. Peck, a farmer, of Milford, October 18, 1823, and had four children—Mary Ann, Sarah Frances, Henry, and John. Mary Ann, the eldest, m. Capt. E. W. Ruggles, and had two children,—Washburn and Richard Whiting. Washburn is a carpenter at Huntington, m. Francelia Beach, of Huntington, and had one daughter, Alice, now two years old. Richard W. d. at the age of fourteen years. Sarah Frances m. E. W. Beckwith, of Cromwell, Ct., of the class of 1847 at Yale. He d. eight years since, in September, 1865, leaving no children. He was a teacher by profession. Henry is unmarried and lives in Texas. John m. Adelaide Morse, as stated above.

6. SUSAN PERRY m. Truman Burt and had two children, who are both dead. They lived at Oswego, N. Y.

4. SAMUEL L. PERRY m. Nancy Dunham, and had one son and three daughters,—Garret, Maria and Charlotte. Garret m. Sarah Birdseye, of Stratford, and had two sons, Frederick and Miles. Maria and Charlotte m. successively, Dr. John Tomlinson, of Huntington, and he had three children,—Samuel, John and Anne Maria. Anne Maria m. Birdseye Blackman, of Stratford, who has a bookstore in the city of New York. She has several children, one of whom, a son, recently died in Paris. Samuel Tomlinson m. Mary Blakeman, of Stratford, resides in New Jersey, and has no children. John Tomlinson m. Harriet Sears. They do not live together; he was out in the rebellion.

16. Capt. Edmund Leavenworth.[3]—THOMAS,[2] THOMAS.[1]

Born in 1725, at Ripton.

Married ABIGAIL BEARDSLEY, of Stratford, now Huntington, about 1750. She was born in 1723, and died March 18, 1804 aged 81, and was buried at Ripton.

He died July 28, 1785, at Huntington, Ct., aged 60 years, and was buried at Ripton.

CHILDREN.

67. ABIGAIL, b. d.
68. GIDEON, b. October 18, 1751, d. April 19, 1816.
69. ANNIE, b. August 19, 1756, d.
70. RUTH, b. d.
71. ABIJAH, b. October 23, 1758, d. November 9, 1777.
72. ELI, b. d.
73. RACHEL, b. July 16, 1761, d. Nov. 19, 1819, at Huntingt'n.
74. SALLY, b. December 28, 1762, d. July 17, 1855. at Roxbury.
75. EDMOND, b. December 14, 1763, or '66, d. January 20, 1857.

All born in Huntington.

May 5, 1734, Capt. Edmund received a bequest from his brother Ebenezer. July 6, 1748, or rather on the death of his father, (that being the date of his will,) he received from his father the whole of his farm at Stratford, where he lived, fronting on the Hoosatonic, saving only certain privileges reserved to his wife; also, all his rights in commonage in Stratford. July 25, 1749, revokes the appointment of Capt. Edmund as his executor.

Capt. Edmund and his son, Gideon, built the Toll Bridge across the Hoosatonic, a short distance above his residence, about the years 1768-9. Capt. Gideon rebuilt it, and it was owned in the family, I think, as long as it continued. He also built and owned many vessels at his boat-yard on the river, just above his dwelling, and just below the stream which enters the Hoosatonic on the Doctor's old farm.

In the spring of 1777 he was the Captain of a company of infantry, raised at Ripton by the authority of the State, called the "Alarm-list Company," or, "Householders," which company belonged to Col. Samuel W. Whiting's brigade. A few days before Danbury was burned, said company was ordered into service and stationed at Fairfield, to guard it, for four months. They guarded the prisoners taken at Danbury, and brought them to Fairfield. At the expiration of the four months, Capt. Joseph Birdseye, of South Ripton Parish, was to relieve said Edmund from the command of the company, but was prevented by illness; and Capt. L. continued in command through the campaign, either in field or garrison. The other officers of the company were John Wooster, First Lieutenant, and John Lake, Ensign, all of South Ripton. In 1779 the company was ordered from Ripton to New Haven, still under command of Capt. L., where they met the enemy, and followed them up the Sound to Fairfield, where the enemy landed and burned the town, with the loss of one man killed.

This was really the fighting family of the name, though none were wanting in their duty in those trying times. Not only was Capt. Edmund in the field, but his two sons, Gideon and Eli, commanded companies and were actively engaged in the war; and his son Abijah, who was a Lieutenant in the army, lost his life by exposure and hardship, and even his son Edmund, though but a boy, served as a soldier.

Thus, every male member of the family, himself and his four sons, were all actively engaged, three of them as Captains commanding companies. Edmund, the father, being over fifty years of age, and Edmund, his son but twelve years of age when he first served, waiting upon his father. All the brothers of Captain Edmund were more than sixty years of age when the Revolution commenced, and too old to engage in the conflict; but there were few of their sons who were not out during some part of the seven years.

17. MEHITABEL, (or Mabel), LEAVENWORTH,[4]—JAMES,[3] THOMAS,[2] THOMAS.[1]

Born July 28, 1721, at Stratford. Married Josiah Wetmore at Stratford. Lived in the north part of Huntington, now Monroe, Ct., (then part of Stratford. Died in 1807, aged 86.

She *probably* had no children, for she seems to have died in 1807; but her relatives now living in Monroe, know nothing of her or her family.

18. TAMER LEAVENWORTH,[4]—JAMES[3], THOMAS,[2] THOMAS[1].

Born May 28, 1727, at Stratford. Died after 1759. Married Samuel Hurd in Stratford, 17 He was a son of Jonathan, son of John 2d. son of John 1st, an early settler of Stratford, Ct. He resided in North Stratford, now Trumbull, Ct. They lived in what is now Monroe, then a part of Stratford.

CHILDREN.

SAMUEL L. Lived over 100 years; was a revolutionary soldier and pensioner, and died about 1864.

19. Samuel Leavenworth.[4]—JAMES,[3] THOMAS,[2] THOMAS.[1]

Born February 21, 1729. Married—— Did he ever marry? Died after 1759, as he was living at the date of his father's will, August 1, 1759.

20. Daniel Leavenworth.[4]—JAMES,[3] THOMAS,[2] THOMAS[1]

Born March 25, 1731, in Stratford.

Married Abigail Beardsley, of Huntington. Born there in 1728. Died March 3, 1810, aged seventy-nine, in Monroe.

Was poor, but noted for honesty and good morals. By trade was a weaver. His wife died May 6, 1801, aged seventy-three. Children all born in the northwest part of Huntington, now Monroe.

April 9, 1761, he bought one hundred and eighty acres of land of his father James, in Blanket Meadow; and March 25, 1785, one hundred and seven acres of Nathan Simmons, also in Blanket Meadow.

CHILDREN.

76. JOHN, b.——— d. young.
77. ELIZABETH, b. about 1754; m. James Winton, d. about 1835.
78. ALVAH, b. about 1757, m. David Hubbell, d. Aug. 22, 1845.
79. ANDREW, b. January 21, 1766, m. Miriam Seelye, d Dec. 18, 1846.

21. ANNE LEAVENWORTH.[4]—JAMES,[3] THOMAS,[2] THOMAS.[1]

Born April 14. 1733, in Stratford. Married Edward Lake, son of Thomas, whe resided in North Stratford, now Monroe. Was living August 1, 1759, the date of her father's will.

22. MARY LEAVENWORTH.[4]—JAMES,[3] THOMAS,[2] THOMAS.[1]

Born August 13, 1735, at North Stratford. Alive and unmarried August 1, 1759, date of her father's will.

23. James Leavenworth.—[4]JAMES,[3] THOMAS,[2] THOMAS.[1]

Born July 8, 1737.

Married Jehodah Moss about 1759, at Ripton. Removed in 1787, to Easton, N. Y., and in 1793, to Johnstown, N. Y., where he died May 6, 1806. His residence was two miles north of Kingsboro. His widow died August 6, 1811, aged seventy-six. He was a loyal son of his Puritan father, religious and strict.

CHILDREN.

80. EBENEZER, b. December 20, 1760, d. October 28, 1811.
81. PRUDENCE, b. ——— 17—, d. ———, m. Josiah Wells.
82. AMARILLA, b. ——— 17—, d. ——— m. Frederick Mills.
83. POLLY, b. ——— 17—, d. ——, m. Charles Hartshorn.
84. CHARITY, b. ——— 17—, d. ——, m. Ezekiel Beardsley.

Probably all born in Stratford, at the White Hills, or in Monroe—probably the latter.

24. ESTHER LEAVENWORTH.[4]–JAMES,[3] THOMAS,[2] THOMAS[1]

Born January 27, 1739-40, in Stratford. Alive and unmarried at the date of her father's will, August 1, 1759.

25. Ebenezer Leavenworth.[4]—JAMES,[3] THOMAS,[2] THOMAS.[1]

Born September 22, 1743, at Stratford. Died before 1759.

28. Nathan Leavenworth.[4]—DAVID,[3] THOMAS,[2] THOMAS.[1]

Born November 1, 1732.

Married Rachel Castle December 12, 1759. She was a daughter of Henry Castle, Jr.; was born November 10, 1737, and died at Hinesburg, Vt., August 7, 1810.

In 1754 he owned lands on Shepaugh River, and lived in Woodbury. He removed with his family to Hinesburg in 1787, from Washington, near New Milford, Ct., and died in Hinesburg February 16, 1809. His house in Washington was about half a mile from the line of New Milford. The children were all born in Washington.

CHILDREN.

85. HENRY, b. September 9, 1760, d. young.
86. HENRY CASTLE, bap. May 8, 1763, d. —— 1799
87. GEN. NATHAN, b. August 20, 1764, d. September 8, 1849.

29. Ebenezer Leavenworth.[4]—DAVID,[3] THOMAS,[2] THOMAS.[1]

Baptized December 29, 1734, at Woodbury.

Married Elizabeth Hurd March 27, 1754. She was daughter of John Hurd; was baptized July 21, 1730, and died March 19, 1822, aged about ninety-two years. He died March 18, 1778, in Woodbury, Ct., of small pox, and administration was granted on *Lieut.* Ebenezer Leavenworth's estate May 5, 1778, 7 Probate vol. p. 280-1; buried at Ruccum. He served in the army of the Revolution. Cothren, p. 783.

CHILDREN.

88. SARAH, b. December 16, 1754, d. in 1833 or '34.
89. DAVID, b. December 19, 1756, d. February 1, 1797.
90. BURZINA, b. September 10, 1758, d. ———
91. BETSEY, b. February 27, 1763, d. at Beloit, Wis., in 1853.
92. REV. EBENEZER ISAAC, b. Sept. 22, 1776, d. Oct. 14, 1851.
93. AZULAH, b. ———, 17—, d. ———
94. ISAAC, b. ——— All born in Woodbury.

30. Capt. David Leavenworth.[4]—JOHN,[3] THOMAS,[2] THOMAS.[1]

Born in 1638, at Woodbury.

Married, 1, OLIVE HUNT, February 8, 1759.
" 2, MARY DOWNS, October 30, 1776.

He was born, lived and died in Woodbury. He died March 25, 1820, aged eighty-two. He was Captain of the Fourth Company, 13th Regiment of the Colony of Conn., in 1776, etc.; served in the army. See Cothren, p. 195-6-7, and 204-8-10 and 11. His will was proved April 10, 1820—13th vol. Prob., p. 4.

CHILDREN.

95. GIDEON, bap. Oct 26, 1759, d. Oct 15, 1827, at Roxbury.
96. MORSE, bap. July 1, 1764.
7. ANNA, bap. November 15, 1767.
98. WHITMAN, b. March 22, 1777, d. young.
99. MARY, b. March 16, 1780, d. young.
100. DAVID, b. April 6, ——— ?
1. ABIGAIL, is mentioned in her father's will.
102. OLIVE, ———

From the pages noted above in Cothren's history, it will appear that he was engaged heart and soul in the war of the Revolution; was called out with his company to New York, and on various occasions, and was one of the active and energetic men of those trying times. Accounts for his services and expenses at Fairfield in 1778, and on other occasions, are on file in the Comptroller's office at Hartford. The account for militia services etc., at Fairfield, amounts to £36 3s. 11d. Another account is £99 3s. 4d.

31. ABIGAIL LEAVENWORTH.[4]—JOHN,[3] THOMAS[2], THOMAS[1].

Born about 1739, at Woodbury.

Married June 29, 1763, John Orton, of Woodbury, b. October 5, 1729. He was the son of John O., bap. December 4, 1692, who was the son of John, bap. 1648, (all of Woodbury), son of Thomas O., b. in 1613, in England. She died before March 4, 1782.

He m. 2d, Patience Warner, March 4, 1782, who d. February 11, 1814. He d. April 2, 1808. See p. 660 of Cothren's Woodbury, vol. 1.

CHILDREN.

1. SARAH, b. April 29, 1765; m. 1st, —— Hurd, 2d, —— Ball, and removed to Canada.
2. MARY ANN, b. July 23, 1768, m. Eli Smith, and settled in Orange, Conn.
3. ESTHER, b. August 2, 1771, m. Hollister Judson.

By his second wife he had—

4. JOHN, b. December 6, 1782.
5. TRUMAN, b. June 16, 1684.

32. John Leavenworth.[4]—JOHN,[3] THOMAS,[2] THOMAS.[1]

Born in 1739; bap. July 19, 1741.

Married November 20, 1769, ABIGAIL PECK, of Newtown. She died at her home in Woodbury, June 30, 1820. Her will was proved July 25, 1821,—13th Prob. vol., p. 47. Her son, John Peck Leavenworth, executor.

He died in June, 1802, in his wagon at Woodbury, just after leaving his home to visit his brother Lemuel, at Whitestown N. Y. He served in the army of the Revolution—Cothren, p. 783. He was a farmer, and was born, lived and died in Woodbury. His will was proved at Woodbury July 19, 1802—10th Prob. vol. p. 104—Russell Leavenworth, executor.

CHILDREN.

103. BETHIA, b. March 14, 1771.
104. CAPT. JOHN PECK, b, November 23, 1772, d. Oct. 13, 1852.
105. LUCRETIA, b. April 18, 1775.
106. RUSSELL, b. January 18, 1777, d. April 17, 1865.
107. AMARILLIS, b. December 11, 1778. She was a twin, the other died.

33. Lemuel Leavenworth.[4]—JOHN,[3] THOMAS,[2] THOMAS.[1]

Born October 9, 1743, at Woodbury.

Marred, 1, SYBIL PARKER, sister of the late Jason Parker, of Utica, about 1769, at Wallingford, Ct. She was born April 9, 1752, and died September 29, 1812, at Whitestown, N. Y.

Married, 2, ABIGAIL JUDSON, August 17, 1814. She was a dauter of Samuel Perry, and widow of Joseph Judson, of Bridgewater, Ct., and was born July 22, 1752, and died November 9, 1818, at Whitestown.

Married, 3, SARAH BOOTH, November 21, 1819, of Woodbury. She was the daughter of David Booth, of Roxbury, and the widow of Dr. Azariah Eastman. She died at Utica, N. Y., aged sixty-two; qu., 82? He died at Whitestown, April 30, 1825, aged eighty-two. He was an early settler at Whitestown, and came in 1785, the first year after the location by Judge White.

CHILDREN.

108. MARY, b. April 9, 1770, d. June 21, 1774.
109. LOVISA, b. August 10, 1771, d. March 27, 1845.
110. REUBEN, b. April 23, 1774, d. February 7, 1829.
111. MARY, b. February 25, 1777, d. June 22, 1859, in her 82d year.
112. LEMUEL, b. July 27, 1780, d. December 14, 1813.
113. COUNT DEGRASSE, b. June 13, 1782, d. May 14, 1791.
114. SYBIL, b. June 1, 1794, and still lives at Utica.

All but Sybil b. in Woodbury.

He was one of those who took up arms to resist the invasion of Burgoyne, and was at the battle of Bennington. He was highly respected for his energy, integrity and benevolence. He was a man of strong convictions, a very decided character, and of some eccentricities. Any member of the Leavenworth family having marked peculiarities, is said to be a "relative of Uncle Lem." He *courted* his second wife before his *first* marriage. She declined to go west with him. When he lost his first wife, and she her first husband, he made a second offer and was accepted.

34. DEBORAH LEAVENWORTH.[4]—JOHN,[3] THOMAS,[2] THOMAS.[1]

Baptized May 8, 1745, at Woodbury.

Married, 1, Joshua Judson, February 27, 1765. He was son of Joseph Judson, of Woodbury, and was b. December 14, 1732. He had previously m. Ann

Walker; and had two children, JOSHUA and MARY. Joshua, Jr., d. early. Joshua J. d. in 1776.

She m. 2, Capt. James Judson, of Woodbury; a farmer and lived and died there.

CHILDREN.

1. DEBORAH ANN, b. May 4, 1766, m. Phineas Smith.
2. JOSHUA, b. November 2, 1772. Removed to Vermont, m. and had children—Sheldon, Nathan, Edward, Harriet, Charlotte and Caroline.
3. RUTH, b. April 2, 1775, m. Nathan, son of Capt. Nathan Stoddard. Her son, the Rev. Judson Stoddard, lives at Center Brook Conn. Capt. Nathan S. was killed by the side of Phineas Smith, who married the sister of Ruth, at Mud Fort, on an island in the Delaware, below Philadelphia, while engaged in a conflict with a British frigate. He was a gallant officer and a truly good man.
4. ISAAC EDWARD, b. after 1776. Was graduated at Yale College in 1803. Went into trade with his brother-in-law, failed, and then went into business in Albany. Died childless.
5. BETSEY, b. after 1776, m William Judson, of Woodbury. Settled in Roxbury and d. there childless.

CHILDREN

And descendants of DEBORAH ANN (JUDSON), wife of PHINEAS SMITH, and daughter of DEBORAH (LEAVENWORTH,) by Joshua Judson, her 1st husband.

PHINEAS SMITH, son of Richard Smith and Anna Hurd, his wife, was born January 1, 1759, and d. November 7, 1839.

DEBORAH ANN JUDSON, (parentage as above), was b. May 4, 1766, and d. May 30, 1850.

PHINEAS SMITH and DEBORAH ANN JUDSON were m. February 19, 1788, and had issue as follows:—

1. TRUMAN, b. November 27, 1791. Yale ollege, 1815.
2. PHINEAS, b. November 19, 1793, d. November 19, 1839.
3. DANIEL SHELDON, b. December 16, 1795, d. November 19, 1849, unmarried.
4. NATHANIEL, b. August 14, 1799.
5. CATHARINE ANN, b. September 23, 1804.
6. NATHAN RICHARD, b. July 2, 1810.

1. TRUMAN SMITH and MARIA COOK, were married at Litchfield, Ct., June 2, 1832, and had issue as follows:—

1. CATHARINE MARIA, b. February 24, 1833, d. August 17, 1834.
2. JANE, b. December 22, 1834.
3. GEORGE WEBSTER, b. May 4, 1837, d. January 13, 1840.

All born at Litchfield.

Maria, wife of Truman Smith, d. April 24, 1849, at Litchfield.

TRUMAN SMITH and MARY ANN DICKINSON were married November 7, 1850, and have issue as follows:—

1. TRUMAN HOUSTON, b. March 30, 1852, d. November 13, 1856.
2. SAMUEL HUBBARD, b. November 18, 1854.
3. EDMUND DICKINSON, b. September 25, 1857.
4. ROBERT SHUFELDT, b. February 4, 1861.
5. HENRY HUMPHREY, } b. August 7, 1863. The last d. August 7, 1864,
6. ALLEN HOYT, } the first August 27, 1864. "Beautiful in their lives, in death they were not divided."

JANE, daughter of Truman Smith and Maria, his wife, m. George A. Hoyt, November 27, 1855, and is childless.

The Honorable Truman Smith was the oldest son of Phineas and Deborah

Ann Smith, and was born at Roxbury, Litchfield county, Conn., November 27, 1791. His father was the oldest son of a family, two of whose members became very distinguished at the Bar, and in public life in Connecticut. One of them, the Honorable Nathaniel Smith, of Woodbury, in Litchfield Co., very early attained to a high rank as a lawyer; was a Member of Congress from 1795 to 1799, and a Judge of the Supreme Court from 1806 to 1819. He died in 1822, aged sixty-two years.

Another brother of the same family was the Hon. Nathan Smith, of New Haven, who was a lawyer of high distinction, and died in Washington in 1835, being at the time of his death a member of the U. S. Senate from Connecticut.

Phineas Smith was a farmer, and in intellectual ability was in no degree inferior to his brothers above named. The subject of this notice was brought up on his father's farm, and owes whatever success he achieved in after life to habits formed, and principles inculcated in the home of his chilhood. He entered Yale College in 1811, and graduated in 1815. The Hon. John M. Clayton, of Delaware, and the Hon. Thomas A. Marshall, of Kentucky, with several others who were afterwards distinguished in public life, were his classmates.

He commenced the study of the law soon after his graduation, and was admitted a member of the bar in Litchfield county, in March, 1818. His classmate Clayton was admitted to the same bar at the same time. In the fall of the same year he opened an office for the practice of his profession in Litchfield, and that was his home till 1854. The bar of Litchfield county then numbered more than forty members, and many of them were very eminent in their profession. Mr. Smith soon felt that at such a bar as this, faithful study and indefatigable labor would alone secure success. To such study and labor Mr. Smith devoted himself strictly; and he soon became known as a young lawyer of marked ability and decided promise. He soon acquired professional employment; and at the end of ten or twelve years he stood among the most talented of his brethren in the management of the most important cases before the higher court.

About the time of Mr. Smith's accession to the bar, a political revolution had taken place in Connecticut, which had displaced from office men who had long and honorably filled the stations of public trust in every branch of the government, and had put in their places untried, inexperienced, and, in many instances incompetent men. The greatest danger was apprehended in the organization of the Judiciary department under the Constitution which the party lately come into power had given the State. The Judges of the Court under the old system of government, were, without exception, eminent jurists, and of pure, unsullied character. It was hoped that some of them might be retained on the new Court; but they were nearly all dismissed from the public service, and it could not be denied that the Court, as constituted under the new order of things, was greatly inferior in ability, and far less possessed of the public confidence than the Court which it had superceded. Chief Justice Hosmer, the only jurist of any distinction retained on the bench, by indefatigable and exhausting labor, gave it some share of respectability; but it could not be concealed from the observation of the bar, that its decisions had lost much of the respect with which those of the old Court were regarded by the Courts of sister States, and in other countries where the common law is the rule of action

To this state of things the attention of Mr. Smith, as his practice increased and his acquaintance with the new Court became familiar, was drawn with anxious solicitude, and it is quite probable that the important bearing that the politics of the State had upon the constitution of the Court, had a strong influence in shaping his conduct in relation to public affairs in the State One prominent reason which he was in the habit of giving in explaining the depth of his interest in politics, was *that he wanted a good Court.* It may be proper to say here that this feeling, in the end, obtained a decided ascendancy in the State, and as vacancies in the Court occurred from time to time, they were filled by the appointment of such men as David Daggett, Roger M. Sherman, Thomas

S. Williams, Clark Bissell, William L. Storrs, and others their successors, who have done honor to their position, and raised the character of the Supreme Court of the State to its ancient eminence.

After a practice of some fifteen years in his profession, Mr. Smith had obtained an eminent position in the county, and had very great popularity with his political friends; in fact, he was the mentor spirit in all their party movements. Up to this time the eminent men of the county were a kind of privileged class, never mingling much with the common people, and known only by their occasional public performances. But Mr. Smith had a far different habit. He welcomed to his acquaintance and sympathy good men of all conditions in society, no matter how humble or obscure the man might be. In that way he became personally well known in every section of the county, and extensively throughout the State. Yet he never took advantage of his social position to obtain preferment for himself. He never packed a convention, never asked for a nomination for any place; never solicited the vote of any man, and never addressed a public assembly in a canvass when his own name was before the people for office. Whenever he gave his consent to receive a nomination at the hands of his friends, he had no competitor for the position. His weight of character, eminent fitness and great abilities, always marked him out as the man for the place, and his nominations were always made with great unanimity. He never failed of an election when he was a candidate, and was usually returned by a strong majority of his district. He was elected a representative from the town of Litchfield in the Legislature of Connecticut for the years 1831-32 and '34, and was a prominent leading member of the house during each of those years. His sagacious counsels were felt in all its deliberations, and had much to do in shaping its measures.

Up to this time, and for several years afterwards, Mr. Smith was engaged in professional employment. He never neglected this duty, however loud the call might be for him to engage in a political canvass. He was a complete master of the science of the law, and his practice was not confined to Litchfield county, but extended to other counties in the State. His manner of conducting trials was peculiar to himself. He was often severe and harsh in his cross-examination of witnesses, especially if he thought they practiced prevarication or dishonesty. He was not what might be called an easy, fluent speaker, but there was a power of thought and strength of argument which attended his oral deliveries which made him a popular advocate, and commanded the strict attention of the hearer.

There was probably no time after 1837 to the time of his election to the Senate, but that Mr. Smith could have held a seat in the House of Representatives of the National Congress, if he would have consented to be a candidate for the position. He was always the first man named for the place, when the matter was talked up among the members of the party; but the demands of clients for his professional services, and the desire that others should share the honors as well as the labors of the position, frequently caused his withdrawal from public life, but in no degree diminished his active labors in the cause which lay near his heart. In 1839, and again in 1841, he was elected to and served in the National House of Representatives. Up to that time the State of Connecticut was entitled to six members, and the county of Litchfield then formed the Sixth Congressional District. Under the apportionment made by the census of 1840, the number of members from Connecticut was reduced to four, and Fairfield and Litchfield counties formed the Fourth District. Mr. Smith was offered the nomination in 1843, for the consolidated district, but declined in favor of the Hon. Thos. B, Osborn, who had represented the Fairfield district during the four previous years. Mr. Osborn was defeated by Dr. Samuel Simons, of Bridgeport, and at that election, every district in Connecticut elected a democratic representative.

In 1844 Mr. Smith was one of the Electoral College of Connecticut, which gave the vote of that State for Henry Clay for President, but who was defeated by James K. Polk, who inaugurated a policy which Mr. Smith believed would prove disastrous to the country, and, in his opinion, subsequent results have fully justified his belief.

In 1845 Mr. Smith was nominated for congress in the consolidated district, and was elected by more than seven teen hundred majority over his competitor, John Cotton Smith, and this, in a district which two years before had given a democratic majority of one hundred and thirteen. At this election the State was completely revolutionized, every district having elected the Whig candidate by a very decided vote.

In 1847 Mr. Smith was reelected by a majority of more than one thousand votes over his democratic competitor; and this was his last term of service in the House of Representatives. During this congress the selection of a candidate for the Presidency, to be supported by the Whig party at the election in 1848 became a matter of great interest, and was attended with no little difficulty. Mr. Smith was a member of the National Whig Convention, at Philadelphia which nominated General Taylor; and although he was willing to support any candidate which the convention should propose, yet he gave it as his opinion from the beginning, that General Taylor was the strongest man for the place, and a majority of the convention concurred in this belief. Mr. Smith was chairman of the Whig committee which had in charge the management of the national canvass, and spent much of his time during its pendency in Washington, superintending the action of the party. In these labors he had the cooperation of Abraham Lincoln, who also was in Washington, as a colleague with Mr Smith during a portion of the time. The efficiency and skill of Mr. Smith in conducting the campaign was acknowledged by all who took an interest in the issue.

In the mean time, the Legislature of Connecticut had elected Mr. Smith to the Senate of the United States for the term commencing with the administration of Gen. Taylor. Before he took his seat in the Senate, President Taylor offered him a seat in his Cabinet, as Secretary of the Interior, but he declined the proposed honor, and turned to his Senatorial position as a more appropriate field for him to occupy in the public service. He continued an active, honored and efficient member of that distinguished body until the 24th day of May, 1854, when, for reasons which he deemed imperative upon himself, he resigned his seat, and has not since been in public life.

Of both branches of the National Congress Mr Smith was an influential member. On every subject to which they were devoted, his speeches contained a great amount of statistical and historical information, and were read with great interest by men of all parties. He was also very successful in harmonizing discordant views among the members of his own party, and in procuring their united action on measures of policy agitated in Congress.

During his term of service in the Senate, besides participating occasionally in debates on minor matters, he addressed to that body able and effective speeches on the subjects following:—

1. On removals from office, delivered March 21 and 23, 1850.
2. On the compromise measures proposed by the Committee of which Mr. Clay was Chairman, delivered July 8, 1850.
3. On the French Spoliation—February 16 and 17, 1851.
4. On the proposition of Mr. Douglass to authorize a levy of tonnage duties by the States for the improvement of rivers and harbors—August 23. 1852.
5. On the construction of a railroad from Missouri to the Pacific coast.—February 17, 1850.
6. On the Nebraska question.—February 10 and 11, 1854.

All those speeches were fraught with good sense and sound logic. That of February, 1854, on the repeal of the Missouri Compromise, expressed the full conviction of its author that the measure foreboded incalculable mischief to the country, and he felt bound to oppose to it an uncompromising resistance. In this, his last speech, Mr. Smith undertook to demonstrate that there was and ever had been, an entire harmony in the elements on which the prosperity of the different sections of the Union depended; that there was an utter impracticability of maintaining an equilibrium between the free and slave States, and how useless such an equilibrium, if attainable, would be to the latter, and that the various slavery questions which, during the few preceding years had made such a disturbance in and out of Congress, were of very inconsiderable importance. Mr. Webster complimented Mr Smith with the remark that he had succeeded perfectly in the effort.

In the fall of 1854 Mr. Smith removed his residence to Stamford, Fairfield county, with the view to open an office in the city of New York, for the practice of law, which he did accordingly, and was so engaged till the fall of 1872, when he retired, except as to two cases before the Supreme Court of the United States, one of which is still pending.

PHINEAS SMITH, JR., and HARRIET JUDSON were married June 30, 1824. She died November 3, 1826, childless.

Yale College, 1816. Studied law and went to Vermont. Settled first at Arlington, then at Rutland, and was eminent in the State; d. there.

PHINEAS SMITH and JANE PENNIMAN were married June 25, 1833, and had issue as follows:—

1. JAMES PENNIMAN, b. May 26, 1834.
2. HENRY PENNIMAN, b. April 13, 1836, d. August 22, 1838.
3. CATHARINE OLIVIA, b. April 13, 1839.

James P. and Catharine O., children of Phineas Smith and Jane, his wife, remain unmarried.

3. DANIEL SHELDON, died unmarried, as already stated.

4. NATHANIEL SMITH and MARILLA S. BENTON were married February 26, 1840, and have issue as follows:—

   1. GERTRUDE AUGUSTA, b December 29, 1841.
   2. MARIA PRESTON, b. August 7, 1847. Both remain unmarried.

5 HENRY N. PAINTER and CATHARINE ANN SMITH, were married November 13, 1838, and are childless.

6. NATHAN RICHARD SMITH and SARAH BLACKMAN were married September 19. 1836, and have issue as follows:—

   1. SHELDON BLACKMAN, b. February 5, 1838.
   2. HENRY PAINTER, b. February 22, 1852, d. April 27, 1852.

SHELDON B. SMITH and MARY BUCKINGHAM were married October 17, 1859, and have issue as follows:—

   1. HOWARD B., b. September 1, 1860.
   2. SARAH E., b. July 15, 1864.

Of the children of Phineas Smith and Deborah Ann, his wife, four are living and two are dead. Of their grand children, nine are living and seven are dead. Of their great-grand children, there are only two and both are living.

35. SYBIL LEAVENWORTH.[4]—JOHN,[3] THOMAS,[2] THOMAS.[1]

Born ——— 1747, at Woodbury.

Married —— Keeler, of Fairfield Co., and had two sons and one daughter.

36. Amos Leavenworth.[4]—JOHN,[3] THOMAS,[2] THOMAS.[1]

Baptized August 9, 1753, at Woodbury.

Married ESTHER WARNER, July 11, 1774, daughter of Thomas Warner. She was born May 21, 1755, or January 28, 1755, and

Eng^d by A. H. Ritchie

Truman Smith

September 12, 1784, joined the first Congregational church at Woodbury. He was executor on his father's estate, February 17, 1785. He removed to Deerfield near Utica, in March 1794, and died there September 2, 1828. He was nine days with his nine children on the way.

CHILDREN.

115. JOSEPH, b. July 19, 1776, d. July 1, 1840, unmarried.
116. SARAH. b. April 29. 1778, bap. December 15, 1784.
117. MARY, born January 23, 1781, bap. December 15, 1784, d. Nov. 13, 1851, unmarried, at her sister Isabel's in Marcy.
118. ESTHER, b. December 6, 1782, bap. December 15, 1784, d. Nov. 10, 1857, unmarried, at her sister Isabel's in Marcy.
119. SUSANNA, b. September 21, 1784, bap. December 15, 1784, d. October, 1841.
120. RALPH, b. June 27, 1786, bap. August 13, 1786, d. November 20, 1852.
121. LORANA, b. Oct. 21, 1788, bap. March 29, 1789, d. October 29, 1826, of typhus fever, at her sister Isabel,s in Marcy.
122. ISABEL, b. April 15, 1791, bap. July 10, 1791, d. November 9, 1796, unmarried.
123. LOVISA, b. January 3, 1793, bap. April 7, 1793, d. unmarried. All born and bap. at Woodbury.
124. ISABEL, b. May 29, 1798, at Deerfield, now in Marcy.
125. *(Daughter)*, b. February 27, 1800, d. same day.

He served in the army of the Revolution. Cothren, p. 783. His farm was in the present town of Marcy, Oneida Co., and fronted on the Mohawk river.

37. AVIS LEAVENWORTH.[4]—JOHN,[3] THOMAS,[2] THOMAS.[1]

Born 1754, at Woodbury. Married Simeon Castle, of Roxbury, and had a large family.

39. Elisha Leavenworth.[4]—JOHN,[3] THOMAS,[2] THOMAS.[1]

Baptized July 3, 1763. No doubt died early.

40. Elihu Leavenworth.[4]—JOHN,[3] THOMAS,[2] THOMAS.[1]

Born June 10, 1763, at Woodbury.

Married DIANTHA BLACKMAN, of Stratford, October 6, 1782.

He was a farmer, lived in Roxbury, Ct.; died there July 1, 1817, and was buried with Masonic ceremonies. She survived him about fifteen years, and died in 1832-3. Her will was proved September 30, 1833, 17th Prob. vol., p. 121. His will was proved at Woodbury, September 18, 1817, 12th Prob. vol., p. 216. John L.. his son, executor.

CHILDREN.

126. JEHIEL, b. October 4, 1783, d. October 11, 1826.
127. JOHN, b. ——— 1786, d. July 10, 1856.
128. DR. ALSON, b. October 12, 1788, d. September 19, 1863.
129. ISAAC, b. June 12, 1791.
130. WILLIAM, b. ——— d. aged 13.
131. CARLOSSY, b. May 3, 1798, d. some years since.
132. LUCY, b. January 1, 1800. All born in Roxbury.

41. MARY LEAVENWORTH.[4]—ZEBULON,[3] THOMAS,[2] THOMAS.[1]

Baptized July 16, 1745.

Married Simeon Hunt April 11, 1769. Removed to Vermont about 1800, and about 1808 to Dayton, Ohio, where both died about 1814. He was a farmer; they had two sons.

CHILDREN.

1. JOHN, b. ——— d. 1845. Had a son Simeon, a merchant at Madison, Ind.
2. NATHANIEL, b. ——— d. about 1830. He was in 1816, a member of the Constitutional Convention of Indiana, and was several years a member of the State Legislature. He had a son Nathaniel, who carried on a tobacco manufactory, and who resided at Madison, Ind.

42. ESTHER LEAVENWORTH.[4] — ZEBULON,[3] THOMAS, THOMAS.[1]

Baptized June 21, 1847, d. in 1749.

43. ESTHER LEAVENWORTH,[4]-ZEBULON,[3] THOMAS,[2] THOMAS[1].

Baptized May 20, 1750. Married Benjamin Kimberly March 23, 1773.

44. Zebulon Leavenworth.[4]—ZEBULON,[3] THOMAS,[2] THOMAS.[1]

Born November 14, 1752, in Roxbury, Ct.

Married LYDIA MARSHALL, of Farmington, Ct., January 21, 1778 Removed to Granville, Mass., in 1786-7. He d. 1795. He was a farmer.

CHILDREN.

133. SARAH, b. August 16, 1779, d. at Leavenworth, Ind., 1820, unmarried.

134. SETH MARSHALL, b. June 13, 1782, d. April 2, 1853.
135. REBECCA, b. August 31, 1784, d. at Jeffersonville, Ind. 1817.
136. RACHEL. b. October 27, 1786, d. at Leavenworth, Ind. in 1832.
137. ZEBULON, b. January 4, 1792, d. at Leavenworth, Ind., September 12-13, 1872, and was buried Sunday, Sept. 15.

45. EUNICE LEAVENWORTH.[4] — ZEBULON,[3] THOMAS,[2] THOMAS.[1]

Born March 2, 1755.

46. ANNA LEAVENWORTH.[4]—ZEBULON,[3] THOMAS,[2] THOMAS.[1]

Baptized August 22, 1757.

47. HULDAH LEAVENWORTH.[4] — ZEBULON,[3] THOMAS,[2] THOMAS.[1]

Baptized May 30, 1759.

48. ALICE LEAVENWORTH.[4]—ZEBULON,[3] THOMAS,[2] THOMAS.

Baptized August 13 1766.

49. Col. Jesse Leavenworth.[4]—MARK,[3] THOMAS,[2] THOMAS.[1]

Born November 22, 1740, at Waterbury, Ct. Graduated at Yale College in 1784.

Married (1) July 1, 1761, CATHARINE FRISBIE, (widow of Capt. Culpepper Frisbie, and daughter of John Conkling, of Southampton, or Easthampton, Suffolk Co., N. Y.) John Conkling's wife was a Scaliger. He m. (2) EUNICE SPERRY. She died in 1835 at Sackett's Harbor.

In his old age, Jesse L. became very infirm. He was at Sackett's Harbor, N. Y., in 1823, decrepid and unable to travel. He died there, probably, on the 12th of December, 1824, though the date of June 29, 1824, is given by one of the family.

CHILDREN.

138. MELINES CONKLING, b. January 4, 1762, d. July 20, 1823.
139. RUTH, b. February 25, 1764.
140. DR. FREDERICK, b September 4, 1766, d. May 17, 1840 at Waterbury.

141. CATHARINE, b. —— 1768, d. June 25, 1815.
142. JESSE, b. August, 1771, d. January 1, 1830.
143. MARK, b. August 31, 1774, d. September 5, 1849.
144. HENRY, b. December 10, 1783, d. July 21, 1834.

The first three were born at Waterbury, the last four at New Haven.

When his father the Rev. Mark, went to Canada, as Chaplain in the French war of 1760, he is supposed to have accompanied his father, and to have held the office of Lieutenant. He was a Captain in the army of the Revolution, and was undoubtedly at Ticonderoga in the spring and summer of 1777, when the fort was abandoned by Gen. St. Clair.

It appears in Hinman's Historical Collection on Conn., in the Revolution, p. 516, that "Capt. Jesse Leavenworth, of New "Haven, under proper orders, gave his deposition respecting the "evacuation of Ticonderoga. The pay table were directed to "settle Capt. Leavenworth's account, etc." This was in Legislative session, January 19, 1778.

I am indebted to the Hon. Frederick J. Kingsbury, of Waterbury, a descendant of Col. Jesse, for the following sketch of him :—

Col. Jesse was the only child of his mother, and was twelve years older than the oldest of his half-brothers. He was graduated at the age of nineteen, and married several months before he attained his majority, and the family tradition is, that they were spoken of as the handsomest couple ever seen at the church in New Haven. All the sons of Rev. Mark appear to have been superior men, both physically and intellectually, taking rank among the foremost wherever they went. For a few years after Col. Jesse's marriage, he lived in Waterbury, carrying on various kinds of business, and at one time keeping a hotel which stood at the corner of Center Square and North Main street, nearly on the ground now occupied by the Citizen's Bank, the building fronting on North Main street.

In February, 1767, he bought a place in New Haven and soon after moved his family there. He soon engaged in commercial affairs, and in Trowbridge's History of Long Wharf, in vol. 1 N. H. Hist. Society papers, his name appears among the most liberal contributors to that enterprise. There was almost no money to be had in those days, and he heads the first list with a subscription of "one hundred bushels of salt," and appears always as a liberal contributor on succeeding lists.

He was a Lieutenant in the "Governor's Foot Guards," the distinguished military company of the State, and of which his neighbor, Benedict Arnold, was Captain. When the news of the battle of Lexington reached New Haven, in the early spring of 1775, Arnold called out his company and asked for volunteers. Forty went—Leavenworth with them. They marched by Pomfret, taking "old Put" along. When they reached camp at Cambridge, their dress and drill were so superior that they were at once detailed to deliver the body of a British officer who had died, and their soldier-like appearance was much admired by the British party whom they met on this occasion. At the end of about three weeks Leavenworth and the company returned. Arnold remained, and began here his career of honor and shame.

Leavenworth's house in those days, was on the water side of East Water street, a little eastward of the site afterwards known as the Pavilion Hotel. In high tides the water came up almost to the rear of the house, and here, during the Revolution, some marauding British soldiers landed, and finding Madame L. alone they robbed the house of such valuables as they could carry, and destroyed other property, ripping open feather beds and emptying them into the sea; also taking the silver buckles out of her shoes, while she stood by and gave them, as she used to say, "a piece of her mind."

She had a keen black eye, and a sharp tongue, and in after years, perhaps not without sufficient cause, she turned it on her husband with such efficacy that he sought shelter in the wilds of Vermont. About 1783 he became alienated from her, and, taking the younger children with him, he left her forever. There may have been fault on both sides, but apparently it was mainly on his, and his memory must bear the blame. He took a woman with him who had been an inmate of the family, and whom he afterwards married, some sort of a divorce having been obtained.

He went first to Caledonia, and at once became a prominent man in that part of the country. He was one of the patentees of the towns of Danville and Peacham, October 27, 1786, and soon settled in Danville on or near the old Hazen military road which runs through the west part of the town. He built mills at West Danville, at the mouth of Joe's pond, and engaged in various other enterprises. He was a member of the Legislature in 1789-91-92 and '98.

He was apparently one of those pioneers of civilization who do more for others than themselves; for though a planner of many enterprises and not wholly unsuccessful he was probably too sanguine and large-minded for his means; at any rate he does not seem to have accumulated much property. He died at Sackett's Harbor, N. Y., whither he had moved some years before Dec. 12, 1824, having moved there on account of his son, Gen. Henry, being at the time stationed there.

While living at New Haven, he took a very prominent and active part in all public affairs. The "Old" or "Red Rock Ferry," was for nearly one hundred and thirty years the only means of communication between New Haven and East Haven and vicinity. Increasing population and business demanded another ferry, and in 1780 Leavenworth's Ferry was incorporated by a grant to Jesse Leavenworth from the General Assembly. It was the shortest route to the business center of New Haven from East Haven, and drew a large portion of the travel for many years, and until in 1791 the bridge over the Quinipiac at Dragon, now Fair Haven, was erected.

50. Mark Leavenworth.[4]—MARK,[3] THOMAS,[2] THOMAS.[1]

Born May 26, 1752. Graduated at Yale College in 1771; was a lawyer in New Haven.

Married Mrs. —— Sherman, widow of William, son of Roger Sherman, the signer of the Declaration of Independence. He went to France with Joel Barlow, U. S. Minister to that country, and died in Paris in 1812, leaving no children.

A daughter of Mrs. Sherman by her first marriage, married Oliver Leicester Phelps, son of one of the partners of the Phelps & Gorham Purchase of western New York. They resided for a time in France, and afterwards in Canandaigua, N. Y., where he died Nov. 2, 1812. *(Turner's Phelps & Gorham Purchase, p. 150.)*

Mark was in mercantile business with his brother Jesse for a number of years before the latter removed to Vermont. They were active and prominent men in the West India trade.

He went to London with Joel Barlow in 1798, and thence to Paris. Here he lived for years in great splendor and prosperity. But eventually he was, as reported, ruined financially by some change of government officers, by the new officers refusing to perform a large contract for iron, made with their predecessors. This, no doubt, was at or about the time of the fall of Napoleon.

He was a member of a Committee appointed by the Legislature of Connecticut, from various parts of the State, to secure relief for the army under Washington. This was in the latter part of 1776 and early part of 1777.

In the Congressional Library at Washington, there is a volume of pamphlets, "in relation to the Revolutionary war of the U. S. of America, 1790," *(J. 459.)* Pamphlets of A. Hamilton, Wm. Van Murray, Dr, Montgomery, Dr. Logan and M. *(Mark)* Leavenworth. And in the Library of the American Phil. Society of Philadelphia, there is a pamphlet No. 288, by Mark Leavenworth, the title page and contents of which are as follows :—

(TITLE PAGE.)

ESSAI.

l' influence de nos vents variables sur la temperature des saisons ainsi que sur la cause de ces vents.

Avec deux Notes relative a la theorie des Marees de l' Ocean.

par M. LEAVENWORTH,

CULTIVATEUR

Paris l' imprimerie des Sciences et des Arts,

Rue Ventadour, No. 5.

1807.

In the preface the writer gives the motives which prompted m to publish, and gives the work as the result of his study and observation.

(The summary of the work preceding first chapter.)

"Essai sur la temperature des saisons en differcules annees, ainsi que sur le cours des vents, particulierement sur l'Ocean

Atlantique dans la zone temperee du nord, et dans les pays situes le long de cet ocean." 74 pages.

The writer then answers the objections made to his theory by some savans.

52. SARAH LEAVENWORTH.[4]—MARK,[3] THOMAS,[2] THOMAS.[1]

Born December 11, 1756. Married Dr. Isaac Baldwin, then of Waterbury, afterwards of Great Barrington Mass. He probably settled at Great Barrington at the suggestion of No. 187, who studied with him at W. He died at Great Barrington February 21, 1814, in the fifty-ninth year of his age.

CHILDREN.

1. SARAH, b. May 24, 1785, m. Dr. Edward Field April 30, 1807, d. August 8, 1808. Dr. F. was a native of Enfield, Conn.

Children.

JUNIUS LEAVENWORTH FIELD, b. February 1, 1808, graduated in Medical Dep't Yale Coll., 1831. Practiced at Wolcott, Conn. M. Mrs. Maria Packard, (*nee* Briggs), moved to Cheshire, Conn., and afterward to Unadilla, Livingston Co., Mich ; d. there November 23, 1867.

Children.

1. James Edward, b. December 20, 1832.
2. Sarah Elizabeth, b. March 18, 1837, d. March 14, 1846.
3. Eugene Briggs, b. May 24, 1840, d. August 9, 1840.
4. Calvin Briggs, b. January 20, 1844, d. September 20, 1847.

1. James Edward, m., first, Loretta Beal, May 5, 1854. She died January 25 1861. M., second, Sarah Beal, November 12, 1863.

Children—James Emery, b. February 23, 1860. Etta Maria, b September 23, 1865. Edward C., b. February 6, 1873, d. July 28, 1873.

2. REBECCA, b. June 23, 1787, d. unmarried January 9, 1844.
3. ESTHER, b. August 21, 1789, m. Dr. Edward Field Jan. 4, 1810.

Children.

HENRY BALDWIN FIELD, b. January 11, 1811, m. Sarah Bulkley, of New Haven, June 14, 2836. He resides in Waterbury, and is Secretary of the Gas Light Co.

Children.

1. A daughter, d. in infancy.
2. Francis Bulkley, b. September 16, 1843, at New Haven. Resides in Waterbury, clerk in a bank ; m. Nov. 22, 1870. Ella S., dau. of George William Cook, of Waterbury, by Rev. F. T. Russell. He has one child, Emily Brintnall, b. May 19, 1873, at Waterbury.
3. Charles Henry, b. March 21, 1849, in Baltimore, now, (1871), living in Rio Janeiro, S. A. Now, (1873), living at Hartford. M. September 20, 1871, Lizzie R. Tremaine, dau. of Charles I. Tremaine, of Hartford, and has two children—Edward Bronson, b. April 27, 1872. Francis Elliott, b. July 21, 1873.

2. SARAH ARIETTA, b. August 27, 1813, d. September 9, 1815.
3. MARY MARGARET FIELD, b March 12, 1817, m. June 30, 1841, Charles Buckingham Merriman, a native of Watertown, Conn., but now residing in Waterbury—a manufacturer—d. October 5, 1866.

Children.

1. Charlotte Buckingham, b. August 21, 1843.
2. Sarah Morton, b. August 7, 1845.

3. Helen, b. January 19, 1848.
4. Margaret Field, b. March 16, 1850.
5. William Buckingham, b. June 11, 1853.
6. Edward Field, b. September 1, 1854.

4. CHARLOTTE ARIETTA, b. December 6, 1819, m. Samuel G. Blackman, February 25, 1851. They reside in New Haven; no children; no business.

5. EDWARD GUSTAVUS, b. December 7, 1822. Studied medicine; now a member of Board of Brokers in New York. Unmarried.

The author well remembers Dr. Baldwin, who was an old gentleman with a wooden leg, and a practicing physician at Great Barrington when the writer was a boy. He was living with his second wife. This was 1810 to 1815, probably.

53. Col. William Leavenworth.[4]—MARK,[3] THOMAS,[2] THOMAS.[1] Born February 23, 1759.

Married HANNAH BRONSON, May 1, 1781. She was daughter of Ezra Bronson. Was born March 26, 1757. He died at Bridgeport, Ct., Nov. 24, 1836. She died March 17, 1836, at Albany, aged 79. In 1782 he was a contractor for procuring soldiers. (Bronson's Waterbury, p. 348.) He was also a contractor for building a church. (ib. 291.) In 1787 he was town clerk of Waterbury; and Oct. 1796 and May, 1798, represented that town in the legislature. He engaged in clock making after the war of 1812—was unsuccessful, and went to Albany. He was at one time interested in the manufacture of copper coin for the colony at New Haven. (Bronson's Waterbury.)

CHILDREN.

145. SARAH, b. June 20, 1784.
146. WILLIAM, b. June 20, 1786.

54. Dr. Nathan Leavenworth.[4]—MARK,[3] THOMAS,[2] THOMAS.[1]

Born December 11, 1761.

Graduated at Yale College in 1778.

He joined the Continental army in 1779, as Sergeant's Mate. Remained in service till the close of the war, leaving West Point in June 1784. In October following he went to Darlington District, South Carolina, and remained there in the practice of medicine till compelled to leave by ill health in 1793. Returned home and lived an invalid in weakness and pain, but cheerful and resigned, till his death on the 9th day of January 1799. He was unmarried.

Leavenworth Post Office, in above District, established near his residence, and discontinued since the rebellion, was named from the Doctor.

In 1789 a petition was presented to the Legislature of South Carolina, asking the enrollment of a volunteer troop of horse for patrol duty, and among the petitioners appears the name of Nathan Leavenworth. He then resided in Darlington District. See "Gregg's History of the Old Cheraw."

55. Joseph Leavenworth.[4]—Mark,[3] Thomas,[2] Thomas.[1]

Born June 15, 1764, at Waterbury, Conn. Died April 16, 1766.

56. Elisha Leavenworth.[4]—Mark,[3] Thomas,[2] Thomas.[1]

Born October 21, 1766, at Waterbury, Conn. (Waterbury records have it October 15.) Died May 3, 1812.

Married, first, Abigail Mather May 15, 17—, widow of —— Mather, and daughter of ———Russell. She died December 13, 1796.

Married, second, Rachel Stone, of Derby, Conn., August, 1798. She was born November 22, 1761, and died March 14, 1852, at the city of New York, to which place he removed in early life. He died May 3, 1812, very suddenly, aged forty-six.

CHILDREN.

147. Nathan, b. October 18, 1792, in New York.
148. Mary Talcott, b. June 25, 1795, d. January 29, 1796.
149. Abigail Russell, b. November 21, 1796, d. Feb. 26, 1797.
150. Child, b. after 1798, d. in infancy.
151. " " " d. "
152. " " " d. "

He was an extensive and wealthy merchant in New York city.

57. Asa Leavenworth.[4]—Thomas,[3] Thomas,[2] Thomas.[1]

Born in 1744, at Woodbury, Conn.; farmer and millwright.

Married Submit Scott, of Watertown, Conn., June 6, 1768. She was the eldest daughter of David and Hannah (Hickock) Scott, who was born at Waterbury, now Watertown, Conn., in 1747, and died at Great Barrington, Mass., February 14, 1814, aged sixty-seven, at the residence of her son David. He died at Binghamton, N. Y., November 19, 1828, at the home of his son, Isaac, aged 84. Was a farmer at Watertown—removed to Canaan, N. Y., about 1795-6, where his son David had settled.

CHILDREN.

153. DAVID, b. September 12, 1769, d. May 25, 1831.
154. JOHN, b. January 23, 1771-2, d. October 10, 1772.
155. JOHN, b. January 23, 1773, d. April 6, 1851.
156. TRUMAN, b. November 22, 1775, d. November 19, 1862.
157. BETSEY, b. April 5, 1778, d. February 1, 1800.
158. ISAAC, b. June 17, 1780, d. February 19, 1860.
159. SALLY, b. March 14, 1788, d. September 19, 1863.

All born at Watertown, Conn.

58. TRIPHENA LEAVENWORTH.[4]—THOMAS,[3] THOMAS,[2] THOMAS.[1]

Born July 3, 1746, and died early.

59. Gideon Leavenworth.[4]—THOMAS,[3] THOMAS,[2] THOMAS.[1]

Born February 21, 1748, in Woodbury, Conn.

Married MARY COLE, of Watertown, Conn., daughter of Thomas Cole. Lived in Watertown, and then in Hamden, in early life, and then removed to the Susquehannah. Then lived for a time in Hamden and in New Marlborough, Mass., and returned to Watertown. He died at Watertown in the old Trumbull House, June 7, 1833. She died at the same place April 2, 1836, aged eighty. About 1823 he visited his nephew, Dr. David Leavenworth, of Great Barrington, Mass. He then lived at New Marlborough, Mass.

CHILDREN.

160. JOHN, b. in Watertown, Sept. 10, 1775, d. Aug. 27, 1822.
161. JARED, b. at the home of his Grand-father, Thomas Cole, (July 17, 1784. Jared L. Pitcher says) at Watertown, in the hard winter of 1781.
162. MARY, b. in Watertown August 1, 1783, d. March 7, 1870, at Woodbury.

He was a remarkably worthy, genial, agreeable and intelligent old man. He was not possessed of much of this world's goods, but was happy and content.

He was remarkably familiar with the genealogy of the entire family, and fifty years since there was scarcely one man of the family, from Dr. Thomas, of Ripton, down, with whose name, residence and business he was not familiar. He furnished a large part of the facts for the Genealogical Tree published in 1840, and made by William and E. W. Leavenworth; and but for him, it is not probable that this genealogy of the family would ever have been written, for this work was commenced only to revise, correct and enlarge that.

The house called the Old Trumbull House was formerly the residence of the Rev. John Trumbull, of Watertown, about a mile below the village, on the Waterbury road. It was the place of birth of John T., his son, the author of McFingal. See a wood cut of it in Barber's Hist. Collection of Conn.

He lived in the enjoyment of a serene and quiet old age, with the partner of his youth, and died, I am sure, at peace with the world and his God. He was a millwright, and built mills in various places, far and near, in early life. He lived at Oxford, Conn. in 1808, and in 1812 moved to Towanda, Penn., from Shephard's Brook, in Hamden.

60. Samuel Leavenworth.[4]—THOMAS,[3] THOMAS,[2] THOMAS.[1] Born 1751 in Woodbury. Removed to Waterbury, Conn. Married SARAH NETTLETON. Died April 12, 1807, in Waterbury, Conn. His wife died March 12, 1840, aged eighty-seven. He bought ninety acres of land in Watertown, of David Brown in 1784, and of his brother Asa, lands in 1787—November 16.

CHILDREN.

163. JOSEPH, b. September 16, 1773, d. April 3, 1866.
164. TRIPHENA, b. September 16, 1775, d. January 28, 1854.
165. HANNAH, b. October 3, 1779, m, David Baldwin January 30, 1800, d. May 14, 1863.
166. SAMUEL, b. December 28, 1783, d. December 12, 1868.
167. SALLY, b. December 10, 1789, m. Hector W. Baird, April 10, 1810.

61. Jared Leavenworth.[4]—THOMAS,[3] THOMAS,[2] THOMAS.[1] Born February 1, 1756. Probably died young.

62. BETTY LEAVENWORTH.[4]—THOMAS,[3] THOMAS,[2] THOMAS.[1]

Born October 27, 1760.

Married Stephen Hurd, July 28, 1783. He was a son of Simeon Hurd, and was born June 28, 1757.

63. Isaac Leavenworth.[4]—THOMAS,[3] THOMAS,[2] THOMAS.[1]

Baptized March 7, 1762. Died young, no doubt.

64. Abel Leavenworth.[4]—THOMAS,[3] THOMAS,[2] THOMAS.[1]

Born January 30, 1765, probably in Woodbury, Conn.

Married LYDIA BARTLETT November 29, 1791, at Charlotte, Vt., daughter of Elihu Bartlett, grand-daughter of Rev. Moses Bartlett, of Middleton, Conn., born at Guilford, Conn., August, 1772. Her mother was Statira Meigs, daughter of Dea. Timothy Meigs, son of James, son of John, son of Vincent, who came from Devonshire, Eng., in 1638. On her mother's side, Mrs. L. was descended from Rev. Abraham Pierson, first President of Yale College.

CHILDREN.

168. MEIGS, b. March 27, 1794, at Charlotte, d. August 20, 1827, at Charlotte, unmarried.
169. MINER, b. May 31, 1796, at Hinesburgh; lives at Bristol, Vt., 1873.
170. LYDIA, b. August 9, 1798, at Charlotte, d. September 8, 1830, at Charlotte, unmarried.
171. Abel, b. November 24, 1800, at Charlotte; lives there, 1873.
172. SABRINA, b. April 1, 1803, at Charlotte; lives at Burlington, Vt., 1873.
173. LAURA, b. December 17, 1805, at Charlotte, d. April 30, 1843, at Madrid, N. Y., unmarried.
174. ARZA, b. July 18, 1809, at New Haven, Vt., d. February 3, 1856, at Norfolk, N. Y.
175. Infant son, b. June 30, 1792, d. June 30, 1792.

Abel L. was a carpenter, settled in northeast part of Charlotte, Vt., when a wilderness with only paths and marked trees for eight miles to the lake. He built a grist and saw mill on the La Plot river. The stones for the grist mill were obtained from flint rocks found in Charlotte, and were worked out by his brother Gideon, who came on from Connecticut for that purpose. His dam was finally swept away by floods; he sold his farm and worked at his trade. The mill stones were purchased by Gen. Nathan Leavenworth, and put in a mill built by him on Lewis Creek river, in the southeast part of Charlotte.

He was a man of energy and skill in his trade, and of integrity of character. He died at Middlebury, Vt. January 25, 1813, where he was engaged in building a large mill, and whither he had removed his family from New Haven Vt., where he owned a farm. His widow returned to New Haven, and thence to Charlotte, where she died June 12, 1853, full of years, respected honored and beloved by all who knew her.

65. Thomas Leavenworth.[4]—THOMAS,[3] THOMAS,[2] THOMAS.[1]

Baptized December 28, 1766, and b. at Oxford, Conn.

Married, first, RUTH JOHNSON, daughter of Alexander Johnson. She died at Charlotte, Vt.

Married, second, MARY MOSIER, at Charlotte, Vt., daughter of Jesse Mosier, of New Milford, Conn., but then of Charlotte. He resided at Hinesburg, Vt., and was a miller. His first wife bore two sons and four daughters. His second wife the same number. He died in July, she in August, 1850, at Brandon, N. Y.

CHILDREN.

First wife.

176. ISAAC, b. ——— ———
177. CALVIN, b. March 9, 1793.
178. POLLY, b. ——, m. Erastus Johnson, of Ohio.
179. SARAH, b. ——, m, Philemon Treat.
180. ROSETTE, b. ——, m. Samuel S. Thompson, of Duchess Co., N. Y.
181. BETSEY, b. ——, m. ———, moved to Rockford, Ill.

Seoud wife.

182. MARIA, b. ——, m. Elander Stevens, of Hopkinton, N. Y.
183. SETH, b. ——, unmarried.
184. MARK, b. April 5, 1814
185. RUTH, b. 1815, m. Judson Wakefield, of Williston, Vt., d. January 1, 1839, at Stockholm, N. Y.
186. MARY, b. 1818, m. Isaac Staples, of Parishville, February 2, 1861.
187. MINERVA, b. 1819, m. said Judson Wakefield, 1842. Died December 25, 1863, aged forty-four.

In early life he lived at Huntington, Conn. About 1797 he

removed to Towanda, Penn. He soon returned to Connecticut and settled at Pines Bridge, town of Oxford. He next removed to Charlotte, Vt., and lived there till 1817, when he removed to Huntington, Vt. Then, in 1838, to Stockholm, N. Y., and from there to Brandon, Franklin county, N. Y., where he died in July, 1850. He was the last of the four Thomas L.'s in a direct line from the immigrant.

66. Dorman Leavenworth.[4]—THOMAS,[3] THOMAS,[2] THOMAS.[1]

Born September 22, (baptized October 28,), 1770, at Woodbury or Waterbury.

Married LUCY TUCKER, at Oxford Conn., December 13, 1794. She was a daughter of Gideon Tucker, a tailor of that place; was born January 4, 1769, and died at Charlotte, Vt., September 15, 1843. He was driven out of Wyoming with his father's family when eight years old; came to Oxford, Conn., and learned the wheelwright's trade, at which he worked till 1808, when he removed to Charlotte, Vt., where he arrived August 28, 1808. He there built a grist mill and saw mill. About 1818 he bought a farm in Charlotte, and resided there till 1839. He then sold to his son Burk, and went to live with his son-in-law, Isaac Sherwood. In two years he returned to Burk's house, and died there May 31, 1861. He lived to see four generations, himself, son, grand-son and great-grand-son, living in one family, and eating at one table. He was a man of remarkably strong constitution, was scarcely ever sick, and bore up under advanced years without showing much the infirmities of age.

CHILDREN.

188. BETSEY, b. October 17, 1796, d. November 27, 1867.
189. BURK, b. January 29, 1801.
190. LUCY, b. October 16, 1804.

He recollected well when the family were driven from the Wyoming Valley—the burying of their pewter plate in a brass kettle—seeing their own dwelling and those of their neighbors in flames from the hills, and the long, tedious, and dangerous journey on foot through the woods and over the mountains back to the frontier settlements and their friends in Connecticut, he carrying a wooden bottle under his arm through the long journey.

67. ABIGAIL LEAVENWORTH.[4] — EDMUND,[3] THOMAS,[2] THOMAS.[1]

Born at Huntington.

Married Dr. Samuel Beardsley, of Stratford, now Monroe, and had five daughters and three sons, all born in Monroe.

CHILDREN.

1. SAMUEL, b. in 1766, m. a Mrs. Hayes and had one son who d. unmarried ; d. December 10, 1823, aged fifty-seven.
2. JAMES, m., first, Ruth Ann Holbrook, of Derby. She d. in childbed ; m. second, Mrs. Lunn, of Oxford.
3. WEBB, d young and unmarried.
4. CHARLOTTE, b. in 1769, d. August 18, 1834, at Oxford, aged sixty-five. She m. Benjamin Hawley, a tailor, and had one son, David, who is married, lives in Ohio, and has no children.
5. ANNA, b. October 9, 1773, and d. November 26, 1836. She m. John Perry, who was b. October 19, 1769; he d. March 13, 1852. They had four children :—
   1. CHARLES, b. April 25, 1796, at Oxford ; d. in the fall of 1861. He m. Mary Ann Paine, and had four children.—Frederick, Charles, Harriet, Adam Clark, all dead but the youngest.
   2. PHILO, b. February 11, 1798, drowned June 12, 1800.
   3. JOHN, b. November 12, 1801, d. July 15, 1839, leaving one child Charles, b. September 20, 1835, d September 12, 1842.
   4. NANCY, b. September 3, 1803, m. Cornelius Pugsley September 14, 1831, and had six children.
      1. Henry, b. July 2, 1834.
      2. Cornelia, b. April 10, 1836, d. April, 62.
      3. Van Allen, b. December 13, 1837, m. Mary Ann Van Valkenburgh, October 3, 1866.
      4. Jacob, b. August 29, 1839, unmarried.
      5. Charles, b. April 27, 1850, unmarried.

6 & 7. SARAH and ELIZABETH, twins, b. September 5, 1779. Sarah m. Isaac Smith, of Oxford ; farmer and had eight children :—

   1. JOSIAH, m. Susan Hayes, and had two sons, now in West Haven. He is dead ; she survives.
   2. SARAH, m. Andrew Pope, had one or two children, and d. in the summer of 1872.
   3. SUSAN, resides at Derby, unmarried.
   4. PHILO, m., first, Betsey Lunn, of Oxford, and had two children. Second, Pamelia Hawkins.
   5. SILVIA, m. Wheeler Bassett, of Oxford ; has one son and two daughters. Lives at Bridgeport.
   6. RUTH ANN, m Frederick Hull, of Birmingham, and has one child.
   7. CAROLINE, m. Julius Wooster, of Derby. Moved to Ohio or Wisconsin, had several children, and d. two or three years since—1868 or '69,—at East Bridgeport, while on a visit east.
   8. GRACE, m. Burton Robinson, of Bethany ; she had no children, and d. in May, 1846, at Derby, at Mrs. Smith's.

7. ELIZABETH, twin to Sarah, b. September 5, 1779 ; m., first, David Smith, of Oxford, farmer and brother of Isaac, and had several children by him. Married, second, Moses Hawkins, of Oxford, and had one dau. Married, third, Adam Lunn, of Southbury, and d. October 23, 1857, aged seventy-eight years.
8. AURELIA, b. April 29, 1785, m. a Downs in December, 1803, and had several children. She d. September 3, 1869, in Michigan.

68. Capt. Gideon Leavenworth.[4] — EDMUND,[3] THOMAS,[2] THOMAS.[1]

Born October 18, 1751, at Huntington, Conn.

Married, first, SARAH WARD, of Stratford, October 20, 1779. She was born February 18, 1761, and died October 27, 1798.

Married, second, MARY ANN HULL, June 10, 1800. She was the widow of Dr. Amzi Hull, of Woodbridge; was born February 19, 1768, and died November 30, 1837. Her maiden name was Mary Ann Kasson.

Capt. Gideon L., was wounded in the thigh at the battle of White Plains, by a musket ball. He was an active and energetic business man, and died April 19, 1816, at Huntington, Conn., and was buried at the White Hills, and his two wives were also buried there.

CHILDREN.

191. ABIJAH, b. October 23, 1780, d. Oct. 14, 1835, at Huntington.
192. NANCY, b. April 19, 1782, d. March 27, 1821.
193. HEZEKIAH, b. December 11, 1784, d. in infancy.
194. SALLY, b. February 6, 1787, d. ———
195. BETSEY, b. June 13, 1789.
196. FANNY, b. June 28, 1791, m. Birdseye Thompson.
197. MARK ELI, b. April 22, 1801.
198. GIDEON HULL, b. April 20, 1804, d. January 1, 1805.
199. MARY ANN, b. November 17, 1805, unmarried and lives in Westport.
200. GIDEON, b. January 30, 1809.
201. SOPHIA AMANDA, b. June 4, 1812, d. February 8, 1816.

The young children who died were all buried at the White Hills.

Capt. Gideon Leavenworth was the second son of Edmund and Abigail Leavenworth (*nee* Beardsley), and grandson of Dr. Thomas Leavenworth, was born October 18, 1751, at Huntington, then in the parish of Ripton, Connecticut. In the old cemetery near the Episcopal church rest the remains of all these ancestors.

Gideon was undoubtedly religiously trained, and is known to have been a member of the church in Ripton, under Rev. Dr. Ely and is believed to have been a true christian.

He was long remembered among his acquaintance for his kindness and generosity, and for the spirit of christian submission and patience with which he bore a confinement of two years and a half, toward the close of his life, from painful rheumatic affection. His children remember his conducting family worship in the old Puritan style, standing at the back of a chair, before he was disabled by his final sickness.

He was a member of the Masonic Institution, but was heard to remark to a brother mason during his sickness, "Ah, brother Tomlinson, masonry never did you and me any good."

He was a man of great energy of character, full of business activity, large-hearted, liberal and kind to the poor. From his own ship-yard, which was directly between his house, (which he built himself,) and the Hoosatonic river, he built and launched eighteen or nineteen vessels. He owned a saw-mill, which stood on a small stream which joined the Hoosatonic, just north of his house, and was largely engaged in the timber business besides a distillery and a large farm on which were apple and peach orchards, and of course had at all times a large number of men in his employ, never refusing the application of any poor fellow who wanted work and wages.

His first marriage was October, 20, 1779, to Sarah Ward of Stratford, Connecticut. Their children were two sons and four daughters viz.· Abijah, Hezikiah, Nancy, Sally, Betsy and Fanny. The last three are still living, and could doudtless relate many things about him.

His second wife was the widow of Dr. Amzi Hull of Woodbridge, Connecticut, [*nee* Mary Ann Kasson at Bethlehem.] She had one surviving child, Aratius Bevil Hull who was afterwards tutor in Yale College, and was then Pastor of the Old South Church in Worcester, Massachusetts, till his death in 1816.

The children of this second marriage, were four sons and two daughters, viz: Mark Eli, Gideon Hull, name forgotten, Mary Ann, Sophia Amanda, and Gideon. Mark is living in Newtown, Conn. Mary Ann has been a teacher for forty-five years, most of the time in Westport, Conn., where she now resides.

Gideon Leavenworth died April 19, 1816, and was buried in the old grave yard on the White Hills, on the road from his home to Ripton, where are also buried his two wives, and some of his children.

He lived on the banks of the Hoosatonic, some two miles above Birmingham, near and just above the residences of his father and grandfather. The house he built is large and spacious, and still remains.

Early in life he was engaged in the war of the Revolution, and was afterwaɹds (1798) a representative of the town of Huntington in the legislature. He commanded a company at the battle of White Plains. He was extensively engaged in lumbering, building bridges, vessels, etc. He rebuilt Leavenworth's Bridge, just above his house, and he and his father first erected it about 1868-9. He suffered much from rheumatism, brought on by exposure and his wounds during the war. He posessed an ample property with large orchards, and sent to market large quantities of fruit and lumber.

He was hospitable, fond of entertaining his friends, particularly clergymen and religious people. He was not only a member of the Congregational church at Ripton, but was active and exemplary. He was on intimate terms with his pastor, the Rev. David Ely, and confided his will to his care. The last year of his life he devoted largely to the reading of the Scriptures "The Afflicted Man's Companion," and "Baxter's Saint's Rest."

His second wife, Mrs. Mary Ann Hull, had in two years lost her husband and three children, and when she married Capt. Gideon had but one child, Aratius Bevil Hull.

69. ANNIE LEAVENWORTH.[4] — EDMUND,[3] THOMAS,[2] THOMAS.[1]

Born August 19, 1756, at Stratford, now Huntington.

Married April 23, 1783, Isaac Hawkins, of Derby, farmer. He died March 18, 1834, aged seventy-three years, eleven months and eight days. Annie H. died June 23, 1843, aged eighty-six years, ten months and four days.

CHILDREN.

1. NANCY, b. January 26, 1784, d. at Derby, August 28, 1854, unmarried, aged seventy years, six months and two days.
2. NABBY, b. October 24, 1786, d. at Derby July 2, or 22, 1787.
3. ISAAC, b. August 24, 1787, d January 2, 1846, aged fifty-nine years, four months and nine days; m. Irene Durand, of Derby, and had three daughters:—
   1. ELIZABETH, who died at fourteen years.
   2. SARAH, who m. William Dibble, of Derby, and now lives in Seymour and has a large family.
   3. MARTHA, who m., first, William Kinney, of Derby, and had children by him. He died, and she m., second, —— Ayres, of Bridgeport, where she now lives.

4. Betsey, b. June 17, 1789, m. March 28, 1841, Ayres Hubbell, of Huntington. He was a farmer, and he d. January 12, 1862, aged seventy-seven years, two months and five days, and she lives with her brother Abijah, at Derby. No children.
5. Sophia, b. April 10, 1791, m. November 25, 1812, Jeremiah Hubbell, who d. July 25, 1848, aged fifty six years, eleven months and three days; a farmer in Huntington, and had one son, Rufus, now, (1872), living in Huntington, a farmer. This son m. Eliza Tucker, of Monroe, and had a daughter Grace. Sophia had four other sons and five daughters, four of whom lived to be women.
6. Annie Maria, b. November 25, 1794, m. January, 1816, Hezekiah Hubbell, of Huntington, a blacksmith, and had children:—
   1. Abijah, farmer of Huntington.
   2. Sarah, m. —— Leavenworth, of Roxbury.
   3. Mary Jane, m. a Hine, and obtained a divorce. She is now m. again and lives at New Haven. Annie Maria H. d. August 20, 1859, aged sixty-four years, nine months and five days.
7. Abijah, b September 14, 1799, m. Hannah Bartholomew, of Derby, where he resides and has a son and daughter, Henry and Cornelia; is a blacksmith. Cornelia m. a Canfield, who died in California. She lives at Derby with her son and daughter. The daughter m —— Miller; the son is m. and has one child. Henry Hawkins m. a Miss Hotchkiss of Oxford, lives in Derby and has two children.
   3. Nicholas Wheeler, of Huntington, a mason. He m. a Miss Downs, of Huntington, and has two daughters, Annie and Maria, both of whom are now at Huntington.
   4. George, m. Urania Hubbell, dau. of Ayres Hubbell. He went to California and d. there; no children.
   5. Caroline, m. Marvin Tuttle, a farmer of Huntington, and has a large family.
   6. Antoinette, m. Jacob Werth, a German, who died in California. She is now a widow there and has no children.
   7. Frank, he is married and insane.
   8. John, m. at Huntington; lives there and has a family of children.

70. RUTH LEAVENWORTH.[4]—Edmund,[3] Thomas,[2] Thomas.[1]

Born —— ——

Married, first, Abijah Booth, of Stratford, February, 1768. He was a son of Zachariah, son of Joseph Booth, and was born January, 1744-5, died 17—

Married, second, Isaac Jennings, of Derby, a farmer.

CHILDREN.

1. Sarah, b. November, 1768, m. Joel Wilcox, a Methodist clergyman.
2. Eli, b September, 1770, m Charity Osborn in 1791.
3. Silas, b. September, 2, 1772, m. Hetty Fenn, of Watertown, Conn.
4. Anna, b. December, 1773, d. young.
5. Gideon, b. April, 1775, a farmer, m. Joan Fairchild, July, 1800
6. Abijah, b. October, 1777, a farmer, m. Abbey Betsey Curtis, dau. of Silas Curtis. He d. in 1855; lived in Stratford. Had five children:—
   1. Emily, who m a Brooks.
   2. Elvira, m. Capt. Levi Wheeler, of Stratford, and has children.
   3. A son who was killed by a tree his father fell on him.
   4. Hannah, unmarried, at Stratford.
   5. Birdseye, m a dau. of Silas Curtiss, Jr., and lives at Stratford, and has a son and daughter

7. Abigail, b. August, 1780, d. young.
8. Hepzibah, b. August, 1782, m. James Booth, a farmer, of Stratford.
9. Julia, b. August, 1788, m. Stephen Allen, a farmer, of Fairfield.

All born in Stratford, and all dead.

71. Abijah Leavenworth.[4]—Edmund,[3] Thomas,[2] Thomas.[1]

Born in 1758, at Huntington, died November 9, 1777. aged nineteen years.

Was a lieutenant in the Revolution, and died from the effects of exposure while in the service—losing his life by standing in deep water a long, cold night, watching the British troops. He took a heavy cold, returned to Ripton, died there, and was buried in the Ripton burying ground.

72. Capt. Eli Leavenworth.[4]—Edmund,[3] Thomas,[2] Thomas.[1]

Born at Huntington, died at Savannah, Georgia.

Married Polly Elliott, of Stonington, probably about the close of the Revolution, in which he served as Captain and Major, and at its close was a Colonel, probably by brevet. After the close of the war, he went South, and died early, at Savannah. He was a baker. The family returned to Connecticut after his death.

CHILDREN.

202. Sally.
203. Fanny.
204. Jenette.
205. Grace.

I learn from Charles J. Hoadley, Esq., of Hartford, State Librarian—to whom I am indebted for so many other facts—that "Major Eli Leavenworth served in the Connecticut line of the Continental army from the commencement of the war till January first, 1781."

Several of the accounts against the State rendered by him at different periods are found in the Comptroller's Office, at Hartford—one from July, 1775 to June, 1776, £1.048. 11. 0—one from July, 1777 to March, 1779, for £1.204. 19. 6—one in March 1781, for £75.

It appears by the records in the Comptroller's office, that he served as a Captain in the Connecticut line of the Continental army, in the Sixth Regiment, commanded by Lieut.-Col. Return J. Meigs, from January 1, 1777 till September of the same year, when he was promoted and served as a Major in the same regiment till January 1, 1781. In 1775 and '76 he served as Captain of the Tenth Company of the Seventh Regiment of the Connecticut line. Capt. Eli and his company were attached to Col. Meigs' regiment, and stationed at Horse Neck in 1777. On the twenty-ninth and thirtieth of October of that year, he was detailed with others and went to Wright's Mills, Westchester county, N. Y., to look after the Cow Boys and Tories who infested that part of the country. They were very successful and returned to Horse Neck November 1. "Hinman's Hist. Collection on Connecticut in the Revolution.

The same work, p. 511, contains the following notice of him:

NEW HAVEN, January 14, 1778.

Thursday the Green Coats taken near Tarrytown, N. Y., passed through New Haven, fifty-two in number, under guard, on their way to Hartford, twenty-seven of whom were taken by Capt. Eli Leavenworth, who, with a party of twenty-seven, surrounded more than thirty of the enemy and killed three, wounded three or four. Among the prisoners was the noted Captain Barnes, and his Lieutenant, Hunt, a New Yorker. Capt. Eli had one man slightly wounded.

[From the Connecticut *Gazette*, New London.

73. RACHEL LEAVENWORTH.[4] — EDMUND,[3] THOMAS,[2] THOMAS.[1]

Born July 16, 1761, at Huntington.

Married David Thompson, of Huntington, farmer, and had nine children. Resided in Huntington; d. November 19, 1819, at Huntington. He was b. November 14, 1756; d. November 17, 1819.

CHILDREN.

1. BIRDSEYE, b. July 17, 1786, d. October 8, 1857, m Fanny Leavenworth, dau. of Capt. Gideon L., and had one son, Birdseye T., who d. at Bridgeport in 1868 or '69. See Fanny L., No. 196.
2. LEWIS, b. June 23, 1788. He was a sea captain and was lost at sea in the West Indies. He m. Betsey Wells, of Huntington.

Children.

1. ELIAS TROWBRIDGE, who d. unmarried.
2. CHARLES LEWIS, of Cleveland, O., unmarried.
3. ANN ELIZA, who m. Edwin Mills of Astoria, and has two daughters,—
   1 Anna, m. George Halsey, and has one child, a son.
   2. Julia, who is unmarried.

3. NANCY, b. April 7, or 17, 1791, d. September 4, 1863; m. Abijah Nichols of Trumbull, October 19, 1809, and had three dau. and two sons. He was b. February 15, 1788.

Children.

1. MATILDA, who m. —— Olmstead, at Bridgeport, who has a son and three daughters.
2. LEWIS PLUM, who d. unmarried at Trumbull.
3. LUCINDA, who m. —— Gould, of Trumbull, and lives at Bridgeport,—widow, no children.
4. LAURA ANN, who m. William Thompson, her cousin, and lives in Fairfield—no children.
5. ELI T., m. Martha Durand, d. of Maria Leavenworth and David Durand, of Derby, in 1857; he d. in 1867, in June, and left no children. She lives in Bridgeport.

4. AMBROSE, b. May 4, 1793, d. August 10, 1816. Was a sea captain; m. September 5, 1813, Laura Ann Botsford, of Newtown, who was b. September 19, 1794, and had one son, Henry William, who d young and unmarried.
5. CUMPHY THOMPSON, b. March 26, 1795, m. Plum Nichols, of Trumbull. Now lives in Ohio and has a family of children.
6. GIDEON THOMPSON, b, March 14, 1797, m. Mariette Wheeler June 12. 1822. She was b. May 13, 1797. Lives in Bridgeport, a retired farmer, and has two children.
   1. DAVID WHEELER, d. young.
   2. FRANCES SARAH, m. Dwight Morris. She was b. in 1823, and d. without children.
7. EDMUND THOMPSON, b. April 9, or 29, 1799; a farmer in Stratford; m. Maria Hyde November 21, 1826—She was b. July 30, 1806,—of Huntington, and had nine children:—
   1. JULIA A., b. November 19, 1828, d. July 29, 1833.
   2. SARAH E., b. August 29, 1830, m. Eliakim L. Walker, of Trumbull; farmer, October 25, 1855. They live in Huntington and have no children.
   3. DAVID L., b. September 18, 1832, m. and lives at the South.
   4. AMBROSE, b. September 1, 1835, d. in U. S. Army, July 22, 1863, m. Sarah M. Jackson, January 6, 1855. Their son Charles H., b. October 16, 1855.
   5. EDMUND T., JR, b. March 19, 1839; farmer; m. Clarissa Beardsley, of Trumbull, where he now lives and has two children.
   6. GEORGE A., b. January 2, 1841; a farmer at Stratford; m. a Miss Sammis, of Stratford, and has one child.
   7. FRANCES M., b. May 21, 1843, m. James Stewart, of Bridgeport. Resides now at Saratoga, N. Y.,—no children.
   8. JULIA A,, b. November 28, 1846, m. in May, 1872, to —— Mallory, of New York, and lives in Bridgeport.

8. JOHN LESTER, b. March 6, 1801; farmer; d. and left children. One is William T., of Fairfield, who m. a dau. of Nancy Nichols.
9. ELI, b. March 8, 1804, m. Frances S. May, June 4, 1829. She was b. June 20, 1811. Has three sons,—
   1. DAVID W., m. P. T. Barnum's daughter, and is in the Custom House and has one dau.
   2. SYLVESTER M., m. Miss Lockwood and has two dau.
   3. DWIGHT W., m. Hattie Mallory, of New Milford, and has no children.

Eli and wife now live in Bridgeport.

74 SALLY LEAVENWORTH.[4]—EDMUND,[3] THOMAS[2], THOMAS[1].

Born December 28, 1762, at Huntington.
Married Samuel Thompson November 21, 1784, of Huntington, and moved

to Roxbury, where they always resided. She died at Roxbury July 17, 1855, aged ninety-two years, six months and nineteen days. She had eight children. He was born May 20, 1762, and died August 15, 1822.

CHILDREN.

1. LAURA, b. July 15, 1785, d. quite young.
2. BENJAMIN, b. July 30, 1787, d. July 29, 1847. He m. Sally Miller, of N. Y., and has a son in Albany.
3. MAHALA, b. January 27, 1790, d. April 6, 1855. She m. John Trowbridge and has children in Roxbury,
4. AMBROSE, b. January 24, 1793, d. June 17, 1855, unmarried ; a merchant, lived at Roxbury.
5. ABIGAIL, b. November 10, 1795, and now lives in Roxbury with a son of Mahala, unmarried.
6. ABIJAH, b. August 20, 1800, d. June 27, 1870, unmarried ; a farmer.
7. ABIGAIL MARY, b. July 8, 1803, d. February, or September, 9, 1808.
8. SAMUEL, b. July 20, 1807, d. November 5, 1863, at Derby ; m. Althea Mitchell, of Woodbury, September 23, 1836, and had two daughters.—
   1. FANNY, m. Bennet Lunn, of Derby, and lives there ; no children.
   2. JOSEPHINE, m. William Gilbert, who lived in Derby. She d. there in 1870. leaving one child.

75. Edmund Leavenworth.[4]—EDMUND,[3] THOMAS,[2] THOMAS.[1]

Born December 14, 1766, at Huntington.

Married, first, MARY JUDSON, of Huntington, January 5, 1786, at Ripton. She was born December 9, 1764, and died at Huntington December 8, 1819. Married, second, AMY TOMLINSON October 26, 1823. She died at Derby, April 30, 1849. He died at Derby, January 20, 1857, aged ninety-one years. He and his two wives, his eldest daughter, and his only son, Edmund, were buried at the White Hills.

CHILDREN.

206. HEPSEY, b. November 17, 1786, d. January 18, 1865, unmarried, at Derby.
207. POLLY, b. August 27, 1789.
208. DELILAH, b. January 1, 1792.
209. MARIA, b. March 13, 1794.
210. LAURA, b. September 29, 1796.
211. EDMUND, b. December 8, 1801. Drowned in the Housatonic, June 13, 1823, aged twenty-one years, six months, and five days.

He was a man of much more than ordinary intelligence, activity and capacity for business. He was kind and benevolent and possessed of great personal popularity. He was elected Selectman of the Town of Huntington for thirteen successive years. Never were the poor of the Town, more carefully cared for. He was genial and warm hearted and strongly attached to his friends and was familiarly known as "Uncle Ed." Probably no man in the town was so generally known. He had a splendid constitution and great muscular power, and was fond of active sports, horse-racing, jumping, hunting, etc., often going to Long Island and bringing home one or more deer. But he was by no means an idler. He was largely engaged in cutting and hauling timber, building bridges, wharves and vessels at his boat yard. He employed in these various works great numbers of men.

He took great pride in fine horses and cattle and no one had better, or was a superior judge. His judgment was quiet and accurate.

He lost two sloops by French Privateers which are covered by the "French Spoliation Bill."

He had great force and pith of expression, and "Uncle Ed" is still often quoted for his pithy remarks, anecdotes and expressions.

His language was a little rough and unpolished and often not very refined, but partaking of the character of those with whom he was much engaged. But there was a religious sentiment within him, handed down, no doubt, from his father and his grandfather, who was Deacon in the First Congregational church at Huntington, and at the close of his life, at his request, his name was enrolled among the members of the Episcopal church in Derby, where he then lived, and in that communion he died.

The following characteristic story of "Uncle Ed." is told by some recent traveler on the Hoosatonic, and is cut from a casual newspaper, by the author. Perhaps it is a little too *broad* to do perfect justice to him, for he was a very kind and benevolent man, and a good and popular citizen :—

The long "Red House" now standing at Leavenworth Landing on the west of Ousatonic Lake, is among our Derby recollections. It was once a favorite "stopping house" between the two counties, when the place was full and lively in ship-building, and thousands flocked thither on a day when a vessel was to be launched. After Leavenworth Bridge, which spanned the river a few rods above, became rickety and unsafe for travel, a sort of public ferry was kept up opposite this "Red House." A blunt, sensible, burly Yankee, familiar to some of our readers in his old age, by the name of "Uncle Ed," officiated as ferryman. On one of these occasions he was aroused from his midnight slumbers by a signal of distress to ferry over a friend from the opposite side The river was high, the night dark and rainy, and the wind blowing a perfect gale

With great effort "Uncle Ed" reached the Derby shore when his tallow candle went out, leaving him in bad humor, and he exclaimed "Who the h—l are you? out this time of night when honest men should be asleep? It is enough to make a minister swear to turn out for a friend such a time as this!" The traveler said not a word but, carefully got himself, horse and wagon, on board when he was told: "now take hold of this rope and pull like the d—l, or we shall go down stream." The order was religiously obeyed, while the ferryman continued his strain of epithets clothed not in the choicest English. Safely over, "Uncle Ed" demanded an extra ninepence, if his friend refused to give his name. "Why," said the stranger, "the man towards whom you have been using such abusive lauguage is your reverend minister from Huntington Center." Oh! yes, parson, I've heard you preach a good many times, but I guess I won't take back anything I've said.

Although but twelve years of age in 1777, when his father, Capt. Edmund, was ordered to Fairfield with his company, he volunteered to go as a private, and served as a waiter to his father during the campaign, joining the company April 2, 1777, as a volunteer private. When his father was again ordered out with his company and sent to New Haven in 1779, his son Edmund again enlisted as a private in his father's company, and accompanied him in the campaign.

All this appears by his own affidavit, made December 13, 1837, in applying for a pension under the act of June 7, 1832. The affidavit is now on file in the War Department at Washington.

77. ELIZABETH LEAVENWORTH.[5] — DANIEL,[4] JAMES,[3] THOMAS,[2] THOMAS.[1]

Born about 1754, in what is now Monroe, Conn.

Married James Winton. Resided in Newtown. She died December 15, 1835, in the State of New York, aged about eighty-one. He died 1824, aged seventy-nine; was a farmer.

CHILDREN.

1. ANDREW, b.
2. JAMES, b.
3. ELI, b.
4. AVIS, b. ——— m. Philo Blakeman, d. in 1868.
5. BEARDSLEY, b. ——— d. in 1869.

All this family are dead; all born in Newtown.

78. ABIAH LEAVENWORTH.[5]—DANIEL,[4] JAMES,[3] THOMAS,[2] THOMAS.[1]

Born about 1757, in the northwest part of Huntington, now Monroe, Conn.

Married David Hubbell, of Huntington, farmer; Revolutionary soldier. Lived in Monroe, Conn He died April 5, 1820, aged sixty-three. She died August 22, 1845, aged eighty-eight.

CHILDREN.

1. CHILD, b. —— d. young.
2. RUTH, b.

3. ANNA, b.
4. CHARITY, b.
5. SALVIA, b.
6. AMARILLIS, b.
7. ASA, b.
8. ELIHU, b.
9. ABIAH, b,
10. REBECCA, b.

All born in Huntington, now Monroe.

79. Andrew Leavenworth.[5]—DANIEL,[4] JAMES,[3] THOMAS, THOMAS.[1]

Born January 21, 1766, in Monroe, (then Huntington,) Connecticut.

Married MIRIAM SEELYE, of what is now Fairfield, Connecticut, November 27, 1792. He died in Monroe, which was set off from Huntington, December 18, 1846, aged eighty years and ten months. She was born May 19, 1767, died in Monroe, June 28, 1853, aged eighty-six years. He was a pillar in the Baptist church. He was a large farmer and had a grist-mill, plaster-mill, saw-mill, store, etc. He was twice in legislature, settled many estates—was Captain of a military company—and many years a selectman of the town of Huntington

CHILDREN.

212. DAUGHTER, b. September 25, 1793, d. in infancy.
213. BETSEY, b. January 19, 1795.
214. DANIEL, b. July 18, 1797.
215. ABIGAIL, b. July 27, 1799, unmarried in 1868.
216. POLLY, b. September 13, 1801, d. February 9, 1838.
217. SEELYE, b. September 25, 1804, d. May 10, 1836, unmarried.
218. ELI, b. March 23, 1809.

All born in Huntington, now Monroe.

80. Ebenezer Leavenworth.[5] — JAMES,[4] JAMES,[3] THOMAS,[2] THOMAS.[1]

Born December 20, 1760, no doubt at North Stratford, now Monroe.

Married, first, MARY ANN MILLS, daughter of Esquire M., of Ripton, Conn., January 27, 1780. She died September 10, 1786.

Married, second, ABIGAIL LAKE, June 3, 1787. Resided at White Hills, in Huntington, Conn., at the time of both marriages; removed to Easton, N. Y., in 1790, and about 1793, after August, to Johnstown, N. Y. Died near Kingsboro, N. Y., October 28, 1811. He was a farmer; of a cheerful, happy temperament. His house and his hand were ever open to those in want.

CHILDREN.

219. ABBY BETSEY, b. September 23, 1780, d. ——— in Wis.
220. SALLY PAMELIA, b May 20, 1783.
221. MARY ANN, b. July 23, 1786.
222. JEHODAH, b. March 29, 1788, d. November 12, 1790.
223. SOPHIA, b. December 3, 1790, at Easton.
224. TREAT MILLS, b. August 10, 1793, at Easton.
225. ELI, b. April 21, 1796, at Kingsboro, N. Y.
226. POLLY, b. May 24, 1797, at Kingsboro.
227. ORRILLA, b. Augnst 4, 1799, at Kingsboro.
228. JEHODAH, b. December 17, 1802, d. March 10, 1805, at Kingsboro.
229. HULDAH, b. April 17, 1805, at Kingsboro, N. Y.

81. PRUDENCE LEAVENWORTH.[5]—JAMES,[4] JAMES,[3] THOMAS,[2] THOMAS[1]

Born in Ripton, Connecticut.

Married Josiah Wells, 1779; farmer, of Ripton. Had five sons and four daughters. The sons are all dead.

CHILDREN.

1. JAMES, b. ——— d.
2. HEZEKIAH, b. ——— d.
3. GUERDON, b. ——— d.
4. JOSIAH, b. ——— d.
5. RANSOM, b. ——— d.
6. POLLY b. m. Post.
7. NANCY, b. m. a Wells.
8. SALLY, b. m. a Johnson.
9. PHŒBE, b. m. William Cozens.

82. AMARILLA LEAVENWORTH.[5]—JAMES,[4] JAMES,[3] THOMAS,[2] THOMAS.[1]

Born in Ripton, Connecticut.

Married Frederick Mills; silversmith. Had three sons and three daughters. The sons were farmers.

83. POLLY LEAVENWORTH.[5]—JAMES,[4] JAMES,[3] THOMAS,[2] THOMAS.[1]

Born in Ripton Connecticut.

Married Charles Hartshorn, a mason, at Easton, N. Y. He was from Providence, Rhode Island, and returned thither, where he was a wholesale merchant.

CHILDREN.

1. William, b. a physician.
2. Sylvester, b. merchant tailor.
3. Sylvius, b. politician.
4. Leander, b. mariner.

84. CHARITY LEAVENWORTH.[5]—James,[4] James,[3] Thomas,[2] Thomas.[1]

Born —— in Ripton, Conn.
Married Ezekiel Beardsley, —— at Kingsboro, N. Y. He was from Huntington, Conn., and a tailor.

86. Henry Castle Leavenworth.[5]—Nathan,[4] David,[3] Thomas,[2] Thomas.[1]

Born at Washington, Conn., May 8, 1763.

He went South before 1787. Was a physician; never married, and died at Wilmington, N. C., in 1799.

87. Gen. Nathan Leavenworth.[5]—Nathan,[4] David,[3] Thomas,[2] Thomas.[1]

Born August 20, 1765, at New Milford, Conn. Removed when a young man with his father to Hinesburg, Chittenden Co., Vt., in 1787, and settled one mile west of the village.

Upon the formation of the first military company in town, in 1788, he was chosen a Lieutenant, the number of men in town not entitling it to a company organization. In 1789, however, he was appointed Captain, and in acknowledgement of the honor, invited the whole town to dine with him.* He subsequently arose to the rank of Brigadier-General.

He represented Hinesburg in the State Legislature in 1796, 1799, 1800, 1802, 1803, 1804, 1805, 1806, 1809, 1810, 1811, 1812, 1813, 1815, 1817, 1818, 1821, 1822, 1827, and 1828; was two years in the State Senate, two years, 1831 and 1832, in the Governor's Council; a Presidential Elector in 1833, and at different times filled every town office, from constable up. In 1824 he was one of the original trustees of the Hinesburg Academy, and in 1822 he was a member of the Constitutional Convention.

---

* Vermont Hist Mag., p. 794-5.

He was twice married, viz:—First, January 30, 1793, ANNE BUCKINGHAM, of New Milford, Conn., daughter of Benjamin B. and Anna Botsford, of New Milford; she was born March 27, 1770, and she died February 5, 1805, in Hinesburg, Vt.

Second, BETSEY HURLBUT, March 6, 1806, daughter of Daniel Hurlbut, born in Waterbury, Conn., and Lucretia Noble, born in Westfield, Mass. They were married at Pittsfield, Mass., removed to Arlington, then to Burlington, Vt., where Betsey Hurlbut was married.

He died September 8, 1849, at Hinesburg, Vt.

CHILDREN.

230. HESTER, b. August 4, 1796.
231. HENRY, b. August 1, 1799, d. May 10, 1854.
232. NATHAN B., b, July 7, 1801.
233. ANNA, b. February 7, 1807, d. August 8, 1809.
234. RACHEL LUCRETIA, b. May 14, 1810.

He was a man remarkable for his integrity, benevolence and kindness of heart. He was tall, dignified, and, in the latter years of his life, venerable in his appearance.

After a most active and useful life of more than sixty years, spent in the town of Hinesburg, filling all the offices in their gift, he died universally respected, beloved and mourned, in the month of September, 1849. Probably no person in this country, who has borne the family name, has been more often and highly honored—more universally respected and beloved, and more unimpeachable in his character and life.

The Historical account of Hinesburg, prepared by the Rev. C. E. Ferrin for the "Vermont Historical Magazine," has the following biographical notice of Gen. Nathan Leavenworth:—

"Gen. Leavenworth was a native of New Milford, Conn., and came to Hinesburg with his father, in 1787, at the age of twenty-three years. He was among the pioneers of the town, and made it his home for three score years. His early life having been spent among the stirring scenes and patriotic struggles of the Revolution, of which, though a mere boy, he was an intelligent and interested observer, his character was formed on the best model of those times. He showed in many ways, the reality and the strength of his regard for his country. He was never absent from the polls at the annual State election, from his first residence in town up to his last sickness. The Rev. O. S.

Hoyt thus spoke of him in a sermon, the Sabbath after his burial:—

'As a member of this community for sixty-two years, how many and conspicuous were the social virtues he exercised! How high a degree of moral worth did he unfold! What an example did he furnish, of enterprise, industry, prudent economy, contentment, meekness, sincerity, truthfulness, affability, kindness, liberality, honesty. His integrity was proverbial. His business transactions were extensive, but I have yet to learn that he ever resorted to the litigations of the law for their final and full adjustment. His distinguished worth did not go unappreciated; he received from this community, and from his fellow citizens at large, unequivocal tokens of their confidence. From 1796 to 1830, he was chosen at twenty-one [20] different times, representative in the Legislature. He was, with emphasis, the man whom the people delighted to honor. He was a member of the Senate of Vermont two years, and once an elector from Vermont of the President and Vice-President of the United States. And when we contemplate his history in the more domestic relations he sustained, how much rises to view most commendable and worthy of imitation.

But there are other and higher grounds of interest in him. In the year 1831 he was led to feel, as never before, that no external morals, however elevated, no amiability of native disposition, no affections merely instinctive, did meet the whole demands of the Divine law. That momentous declaration of the Savior, 'Except a man be born again he cannot see the kingdom of God,' came, with a new and mighty power, home to his soul. He publicly avowed his confidence in the Savior, and his supreme attachment to him, by connecting himself with the Episcopal church. Still, he was most free and liberal in aiding us in sustaining all the institutions of the gospel among the people. (There was no Episcopal church in Hinesburg.) There was nothing sectarian in his spirit, or in his efforts; he loved all who bore the image of the Savior. With them he was at home, and around the communion table, in social conference, and in the prayer meeting, as well as in all the more public movements of the church. Punctually and habitually he honored the sanctuary. Humbly and prayerfully there, in the bible class, he studied the oracles of God. And at last, death had no terrors. He who is the resurrection and the life was his refuge, and he was at rest.' "

88. SARAH LEAVENWORTH.[5]—EBENEZER,[4] DAVID,[3] THOMAS,[2] THOMAS.[1]

Born December 16, 1754, in Woodbury, Conn.
Married, first, Lemuel Downs, March 2, 1778.
Married, second, Dea. Thomas Abbott, who lived with her about 1820, in La-

Fayette, Onondaga Co., N. Y., about half a mile north of the resting-place of the Cardiff Giant. He was a farmer, and died there before 1830. She died in Orleans county. at her son Lemuel's, about 1833-4, or possibly at her son-in-law's house—they both lived in Orleans county.

Her children by her first husband were as follows —:

CHILDREN.

1. LEMUEL, b. —— ; was a farmer in Fabius, Onondaga county. Mrs. D. came to live with him after the death of her first husband. Here she was married to Deacon Abbott. The son moved to Orleans county, and then to Marshall, Mich., and died there.
2. ANN, b. ——, m. —— Gates, in Fabius; moved to Orleans county and d. there. She had four or five children.
3. MARIA, b. ———, m. an Eldredge, at Fabius, and went West. She had three children, and d. at Marshall, Mich., at her brother Lemuel's; also her two daughters.
4. BETSEY, m. in Conn., ——— Downs for her second husband. He d. leaving one son, William, three months old, who m. Orpha Winchell, dau. of Joseph Winchell, of LaFayette, Onondaga county, April 2, 1831; he d. at Syracuse, leaving three children.
   1. HARRIET, b. in 1821, m. Peter Waggoner, of Syracuse, and lives there.
   2. LEMUEL HUDSON, b. in 1823, lives in St. Louis, has three children.
   3. JULIA, b. in 1825, m., and d. in 1860, at Dunkirk, leaving three children.
5. AMY, b. ———, m. a Horton about 1820, in Fabius; went to Ohio; had no children.

She, (Sarah), had no children by Deacon Abbott. After Deacon Abbott's death, about 1833, she lived one season with her grandson, William Downs, of Tully—from spring to fall—then he took her to her son-in-law, Mr. Gates, in Orleans county, where she died in the winter of 1833-4, at the house of her son Lemuel.

89. David Leavenworth.[5] — EBENEZER,[4] DAVID,[3] THOMAS,[2] THOMAS.[1]

Born December 14, 1756, in Woodbury, Conn.

Married MARY DOWNS October 30, 1776. She was born February 15, 1756, and died October 16, 1799; he died February 1, 1797.

He resided in Woodbury and New Milford until 1781, when he removed to Sandgate, Vt., and in 1784 to Canaan, Columbia county, N. Y. In 1784 he settled in Nassau, Rennsalaer Co. where he resided until his death, which was occasioned by being thrown from a horse, while racing on frozen ground.

He was a farmer and owned the farm at East Nassau, where his daughter Mary now (1870), resides.

CHILDREN.

235. WHITMAN, b. November 22, 1777.
236. MARY, b. March 17, 1780.
237. DAVID DOWNS, b. May 3, 1782.

Nathan Leavenworth

238. Anna, b. February 7, 1785.
239. Sarah, b. February 11, 1788.
240. Isaac, b. September 22, 1790.
241. Ebenezer, b. May 28, 1793, d. October 19, 1863.

90. BURZINA LEAVENWORTH.[5] — Ebenezer,[4] David[3], Thomas,[2] Thomas.[1]

Born September 10, 1758, in Woodbury, Conn.

Married Elijah Hurd, January 22, 1779. He was born April 10, 1755, and was the son of Simeon Hurd of Woodbury. They resided in Sandgate, Vt., where she died.

91. BETSEY LEAVENWORTH.[5] — Ebenezer,[4] David,[3] Thomas,[2] Thomas.[1]

Born February 27, 1763, at Woodbury, Conn.

Married Elijah Peet, of New Milford, Conn., and in 1830 they lived at Euclid, six miles east of Cleveland, Ohio. He was born July 28, 1765. She died at Beloit, Wis., in 1853. He died in 1814, at Lee, Mass.

Did not Mrs. P. marry a Hurd for her first husband. The family records of the Peet family show that Mr. P. married Betsey Hurd·

CHILDREN.

1. William Leavenworth, b. November 19, 1788.
2. Beulah, b. August 24, 1790.
3. Elijah, Jr., b. May 6, 1793.
4. Stephen, b. February 20, 1797. Yale College, 1823.
5. Minerva, b. June 23, 1800, at Sandgate, Vt., m. at Lee, Mass., Fuller and resides at Concord, N. H.

Stephen. P. prepared for college with Rev. Ralph Emerson at Norfork Conn. Studied theology at Princeton, New Haven and Auburn. Was ordained at Euclid, Ohio, February 22, 1826 ; m. Martha Dennison Sherman, May 1, 1829.

He remained a pastor at Euclid seven years—years of great labor, activity and success. He then spent four years laboring with sailors and boatmen on the western waters. In 1837, he was settled over the only Presbyterian church then in Wisconsin. In the fall of 1839, he took charge of the first Presbyterian church of Milwaukee where he remained till 1841. He was then appointed General Agent of the American Home Missionary Society of Wisconsin. In this position he was active, influential and judicious, and remained in it seven years. He was the originator and most able defender of the plan of union between the Presbyterian and Congregational churches of Wisconsin, which has been so beneficial He was mainly instrumental in founding both the College at Beloit, and the Theological Seminary at Chicago, and on his death the trustees of the College thus express their appreciation of his work :—

"We record our conviction that to the sagacity and wise, christian perseverance of onr departed brother, this College, under God, pre-eminently is indebted, for its existence and the success of its early history, and in his removal we mourn the loss of a judicious counselor, and an efficient helper, and of a personal friend."

He died at Chicago on the 21st day of March, 1855, on his return from the east, where he had been actively engaged for his great enterprises, and was buried in the cemetery, on the same hill with the College, where a monument was erected to his memory by his many friends.

92. Rev. Ebenezer Isaac Leavenworth.[5]—EBENEZER[4], DAVID,[3] THOMAS,[2] THOMAS.[1]

Born September 22, 1776, at Roxbury. Conn.

His father died when he was one and a half years old, and he went to live with his uncle Nathan. Graduated at Williams College 1804. Had united with the church in Hartland in 1799. Was licensed to preach by the Berkshire Association, 1805; took second degree at Williams College in 1807.

Married SARAH WHITTLESEY September 28. 1808, daughter of Eliphalet, at Old Stockbridge, Mass.; labored as a missionary of the Presbyterian church in Pennsylvania and New York, part of 1806-7-8. Resided at Watertown for a time. Ordained at Camden, N. Y., 1809; was dismissed from Camden October 6, 1813. Lived a short time at Rome, N. Y. On the 6th of Cctober, 1814, he was installed pastor of "Manlius First". and "Pompey Third" churches, in connexion. The former was at Morehouse's Flats, near the gate east of Jamesville, in the town of Manlius, and was organized " very early." The latter was at LaFayette Square, and was organized in 1809. It was then called "Pompey West Hill. He was dismissed February 4, 1818, from Manlius, and from Pompey in 1819, and in May, 1819, was settled over the church of Onondaga Hollow. He became connected with the Cortland Presbytery in 1825, and settled in Lincklaen in 1826, and afterwards in Newfield. His residence at Onondaga was on a farm two and a half miles southeast of Syracuse. Removed to Brownhelm, O., from Newfield, and died there October 14, 1851. His wife died there February 24, 1856, aged seventy-two years.

CHILDREN.

242. LORENZO W., b. July 17, 1809, d. October 16, 1830, at Brownhelm.
243. EBENI, b. October 16, 1811.
244. SARAH ELIZABETH, b. November 6. 1813.
245. CHARLES, b. March 25, 1816, d. April 11, 1858.
246. HEMAN E., b. October 7, 1820.
247. MARY, b. September 16, 1822.
248. MARTHA, b. April 20, 1825, d. June 30, 1825.
249. MARTHA, b. November 16, 1830, d. December 20, 1862.

My learned antiquarian friend, Henry C. Van Schaack, of Manlius, has called my attention to—

"A sermon on the influence of good and bad Rulers, by Ebe-"nezer I. Leavenworth, pastor of the united congregations of Man-"lius and Pompey. Published at the request of said societies.

"MANLIUS:

"PUBLISHED BY KELLOGG & CLARK,

"In the Stône House, corner of Seneca and Cherry Valley Sts.

"1817."

He was a man of very respectable abilities, of most exemplary life, and most devoted to his profession, and to every duty growing out of it. He spent much of his life in missionary labor among the early settlers of New York, and when not a settled pastor he thus spent the intervals.

93. AZUBAH LEAVENWORTH.[5] — Ebenezer,[4] David,[3] Thomas,[2] Thomas.[1]

Born from 1776 to 1780, in Woodbury, Conn.

95. Gideon Leavenworth.[5]—David,[4] John,[3] Thomas,[2] Thomas.[1]

Born October 26, 1759, in Roxbury, Conn. Baptized October 26, 1764.

Married Loisa Hunt October 16, 1775. She died in 1828, and her will was proved October 6, 1828—12th Prob. vol., 249. He was a farmer, and died in Roxbury October 15, 1827, of paralysis. He served in the army of the Revolution—Cothren, p. 783, and was a commissary under LaFayette. He was a member of the Legislature in 1806, from the town of Roxbury. Will proved October 22, 1827, Russell and Sheldon L., executors—15th Prob. vol., p. 199.

CHILDREN.

250. Charlotte, b. November 12, 1778, d. April 14, 1858.
251. Russell, b. October 16, 1781, d. March 12, 1866.
252. Lovina, b. December —, 1784, d. in Plymouth, Ct., 1861.
253. Anna, b. May 23, 1789, m. Ralph Revillo Keeler.
254. Sheldon, b. January 27, 1801, d. February 25, 1869.

96. Morse Leavenworth.[5]—DAVID,[4] JOHN,[3] THOMAS,[2] THOMAS.[1]

Born July 1, 1764, in Roxbury, Conn.

Married SARAH BENEDICT, of New Milford, December 25, 1783. She was daughter of Jonathan Benedict, Esq., who was born in 1723, and she was born in New Milford, January 30, 1760, and died in Roxbury January 29, 1856, aged ninety-six years. He died November 12, 1822, in Roxbury, Conn., aged fifty-eight years; a farmer. His will was proved December 3, 1822—13th Prob. vol., p. 138; he was a soldier in the army of the Revolution—Cothren, p. 783. Built, lived and died in the house now owned and occupied by his grandson, John H.

CHILDREN.

255. MARTIN, b. January 12, 1785, d. February 16, 1813.
256. TRUMAN, b. Aug. 18, 1786, d. March 26, 1852, in Roxbury.
257. PHILO, b. ——, d. in 1835, in Roxbury.
258. WAIT, b. September 12, 1792, still living, (1874), in Roxbury.
259. HARRIET, b. October 30, 1796, " " in Bridgeport.
260. MORSE, b. July 27, 1805, d. November 23, 1852, at Roxbury.

97. ANNA LEAVENWORTH.[5]—DAVID,[4] JOHN,[3] THOMAS[2], THOMAS.[1]

Born November 15, 1767, in Roxbury, Conn.
Married Samuel Cowell, moved to Greenville, Vt.

98. Whitmore C. Leavenworth.[5]—DAVID,[4] JOHN,[3] THOMAS[2], THOMAS.[1]

Born March 22, 1777, in Roxbury, Conn. No doubt died young, as his birth is not now known in the family of Leavenworth's at Roxbury.

99. MARY LEAVENWORTH.[5]—DAVID,[4] JOHN,[3] THOMAS[2], THOMAS.[1]

Born March 15, 1780, died, probably, early.

100. David Leavenworth.[5]—DAVID,[4] JOHN,[3] THOMAS,[2] THOMAS.[1]

Born April 6, ——, in Roxbury.

Married SARAH NETTLETON. She died at her daughter's Mrs. Ryan's at Huron, O., and was buried there.

Being the youngest son, he was left the farm in Roxbury, that had been owned by his father. He sold this, and bought another in Woodbury. He died at Chatham, Ill., at his son, David B.'s, in the spring of 1858. He was out in the war of the Revolution, according to Cothren, p. 783.

CHILDREN.

261. EMELINE, b. April 7, 1804, d. ——, m. Horace Miner.
262. ELIZA, b. March 22, 1806, m. David Beard.
263. DAVID BIRDSEYE, b. ——, m. 1, Almira Stow,—2, Aurelia Parmeter.
264. SARAH, b. ——, m. Charles N. Ryan.
265. EDWIN ALONZO, b. about 1818-19, d. at New Orleans about 1840.
266. WOLCOTT, b. October 20, 1821, m. Mary Calkins, of Earlville, N. Y.
267. BEARD, b. ——, m. Kate E. Coman, of Eaton, N. Y.

101. ABIGAIL LEAVENWORTH.[6]—DAVID,[4] JOHN,[3] THOMAS,[2] THOMAS.[1]

Married Josiah Rundle, and moved into the State of New York—Whitestown, as supposed. She is mentioned in her father's will, vol. 13, Prob., p. 4.

CHILDREN.

1. FANNY. 2. SALLY. 3. DELILAH. 4. NELSON.

102. OLIVE LEAVENWORTH.[5]—DAVID,[4] JOHN,[3] THOMAS[2], THOMAS.[1]

Born ot Woodbury.
Married Nathaniel Galpin, of Roxbury.

CHILDREN.

1. ABIGAIL, b.
2. BENJAMIN, b.
3. NATHAN, b.
4. OLIVE, b. ——, m. Martin Booth, of Woodbury.
5. CURTISS, b. —— 1816. All born in Roxbury.

Mrs. G. in her old age, lived with her daughter, Olive, at Warren, Macomb Co., Ohio, and died there.

103. BETHIA LEAVENWORTH.[5]—JOHN,[4] JOHN,[3] THOMAS[2], THOMAS.[1]

Born March 14, 1771, at Woodbury.
Married, first, George Gordon, of Woodbury, a wagon-maker. They lived at

Woodbury many years, and finally separated. He died before 1807. She went first to her father's, and in 1820 was keeping house at W.

Married, second, Nehemiah Judson, of Woodbury, at Middleville, N. Y., in the winter of 1829-30, (where she was then living with her son), and returned to W. and died there.

CHILDREN.

By first husband.

1. HENRY, b. at Woodbury.
2. ALTHÆA, b. "
3. JULIA, b. "

Her son Henry went west when a young man, and about 1818 married Maria Cheever, of Utica, and settled at Middleville in Herkimer Co. He was a machinist. He had two sons, Frederick and George, one born in February, 1819. He afterwards moved into Otsego Co., and he and his wife both died there. He owned or was interested in a cotton factory at Middleville.

Althæa m. —— Smith, of Fairfield, Herkimer county.

Julia m. Daniel Brayton, from near Eatonville, and had a dau. who m. Cornelius Christ, and lived at Middleville. Althæa and Julia are both dead.

104. Capt. John Peck Leavenworth.[5]—JOHN,[4] JOHN,[3] THOMAS,[2] THOMAS.[1]

Born November 23, 1772, in Woodbury, Conn.

Married MARY JUDSON April 20, 1797. She was born February 9, 1779, and died March 11, 1861; daughter of Jonathan Judson, of Woodbury, and he married Ruth Minor. They lived in Woodbury some years, then removed to Rush, N. Y., in 1823; he was a farmer. Died October 13, 1852, in the town of Rush.

CHILDREN.

268. CHARLOTTE, b. January 28, 1798, in Woodbury.
269. WILLIAM CURTISS, b. March 23, 1799.
270. SARAH, b. July 15, 1801, d. July 3, 1865.
271. THADDEUS MINOR, b. April 15, 1803.
272. KEZIAH, b. February 3, 1805.
273. CHARLES, b. January 5, 1807, d. February 9, 1813.
274. CHAUNCEY, b. November 6, 1808.
275. RUTH, b. Sept. 14, 1810—Mrs. Brown says Sept. 5, 1811.
276. BENJAMIN, b. February 25, 1813, d. May 19, 1819.
277. HOBART, b. April 4, 1815.
278. MARY JANE, b. July 2, 1820.
279. BENJAMIN JUDSON, b. July 1, 1822, d. June 4, 1853.

He was a man of ability and marked character. Three of his sons became clergymen, and one a lawyer. Benjamin J., the youngest, remained on the farm with his father. The whole family were distinguished by high moral and religious character.

105. LUCRETIA LEAVENWORTH.[5]—JOHN,[4] JOHN,[3] THOMAS,[2] THOMAS.[1]

Born April 18, 1775, in Woodbury, Conn.

Married Adin Maltby, a brother of the husband of her sister Amarillis: a farmer. They went west at an early day, into the eastern part of the State of New York, and settled at Bethel. She had a large family of children. She died in 1829, at Bethel, of consumption.

CHILDREN.

1. MARCUS. 2. MARIETTA. 3. BETSEY. 4. JOHN.
5. HARMAN, d. quite a number of years since, at Bethel, Sullivan Co.;
6. HIRAM. 7. DAVID.

106. Russell Leavenworth.[5]—JOHN,[4] JOHN,[3] THOMAS,[2] THOMAS.[1]

Born January 18, 1777, in Woodbury, Conn.

Married, first, ALTHÆA DEFOREST, February 5, 1802. She was born September 7, 1779, and died February 21, 1814. She was a daughter of Joseph DeForest, of Woodbury.

Married, second, POLLY WARNER, of Newtown, September 13 1815, daughter of Noadiah W., a clergyman of Danbury, then at Newtown. He was a mechanic. Removed about 1824 to Newtown, Conn., and died April 17, 1865; lived in New Milford in 1827, on a farm; in 1830 in Bridgewater, Litchfield county.

CHILDREN.

280. JOHN D., b. January 2, 1803,
281. ABIGAIL, b. June 4, 1804, d. February 28, 1866?
282. EMELINE, b. August 14, 1807.
283. MARK, b. March 25, 1809.
284. LORENZO W., b. July 2, 1821.

All born in Woodbury.

Russell kept the homestead of his father until after his mother's death.

107. AMARILLIS LEAVENWORTH.[5] — JOHN,[4] JOHN[3], THOMAS,[2] THOMAS.[1]

Born December 11, 1778, at Woodbury.

Married December 2, 1798, Frederick Maltby, of Woodbury, brother of Adin M., husband of Lucretia. Frederick M. was born at Litchfield, December 4, 1776. They were the sons of John M., a hatter.

He moved to Lanesboro, Mass., in 1800, after the birth of his first child. Then to Ulster Co., N. Y., in 1805, and in 1819 on to a farm four miles west of Shawneetown, Ill.

CHILDREN.

1. SOPHIA, b. December 19. 1799 at Woodbury; m. William Lowell, of New Madrid, Mo., February 22. She d. January 29, 1823, at New Madrid.
2. MARTHA, b. June 10, 1802, at Lanesboro, Mass.; m. March 17, 1828, Wm.

Siddall, who was from Manchester, England. He came to this country in 1805, and was a merchant. He was b. January 30, 1802, and d. January 28, 1867. Mr. and Mrs. Siddall moved to Equality, Ill., in 1829.

Children.

1. JOHN MALTBY, b. August 28, 1829; farmer; lived in Arkansas sixteen years; driven out by rebellion; now at Equality; m. Elizabeth Jaques, April 13, 1853. *Children.*—Mary, b. Feb. 22, 1853, in Equality; d. Sept. 19, 1855, in Arkansas. Martha E., b. March 28, 1856, d. March 2, 1861. Sarah A., b. Nov. 7, 1858. Willie, b. June 24, 1860, d. May 1, 1864. John b. May 12, 1864, d. Aug. 9, 1866. George Emerson, b. December 28, 1865. Robert, b. April, 1869.
2. FREDERICK, b. January 22, 1831, d. February 16, 1835.
3. JOSEPH ROBERT, b. November 30, 1832, m. Ann V. Gilham, October 25, 1858. *Children.*—Son, b. — d. early. Martha Susanna, b. April 20, 1864. His wife d. February 22, 1865.

Married, second, January 9, 1867, Rebecca Mc. Garr, at Shawneetown, Ill. *Children.*—Annie Bell, b. April 9, 1868. Ida May, b. Oct. 22, 1870, lives at McLanesboro, Hamilton Co., Ill., twenty-eight miles from Equality; a tinner.

4. WILLIAM ALLEN, b. April 1, 1835, m. Elizabeth Morford, of Penn., July 21, 1861. Lives at Washington, Iowa; a tinner. No children.
5. PARMENAS, b. June 17, 1837, m. October 4, 1866, Joanna Probusco, from Geneva, N. Y. *Children.*—Florence Edna, b. November 19, 1867. Jacob Probusco, b, August 20, 1869. lives at Equality; a tinner.
6. ELIZABETH ANN, b. January 6, 1840, m. Miller J. Hine, machinist, of Equality, Feb. 16, 1764. *Children.*—Harry Siddall, b. Dec. 2, 1864, d. August 2, 1865. William, b. at Cairo, Ill., Dec. 18, 1866, d. January 9, 1807, at Equality. James P., b. Dec. 2, 1868, at Equality. A daughter b. Jan. 11, 1872, at Equality.
7. MARTHA AMARILLIS, b. November 8, 1842, m. April 4, 1864, Marcus W. Ross, of Princeton, Ill., d. January 20, 1865, bearing a son, George Siddall, six days old, who d. July 20, 1865.

3. DARWIN, b. March 16, 1804, at Lanesboro, Mass., d. in Ill., September 11, 1822, near Shawneetown.
4. ERASMUS, b. July 3, 1806, in Ulster Co., d. at Cincinnati, O., April, 1865. m. in 1829—(Mrs. S. don't recollect her name).

Children.

1. SOPHIA, b. in 1830, d. in 1848, m. Jo. Coffin, in December, 1847, d. in 1848, leaving twin babies two weeks old; d. in nine months of cholera, both the same day.
2, ELIZA, b. in 1832, m. Jo. Coffin in 1853.
3. SARAH ANN, b. in 1834, m. William Cooper in 1854. *Children.*—Child, d. an infant in 1836. George, b. in 1838. Amarillis, b. in 1842-3, d. 1850.

5. ALEXIS, b. July 25, 1808, in Ulster Co., m. Narcissa Mason in September, 1833, and lived near Equality. They lost a daughter, Amarillis and a son Hannibal, in infancy. Narcissa d. in January, 1850, on a farm.

Children.

1. FREDERICK, M., b. in 1835 d. in 1864.
2. THOMAS, b. Dec. 1839, d. in January 1868, in Equality.
3. COLUMBUS, b, spring of 1842.
4. MARTHA HARRIET, b. in 1844.
5. ISAAC DARWIN, b. in 1846 d. in 1857.
6. CYRUS b. in January, 1869. He is a physrcian and now a widower living in Texas.

The last three were born four miles west of Equality on a farm.

109. LOVISA LEAVENWORTH.[5]—LEMUEL,[4] JOHN,[3] THOMAS,[2] THOMAS.[1]

Born August 10, 1771, at Woodbury.

Married Rufus Case, of Whitestown, N. Y. Case lived in Paris, Oneida Co., N. Y., but came from Adams, Mass. Rufus Case lived in New Haven, Oswego Co., and died there. They had four children. In 1843, she moved to Naples Ontario Co., N. Y., and died there March 27, 1845.

CHILDREN.

1. LAURA. 2. SUSAN. 3. MARY. 4. RUFUS.

Laura married John Dickinson. Mrs. Case lived with them at Naples.

110. Reuben Leavenworth.[5]—LEMUEL,[4] JOHN,[3] THOMAS[2], THOMAS.[1]

Born April 23, 1774, at Woodbury.

He was a lawyer; studied with Thomas R. Gold, and practiced his profession at Whitestown. Died February 7, 1827, at Whitestown, unmarried.

111. MARY LEAVENWORTH.[5]—LEMUEL,[4] JOHN,[3] THOMAS[2], THOMAS.[1]

Born February 25, 1777, at Woodbury.

Married Reuben Foster, of Whitestown, b. August 11, 1771. He died April 16, 1844. aged seventy-four. She died June 22, 1859. All this family except Elizabeth Webb, are dead.

CHILDREN.

1. MARY, b. ——, d. ——, m. Medad Harvey, one child.
2. SABRINA, b. ——, d. ——, m. Benedict Joselyn, one child.
3. ALEXANDER, b. ——, d. ——, m. Abbey ——, of Auburn, have 4 children.
4. REUBEN, b. ——, d. ——, m. Jane Curtiss, four children.
5. SAMANTHA, b. in 1807, d. at Bellows Falls February 7, 1839, aged thirty-two; m. Luther Fuller, three children.
6. SYBIL, b. ——, d. at New York Mills, Oneida county in 1854, m. Ira Hand
7. ELIZABETH, b. August 27, 1813, lives at Bellows Falls, and m. September 23, 1839, Joseph Webb, three children.
8. MILTON DEGRASSE, b. 1816, m. Patience B. Marsh, March 16, 1844. He d. March 23, 1850, aged thirty-four. Children—Samantha, b. December 17, 1844, Eliza, b. February 24, 1847.
9. HELEN, b. ——, d. at Canton, Mich., September 26, 1847, m. Philemon Phelps, five children.

They were all born in Herkimer except Milton DeG. and Helen, who were born in Whitestown.

112. Lemuel Leavenworth.[5]—LEMUEL,[4] JOHN,[3] THOMAS[2], THOMAS.[1]

Born July 27, 1780, at Woodbury.

Married MARY ROGERS, daughter of Capt. Jonathan Rogers,

who removed from Westfield, Mass., and became one of the first settlers of Lowville. Lemuel L. enlisted under Capt. Ketchum of the 25th U. S. Infantry, February 13, 1813; was wounded November 11, at French Creek, and died in service December 14, 1813. His widow subsequently married William Way, who died at Lowville. She married Arnold Stone as a third husband, and died in Rodman, N. Y., March 18, 1844; aged sixty-three years.

CHILDREN.

285. ELIZABETH DANKS, b. September, 1800, at Whitestown; d. January 6, 1821, at Lowville, N. Y., unmarried.

286. LUCY PARKER, b. August 25, 1803.

114. SYBIL LEAVENWORTH.[5]—LEMUEL,[4] JOHN,[3] THOMAS,[2] THOMAS.[1]

Born June 1, 1794, at Whitestown.

Married Abner Burton November 10, 1829. He died before 1845. She left him and then lived with her married daughter in the city of New York, and now, 1870, with the same daughter, who married James Finkle, and lives in Utica.

CHILDREN.

1. CORNELIA BURTON, b. October 24, 1833, m. James Finkle November 4, 1853, at Utica, in the house where she now lives, No. 25 Rutger street; has one son, Frank M. Finkle, born January 5, 1855.

115. Joseph Leavenworth.[5]—AMOS,[4] JOHN,[3] THOMAS,[2] THOMAS.[1]

Born July 19, 1776, at Woodbury, Conn., and moved with his father to Deerfield, N. Y., in March, 1794.

He lived for a time in Truxton, Cortland Co., N. Y. Was not married. He died there July 1, 1845, at the house of his sister, Mrs. Alexander Pope. He was a farmer.

116. SARAH LEAVENWORTH.[5]—AMOS,[4] JOHN,[3] THOMAS[2], THOMAS.[1]

Born April 29, 1778, at Woodbury. Baptized December 15, 1784.

Married Lemuel Barnard, at Whitestown, where he lived and died,

CHILDREN.

1. MABEL.
2. WARNER.
3. WILLIAM, } Twins
4. WINDSOR, } Windsor went to California many years since—not heard from.
5. SARAH ANN.
6. AMOS L.

WARNER, lives near Syracuse.

The daughter, Sarah, Mrs. Irwin, lives in St. Louis. They were all born at Whitesboro.

119. SUSANNA LEAVENWORTH.[5]—Amos,[4] John,[3] Thomas,[2] Thomas.[1]

Born Sept. 21, 1784, at Woodbury, d. Oct.1841. Baptized December 15, 1784. Married Daniel Gazly, of Edmeston, Otsego County, N. Y., a harness maker, March 20, 1802; married at Deerfield. He was born at Poughkeepsie, Duchess Co., N. Y., May 8, 1778. She died at Edmeston October 2, 1841. He at Mainville, Cook Co., Ill., May 6, 1847.

CHILDREN.

1. Ann Eliza, b. October 9, 1806, m. Nicholas Sherman, and d. in Illinois.
2. Ralph, b. May 14, 1808, m. Harriet Hart, is now living at Bridgewater, Oneida, Co., and has four children.
3. Mary Louise, b. March 31, 1810, m, a Mr. Townsend, of Iowa; no children; now a widow.
4. Erasmus Darwin, b. April 17, 1812. Is living in Iowa.
5. Esther, b. April 4, 1814, m. first, Mr. Whitmarsh, and had three children; second, Deacon Severance, of Truxton, and had a daughter; is now a widow, at Fabius.—d. 1873.
6. John, b. April 24, 1817, lives in Michigan.
7. Cornelia, b. October 15, 1819; lives at the West.
8. Amos, b. August 7, 1822, d.——

Ann Eliza Gazly, m. Nicholas Sherman March 13, 1837. She lived in Chicago and had two children—Ann Eliza aud Jeremiah. Jeremiah, only is living.

Ralph L. Gazly m. Harriet E. Hart, in Ohio, March 18, 1837. *Children*—Susanna L., b. September 8, 1838. Judah H.. b. February 13, 1842. Celia O., b. October 30, 1844. Amos H., b. September 6, 1847, and Esther F., b. February 10, 1854. Amos H. d. September 26, 1848.

Esther Gazly m. William Whitmarsh October 14, 1839. *Children*—1. Emma Ambrosia, b. September 15, 1840, at Cuyler, N. Y., m. Luzerne Mallory January 14, 1864, at Truxton. Their only child, Nellie E., b. at Cincinnatus, N. Y., March 28, 1865. Emma d. September 8, 1868, at Ypsilanti, Mich.
Lnzerne Mallory d. at the same place February 12, 1872,

2. Melvin N, Whitmarsh, b. September 25, 1842, at Cuyler, and d. Chicago, August 14, 1844.
3. Mary Louise Whitmarsh, b. at Cuyler April 4, 1844.

William Whitmarsh d. at Chicago August 16, 1846.

Mrs. Whitmarsh m. second, August 28, 1858, John Severance, of Truxton, who d. there June 15, 1869. She now resides at Franklin village in Fabius, Onondaga county, N. Y., 1872.

120. Ralph Leavenworth.[5]—Amos,[4] John,[3] Thomas,[2] Thomas.[1]

Born June 27, 1786, at Woodbury, Conn. Baptized August 13, 1786.

Married Mary B. Hunt, November 11, 1819. She was born in Williamson Co., Tenn., October 15, 1800, daughter of Noah Hunt, who was from S. C. He died November 20, 1852, in St. Genevieve Co., Mo., on a farm some fifteen miles from the town of St. G. He went thither from New York in 1818, as a millwright; was a mill owner several years, but became a farmer.

CHILDREN.

287. Amos Warner, b. September 21, 1820.
288. Ralph Baptist. b. December 3, 1822, d. June 18, 1865.
289, Mary Ann, b. December 27, 1824.
290. Noah Hunt, b. October 7, 1826.
291. Franklin, b. September 13, 1828.
292. Rebekah Ann, b. April 10, 1830, d. February 11, 1838.
293. Milton Bailis,b. September 20, 1831,d. February 20, 1838.
294. Nancy Caroline, b. September 5, 1834, d. Feb. 5, 1838.
295. Joseph Harrison, b. April 27, 1841.

123. LOVISA LEAVENWORTH.[5]—Amos,[4] John,[3] Thomas[2], Thomas.[1]

Born January, 3. 1793, at Woodbury, Ct. Baptized April, 7. 1793, at Woodbury.

M. Alexander Pope son of Joseph and Hannah P., at Deerfield Aug. 11,1811. He d. in Truxton which was their residence. He was a farmer. She resides at Fabius, N. Y. but formerly and for many years at Truxton, N. Y. She never had a child.

He was born at Bridgewater, in the Co. of Plymouth, Mass. June 5. 1788. and d. December, 8. 1831.

124. ISABEL LEAVENWORTH.[5]—Amos,[4] John[3], Thomas[2], Thomas[1].

Born May 29. 1798, at Deerfield, Oneida Co., N. Y.

Married February 1, 1819, at Rome, N. Y. to Jacob Edic, who was born January 28. 1782, and was the son of Jacob Edic and Elizabeth Weaver.

He was a farmer. He died at Marcy (formerly a part of Deerfield) April, 4. 1859, aged seventy-seven years.

CHILDREN.

1. James C , b. 1819, m. Helen Shaw of Deerfield, February, 1847, and has seven children,Emily, Caroline' Charles, Franklin, Pearl, Martha and Robert. He lives in Augusta, and is a farmer.
2. Emily, b. June 13, 1821, d. October 16, 1843, unmarried.
3. Henry, b. April 2, 1823, m. Eliza Kip, of Floyd in 1825, and has three children—George, Hattie and Frederick. He is a farmer.
4. Jacob William, b. December 14, 1824, d. February 9, 1825.
5. Isabel Louisa, b. August 19, 1826, d. September 30, 1832.
6, Amos Leavenworth, b. May 21. 1828, m. Calista R. Payne, of Deerfield, September 20, 1854, and has five children—Eddie, Albion, Leila, Willie and Ella. He is a farmer.
7. Mary Esther, b. September 20, 1830, m. October 18, 1859, Ephraim B. Horne, of Marcy, and has three children—Nellie, Franklin and William. He is a farmer.

8. CHARLES JAY, b. October 12, 1832, is unmarried and lives on the homestead with Mrs. Edic; a farmer.
9. B. FRANKLIN, b. September 19, 1834, lives near Chicago and is unmarried. A farmer.
10. JOHN JACOB, b. September 21, 1836, is a physician and lives in Leavenworth, Kansas. He is unmarried.
11. ANTOINETTE M., b. October 9, 1838, m. December 1, 1858, Franklin Hannahs, Professor of Languages in Fairfield Seminary. Her husband entered the army and died at Harrison's Landing in 1862, leaving her and two children, Mary and Franklin. She resides at Fulton, Oswego Co., N. Y.
12. ISABELLA L., b. July 4, 1841, is unmarried.

126. Jehiel Leavenworth.[5]—ELIHU,[4] JOHN,[3] THOMAS,[2] THOMAS.[1]

Born October 4, 1783.

Married LAURA THOMPSON, in 1803, at Woodbury, Conn. She died at Canaan Falls, Conn., March 2, 1843. He died at the same place October 11, 1826. He was a farmer and resided at Salisbury, Conn., and at Canaan Falls.

CHILDREN.

296. ELIHU, b. ——, 1805, in Woodbury.
297. LE GRAND, b. April 28, 1807, at Woodbury.
298. WILLIAM C., b. ——, 1809, d. November 8, 1826.
299. SALLY MEBOLD, b. December 8, 1811, in Woodbury.
300. CAROLINE DIANTHA, b. ——, 1813, in Woodbury, d. 1837.

127. John Leavenworth.[5]—ELIHU,[4] JOHN,[3] THOMAS,[2] THOMAS[1].

Born in 1786, in Roxbury.

Married MARIA JUDD, daughter of Hollister Judd. She was lost on the steamer "Golden Gate," on her return from California, where she had been on a visit to her daughter. The vessel was lost in July, 1860, on the Pacific coast. He was a farmer, and died July 10, 1856; was buried at Roxbury. He lived on Good Hill, between Roxbury and Woodbury, the line ruuning through his house.

CHILDREN.

301. FREDERICK J., b, October 1829, d. May 27, 1836, aged, seven years and seven months.
302. MARGARET J., b. ——, m. John C. Booth, of New York, a merchant. She had a daughter, Etta.

Margaret's husband died in California about 1860, when she

married Judge Leonard Ferris, of San Francisco, Cal. She is now, *(1872)*, living at Virginia City, Nevada.

His residence was probably the homestead of the first Thomas. John and his son, Frederick, are both buried in the new cemetery at Roxbury.

128. Dr. Alson Leavenworth.[5] — ELIHU[4], JOHN,[3] THOMAS[2], THOMAS.[1]

Born October 12, 1788, in Roxbury, Conn.

Married SALLY CANFIELD, of Woodbury, October 7, 1811. She was a daughter of Elisha and grand-daughter of Rev. Thomas Canfield, of Woodbury. He studied medicine in Philadelphia, graduated in 1813; was appointed a surgeon in the war of 1812-15, by the General Government, and removed to Cattaraugus Co., N. Y., in 1818. Died September 19, 1863, at Cattaraugus, Cattaraugus Co., N. Y. Mrs. L. died in Chicago at the residence of her son Alson E., on the 10th day of June, 1871.

CHILDREN.

303. SARAH CAROLINE, b. June 8, 1817, in Roxbury, Conn., unmarried.

304. ALSON E., b. May 17, 1831, at Little Valley, Cattaraugus Co., N. Y., m. Hannah M. Egert.

He commenced the practice of his profession in the village of Woodbury in 1811, but in the fall of 1812 entered the University at Philadelphia, attended the last course of lectures delivered by the celebrated Dr. Rush, and was graduated in the spring of 1813, having been licensed to practice in Conn. in May, 1811. He returned to Woodbury and resumed his practice, and soon after received the appointment of surgeon in the Connecticut line of militia, and ordered into the service of the United States in the war then pending. But owing to the dispute between the State and General Government as to the right to appoint, he never acted under it.

In the spring of 1818, Dr. Leavenworth resolved to migrate to the Connecticut Reserve. Purchasing a yoke of cattle, and preparing a large covered wagon, properly fitted up, in June he bid farewell—then deemed a *final* farewell—to Connecticut, commenced his journey, and four weeks found him at Batavia,

Alson Leavenworth

in the county of Genesee. There he halted to rest, became acqnainted with the agents of the Holland Land Company, and under their advice changed his course towards Cattaraugus, and in about a week found himself at what is now the village of Ellicottville.

Here the Doctor unloaded his covered wagon, and, with Mrs. L., began the battle of life in the wilderness. His practice soon extended over the county of Cattaraugus, from the Pennsylvania line to that of the county of Erie.

On the 25th of January, 1823, he was appointed First Judge of the County Court of Cattaraugus County, which office he continued to hold till February 15, 1833, when he was succeeded by the Hon. Benjamin Chamberlin. He was also one of the Commissioners to erect the county buildings of Cattaraugus county, and to lay out the roads on the Allegany Indian Reservation. He was one of the original projectors of the Randolph Academy, and a liberal contributor to its funds.

The biographical sketch of Dr. L. in the history of Cattaraugus county by the Hon. John Manly, now (1873) an honored member of the Legislature from Cattaraugus county: which was published in 1857, thus concludes ;—

"Judge Leavenworth by diligence, liberal economy and judicious investments is in possession of a competency. Long may he live to enjoy the fruits of his well filled cornucopia. Whoever has traveled on the New York and Erie Rail Road, has, of course, as the cars swept around the crescent at Cattaraugus Station noticed the elegant brick mansion resting on the southern edge of a hundred acres of table land, forming the handsomest plateau on the line of the road. That is the homestead of Judge Leavenworth—there he enjoys life, pets his fine herd, hospitably entertains his friends; can tell many a pleasant anecdote of the early pioneer life in the county; and there, as elsewhere, in his green old age, perhaps no man in the county is more sincerely esteemed."

Most of the facts above stated are taken by the author from said sketch by the Hon. Mr. Manly.

He had an extensive practice in his profession, and was usually in some official position. He was Supervisor of Ellicottville, Cold Spring, and New Albion, the three towns in which he resided at different times, and Loan Commissioner of the county. He was a gentleman of great integrity and kindness of heart, and possessed in a high degree the confidence, respect and affection of his fellow citizens.

129. Isaac Leavenworth.[5] — Elihu,[4] John,[3] Thomas[2], Thomas.[1]

Born June 12, 1791, in Roxbury, Conn.

Married, first, Mrs. Olive Lum, in 1823, of Washington, Ct. She died September 26, 1827, at Roxbury, and was buried in the new cemetery.

Married, second, Olivia Newton, of Woodbridge in 1829.

Resides in New Haven and is a lawyer. He has no issue, but has adopted a child.

131. CARLOSSY LEAVENWORTH.[5] — Elihu,[4] John[3], Thomas,[2] Thomas.[1]

Born May 3, 1798, in Roxbury, Conn.

Married Emery Blodget, at Ellicottville, N. Y., in 1827. Lived at Alexander Genesee county, where he was an inn-keeper and merchant. Both are dead.

CHILDREN.

1. Julia, b
2. Laura Ann, b,
3. Isaac Kasson, b.
4. Alson, b.
5. Monroe, b.

132. LUCY LEAVENWORTH.[5]—Elihu,[4] John,[3] Thomas[2], Thomas[1]

Born January 1, 1801, in Roxbury, Conn.

Married, first, September 27, 1829, Welcome Smith, at Borodino, at the house of Lloyd Nichols, by Rev. Mr. Darling. A tanner, and a licensed Methodist exhorter. Resided at Borodino, Onondaga Co., N. Y., some years. He removed to Cattaraugus Co., and died March 3, 1837.

Married, second, Clark Holmes, about July 1, 1848, at Mansfield, Cattaraugus county; a farmer, and also a Methodist clergyman, of Otto, Cattaraugus Co., N. Y. Now, 1870, at Cattaraugus Post Office, Cattaraugus Co., N. Y.

CHILDREN.

1. Hobart Alson, b. February 26, 1832, at Spafford, d. February 10, 1856, at Otto, Cattaraugus Co.
2. Eliza Ann, b. May 3, 1834. at Spafford, d. October 19, 1870, at Otto, Cattaraugus Co. She m. at New Albion, September 18, 1853, William Garlock, of Otto, and had three children. He enlisted in the army during the Rebellion. *Children*—Lilly, Fremont, and Welcome.

133. SARAH LEAVENWORTH.[5] — Zebulon,[4] Zebulon[3], Thomas,[2] Thomas.[1]

Born August 16, 1779, at or near Hartford, Conn. Died at Leavenworth Ind. about 1820. Never married.

Zebulon Leavenworth

134. Seth Marshall Leavenworth.[5]—ZEBULON, ZEBULON[3], THOMAS,[2] THOMAS.[1]

Born June 13, 1782-3, in Roxbury, Conn.,—his son John says Hartford, Conn.

Married ESTHER MATHEWS, daughter of Elijah M. and Sabbiah Howd, of Cape May, N. J., at New Albany, Ind., June 15, 1820. She was born at Cape May, N. J., February 28, 1799.

He removed to Cincinnati, O., in 1809 or '10. Taught school and studied law. He was four years, 1828 to 1832, in the Indiana State Legislature, and located in the town of Leavenworth, Ind., having removed to Leavenworth in 1818. In 1850 he removed to St. Louis, Mo., where he died April 2, 1853. His widow resides there, 1865. He was a lawyer by profession. He was graduated at Williams College in 1808.

CHILDREN.

305. SETH M., b. July 30, 1821, at Leavenworth, Ind., and d. at Mt. Vernon, Ind., November 21, 1868.
306. FRANCIS P., b. January 27, 1824, d. at St. Louis May 17, 1857, unmarried.
307. MARK, b. December 6, 1825, d. at St. Louis February 17, 1865, unmarried.
308. MARTHA HELEN, b. March 6, 1828, at Leavenworth.
309. ZEBULON, b. June 2, 1830, at Leavenworth.
310. JOHN M., b. March 26, 1835, at Leavenworth.
311. WILLIAM E., b. July 1, 1837, d. June 19, 1841, at Vicksburg, Miss.

He was extensively engaged in mercantile business at Leavenworth, and built mills there, and also at Milltown, twelve miles north of Leavenworth, on the Big Blue river.

He was a man of great activity, energy and enterprise; sanguine in his temperament, and public spirited and ready to engage in all new enterprises for the public good.

135. REBECCA LEAVENWORTH.[5]—ZEBULON,[4] ZEBULON[3], THOMAS,[2] THOMAS.[1]

Born August 31, 1784, at Roxbury Conn.

Married Joseph N. Phelps at Torrington, Conn., about 1802. Died about 1817, at Jeffersonville, Ind.

CHILDREN.

1. JOSEPH N. PHELPS, JR., never m., left Leavenworth just before 1850, and was never heard of afterwards.
2. SARAH L. PHELPS, m. Eben Edson, of Mt. Vernon, Ind., and had two sons —Joseph P. Edson and William P. Edson.

136. RACHEL LEAVENWORTH.[5]—ZEBULON,[4] ZEBULON[3], THOMAS,[2] THOMAS.[1]

Born October 27, 1786, at Roxbury.

Married William Bounds, at Torrington, Conn., in 1810. He died at Leavenworth about 1832, and she then m. —— Baily. She had seven children and died in Iowa in September, 1870.

CHILDREN.

1. LYDIA RATHRACH
2. OLIVER.
3. SARAH,
4. ALMIRA, } Twins.
5. ALVIRA, }
6. SETH.
7. ESTHER,

137. Zebulon Leavenworth.[5]—ZEBULON,[4] ZEBULON,[3] THOMAS,[2] THOMAS.[1]

Born January 4, 1792, at Granville, Mass.

Married MARGARET PATTERSON, January 11, 1821, at Leavenworth. She was born in the State of Delaware, December 28, 1802. Her father removed to Buffalo, and was there in the war of 1812-15. Removed to Leavenworth, Ind., in 1819, and in 1820 to Vandalia, Ill. He is a carpenter.

Zebulon L. removed to Cincinnati, O., in 1811; taught a year; studied law with Judge Scott, of Chillicothe, a year; went on a surveying tour for the Government, in Illinois; returned to Cincinnati in 1814, and engaged in trade with his brother Seth. In 1816, came down to Jeffersonville, Ind. In 1818 they purchased 400 acres of public lands, and laid out the town of Leavenworth, Ind., built a merchant and saw mill on Big Blue river and afterwards a steam mill. He has been several years a magistrate and county officer, and has served three years, 1831-33 and '34, in the Indiana State Legislature.

CHILDREN.

312. MARY JANE, b. November 9, 1822,
313. ZEBULON, b. Nov. 29, 1824, d. at Leavenworth, Jan. 1826.
314. LYDIA ISABEL, b, September 10, 1830.
315. PRESERVED MARSHALL, b. December 14, 1833, d. at La Grange, Mo., June 12, 1850.
316. MAGGIE RUTH, b. Jauuary 24, 1836.

317. Oliver Solon, b. September 2, 1838.
318. Sarah Jenette, b. February 12, 1842.
319. Elias P., b. June 12, 1845.
320. William Thaddeus, b. December 10, 1847, d. at Leavenworth March 9, 1849.

They were all born at Leavenworth.

He died at Leavenworth September 12 or 13, 1872, and was buried there on Sunday, the 15th.

Like most members of the family, he was a man of a large and vigorous frame, capable of great effort, both mental and physical. He was a man of excellent judgment, full of enterprise and sagacity. He was patient and persevering, and, therefore, in the end generally successful. He enjoyed during a long life, the confidence, respect and esteem of his fellow citizens, and died universally regretted.

In the Leavenworth Independent, of January 14, 1871, was published the following account of his "golden wedding":—

THE GOLDEN WEDDING.

A Half Century of Wedded Life—The Dinner, Speech, Supper and Presents—A Rare Occasion and a Splendid Time.

The first Golden Wedding ever celebrated in Crawford county, took place at the residence of Mr. Oliver Leavenworth, near this place on Wednesday evening last. The parties celebrating their fiftieth anniversary of wedded life, were Mr. Zebulon Leavenworth, aged seventy-nine years, and his wife Margaret, aged sixty-nine. At the dinner party given on Wednesday at noon, to the members of the family and a number of the old citizens of the place, Mr. Leavenworth arose, and in a voice full of feeling and emotion, gave a brief history in verse of the life of himself and wife during the past fifty years. The poem was full of pathos and sublime thoughts, and when the aged gentleman resumed his seat, every eye was suffused with tears. Below we give the address of Mr. Leavenworth in full:—

Ladies, Gentlemen, and Children,—

I have the gratifying pleasure to say to you all that my wife and I have lived happily together for fifty years, and there never has an angry word passed between us, and I hope you may all have the same pleasing intelligence to communicate to us. You all know that I am not an orator, and for that reason I thought that I would recite a few lines, in a conversation with my wife, which might suit the present occasion as well as anything else that I could say to you at this time. I will call it a short history of our journey through life:—

Fifty years through shine and shower,
  Fifty years, my gentle wife,
You and I have walked together,
  Down the rugged road of life.
From the hill of Spring we started,
  And through all the Summer land,
And the fruitful Autumn country,
  We have journeyed hand in hand.

We have borne the heat and burden,
  Willingly, painfully and slow,
We have gathered in our harvest
  With rejoicing long ago.
Leave the upland for our children,
  They are strong to sow and reap;
Through the quiet, wintry lowlands,
  We our level way will keep.

'Tis a dreary country, darling,
  You and I are passing through,
But the road lies straight before us,
  And the miles are short and few.
No more dangers to encounter,
  No more hills to climb, true friend,
Nothing now but simple walking
  Till we reach our journey's end.

We have had our time of gladness;
  'Twas a proud and happy day:
Ah! the proudest of our journey,
  When we felt that we could say
Of the children God has given us,
  Fondly looking on the six.—
"Lovely women are our daughters,
  And our sons are noble men."

We have had our time of sorrow—
  Our time of anxious fears,
When we could not see the milestones
  Through the blindness of our tears.
In the sunny Summer country,
  Far behind us little Zebie, Thaddie,
And Marshall, too, grew weary,
  And we left them on the way.

Are you looking backward, mother,
  That you stumble in the snow?
I am still your guide and staff, dear,
  Lean your weight upon me—so.
Our road is growing narrow,
  And—what is that you say?
Yes, I know your eyes are dim, dear.
  But we have not lost our way.

Cheer thee, cheer thee, faithful hearted,
  Just a little way before
Lies the great Eternal City
  Of the King that we adore.
I can see the shining spires,
  And the King—the King, my dear;
We have served hin long and humbly—
  He will bless us—never fear.

Ah! the snow falls fast and heavy;
  How you shiver with the cold;
Let me wrap your mantle closer,
  And my arm around you fold.
We are weak and faint and weary,
  And the sun's low in the west;
We have reached the gate, my darling,
  Let us tarry here and rest.

Mr, L. (from whom the town of Leavenworth derived its name) first settled in this country in 1821, and since that time he has been engaged in business in this place, either in the mercantile trade or farming. Mr. L. and his lady are both in excellent health, and bid fair to live to celebrate their diamond wedding, twenty-five years hence.

Of the relatives present at the celebration there were Oliver Leavenworth and wife, Elias Leavenworth and wife, of this place; Edward Sullivan and wife of Mt. Vernon, Jos. H. Thornton and wife, of Cincinnati ; J. A. Lyon and wife, of this place, and Mrs. J. A. McCoon, of Staunton, Kansas.

There were also present about seventy-five invited guests, principally residents of the town. When the refreshments were announced the assembled guests formed in couples and marched past the venerable couple, shaking hands,congratulating, and wishing them a still longer lease of life. On arriving at the large and spacious dining room, we found there prepared a feast fit for kings.

It is useless to say that ample justice was done to the rich viands prepared for the occasion. The merry laughter of the happy party made the occasion a scene of beauty and splendor.

The presents to the aged pair were magnificent and very valuable, consisting of gold watches, cups, rings, pens and penholders, spectacles, etc., all of the purest gold and finest finish.

As the "wee sma' hours" of morning approached, the party dispersed to their homes to dream of golden weddings, long life, costly presents, and huge cakes. We wish the venerable couple yet a long life of usefulness and happiness.

May their last days be their best aud pleasantest, and when their days of usefulness are ended here, may they find a happy resting place in that beautiful land, " where the wicked cease from troubling, and the weary are at rest."

138. Melines Conkling Leavenworth.[5] — Jesse,[4] Mark[3], Thomas,[2] Thomas.[1]

Born January 4, 1762.

Graduated at Yale College in 1784; went to Augusta, Ga., and became a planter.

Married Mrs. Anne Lamar, ———, 1801, of Augusta, and resided at that place until his death, July 20, 1823. He left no issue. His house and home was in South Carolina, a little below Hamburgh, which is opposite to Augusta.

Gov. Milledge married the daughter of Mrs. Lamar, by her first husband.

139. RUTH LEAVENWORTH.[5]—Jesse,[4] Mark,[3] Thomas[2], Thomas.[1]

Born February 25, 1764, at Waterbury.

Married Moses Elkins at Peacham, Vt., in 1785. Removed to Potter, Lower Canada, in 1797, where they resided until their deaths, Moses dying August 9, 1838, and Ruth November 1, 1824. They had eight children—Samuel, Mark Leavenworth, Hannah, Catharine, Sabra, Moses, Judith, and David.

1. Samuel, b. July 25, 1786; merchant at New Orleans, La., where he d. February 19, 1835, unmarried.

2. MARK LEAVENWORTH, b. November 25, 1788 m. Lydia Skinner, of Craftsbury, Vt., November, 1815, farmer resides at Potter, Canada East. His children are eight,—Ruby, Louisa, Catharine, Samuel, Ruth, Mark Leavenworth, Jr., Lydia Maria and Ann Almira.

1. RUBY, b. September 17, 1816, m, Joshua Rines, of North Troy, Vt., April 1838, d. November 30, 1840, without children.
2. LOUISA, b. January 10, 1818, m. November 7, 1834, S. C. Moore, M. D., Reside at North Troy, Vt. Her children are 1. Harry, b. Nov. 1835; d. March, 1864; 2, Ruby Ann, b. Oct., 1840; 3, Emurgene ,Catharine, b. March, 1844, m. Robert Chandler, of North Troy, Vt., Aug., 1860; has children—Frances, b. Sept., 1865; Bnrton Moore, b. Dec., 1867.
3. CATHARINE, b. Nov. 17, 1820, m. Newton Hitchcock, of Westfield, Vt., 1854. Has one child, Mark Newton, b. April, 1860.
4. SAMUEL, b. May, 1823, m. Eveline Horner, of North Troy, Vt., February, 1844; farmer, resides ———, Wis. His children are Emeline, b. November, 1844; 2, Lydia, b. February, 1847; 3, Eveline, b. 1850.
5. RUTH, b. May, 1825, m. Andrew Rankin, of Windsor, Canada East, 1847. Her children are 1, Fanny, b. July, 1848, m. James Frasier, of Windsor, January, 1870; 2, Henry, b. March, 1850; 3. Nellie, b. 1857; 4. John, b. March, 1860; Burton, b. March, 1862.
6. MARK LEAVENWORTH, JR., b. February, 1828, m. Jane Hardy, of Potter, Oct., 1851; farmer, resides in Potter. His children are Ruth, b. Nov., 1852; 2, Samuel, b. November, 1855; 3, James, b. November, 1858; 4, Emily, b. May, 1863; 5, Lydia Maria, b. August, 1866; 6, Julia. b. April, 1869.
7. LYDIA MARIA, b. July, 1831, m. Abijah Hardy, of Potter, June, 1858. Her children are—1, Grace, b. January 17, 1859; 2, Bertha, b. May, 1862; 3, Lydia Maria, b. September 25, 1866.
8. ANN ELMIRA, b. May 8, 1834, m. ——— Richardson, of Topsham, Vt., September, 1856. Her children are—1, Nellie, b. June, 1858; 2, Flora, b. March, 1867.

3. HANNAH, b. April 9, 1791, m. Jesse Corsair, of Sutton, Canada, January, 1812, d. August 22, 1865. Her children are eight—Simeon, Catharine, Ruth, Moses, Judith, Harvey, Ephraim and George.

1. SIMEON, b. October, 1815, m. Betsey Morgan, of Sutton; d. June, 1860, farmer, resided at Sutton. His children are—1, Hannah, 2, Jane; 3, Richmond, of whom I know nothing.
2. CATHARINE, b. 1816, m. Hiel Chappell, of Potter, December, 1838. Her children are—Charles, Eliza, Jesse, Nancy and George.
3. RUTH, b. July, 1817, m. John Morgan, of Sutton, March, 1849. Her children are—Lucrecia, Oscar, Judith and Jane.
4. MOSES, b. June, 1819, m. Susan Lucas, 1840; farmer, resides at Sutton, and has one child, Harvey.
5. JUDITH, b. 1821, m. Austin Chamberlain, of Sutton, 1843. Her children are—William, Oscar, Harvey and Orin.
6. HARVEY, b. July, 1822, m. Rosanna Cook. 1842; farmer, resides in Sutton. His children are Henslow, Harvey, Therisa.
7. EPHRAIM, b. December, 1832, m. Phoebe Wilson, 1851. His children are—Henry, Ephraim and Harry.
8. GEORGE, b. 1838, m. 1864.

4. CATHARINE, b. April 14, 1794, m. Thomas Wallace, of Berlin, Vt., December 1810, d. April 29, 1845. Her children are—Margaret and Mathew Pike.

1. MARGARET, b. June 11, 1811, twice m., (1,) 1836 to John B. McClane, Esq., of Cabot, Vt., ———, *(2)* to Carlos Bancroft, of Montpelier, Vt. No children.

2. MATTHEW PIKE, b. April, 1813, m. Mary Tucker, of Calais, Vt., January, 1840; physician, resides at Cabot, Vt. Has one child, Isadore, b. July, 1841, m. Luke Fisher, of Cabot, 1869.

5. SABRA, b. December 30, 1797, m. Stephen Tree, of Stanbridge, Canada, 1823, d. at Savannah, Ga., where she had gone for her health, April 6, 1841, Her children are three—Eber, Ruth and Moses.

1. EBER, b. March, 1855, resides at Dunham, Canada.
2. RUTH, b. 1834, d. 1840
3. MOSES, b. 1837.

6. MOSES, b. March 16, 1800, m. Eliza Miltimore July, 1824, d. April 21, 1868; farmer, resided at Potter. His children are eight—Thomas Wallace, Nancy Jane, Susan, Sarah, Mathew Wallace, George, Mary and Horace.

1. THOMAS WALLACE, b. August, 1825, m. Caroline Hardy, June, 1848; farmer, resides at Potter. His children are—1, Elizabeth, b. 1850; 2, Susan, b. 1852; 3, Flora, b. 1854; 4, Mary, b. 1858: 5, Eugene, b. 1860; 6, Homer, b. 1862.
2. NANCY JANE, b. January, 1827, m. Josiah Bailey, of Potter, October 3, 1846. Has no children.
3. SUSAN, b. 1828, m. Harvey Jenks, of Potter, 1847. Her children are—1, Eliza Jane, b. 1849; 2, Mary, b. 1852; 3, Millie, b. 1854.
4. SARAH, b. November, 1830, m. John Green, of Potter, 1847. Her children are—1, Moses, b. 1850; 2, Eliza, b. 1851: 3, John, b. 1869.
5. MATTHEW WALLACE, b. March, 1835, m. Ellen Mason, 1856, His children are—1, William, b. 1856; 2, Hattie, b. 1861,
6. GEORGE, b. October, 1836, m. Ann Pike, of Potter, 1858. His children are—1, Frank, b. 1859, 2, Frederick, b. 1861, 3, Addie, b. 1864.
7. MARY, b. May, 9, 1838, m. Franklin Esty, of Potter, 1856. Her children are—1, Irene, b. 1863. 2, Jennie, b. 1868, 3, Susan, b. June, 1870.
8. HORACE, b, 1840, m, Mary Upton, of Troy, November, 1861. Has no children.

7. JUDITH, b. March 26, 1803, m. Farrand Livingston, of Washington, Connecticut, March, 15, 1825; resides at Potter.
Her children are six — William Wallace, Ruth Ann, Ellen Eliza, Loudon Bard, Henry Farrand, George Adelbert.

1. WILLIAM WALLACE, b. Dec. 15, 1832, m. Martha Everts Tracy, of Andover, Massachusetts, May 17, 1860; Congregational clergyman, missionary of the A. B. C. F. M. stationed at Sivas, Turkey, Asia. His children—1, Alice, b. March, 1, 1861, 2, William Farrand, b. July, 5, 1862, 3, Stephen Tracy, b. December, 29, 1864, 4, Rebecca, b. September, 10, 1867, 5, Edward McCallum, b. August, 14, 1869.
2. Ruth Ann, b. July 19, 1835.
3. ELLEN ELIZA, b. September 27, 1838, m. Stephen Boswell, of Potter, June 18, 1867. Has one child, Eliza Ann, b. April 13, 1869.
4. LOUDON BARD, b. September 23, 1840, m. Hattie Chamberlain, of Sutton, December 19, 1865; farmer; resides at Potter, has no children.
5. HENRY FARRAND, b. April 19, 1843; physician, Indian Agent, stationed at Fort Thompson, Dakota Territory.
6. GEORGE ADELBERT, b. May 8, 1846, m. Addie Abbott, of North Troy, Vt. February 12, 1868; farmer, resides at Potter. Has one child, Asa Walter, b. October 30, 1868,

8. DAVID, b. April 14, 1806, m. Martha Wakefield July 31, 1827, d. November 30, 1857; farmer, resided at Potter. His children are nine—Paul Richmond, Betsey, Moses Martin, Susan, Henry, David, Cassius, William and Addie.

1. PAUL RICHMOND, b. April 13, 1828, m. Rosette Hayward May 1, 1848; farmer, resides at ——, Iowa. His children are—1, Charles, b. April,

1850 ; 2, Mary, b. 1852, d. 1856 ; 3, Lucy, b. 1854, d. 1864 ; 4, Jedediah, b. 1856.

2. BETSEY, b. March, 1832, m. Benjamin Homer, of North Troy, 1857, d. August 6, 1865. Has one child, Frank, b. 1864.
3. MOSES MARTIN, b. 1833, m. Emeline Johnson, of Albany, Vt., March 1857, d. while a prisoner at Andersonville, 1864 ; Farmer, resided at Potter. His children are—1, Eva, b. March, 1858 ; 2, Lydia, b. March 1860.
4. SUSAN, b. Sept. 20, 1836, m. Austin Morse, of North Troy, Vt., 1853. Her children are—1, Cynthia, b. February, 1855 ; Hattie, b. April, 1857; Mason, b. 1859.
5. HENRY, b. June, 1839, m. Eliza Brown, 1866 ; farmer, resides at Joy, Vt. His children are— 1, Ami, b. July, 1868 ; Charles, b. July, 1870.
6. DAVID, b. October, 1841, m. Augusta Whitcomb, 1867 ; farmer, resides at Potter. His children are— 1, Pliny, b. 1868 ; Maud, b. 1869.
7. CASSIUS, b. May 9, 1844, m. Ruby Riter August. 1863 ; farmer, resides at Sutton, Canada, His children are— 1, Rodney, b. 1865 ; 2, Edith, b. 1866: 3, Clinton, b. August, 1868.
8. WILLIAM, b. June, 10, 1847, m. Lucretia Titus, September, 1869 ; mechanic, resides at North Troy, Vt.
9. ADDIE, b. March, 1854.

140. Dr. Frederick Leavenworth.[5]—JESSE[4], MARK,[3] THOMAS,[2] THOMAS.[1]

Born September 4, 1766, at Waterbury, Ct. d. May 17, 1840, at Waterbury.

Married FANNY JOHNSON, May 19, 1796, daughter of Abner Johnson, of Waterbury. She died there May 14, 1852, aged 75.

He was a physician at Waterbury, and engaged in manufactures. He spent his life there.—Bronson's Waterbury, p. 429.

CHILDREN.

321. LUCIA, b. March, 24, 1797, m. Rev. Asa M. Train of Milford Conn.

322. ELIZA, b. December, 17, 1798 ,m. Charles D. Kingsbury, March, 5, 1821, d. November, 16, 1852.

323. FREDERICK, AUGUSTUS, b. June, 13, 1801, d. December 24, 1809.

324. ABNER JOHNSON, b. July 12, 1803, d. February, 12, 1869.

325. FANNY AUGUSTA, b. June, 1, 1812, m. N. S. Wordin, May 29, 1839.

326. ELISHA. b. March, 15, 1814, unmarried.

When quite young his parents moved to New Haven. His father resided for some years in a house ou the southward or water side of Water street, nearly opposite to the building known for many years as the "Pavillion Hotel". Jesse L. was engaged in commerce, and owned the ferry to East Haven, where Tomlinson's Bridge and Wharf now are, (Steamboat wharf). He once lost a sloop in Hurlgate laden with flax seed. He was Lieutenant in a militia company, of which Benedict Arnold was Captain. Frederick remembered when the company left for the American army at Cambridge, in 1775, and followed them to the outskirts of the town. The father returned not long after. The mother, was a resolute and fearless woman. When the British troops landed at New Haven, her husband was absent. She refused to leave the house, which stood directly by the water; the British sailors landed there, pillaged the hous,e took her silver buckles off her shoes, ripped open her feather beds and emptied them into the sea, while she took what revenge a woman could, by giving them "a piece of her mind."

She is said to have had, at times, a sharp tongue. Perhaps her husband found it so, for before Frederick was seventeen years of age, the father left the mother, taking with him a part of the children, and never returned. Frederick, being thus left to himself, and being desirous to assist his mother, shipped on board a vessel belonging to Capt. Helms, of New Haven. He made several voyages as mate and super-cargo, to the southern ports of the U. S., to the West India Islands, and to what was then called the "Spanish Main." On his last voyage he entered into the employment of a Scotch merchant named Anderson, in the Island of Trinidad, where he remained some time. A portion of this time he was several miles inland, on a small river, where for months he did not see a white face. He located some government lands, in connection with a brother-in-law of Anderson's, and proposed to make a permanent settlement; but he was attacked by the yellow fever, and his constitution so much affected that he did not anticipate an ultimate recovery. In this condition he embarked for home, hoping for nothing more than to die among his friends. He was greatly benefitted, however, by the voyage, and before long entirely recovered.

He pursued the study of medicine, first with a Dr. Phelps, at or near Danville, Vt., and afterwards with Dr. Isaac Baldwin, of Waterbury, his uncle by marriage, and a man of superior ability. He practiced a short time in connection with Dr. B. He then married and located in West Stockbridge, Mass. At the end of about two years, Dr. Baldwin having decided to leave Waterbury, Dr. Leavenworth returned to take his place, and practiced his profession for several years. He was considered skillful, and had especial repute for treating the diseases of children, more than ordinary knowledge of *materia medica* for those times, and much mechanical ingenuity. He was not fond, however, of the drudgery of practice, and probably through the influence of his brother Melines, who then resided in Georgia, he undertook various commercial adventures, dealing in horses, cotton, etc., or what was then known as "Southern trade." For some years his winters were spent in Georgia, and his summers with his family in Connecticut.

In 1811, he engaged in manufacturing in Waterbury, and subsequently in mercantile business in connection therewith. He did not entirely relinquish his southern trade, and at the close of the war of 1812, met with a severe loss by the fall in the price of cotton, in which he had invested somewhat largely. He was not, however, a man to be daunted by reverses, and he pursued his business with industry; but he had nothing more to do with southern trade. In 1827 he sold out his manufacturing interest, and thenceforward was engaged exclusively in mercantile business, mainly dealing in drugs and medicines. He, however, carried on farming somewhat extensively and successfully.

He held the office of post master in Waterbury for upwards of twenty years prior to his death. He was a man of extensive and varied knowledge, gained by reading and observation, and possessed of quick insight into men and things. He had a keen sarcastic wit, and a strong sense of humor. His opinions were deliberately formed, but were expressed decidedly, and held with much tenacity. Though very independent in his judgments and action, he was a man of quick sympathies, and prized the respect and esteem of his fellows. His religious opinions, very positively held, were not those of most of his friends and associates, and the writer of this sketch is of the opinion that a want of sympathy arising from this fact, was keenly felt by him, and probably resulted in his later years, in a certain studied disregard of some conventionalities, amounting to something like eccentricity.

For this notice of Dr. Frederick, I am again indebted to his grandson, the Hon. Frederick J. Kingsbury, of Waterbury.

141.* CATHARINE LEAVENWORTH.[5] — JESSE,[4] MARK,[3] THOMAS,[2] THOMAS.[1]

Born in 1768 at New Haven.
Married, first, ——— Dennis. Second, Thomas Peck.
She died June 25, 1815.

CHILDREN.

1. KATHARINE, (DENNIS, b. ——, m. (1) —Flock, 2d, — York, d. at Waterbury. Had one daughter, Jane. m. Garry Arntz, of Naugatuck. At last accounts they were living somewhere in Bradford county, Pa.
2. HARRIET (PECK), b. ——, m. ——— Sanford. Had one child, which died. She was living at New Haven at last accounts.
3. CHARLES (PECK), b. ——, went to Macon, Ga., when a young man, has not been heard from in many years.

142. Jesse Leavenworth.[5]—JESSE,[4] MARK,[3] THOMAS,[2] THOMAS.[1]

Born August 17, 1771, in New Haven, Conn.

Married, first, NANCY POPE, February 20, 1791. She was born June 26, 1769. She died September 8, 1814, leaving six children.

Married, second, MARTHA MORRILL. She survived him and afterwards married John Sleeper, of Newark, Vt. Both are now dead; she died September —, 1864.

He removed in early life to Danville, Vt., where he resided until about 1820, when he removed to Wheelock, and died there January 1, 1830.

CHILDREN.

327. CATHARINE, b. May 1, 1792, m. Enoch Hazeltine, November 3, 1812, d. February 28, 1855.
328. DR. FREDERICK, b. May 11, 1794, d. December 12, 1855.
329. NANCY, b. September 27, 1797, d. February 10, 1820, unm.
330. FANNY POPE, b. November 27, 1800, m. Edward N. Darling.
331. MARIA, b. February 17, 1803, d. March 13, 1823, unm.
332. MELINA LAMAR, b. June 19, 1805, d. Sept. 2, 1830, unm.
333. MARY JANE. b. —— 1817, m. Orrin Cutler.
334. MARK, b. December 11, 1828, at Wheelock, Vt.

He died greatly respected, and had been post master at Wheelock for quite a number of years before his death.

143. Mark Leavenworth.[5]—JESSE,[4] MARK,[3] THOMAS,[2] THOMAS.[1]

Born August 31, 1774, in New Haven, Conn.

Married. first, ANNA COOK, daughter of Moses Cook, son of Moses, in 1795. She was born March 8, 1778. and d. April 9, 1842.

Married, second, SUSAN JUDSON COOK, October 27, 1844, daughter of Joseph Cook, was born October 25, 1797, and died December 15, 1848.

Went with his father to Vermont, when he was ten years old, but returned in four years on foot to Connecticut. He became engaged in manufactures at Waterbury, and died there September 5, 1849.

CHILDREN.

335. DR. MELINES CONKLING, b. January 15, 1796, d. November 18, 1862.
336. ANNA MARIA, b. February 10, 1798, d. May 6, 1870.
337. MARK MORTIMER, b. May 13, 1800, d. July 22, 1825.
338. BENJAMIN FRANKLIN, b. July 27, 1803, d. October. 1851.
339. HARRIET, b. July 19, 1807, d. May 25, 1808.
340. HARRIET H., b. May 19, 1810, d. March 23, 1833, unm.
341. CATHARINE E., b. August 1, 1816, d. February 9, 1855.

For the following sketch of Mark Leavenworth, I am indebted to Bronson's History of Waterbury. where it will be found, p. 425.

"Mark Leavenworth was born in New Haven, August 31, 1774 and died in Waterbury September 5, 1849, aged 75 years. His father, Jesse Leavenworth, a graduate of Yale College, and a Captain in the Revolution, was a man of much enterprise, and previous to the war, was largely engaged (for the times), in the shipping interest. His mother, Catharine Leavenworth, was a woman of great spirit and firmness, as was instanced by her insisting on remaining at her residence during the invasion of New Haven by the British, while her husband was absent carrying their children to a place of safety, and when nearly all the inhabitants had fled. At the age of ten years, the subject of this notice removed with his father to the county of Caledonia, in Vermont, at which time there was not a white man living within thirty miles in the direction of Canada. and but one family within many miles of their residence. The father owned what are now the towns of Danville and Peacham.

Mark Leavenworth

At the age of fourteen, becoming dissatisfied, he determined to return to Connecticut; he performed the journey on foot and alone; the distance was near three hundred miles. After his return to New Haven, he resided in the family of his Uncle, Mark Leavenworth, Esq., who sent him to a school, (Mansfield's) where he studied geometry, navigation, and surveying, intending to go to sea, an idea which he afterwards relinquished. Further than this, his school education was limited, being confined to reading, writing, geography, and a good knowledge of arithmetic. After leaving school he was engaged in mechanical pursuits. He was employed for a number of years with Jesse Hopkins, of Waterbury, in that branch of the silversmith business which was applied to making knee and shoe buckles.

Near the period of his majority, the fashions having changed, this branch of the business became worthless. At the age of 21 years he married Anna, daughter of Moses Cook, of Waterbury, a woman of placid temper, excellent sense, and great moral worth, and commenced life with no other capital than great energy, a determined will, and uncommonly industrious habits. They had seven children, six of whom arrived at the age of maturity, of whom the eldest two survive. After his marriage he engaged in the manufacture of axes and steelyards, and also the mountings of small arms, (guns), such as ramrods, barrels and bayonets. At this business he employed a number of hands until the year 1800. In the fall of that year he left for South Carolina and Georgia, with steelyards and axes. This was an adventure which at the time called forth more remark, and excited more wonder than the circumnavigation of the globe would in our day. In the year 1801, in company with his brother, Dr. Frederick Leavenworth, he collected a drove of mules in Vermont and New Hampshire, which were driven to South Carolina and Georgia. He continued in this business about five years. He returned in the Summers and employed himself in constructing one or more of Whitney's cotton gins. The gin was then a recent invention. After ceasing to go South, he commenced the manufacture of clocks, in which business he was for many years extensively engaged. In 1829, in addition to the clock business, he became interested with his son, B. F. Leavenworth, and his son-in-law, Green Kendrick, in the manufacture of gilt buttons. In 1835 he ceased to manufacture clocks, and engaged personally in the manufacture of gilt and cloth buttons, with his son-in-law, C. S. Sperry, which he continued till his death.

He was a pioneer in manufacturing in the town of Waterbury. By reading and observation he became a man of much intelligence. He was benevolent and public-spirited. He was a member of the Congregational church, with which he and his wife united in 1817. She died April 9, 1842.

In person Mr. Leavenworth was of middle stature, his frame compactly and firmly knit together, and his constitution good. Though not always fortunate in business, he was a man of untiring industry, and indomitable energy and perseverance. It was when laboring under embarassment that these traits were most conspicuous. When others would have despaired, he saw reason for redoubled effort and more untiring application. Under a load that would have broken the back or crushed the spirit of an ordinary man, he moved with freedom and cheerfulness. If bad luck overtook him, he was always ready to try again, and never failed to find something to comfort him. When the storm came upon him in 1837, and he was obliged to yield, he consoled himself with the reflection that he stood it longer than the United States Bank, and, it may be, added that he recovered sooner.

Mr. Leavenworth had one of the kindest of hearts. He was well informed, sociable, sensible and shrewd. There was sometimes an archness, a dry humor in his remarks, particularly on character, which rendered his familiar conversation quite attractive.

144. Gen. Henry Leavenworth.[5]—Jesse,[4] Mark,[3] Thomas[2], Thomas.[1]

Born December 10, 1783, at New Haven, Conn. Removed in childhood, with his father, to Danville, Vt.

Married, first, Elizabeth Eunice Morrison. Left Vermont for New York State, and obtained a divorce. He had two children by this marriage—a son and daughter. Studied law with Gen. Erastus Root, at Delhi.

Married, second, Electa Knapp, daughter of Cyrus Knapp, of Delhi, N. Y., who died June 12, 1811, aged eighteen years, and twenty-five days, within a year after marriage,

Married, third, Harriet Lovejoy, in the winter of 1813-14. She was of Blenheim, Schoharie Co.; born in 1791, and died at Barrytown, N. Y., September 7, 1854, aged sixty-three. His daughter Alida also died at Newburgh, where Mrs. L. lived after the death of the General, on the 29th day of January, 1839.

He was appointed Captain of the 25th Infantry, April 25, 1812, and Major of the 9th Infantry August 15, 1813. Commanded his regiment, and was brevetted Lieut.-Colonel for distinguished services at Chippewa, July 5, 1814. August, 1814, he commanded regiment and was brevetted Colonel, for distinguished services at Niagara, in which he was wounded, July 25, 1814. retained, on the peace establishment, May 25th, 1815, in the Second Infantry. Lieut.-Colonel in 5th Infantry February 10, 1818. Commanded and was distinguished in an expedition against the Arickaree Indians, seven hundred miles above Council Bluffs, on the Missouri river. Brevet Brigadier General for ten years faithful service, July 25, 1824. Colonel of the 3d Infantry, December 16, 1825, was made a Brigadier-General in the army in 1833, and died at Cross Timbers, near the Falls of Washita, in an expedition against the hostile Pawnees and Camanches, July 21, 1834. He was elected a Member of the Assembly for Delaware Co., N. Y., in 1815. He was buried at Delhi, N. Y.

CHILDREN.

342. JESSE HENRY, b. March 29, 1807, at Danville, Vt.
343. EUNICE ELIZA, b. ———
344. ALIDA YATES, b. ——, d. at Newburgh, N. Y., Jan. 21, 1839
345. DAUGHTER, ———

Early in life he left Danville, went to Delhi, Delaware Co., N. Y., and commenced the study of law with Gen. Erastus Root, then the leading lawyer in that county, and afterwards Lieut.-Governor of the State. On being admitted to the bar, he formed a partnership with General Root, which continued until he received a Captain's commission, and entered the army in April, 1812.

He married his second wife, Electa Knapp, of Delhi, in the spring or summer of 1810, and she died within a year thereafter.

In leaving his profession he abandoned a large and lucrative practice, and the most flattering prospects.

It is stated in Gould's History of Delaware County, that he took with him from that county, four hundred and thirty men to the army, of whom twenty-eight only finally returned.

His merits were early appreciated by his superior officers, and on the 15th of August, 1813, he was appointed a Major in the 9th Infantry, and as such had command of that regiment and a part of the 22d, at the battle of Chippewa, on the 5th of July, 1814, and at the battle of Niagara, on the 25th of the same month. For his gallant services at Chippewa, he was brevetted Lieut.-Colonel in August, 1814; and for similar good conduct at Niagara, he was brevetted Colonel in November, 1814. It is stated in above history, that two horses were killed under him in those bloody battles. He was wounded and fell from his horse, from the effect of a spent ball. See Lossing's Field Book of the war of 1812, ps. 809-816, and onwards.

On returning from the war, and in the fall of 1815, he was elected by the people of Delaware to represent that county in the Legislature, where he became at once an active and influential member.

Being retained on the peace establishment, May 25, 1815, he was, in 1816 or '17, appointed Indian Agent for the northwestern territory, with his headquarters at Prairie du Chien. He left his wife and young daughter at the east, and after some years they joined him at Prairie du Chien, going by the way of New Orleans and St. Louis. At the latter place, they were met by fourteen Indians with a palanquin, sent by Col. L. for their escort on their journey of seven hundred miles through the then unbroken wilderness. Four of them carried the palanquin, five marched in front and five in the rear. Two stood as watchmen each night, and all were polite, kind and obliging. They arrived safely on the thirty-fourth day. She is said to have been the first white woman who traveled through the wilderness to that remote station.

Remaining in the army, he spent the remainder of his life in the valley of the Mississippi, guarding the frontiers from the hostile Indians. For a time he had charge of the school for infantry practice at Jefferson Barracks. He built Cantonment Leavenworth, on the Missouri, directly above and adjoining the city of Leavenworth—hence its name.

At the time of his death he was stationed at Fort Jessup, and his wife and daughter were with him, when he was not absent on expeditions against the Indians.

While on his last pursuit of the hostile Pawnees and Camanches, he was seized with a violent fever, it being in the month of July, and he died in the full possession of all his faculties, lying in his wagon, while the troops were halted upon the open prairie. He was taken to the camp on the False Washita, and was temporarily buried at a place called the Cross Timbers. He had the possession of his faculties to the last, and gave directions as to his affairs, expressing a particular desire that his remains might

H. Leavenworth

LEAVENWORTH, KANSAS

be taken to Delhi and buried there, for the reason that he was indebted to the people of Delaware for all that he had been in life. His remains were brought from their brief resting place by his wife, and arrived at Catskill on Friday, the 22 of March, 1835, under the care of Major Belknap, of the U. S. army, his intimate personal friend. The Delaware Dragoons met the remains at Catskill, and escorted them to Delhi.

On the 17th of March a public meeting of the citizens of Delhi was held, for the purpose of taking suitable action in relation to the funeral of General Leavenworth. Gen. Erastus Root, Hon. Charles Hathaway, and others, were appointed a committe of arrangements. A series of most flattering resolutions was passed at the meeting, and General Root was selected to deliver the address at his funeral, which took place at Delhi, on Saturday, the 23d day of March, in the presence of an immense concourse of the people of the county of Delaware, composed of his former clients, constituents, friends and admirers. The Rev. Mr. Fenn conducted the religious exercises. The eulogy pronounced by General Root was published in the papers of Delaware county, but the author has been unable to procure a copy. But, by the kindness of the Hon. Norwood Boune and the Hon. Charles Hathaway, of Delhi, he has been furnished with files of the papers of the day, and with a copy of the History of Delaware county, and with facts in relation to Gen. L; and from these sources much of the above has been derived, and some of it from an article in said history on Gen. L. and his wife, by a daughter of E. B. Fenn, Esq., of Delhi.

General Leavenworth was, by nature, endowed with great activity, energy and power. He was a polished gentleman, a public spirited and patriotic citizen, a reliable friend, and faithful in the performance of all the duties of life. He had in a few years greatly won the confidence and love of the people of Delaware county, and died by them universally respected, beloved, honored and mourned.

His remains were deposited in the *old* cemetery at Delhi, and his regiment erected to his memory a beautiful white marble monument, twelve feet high—the "Broken Column."

The lot within which repose also, the remains of his second wife, is surrounded by an enclosure, composed of heavy cannon connected with chains. The inscriptions upon the four sides of the die, are as follows ;—

1st. "In memory of Henry Leavenworth, Colonel of the U. S. Infantry, and Brigadier-General in the army."

2d. Born at New Haven, Conn., December 10, 1783. Died in the service of his country, near the Falls of Washita, July 21, 1834.

3d. For his civic virtues, his fellow citizens of Delaware Co. honored him with a seat in the Legislature of New York. The fields of Chippewa, Niagara and Aurickaree establish his fame as a soldier.

4th. As a testimonial to his public and private worth, his regiment have erected this monument.

After the death of General Leavenworth, his widow and daughter resided for a time at Delhi, and afterwards mostly at Newburgh, spending more or less time at Barrytown, where she had spent some of the earlier years of her married life; and when she died, September 7, 1854, aged sixty-three years, she was buried at Newburgh, and upon the north side of the same monument erected over the grave of her daughter Alida, is the following inscription :—

HARRIET LEAVENWORTH,

WIDOW OF THE LATE BRIGADIER-GENERAL LLAVENWORTH, OF THE U. S. ARMY.

Died at Barrytown, Duchess Co., N. Y.,

Sept. 7, 1854, Æ. 63 years.

145. SARAH LEAVENWORTH.[5]—WILLIAM,[4] MARK,[3] THOMAS[2], THOMAS.[1]

Born June 20, 1784, at Waterbury.

Married October 28, 1804, Joel Walter, son of William Walter, of New Haven.

Died February 6, 1860, at the house of her daughter, then Mrs. Hagood, at Barnwell C. H., South Carolina. Joel Walter graduated at Yale College in 1800. Editor and publisher in New Haven. Died at Hamden, near New Haven, January 16, 1832.

CHILDREN.

1. LOUISA, b. April 15, 1806, d. same day.
2. CHARLES PIERPONT, b. June 5, 1807, m. September 11, 1836, Lucy Jane Harris, d. February 21. 1860, at Albany, N. Y.

Children.

1. WILLIAM PIERPONT. 2. ELLEN COCKRAN. 3. SARAH CORNELIA. 4. CHARLES,

3. REV. WILLIAM HENRY, b. November 20, 1808. Trinity College 1828.

Episcopal clergyman at Troy, N. Y., where is his monument; m. June 3, 1840, Ellen Cochran, of Schenectady, N. Y., d. at N. Y., May 12, 1846, suddenly, on his way south for his health.

Children.

1. GERTRUDE COCHRAN, b. in Schenectady April 1, 1841. She is deaf and dumb. Educated at the N. Y. State Deaf and Dumb Asylum at Washington Heights. Now living in New York, No. 60 Clinton Place, but often at her great-uncle's, Gerrit Smith, of Peterboro, N, Y.
2. WALTER COCHRAN, b. in New York April 30, 1844, d. August 16, 1845.

4. GEORGE, b. November 9, 1810, m. September 21, 1835, Juliana Oaks, of New Haven. She d. at Harrisburg, Pa., October 8, 1862. Married, second, —— ——

Children.—All of first wife.

1. JULIA MARTHA, b. at New Haven, May 31, 1837.
2. GEORGE LEAVENWORTH, d. at Bridgeport, March 6, 1839. Local editor Daily State Journal, Harrisburg, Pa.
3. WILLIAM GREEN, b. at Bridgeport December 2, 1841, m. June 6, 1866, Isabella Lybrand Sayford, of Harrisburg, Pa.; is clerk for a railroad Co., has had two children,—1. Joseph Oakes, b. April 2, 1868, d. May 26, 1868. 2. Adaline Sayford, b. August 16, 1869.
4. ELIZABETH BRAINERD, b. at Bridgeport July 4, 1843, m. January 19, 1869. F. O. Whitman, of Harrisburg. One child—H. D., b. Oct. 26, 1869.
5. EDWARD BOWDITCH, b. July 4, 1844, d. August 5, 1844.
6. HARRIET HOWELL, b. May 24, 1845.
7. FREDERICK BOWDITCH, b. April 30, 1847, clerk for Railroad Co.
8. MARY DAYTON, b. at Milton, N. Y., January 8, 1850, d. July 23, 1851.
9. ESTHER SUSAN, b. in Georgetown, Md., February 16, 1854.

5. JOHN BAKER, b. November 12, 1812, d. September 9, 1813.
6. FRANCIS JOHN, b. November 15, 1814, d. September 24, 1815.
7. THEODOSIA LOUISA, b. May 4, 1816, d. February 4, 1817.
8. JAMES, b. January 27, 1818, m. November 28, 1842, Martha Kinney, at Boonville, Mo., d. February 22, 1860. Merchant and steamboatman.

Children.

1. DUNCAN CARTER, b. at Madison, Ind., September 5, 1843, d. June 24, 1844, at Booneville.
2. MARGARET CORNELIA, b. at Booneville October 6, 1846, d. Feb. 16, 1847.
3. JAMES ADAM MODENWELL, b. April 29, 1848, d. September 11, 1848.
4. WILLIAM AUGUSTUS, b. March 17, 1850, d. March 25, 1852. His widow has married Dr. Milton McCoy, of Booneville, Mo.

9. ELIZABETH MARIA, b. June 15, 1820, d. November 2, 1821.
10. ELIZABETH MARIA, b. January 6, 1822, d. at Albany, May 11, 1831.
11. CAROLINE SARAH, b. February 3, 1819, m., first, William J. Hagood, of Charleston. S. C., at Aiken, S. C., April 26, 1853. He died.

Children.

1. WILLIAM WALTER. b. March 15, 1854, d. July 27, 1854.
2. WALTER LEAVENWORTH, b. October 9, 1855, d. October 29, 1858.
3. ROBERT BROWNELL, b. April 21. 1858, d. January 8, 1859.
4. WILMOT JOHNSON, b. September 19, 1860, d. September 21, 1860.

Married, second, February 25, 1863, at Barnwell C. H., John E. Thornton, of Ga.

Married, third, Andrew W. French, formerly of Milford, Conn.

12. CORNELIA LOUISA, b. March 1, 1824, m. June 10, 1858, at Booneville, Mo. John F. Zeigler, of St. Louis, Mo. He d. at Baltimore, January 30, 1868. No children.

146. William Leavenworth.[5]—William,[4] Mark,[3] Thomas[2], Thomas.[1]

Born June 20, 1786, at Waterbury. Conn.

Married Fanny Porter, daughter of Abel Porter, at Waterbury, October, 1808. Died at Albany July 29, 1829, aged forty three years. She died at Akron, O., May 13, 1867; buried at Waterbury.

CHILDREN.

346. Sarah Hannah, b. at Albany, June 16, 1818; m., first, Benjamin P. Watrous; second, F. A. Nash.

147. Nathan Leavenworth.[5]—Elisha,[4] Mark,[3] Thomas[2], Thomas.[1]

Born October 18, 1792, in New York.

Married Alice Johnstone October 4, 1827. She was dau. of John Johnstone of Scotland, and AnneFleming of N. Y., and was born at Geneva, N. Y., October 27, 1803, and was neice of Chas. King, President of Columbia College, N. Y. They were married at Grace Church. New York city, by Rev. Dr. Wainwright.

He died in New York June 16, 1861. She died August 9, 1869, at the house of her son-in-law, R. M. Cameron, on Staten Island.

CHILDREN.

347. Edward, b. January 16, 1829.

348. Capt. Mark Frederick, b. at Bennington. Vt., October 17, 1832, d. March 18, 1864.

349. George Henry, b. at Bennington, Vt., September 12, 1835, d. July 9, 1865.

350. John Johnstone, b. August 16, 1837, at the Bennington Iron Works, d. February 18, 1868, at Hartford.

351. Anne Fleming, b. March 4, 1839, at Elizabethtown, N. J.

Early in life he was extensively engaged in the manufacture of iron at the Bennington Iron Works, in Vermont. He subsequently returned to New York, but resided at Elizabeth, near Mrs. L. uncle's the late Charles King. But the last years of his life were spent in New York. He was engaged in fire insurance in connection with some one of the large English companies.

Residence of HON. DAVID LEAVENWORTH
Great Barrington, Mass.
Erected 1820.

153. David Leavenworth.[5]—ASA,[4] THOMAS,[3] THOMAS,[2] THOMAS.[1]

Born September 12, 1769, at Waterbury, now Watertown, Ct.

Married LUCINDA MATHER, at Torringford, Conn., January 16, 1794. She was the third child of Zachariah and Lucy Gaylord Mather, and was born at Torringford, May 6, 1775. Her father was born at Suffield in 1736, and died at Romulus, Seneca Co., N. Y., September 17, 1813. Her mother, Lucy Gaylord, eldest daughter of Dea. Nehemiah Gaylord, and Lucy Loomis, was born at Torringford, 1742, and died at Middlesex, N. Y., July 4, 1837, aged ninety-six. The parents of Lucinda M. were married in 1759. David Leavenworth died May 25, 1831, at Great Barrington, and his widow, Lucinda, at Syracuse, N. Y., February 3, 1866, aged ninety-one years, less three months and three days. The following notice of her death was sent to her numerous relatives and friends:—

"DIED.

"At the residence of her son, the Hon. E. W. Leavenworth, at Syracuse, on Saturday, February 3, 1866, and in the 91st year of her age, Mrs. Lucinda Leavenworth, widow of the late Dr David Leavenworth, of Great Barrington, Mass.

"She died happily and quietly, of the gradual decline of her vital powers, without sickness or suffering, surrounded by her family, and at peace with the world and her Lord,

> "Like one who wraps the drapery of his couch
> About him, and lies down to pleasant dreams."

CHILDREN.

352. CHARLES, b. January 26, 1796, d. January 15, 1829, at Egremont, Mass.

353. WILLIAM, b. Novembr 10, 1799, d. May 6, 1860, at Allentown, N. J.

354. ELIAS WARNER, b. December 20, 1803.

All born at Canaan, Columbia Co., N. Y.

He was a physician in early life and studied his profession with Dr. Isaac Baldwin, of Waterbury, Conn., who married Sarah, daughter of Rev. Mark Leavenworth, of Waterbury.

After he was admitted to practice, he spent a year more or less, at Torringford—probably in 1793. After his marriage he spent a year at Roxbury, at the solicitation and by the advice of General Hinman, father of the late Ralph Hinman, of Hartford

Secretary of State of Conn. He then turned his steps west, and in 1795 went as far as Canandaigua, but returned and settled at New Canaan, Columbia county, N. Y. Here he injured his health in the duties of a large country practice, and about 1798-9 was made State printer, through the influence of his friends, Elisha Williams, Jacob Rutger Van Renselaer, and others, and he went to Albany and formed the firm of Leavenworth & Whiting, booksellers and stationers, and did business on the northwest corner of State and North Pearl streets, under the shade of the still existing and celebrated old Elm.

A change of politics deprived him of the State printing in 1802-3, and in the last year he returned to Canaan, and in 1805-6 settled at Great Barrington, Mass., and went into the business of a merchant with his youngest brother Isaac, under the firm of D. & I. Leavenworth. Here he spent the residue of his life, in the business of a merchant.

He was a man of high personal character; an active and consistent member of the Congregational church; of unquestioned integrity; great firmness of purpose, and strong, active and vigorous powers of mind. He was energetic and public spirited and took a prominent part in every enterprise for the improvement of the town.

He was repeatedly a member of the Legislature in the high political time of 1812-13, etc., and for many years before his death was the Moderator of the town. On the 18th of June 1819, he was appointed one of the Justices of the peace within and for the county of Berkshire, for seven years from that date "if he shall so long behave himself well in said office". The commission was signed by John Brooks, Governor, and Alden Bradford, Secretary of the Commonwealth, etc., and the oath was taken by and before Moses Hopkins, (son of the celebrated Dr. H.) and Gen. John Whiting, thereunto empowered by a "Didimus potestatem."

He had a farm about, and near to, his residence at Great Barrington, which he greatly enjoyed, and to which he devoted much of his time and thought. He was often a competitor for prizes at the Berkshire Agricultural Society, not only on his farm, but on his cattle and sheep, and frequently successful. He took much pride and pleasure in all matters connected with his farm. He was also very fond of horticulture, and several acres of ground about his residence were always filled with the choicest varieties of apples, pears, peaches and plums, and in the greatest abundance. And yet, notwithstanding these various demands upon his attention, his leisure was largely devoted to choice books with which his library was at all times liberally supplied.

His life was one of great activity and usefulness and he died in the full enjoyment of the love and respect of his neighbors and fellow citizens, and with perfect trust in the mercy of his Savior.

155. John Leavenworth.[5]—ASA,[4] THOMAS,[3] THOMAS,[2] THOMAS.[1]

Born January 23, 1773, at Watertown, Conn.

Married POLLY DENNISON September 10, 1795, at Greenfield, Saratoga Co., N. Y. She was born at Stonington, Conn., December 27, 1778. He died April 39, 1851, at East Genoa, Cayuga Co., N. Y., where he had lived for nearly fifty years. He was a farmer; went from Watertown to Milton, Saratoga Co., early in 1793, in 1795 to Canaan, Columbia Co., and in 1800 to Genoa. In 1800 he bought a farm in what is now the town of Lansing, Tompkins Co., about three miles southeast of East Genoa, and in 1809 he bought the farm on which he lived and died, and on which his son Horace still resides, at East Genoa.

CHILDREN.

355. HIRAM, b. August 25, 1797, at Canaan, Columbia Co.
356. POLLY, b. December 26, 1799. " "
357. FANNY, b. August 1, 1803.
358. CLARA, b. June 28, 1808.
359. OLIVIA, b. May 9, 1810.
360. HORACE, b. July 8, 1817.

All born at East Genoa, except the first two.

He went on to the frontier as Lieutenant, at Niagara in 1814, in Col. John Harris' regiment, and was afterwards elected Captain, and filled many offices in town. He was a man of great integrity, and universally respected and beloved.

156. Truman Leavenworth.[5]—ASA,[4] THOMAS,[3] THOMAS,[2] THOMAS[1].

Born November 22, 1775, in Watertown, Conn. Removed to Canaan, N. Y., in 1796, with his father and family.

Married CLARISSA CLEVELAND September 10, 1817. , She was a daughter of Amasa Cleveland, who died July 1, 1833, aged 77. She was born in Williamsburg, Mass., February 15, 1783. She still lives—1873. He died December 19, 1861. He was a farmer.

CHILDREN.

361. EVELINE THEODOSIA, b. August 25, 1818 at Canaan, N. Y.
362. EDWIN WALDO, b. April 3, 1822, " "

He was a large, heavy man, weighing nearly or quite two hundred and fifty pounds. He was a farmer, and spent his life at Canaan four corners, in a quiet manner. He was industrious, frugal, kind and inoffensive, spending his days at his own home and devoting a large part of his time to books.

157. ELIZABETH LEAVENWORTH.[5] — ASA,[4] THOMAS[3], THOMAS[2], THOMAS[1].

Born April 5, 1778, at Waterbury, now Watertown, Conn. Came in early youth with her parents to New Canaan, Columbia Co,, N. Y., about 1795-6.

Married Arthur Hotchkiss early in 1797, at Canaan, N. Y. Resided at Lansingburg a year, and then removed to Albany, where she died February 1, 1800. He was for some years a merchant tailor.

CHILDREN.

1. ADELINE, b. December 24, 1797, at Canaan, N. Y., m. Henry Moschell, and lived many years at Cazenovia.

Children.

1. GERTRUDE, m. Julius Hill, of DeRuyter.
2. JACOB LEAVENWORTH, lives at Homer.
3. ELEANOR. b. August 15, 1833, at Cazenovia, m. Henry Brown.

Henry Moschell d. at Cazenovia in 1844.

2. NANCY, b. March 10, 1799, at Lansingburg, N. Y.; m. Fletcher Norton Oman, a Scotchman, and by trade a tailor. He d. October 18, 1828. His widow resides at North Lee, Mass., and has a son, Thomas Arthur, b. in Bethlehem, and some daughters b. in Albany.

Children.

1. MARY, b. April 1819, at Albany, d. August 21, 1857.
2. ELIZABETH, b. December 3, 1821.
3. ADELINE, b. September 3, 1823.
4. THOMAS ARTHUR, b. March 27, 1826. He is married and resides at at North Lee, Mass.

3. WILLIAM, b. after 1801, by a second wife.

He was a member of the New York Constitutional Convention of 1846, and of the State Senate in 1856-7, and then resided in Chester, Warren Co. In 1863-6, he was a clerk in the Bureau of Military Statistics, at Albany. Present residence, Glens Falls, N. Y.

Isaac Leavenworth

WOLCOTT, N.Y.

158. Isaac Leavenworth.[5]—ASA[4], THOMAS,[3] THOMAS[2], THOMAS.[1]

Born June 17, 1781, at Watertown, Conn.

Married ANN LEE October 15, 1811. She was born at Pittsfield, Mass., November 11, 1792, and died at Wolcott, N. Y., January 24, 1861. He died at Wolcott, N. Y., February 29, 1860. She was the daughter of Dr. Jonathan Lee, and Mabel Little, of Pittsfield, Mass., and Salisbury, Conn.

CHILDREN.

363. CAROLINE EMILY, b. August 27, 1812, at Great Barrington, Mass.

364. ELISHA LEE, b. September 20, 1814, at Great Barrington, Mass., d. November 16, 1860, at Wolcott, N. Y.

Isaac Leavenworth was a gentleman of uncommon merits. He was active, energetic, sagacious and successful in his business enterprises; frugal and prudent in his personal expenses: kind, liberal and benevolent towards the poor and afflicted; remarkably public spirited and generous in all enterprises aiming at the public good. What he accumulated by the exercise of one class of virtues, was expended in doing good through another class. His whole life was that of an active, cheerful, liberal christian gentleman.

Some years before his death, he sent for the author, to draw his will, by which he proposed to leave liberal bequests for the benefit of the people of Wolcott, and of the Presbyterian church, of which he was long an active, liberal and exemplary member. The author advised him not to make any will, which seemed superfluous, but, as he was in good health, to administer upon his estate himself, and do in his lifetime what he proposed to provide for by his will. He accepted of the advice, and the result was, that at his own expense he built a commodious and tasty Lecture Room for the church, at an expense of some fifteen hundred dollars; he purchased a lot for a parsonage at a cost of five hundred dollars, upon which his widow, after his death, built a parsonage at an expense of some two thousand dollars: he conveyed to the Society a block of three stores in the village of Wolcott, for the support of the Society after his death, and gave to them, also, a small cemetery, which he had laid out for the convenience of the village. He also joined with the citizens, and paid one-half of the expense of building the "Leavenworth Institute," and furnishing the library and chemical and philosophical apparatus, in order that it might be taken under the care of the Board of Regents. This was an academical institution at the village of Wolcott, and was so named by the citizens, out of compliment to his liberality.

He lived to a good old age, still active and full of good works, and died at Wolcott February 29th 1860, universally respected and beloved.

He was a member of the Legislature from the county of Wayne in the year 1849. A gentleman who had been spending some weeks at Wolcott on his return home, published the following sketch of Mr. L.:—

"Of all the men Wolcott has ever known Hon. Isaac Leavenworth claims, obtains, retains and maintains the first place in the affection of her inhabitants and he has spent a life of energy and uprightness in the advancment of her comforts and interests. If a poor man wants aid in business Mr. Leavenworth is not appealed to in vain; if a poor man is sick and in distress Mr. Leavenworth will find him out and assist him. If a merchant or master mechanic finds business drags Mr. Leavenwoth counsels him as a friend, cheers him by his advice and assists him by his support, bids him keep up a brave heart and all will be well. If a public benefit is mooted, Mr. Leavenworth heads the list with a liberal contribution. Look at the splendid new church the Presbyterians have; look at the very nice acadamy just about completed. They both owe their existence and completion to his pecuniary aid. Not only in such enterprises is he found active; smaller things for the benefit of the community occupy his attention. If a town pump wants repairing he don't solicit subscriptions but does it himself at his own expense. Turn where you will you see evidences of his generosity, enterprise and public spirit, and where is his reward? Go and ask every citizen of Wolcott and you can't find a man of any character but has a fellow feeling in his bosom for Hon. Isaac Leavenworth. We never knew till this visit that one man could so wholly engross the good will of a whole village as does this gentleman. We were delighted to find that the people so generally appreciated his worth and we sincerely hoped that every rich man could walk through his own village amid so much love and respect, and feel the happiness of dispensing the bounties which God has showered upon them during their life time, instead of waiting till after death, when there is no choice but to leave their riches behind, Never did we more realize the text "Inasmuch as ye do it unto one of these little ones, ye do it unto me." Nor that great commandment of our Savior's, "Love thy neighbor as thyself."

159. SALLY LEAVENWORTH.[5]—ASA,[4] THOMAS,[3] THOMAS[2], THOMAS.[1]

Born March 14, 1788, at Watertown, Conn.

Married Jeremiah Magraugh, December 2, 1812. He died November 11, 1850. She died September 19, 1863. Married at Canaan, Columbia Co. N. Y. Died at Wellington, O.

CHILDREN.

1. MARY, b. September 11, 1813, m. John M. Tuttle November 8, 1832. She d. at Wolcott, N. Y., November 4, 1841.

2. Asa, b. July 12, 1815, d. December 2, 1817.
3. Elizabeth, b. June 9, 1818, married, first, Joseph Webster, June 15, 1841. He was b.———, d. April 2, 1845. Married, second, Thomas Stewart, September 10, 1853, in Wellington, Ohio.
4. Adaline, b. April 30, 1820, m. Edward S. Tripp, October 19, 1845.
5. John, b. October 11, 1822, m. Sarah A. Elliott, April 2, 1849.
6. Sarah, b. August 10, 1825, married, first, John A. Nightingale April 20, 1851. He d. October 2, 1851; m., second, James A. Hutchinson June 29, 1853. Resides in Pittsfield, Mass.

160. John Leavenworth.[5] — Gideon[4], Thomas,[3] Thomas[2], Thomas.[1]

Born September 10, 1775, at Watertown, Conn.

Married Rachel Tamer October 17, 1799, of Watertown, Ct. She was born May 11, 1775. He lived first at New Haven, then at Hamden, and was a carriage maker. Then moved to Towanda, Pa., in 1812, and about three years after to Genoa, N. Y. He was a contractor on the Erie canal at Clyde, where he died August 27, 1822. His wife died December 14, 1848, at Genoa, N. Y. Remains removed to Rushville.

CHILDREN.

365. Mira, b. November 30, 1800, d. June 6, 1817, at Genoa, unmarried.

366. Lucius. b. May 1, 1802, m. Hannah Gates. He d. in 1863, at Trumansburg, N. Y.

367. Caroline, b. February 19, 1806.

368. Harriet, b. June 5, 1807, d. April 10, 1822, at Clyde, N.Y.

369. Betsey, b. November 28, 1808.

370. Mary Eliza, b. February 12, 1812.

371. Rachel, b. September 17, 1815.

All born at New Haven, except Rachel, who was born at Towanda.

161. Jared Leavenworth.[5] — Gideon,[4] Thomas,[3] Thomas[2], Thomas.[1]

Born March 8, 1780, at Watertown, Conn.

Married, first, May 2, 1800, Mary Osborn, of Hotchkisstown, near New Haven. She was born at New Haven, August 30, 1782. She died at Savannah, Georgia, September 9, 1812.

Married, second, February 3, 1814, Jane Strope, of Wysox, Pa. She was born at Wysox, Bradford Co., Pa., February 16,

1792. She died December 31, 1841, at Towanda, Pa. He died and was buried at Albany, N. Y., May 30, 1829, but was then a resident of Philadelphia, and was a contractor on the Delaware and Chesapeake canal. His business was that of a contractor on public works, and he had been so engaged on the Erie canal.

CHILDREN.

372. SUSANNA, b. March 16, 1801, at Hamden, Conn., d. September 12, 1802, at New Haven Conn.
373. SUSANNA, b. October 18, 1804, at New Haven, Conn.
374. HENRIETTA, b. January 12, 1806, " " "
375. MATILDA E., b. March 31, 1816, at Genoa, d. January 23, 1844, unmarried, at her aunt's, Catharine Hewitt, East Genoa, N. Y.
376. ELMA ANN, b. July 31, 1818, d. April 15, 1822, at Clyde, while her father was there as a contractor.
377. FRANKLIN JAMES, b. January 24, 1827, in Delaware City, Del., while his father was engaged on the Delaware and Chesapeake canal.

162. MARY LEAVENWORTH.[5]—GIDEON,[4] THOMAS,[3] THOMAS[2], THOMAS.[1]

Born July 17, 1784, at Watertown, Conn.

Married Jonathan Pitcher, the fourteenth child of James P., of Washington, Conn. He died at Wabash, on the Wabash river, in 1825. She married, second, Stephen Allen, of Woodbury, and died March 7, 1870, at Woodbury, Ct., leaving no other child than Jared L. She was aged eighty-six years, seven months and seven days.

CHILDREN.

1. JARED L., b. April 20, 1808, at Oxford, Conn. ; m. February 15, 1836, Mary daughter of Thomas and Polly Adams, at Pittsford Vt.

Children.

1. MIRA L., b. in Naugatuck August, 1839, d. August 13, 1870, at North Pownal, Vt.

J. Pitcher moved from Oxford to Hamden before Jared L.'s recollection; then to Towanda, Pa. Jared L. resides at North Pownal Vt., and is a storehouse of traditions and family legends, handed down largely from his grandfather, Gideon.

163. Joseph Leavenworth.[5]—SAMUEL,[4] THOMAS,[3] THOMAS[2], THOMAS.[1]

Born September 16, 1773.

Married TAMER, daughter of Benjamin Prichard, January 12,

1797. Still living in her 94th year, 1870. Retained the homestead in Waterbury. He died April 3, 1866, at Waterbury.

CHILDREN.

378. HARRIET, born November 19, 1798, m. William Lockwood of Watertown, d. July 17, 1870.
379. HANNAH P., b. September 16, 1800, m. Lyman Bradley January 20, 1820, d. February 25, 1864.
380. JOSEPH STANLEY, b. December 2, 1802, d. Dec. 28, 1841.
381. SAMUEL E., b. August 11, 1805, d. February 20, 1814.
382. REBECCA, b. February 9, 1811, m. William R. Hotchkiss, of Watertown, d. April 11, 1838.
383. MARY G., b. September 6, 1814, m. William Newton.
384. SARAH ANN, b. August 9, 1817, m. Joseph Wheeler.

All born in Waterbury, Conn.

164. TRYPHENA LEAVENWORTH.[5]—SAMUEL,[4] THOMAS[3], THOMAS,[2] THOMAS.[1]

Born September 16, 1775, at Waterbury, Conn.

Married Ephraim Warner, —— 1798, at Waterbury. He was born July 3, 1775, and died at Summit, Schoharie Co., N. Y., February 20, 1815. She died January 28, 1854, at Phoenix, Oswego county, N. Y. They removed to Schoharie Co., N. Y., where he was émployed as a machinist and millwright.

CHILDREN.

1. PHILA, b. March 27, 1799, in Waterbury, d. March 13, 1813, in Schoharie Co
2. REBECCA, b. March 28, 1801, in Waterbury, m. —— ——, a farmer, and d. in the township of Van Buren, Iowa, September 9, 1845.
3. BENNET, b. July 28, 1806, in Summit, N. Y., was a carpenter, and d. September 20, 1835, in Medina, Ohio.
4. WILLIAM, b. March 6, 1809, in Summit, N. Y., is a tailor and resides at Fulton, N. Y. His youngest son starved to death in Andersonville prison October 10, 1864. He was captured at Plymouth, N. C., was wounded on the head by a fragment of a shell, and lived from April 20, 1864, a prisoner in the hands of the rebels.
5. EPHRAIM, b. February 9, 1811. Removed to Alexandria, Mo., and was a contractor; was in the Confederate service.

165. HANNAH LEAVENWORTH.[5]—SAMUEL,[4] THOMAS[3], THOMAS,[2] THOMAS.[1]

Born October 3, 1779, at Waterbury, Conn.

Married David Baldwin January 30, 1800, at Waterbury. He was a carpenter, joiner and farmer. He was born December 29, 1775. Died March 15, 1842. She died May 14, 1863.

CHILDREN.

1. LOVISA, b. November 15, 1800, d. November 14, 1813.
2. MELISSA, b. June 17, 1803, m. Garry Hull, of Waterbury.

3. JULIA, b. July 5, 1805, m. Samuel D. Chipman, of Waterbury.
4. DENISON, b. April 30, 1811, d. November 20, 1813.
5. DAVIS, b. November 19, 1815, unmarried ; lives where his father did.

Melissa Baldwin, b. June 17, 1803, m. February 15, 1825, Garry Hull, farmer, of Waterbury. He d. May 26, 1865, b. January 10, 1804.

Children.

1. ELLEN L., b. April 30, 1826, m. August 31, 1847, Beri J. Bristol, of Waterbury. He d. August 11, 1864.
2. HARRIET M., b. May 7, 1828, m. November 29, 1847, Burritt H. Lewis. *Children*—Harriet A., b. May 28, 1850 ; Ida M., b. October 25, 1857.
3. STYLES D., b. November 19, 1830, d. March 22, 1832.
4. DAVID B., b. February 21, 1833, m. October 7, 1855, Harriet A. Lines. *Children*—John B., b. May 7, 1862.
5. JOHN L., b. January 22, 1838, d. April 1, 1858.

Julia Baldwin. b. July 5, 1805, m. April 21, 1828, Samuel D. Chipman, of Waterbury, farmer. He was b. December 29, 1804.

Children.

1. MARTHA A., b. July 30, 1832, unmarried.
2. JOHN B., b. March 18. 1836, m. October 4, 1856, Mary A. Hoffman. She was b. April 22, 1841. *Children*—1. Mary J., b. January 29, 1858. 2. Irwin F., b. July 24, 1862. 3. Samuel A., b. March 15, 1870.
3. HENRY M., b. April 19, 1840, m. Emma E. Wooster, December 6, 1868. She was b, March 2, 1844.

All the above lived in Waterbury, Conn.

166. Samuel Leavenworth.[5]—SAMUEL,[4] THOMAS,[3] THOMAS[2], THOMAS.[1]

Born December 28, 1783, at Waterbury, Conn.

Married ESTHER PARDEE January 1, 1804, daughter of Jonathan Pardee. She died May 16, 1850, at Ann Arbor, Mich. He died December 12, 1868, at the same place. She was born September 11, 1783.

CHILDREN.

385. LYMAN, b. February 5, 1805, in Waterbury, Conn.
386. BETSEY, b. February 8, 1808, " m. Philip Baker.
387. DAVIS, b. April 23, 1810, at Genoa, Cayuga Co., N. Y.
388. JOSEPH, b. August 10, 1813, d. 1815, at Prattsburg, N. Y. where he was born.
389. MARY. b. February 14, 1817, at Pike, N. Y., unmarried.
390. EDMUND, b. November 5, 1820, at Prattsburg.
391. JOSEPH, b. July 7, 1822, at Prattsburg.
392. SAMUEL, b. July 20, 1825, d. January 4, 1826, at Batavia, N. Y.. where he was born.

167. SALLY LEAVENWORTH.[5] — SAMUEL,[4] THOMAS[3], THOMAS,[2] THOMAS.[1]

Born December 10, 1789.

Married Hector W. Baird April 10, 1810, at Waterbury, Conn., a farmer. She is still living at Waterbury, (Oakville). He died at Bridgeport some years since.

CHILDREN.

1. SAMUEL, b. January 25, 1811, m. Harriet Blakeslee, d. April 26, 1856, no ch.
2. DAVID, b. October 3, 1816, d. October 20, 1845, unmarried.
3. JOSEPH H., b. December 9, 1827, m. Myra Paul February 27, 1854, machinist, at Oakville, Waterbury. *Ch.*—LENA, b. May 24, 1855.

168. Meigs Leavenworth.[5] — ABEL,[4] THOMAS,[3] THOMAS[2], THOMAS.[1]

Born March 27, 1794.

He was an invalid from his birth, and never married. His father deeded him eighty acres of land, in Charlotte, on account of his want of health, which, after the loss of his mills, etc., became the support and home of the family.

169. Miner Leavenworth.[5] — ABEL,[4] THOMAS[3], THOMAS[2], THOMAS.[1]

Born May 31, 1796, at Hinesburgh.

Married MARY MYERS September 15, 1841, daughter of John Myers, of Bristol, Vt. She was born March 29, 1796, on the Mohawk, and died at Bristol April 20, 1854, beloved and respected. He resides in Bristol, and is a miller by occupation. He followed his business in Vermont and northern New York, for some years, then purchased a mill in Bristol, and married. He has no children. He is a good citizen, and shows in his daily life, his christian purity and integrity.

171. Abel Leavenworth.[5]—ABEL,[4] THOMAS,[3] THOMAS,[2] THOMAS.[1]

Born November 24, 1800, at Charlotte, Vt.

Married January 12, 1826, ANNA HICKOK, daughter of Amos Hickok and Anna Foote, grand-daughter of Dr. Samuel H., of Cooperstown, N. Y. She was born at Washington, Conn., December 13, 1802, and died at Charlotte, Vt., December 19, 1849. She was a woman of rare worth, and of superior culture and information for her times, and was devoted to the work of training her children in the fear of the Lord, and for lives of usefulness.

CHILDREN.

393. INFANT SON, b. August 22, 1826, d. same day.

394. " b. August 18, 1827, " "

395. ABEL EDGAR, b. September 3, 1828. Lives at New Haven, Vt.

396. LYDIA ANNA, b. Jnne 28, 1830. Lives at Charlotte, Vt.

397. LOUISA MILLER, b. July 10, 1832. Lives at Saginaw, Mich.

398. LUCY JANE, b. August 26, 1834, d. November 19, 1865, at Decker, Ill.

399. CHARLOTTE LAURA, b. August 17, 1837. Lives at Carlyle, Ill.

400. SARAH SABRINA, b. February 17, 1840. Lives at Carlyle.

401. MARY AMY, b. June 6, 1842, d. at Madrid, N. Y., March 21, 1843.

The last five were born in Madrid, N. Y., the others in Charlotte, Vt.

After the death of his father in 1813, he, in connection with his mother, was largely the support of the family. By his own labor at fourteen, he purchased a yoke of steers and helped clear the eighty acres of his brother Meigs. His mother resided with him, for the most part, till her death. His house was always a home for all the family. For a few years in early life, he was a marble manufacturer at the old mill site of his father's. He then purchased of his father-in-law, the old farm of his father's, where he was born, and afterwards re-sold it to Mr. H., and purchased a farm in Madrid, N. Y., where he resided twelve years, till 1844, enjoying the confidence and respect of the community, when, on account of the health of his family, he returned to Charlotte, and finally re-purchased the old farm of his father's, on which he still resides, enjoying the good-will of all his neighbors, and often holding places of trust and honor, but declining a seat in the Legislature, as not suited to his tastes and pursuits.

After the death of his first wife in 1849, he married Mary Elizabeth Joslyn, April 10, 1851, at Charlotte, widow of Samuel C. Alexander, of Williston, Vt., born at Essex, Vt., April 11, 1817; married Samuel C. A., May 29, 1835. By him she had three sons and one daughter. One son died at twelve, and two gave their lives to their country, in the Sixth and Tenth Vermont regiments, in the army of the Potomac. Samuel C. A. died September 13, 1842.

Abel Leavenworth and Mary Elizabeth Joslyn had three children, all born at Charlotte, Vt.

402. MARY ELIZABETH, b. February 11, 1852, d. December 25, 1866, at Charlotte.

403. AMY JEANNETTE, b. August 9, 1854; student and teacher.

404. ELLA MARIA, b. December 6, 1856, d. December 23, 1867 at Charlotte.

172. SABRINA LEAVENWORTH.[5] — ABEL,[4] THOMAS[3], THOMAS,[2] THOMAS.[1]

Born April 1, 1803, at Charlotte, Vt.

Married John Matthews, at Madrid, N. Y., January 14, 1841. He was a widower, of Norfolk, N. Y., with a large family. She resides in Burlington, Vt.

CHILDREN.

1. SABRINA JANE, b. at Norfolk, N. Y., October 27, 1841. Resides now at Burlington, Vt., and her mother with her. She keeps a boarding house.

Mrs. Matthews was treated so badly by her husband that at the expiration of two years she left him, went to Hinesburg, and devoted herself to the care and education of her daughter Sabrina.

She commenced life as a teacher, and then became a milliner at the village of Columbia in the town of Madrid, St. Lawrence Co., where her brother Abel resided, and from there removed to Belleville, in Canada. She was so much interested and active in aiding the patriots in 1840, that she thought it prudent to return to Columbia.

Sabrina Jane Matthews married John Henry Ray, of Hinesburg, Vt., by whom she had one child, Elizabeth Jane.

174. Arza Leavenworth.[5] — ABEL,[4] THOMAS,[3] THOMAS,[2] THOMAS.[1]

Born July 18, 1809, at New Haven, Vt.

Married MARY CLAFLIN, December 17, 1834, at Middlebury, Vt., born in Charlotte January 31, 1816. Died February 3, 1856, at Norfolk, St. Lawrence Co., N. Y.

He was a blacksmith and learned his trade at Charlotte. Resided at Madrid before going to Norfolk, in the village of Columbia. Moved from Vermont in 1835, to Madrid. Remained three years, and then moved to Norfolk.

CHILDREN.

405. HENRY ARZA, b. October 19, 1835, at Madrid, St. Lawrence Co., N. Y.

406. Sidney Burk, b. August 5, 1841, at Norfolk, St. L. Co.

Mary Clafiin was the daughter of Clark Claflin and Polly Whitney, both of New Hampshire. She was born at Hancock, Vt., January 31, 1816. Her father afterwards lived in New Haven, Vt. She lives now at Sandy Creek, N. Y., with her two sons.

By a change in the channel of the New Haven river in the town of New Haven during the night between the 26th and 27th of July, 1830, several buildings containing families were isolated and afterward swept away by the waters. Of the twenty-one persons who were thus surprised and washed away, seven only escaped, the remaning fourteen found a watery grave. Mr. Claflin's home was one of those isolated,and threatened with destruction. On finding his dwelling surounded, he fled with his family to the chambers. Fortunately a large tree stood near the house, whose branches could be reached from the chamber windows. Mr. Claflin passed his family into the branches of this tree, where they passed a night of sleepless terror. Mary was one of these children. Fortunately the main current did not strike the house, or uproot the tree and in the morning they were all rescued from their danger.

176. Isaac Leavenworth.[5]—Thomas,[4] Thomas,[3] Thomas[2], Thomas.[1]

Born October 9, 1791.

Married November 8, 1812, Ruth Clark, who was born July 30, 1793, died July 29, 1864. He was a blacksmith. His three sons were auger makers at West Haven.

CHILDREN.

407. Levi C., b. April 12, 1814, d. June 3, 1814.
408. Edmund S., b. October 1, 1815.
409. Caroline E., b. February 26, 1818.
410. John L., b. December 15, 1821, d. February 24, 1859.
411. Clark, b. May 12, 1827, lived at Chester.

177. Calvin Leavenworth.[5]—Thomas,[4] Thomas,[3] Thomas,[2] Thomas[1].

Born March 9, 1793, at Derby, Conn.

Married, first, Sophia Wooster, in Oxford, Conn., 1812. She was born May 25, 1795. She died September 20, 1839.

Married, second, Esther Beecher, in Oxford, Conn., September, 1840. She died April 11, 1857.

Married, third, Mary Wooster, of Oxford, Conn., December 25, 1859. She had no children.

He was drafted into the army in 1813. Was a shoemaker and afterwards a farmer; lived at Pine's Bridge, Oxford, Conn , and died April 8, 1861.

CHILDREN.

412. David J., b. November 24, 1813.
413. Eliza, b. February 29, 1816, m. Elisha Wheeler, of Southbury.
414. Thomas B., b. December 14, 1821, (his sister Eliza says 1820.
415. Maria, b. November 23, 1822.
416. George, b, January 30, 1826.
417. Calvin Bennet, b. September 11, 1829.
418. Julia S., b. August 1, 1846. She married March 23, 1869.
419. Sarah, b. October 1849. Lives with Calvin B., in Iowa.
420. Mary R., b. in 1851, d. February 21, 1854.

All born at Oxford.

178. POLLY LEAVENWORTH.[5]—Thomas,[4] Thomas,[3] Thomas[2], Thomas[1]

Born 1802 to '4. Married Erastus Johnson, of Ohio.

Removed to Ohio. She lived at Charlotte, Vt., from about fourteen years of age, till she was about twenty-one, with Amos Tomlinson, and then returned to Connecticut, and a few years after was married.

179. SARAH LEAVENWORTH.[5] — Thomas,[4] Thomas[3], Thomas,[2] Thomas.[1]

Born before 1800. Married Philemon Treat, of Oxford, Conn., clockmaker.

CHILDREN.

1. Philo.
2. Horace.
3. Polly.
4. Henry.
5. Sarah.
6. Rosette.

180. ROSETTE LEAVENWORTH.[5] — THOMAS,[4] THOMAS,[3] THOMAS[2], THOMAS.[1]

Born ——— ——. Married Samuel Slee Thompson, of Stamford, Duchess Co., N. Y, Farmer, removed to Rockford, Ill. Has several children.

1. OTHO, b. ———

181. BETSEY LEAVENWORTH.[5] — THOMAS,[4] THOMAS,[3] THOMAS,[2] THOMAS.[1]

Born —— ———. Married —— Straw. Removed to Ohio,

CHILDREN OF SECOND WIFE.

182. MARIA LEAVENWORTH.[5] — THOMAS,[4] THOMAS,[3] THOMAS[2], THOMAS.[1]

Born May 29, 1828, at Huntington, Vt.

Married Elander Stevens, of Hopkinton, St. Lawrence Co., N. Y. Cabinet maker; he was born in 1813.

CHILDREN.

1. AMANDA MARIA, b. in 1857, in Hopkinton.
2. DELILAH, b. in 1863, "
3. MARIA L., b. in 1865 "
4. RUFUS, b. in 1867, " d. in 1869, aged 18 months.

183. Seth Leavenworth.[5] — THOMAS,[2] THOMAS[3], THOMAS,[2] THOMAS.[1]

He enlisted during the rebellion in one of the Vermont regiments, and when last heard from was still in Vermont, unmarried.

184. Mark Leavenworth.[5]—THOMAS,[4] THOMAS,[3] THOMAS[2], THOMAS.[1]

Born April 5, 1814, at Huntington, Vt. Is a farmer.

Married EUNICE SPRAGUE October 16, 1836, at Huntington. He formerly lived in Stockholm, St. Lawrence Co., N. Y. Now in Brandon, Franklin Co. P. O. address, Bangor. Lives about three miles from there. He has three children and has lost seven.

CHILDREN.

421. BETSEY, b. November 4, 1837, at Huntington, Vt., m. William McIntosh.

422. JAMES, b. February 3, 1845, at Bangor, Franklin Co., N.Y.

423. HENRY, b. August 13, 1850, at Brandon, " " "

185. RUTH LEAVENWORTH.[5]—THOMAS,[4] THOMAS,[3] THOMAS,[2] THOMAS.[1]

Born in the year 1815, d. January 1, 1839, aged twenty-three.

Married Judson Wakefield, of Williston, Vt., a farmer, son of Isaiah W., who was born November 12, 1777, and d. August 4, 1814. Judson Wakefield was born May 12, 1808, in Vt., d. in Stockholm.

CHILDREN.

1. JANE, b· ——, d. in Stockholm.
2. CHARLES, b. ——, d. in Stockholm.
3. ORRIN, b. in Stockholm October 10, 1838.

He is a carpenter; now in California, unmarried, at Timber Cove, Sonoma Co., Cal.

186. MARY LEAVENWORTH.[5]—THOMAS,[4] THOMAS,[3] THOMAS,[2] THOMAS.[1]

Born in 1818, at Huntington, Vt.

Married Isaac Staples February 2, 1861, a farmer of the town of Parishville, St. Lawrence Co., N. Y. She resides in Hopkinton and has no family.

187. MINERVA LEAVENWORTH.[5]— THOMAS,[4] THOMAS,[3] THOMAS,[2] THOMAS.[1]

Born in 1819, died December 25, 1863, aged forty-four.

Married Judson Wakefield in 1842; a farmer. He died at Stockholm December 9, 1855, in his forty-eighth year, and was born May 12, 1808.

CHILDREN.

1. CHARLES A., b. October 4; 1842, and lives in Hopkinton, N. Y.
2. CLARINDA, b. April 1, 1846.
3. LUCY L., b. April 26, 1850.
4. CARRIE M., b. December 8, 1854.

The last three live at Oxford Mills, Canada West.

188. BETSEY LEAVENWORTH.[5]—DORMAN,[4] THOMAS,[3] THOMAS,[2] THOMAS.[1]

Born October 17, 1796, in Oxford, Conn. Removed with her father's family to Vermont in 1808.

Married William Orson Barker January 2, 1817, in Charlotte, Vt. He was a son of William, who died at Champlain, N. Y., August 22, 1796, in the twenty-sixth year of his age. He was born at Champlain, N. Y., July 6, 1795. He dealt extensively in horses in early life, taking them from Vermont to the Hartford market. He lived mostly in Charlotte, where he subsequently devoted his time principally to agriculture. He died November 10, 1862, and his wife Betsey died November 27, 1867.

CHILDREN.

1. WILLIAM ORSON, b. May 12, 1818, d. August 9, 1835.
2. SARAH JENNETTE, b. February 3, 1820.
3. HARRY, b. March 12, 1822, d. April 16, 1822.
4. ALONZO HICKOK, b. March 6, 1823.
5. DORMAN, b. July 3, 1825, d. May 16, 1826.
6. LUCY ANN, b. February 24, 1827.
7. JANE LYDIA, b. February 1, 1830.

8. DORMAN LEAVENWORTH, b. February 6, 1832, d. August 9, 1835.
9. GEORGE CASE, b. March 25, 1835, d. August 3, 1835.
10. ORSON, b. August 17, 1840, d. August 18, 1840.

189. Burk Leavenworth.[5]—DORMAN[4], THOMAS,[3] THOMAS,[2] THOMAS.[1]

Born January 29, 1801, at Oxford, Conn. Removed to Vermont in 1808.

Married, first, CHARLOTTE SHERMAN, December 28, 1825. She was a daughter of George Sherman, farmer of Charlotte, and was born November 27, 1806. She died October 11, 1860.

Married, second, MRS. RACHEL BARTON, February 25, 1863. She was the widow of ——— Barton, and daughter of Elijah Alexander, of Charlotte; farmer. She was born June 2, 1814.

He represented Charlotte in the Vermont Legislature two years—1842-3. He was also a Justice of the Peace. A man of character, standing, and a large farmer.

CHILDREN.

424. HENRY CLAY, b. July 28, 1827.

190. LUCY LEAVENWORTH.[5] — DORMAN,[4] THOMAS[3], THOMAS,[2] THOMAS.[1]

Born October 16, 1804, at Oxford Conn. Removed with her father's family to Charlotte, Vt., in 1808.

Married Isaac Sherwood —— 1822, at Charlotte. He was born November 5, 1797, in Herkimer county; N. Y., and was a son of Jeremiah S., a farmer, who died at Geneva, N. Y., in 1822.

Isaac S, was a clothier, and ran a woolen factory in Hinesburg, Vt., for a few years, then went to Burlington, Vt., and kept an auction store; was deputy sheriff of Chittenden Co., Vt., several years, and about 1855 removed West. He resides, 1867, at Fond du Lac, Wis., and is in the auction and commission business with his son Edwin.

CHILDREN.

1. WILLIAM HENRY, b. April 6, 1823.
2. BURK, b. July 29, 1825.
3. EDWIN, b. February 25, 1828.
4. RALPH, b. March 27, 1830.
5. LUCY JANE, b. March 25, 1834.
6. MARY ANN, b. March 5, 1837.
7. EMELINE ELIZA, b. March, 29, 1839.
8. GUY, b. May, 23, 1840. Enlisted in the Union Army and was killed in the battle of Gaines Mills, Va. June, 28, 1862.

191. Abijah Leavenworth.[6]—Gideon[4], Edmund[3], Thomas[2], Thomas.[1]

Born October 23, 1780, at Huntington.

Married Alpha Dinah Beardslee, of Huntington, February 6, 1808. He died at Huntington, Conn., October 12, or 14, 1835 She died December 25, 1835, both at Huntington. He represented the town of Huntington in the Legislature in 1821. He and his wife are buried at the White Hills.

CHILDREN.

425. Fanny Maria, b. October 15, 1808, at Huntington.
426. Emeline Eliza, b. January 11, 1812, d. January 19, 1834.

192. NANCY LEAVENWORTH.[5] — Gideon,[4] Edmund,[3] Thomas,[2] Thomas.[1]

Born April 19,1782' at Ripton

Married January 6,1805, Nathan Shepherd of Newtown, Conn. Mrs. Shepherd died at Derby March 21, 1827, aged 45, and was buried at White Hills. Mr. S. died March 31, 1858, aged 81, and was buried at the same place.

CHILDREN.

1, Truman, b. May 18, 1806, m. December 25, 1839, Mary Ann Webster, who was b. March 15, 1819, d. February 25, 1866.

Children.

1· Zilpha, b, April 28, 1841.
2. Mary Ann, b. April 15, 1843-5.
3. Truman, b. June 25, 1848, d. April 18, 1849.
4. Naaman, b. April 20, 1850. All born at Roxbury.

Truman Shepherd is a widower and lives in Roxbury. Zilpha married Charles Bradley, a farmer of Newtown, living in a place called "Ragged Corner". Naaman is a teacher in a school at Sing Sing, N. Y.

2. Sarah, b. November 16, 1807, m. Joel Sherman of Newtown, farmer who was b. December 10, 1800, and had two sons—Charles and Albert, She d. July 25, 1873.

Charles Sherman m. Anna Coles and they had three children. She left him and he procured a divorce. He is a carpenter.

Albert Sherman m. Elizabeth Carr of New Haven. He has gone to parts unknown.

3. Carlos, b· —— lives(1870)at Hamilton, Ohio, unmarried."
4. Caroline, b. May 2, 1815, m. Mason S. Abbott, who is a carriage maker, and lives at Black Rock, Bridgeport, Conn. No children.
5. Augusta, b. February 27, 1817, m. February 22, 1835, Bennett Platt, of Newtown, a farmer and lives there. He was b. October 4, 1800.
6. Eliza, b. —— m. Ephraim Wheeler. She lives in Iowa, a widow.
7. Harriet Nancy, b. December 20, 1820. Lives in New Haven, unmarried.
8. Nathan, b. December 10, 1824, m. Fanny Hill, October 13, 1850. She was b. June 6, 1812. He is a shoemaker.

Children.

1. Carlos, b. June 3, 1852, d. August 18, 1865.
2. Emma. b. January 20, 1855.

The eight children of Nancy L. and Nathan S., were mostly born in Newtown.

194. SALLY LEAVENWORTH.[5] — GIDEON,[4] EDMUND,[3] THOMAS[2], THOMAS.[1]

Born February 6, 1787.

Married James Smith January 6, 1806, and lives now, 1870, with her daughter Sally Hodge, at Roxbury.

CHILDREN.

1. SALLY, b. December 20, 1806, at Newtown. Married Philo N. Hodge, of Roxbury, November 19, 1835. Had two sons and one daughter,—
   1. BRUCE, b. December 25, 1836.
   2. ELLEN, b. March 5, 1843.
   3. CHARLES, b. November 12. 1844, d. October 30, 1860.
2. ELIZA, b. January 15, 1811, d. young.

195. BETSEY LEAVENWORTH.[5] — GIDEON,[4] EDMUND[3], THOMAS,[2] THOMAS.[1]

Born June 13, 1789, at Huntington, Conn.

Married (1,) January 25, 1807, Elisha Patterson, b. at Oxford, January 27, 1777. He died at Roxbury, October 21, 1826, aged forty-nine.

Married, second, February 26, 1833, at Roxbury, Enos Stoddard, of Litchfield.

CHILDREN.

1. JENNETTE, b. August 30, 1807, m. Samuel Tomlinson, of Woodbury, November 8, 1827. He died. They had five children—two sons and three daughters :—

   1. JANE. 2. BETSEY. 3. ELISHA. 4. HOMER. 5. ELLEN, who is d.

In 1870 she was a widow, living at Woodbridge.

2. ANGELINE, b. January 14, 1812, m. Edwin C. Prindle, of Roxbury, February 20, 1833, and has had three children :—

   1. JULIA E., d. 2. CYRUS E. P. 3. IDA A. P.

Mr. Prindle represented the town of Roxbury in the Legislature of 1869.

3. ABIGAIL, b. January 8, 1815, m. Thomas W. Sanford, of Roxbury, December 4, 1839, and had two sons aud two daughters : —

1. ELLIOTT. 2. ANDREW. 3. MAHALA, d. 4. MARY ANN, d.

Thomas W. Sanford died, and she married, second, Henry Peck, of Woodbury.

4, SARAH MARIA, b. Juue 16, 1820, m. Deacon Truman H. Judson, of Woodbury, June 16, 1842. They live in Roxbury, or Woodbury, and have two sons—Franklin and Albert,

196. FANNY LEAVENWORTH.[5] — GIDEON,[4] EDMUND[3], THOMAS,[2] THOMAS.[1]

Born June 28, 1791, at Huntington

Married Birdseye Thompson, January 14, 1811. He was born July 17, 1786, and died at Bridgeport October 9, 1857. Son of David and Rachel Thompson.

CHILDREN.

1. CUMPHY MARIA, b. June 4, 1812, m. —— ——
2. WILLIAM HENRY, b. May 31, 1814, m. November 23, 1848, Caroline Curtiss of Bridgeport.
3. SARAH ANN, b. October 26, 1817, m. July 4, 1842, Daniel Hoadley, of Ansonia.
4. JENETTE ADELINE, b, March 28, 1819, m. November 22, 1842, P. H. Sperry of Bridgeport.
5. BETSEY, b. March 6, 1820, m. November 10, 1845, Frederick Godfrey, of Bridgeport.
6. GEORGE, b. July 29, 1822, m. first, November 19, 1846, Delia Smith; m. second, June 12, 1865, Harriet T. Sacwell.
7. BIRDSEYE, b. February 10, 1824, m. March 11, 1866, Josephine Hawley. He d. February 1, 1869. She d. October 18, 1870, yged 28 years.
8. MARIETTA, b. March 31, 1829, m. September 28, 1848, George Hurd, and had two children, then obtained a divorce, and is now m. second, to Lafield, of Bridgeport.

197. Mark Eli Leavenworth.[5]—GIDEON,[4] EDMUND,[3] THOMAS,[2] THOMAS.[1]

Born April 22, 1801, in Huntington; was a blacksmith.

Married CATHARINE THIRZA BEARDSLEE, of Huntington, March —— 1824. She died April 14 or 23, 1865, at Newtown, Conn. Resides at Newtown.

CHILDREN.

427. ELI, b. August 19, 1824, in Huntington Conn.

428. ABIGAIL, b. April 25, 1826, at Newtown, Conn., d. May 21, 1854.

429. ELIZABETH, b. December 31, 1827, at Newtown, Conn. unmarried.

199. MARY ANN LEAVENWORTH.[5]—GIDEON,[4] EDMUND[3], THOMAS[2], THOMAS[1]

Born November 17, 1805, at Huntington, on the bank of the Housatonic, two miles above Birmingham.

She has spent her life actively and most usefully, engaged in the cause of education. And now, having seen almost her three score and ten, she is still engaged in the same high calling with all the diligence and enthusiasm of her early youth, at Westport, Conn.

200. Gideon Leavenworth.[5]—GIDEON,[4] EDMUND,[3] THOMAS[2], THOMAS.[1]

Born January 30, 1809, at Huntington, Conn.

Married MARTHA ELEANOR DANNELS, of Rochester, N. Y., December 3, 1840. She was the daughter of George Dannels, one of the early settlers of Rochester, and was born July 8. 1816.

CHILDREN.

430. GEORGE GIDEON, b. December 2, 1841.
431. CHARLES FREDERICK, b. October 2, 1845.
432. FRANK BURTON, b. January 21, 1847.
433. BEVIL HULL, b. August 4, 1850, d. in infancy.

All born at Rochester.

434. EMMA, (Adopted child,) b. September 12, 1853. Took the name of Leavenworth.

202. SALLY LEAVENWORTH.[5]—ELI,[4] EDMUND,[3] THOMAS[2], THOMAS.[1]

Born 1780 to 1790, probably. Was born, probably, at the South, soon after the Revolution. Returned to Connecticut soon after her father's death.

Married, first, John Jeffers, and had two sons, and lived many years at Albany. One of her sons was John.

Married, second, King Lampson, and died at Cincinnati.

203. FANNY LEAVENWORTH.[5]—ELI,[4] EDMUND[3], THOMAS,[2] THOMAS.[1]

Born 1780 to 1790. Married Isaac Lum, of Derby, a confectioner, and had five children. She died at Cambridgeport, Mass., about 1868.

CHILDREN.

1. SALLY JENETTE, m. a Faulkner and had one son, Frank, who lived at Derby, and married there, and now lives at Springfield, Mass.
2. ANGELINA, d. young.
3. CHARLOLTE ELIZA, m. Sherman Canfield, of Derby, a merchant, in 1831, and had three children, all of whom d. young. She is still at Derby.
4. ISAAC ELI, lives at Cambridgeport, Mass., and is married.
5. FANNY, m. a Hyde, of Boston, and d. childless.

204. JENETTE LEAVENWORTH.[5] — ELI,[4] EDMUND,[3] THOMAS,[2] THOMAS.[1]

Born 1780 to 1790, at Huntington, or at the South.

Married ——Van Denburgh, on the Hudson river, and had a son, who is dead, and a dau. The son lived at Cincinnati, O., and the daughter at Columbus, O.

205. GRACE LEAVENWORTH.[5]— ELI,[4] EDMUND,[3] TOHMAS[2], THOMAS[1].

Born at Huntington, probably during the Revolution.

Went South with her father, and soon after returned to Conn.,—soon after her father's death; married, September 4, 1794, Enoch Johnson, at Woodbury.

CHILDREN.

1. SEYMOUR, b. May 11, 1795, at Woodbury.
2. MARSHALL, b. December 20, 1797, at Woodbury. See Cothren's Woodbury, p. 602.

Mrs. David Shelton, of Huntington, says Eli had no daughter Grace. If so, whose daughter was the Grace mentioned by Mr. Cothren?

207. POLLY LEAVENWORTH.[5] — EDMUND,[4] EDMUND[3], THOMAS,[2] THOMAS.[1]

Born August 27, 1789, at Huutington.

Married March 6, 1809, Azariah Hawley Perry, of Oxford, farmer. He died November 21, 1826, at Huntington, where he always lived after his marriage, aged forty-six years. He was born September 21, 1780, at Oxford, son of Yelverton Perry and Patience Tomlinson. Polly Leavenworth died May 31, 1871, aged eighty-one years.

CHILDREN.

1. JANE P., b. March 18, 1811, at Huntington; m. David Shelton, of Huntington, May 4, 1830. He was the son of Agur Shelton and Abigail Newton, who was the daughter of the Rev. Christopher Newton, an Episcopal clergyman. David Shelton d. June 2, 1872, at Huntington, aged seventy-two. They had one child, a daughter, b. February 8, 1833, at Huntington—Mary Jane. She m. Edwin Wooster, son of Sheldon Wooster and Sally Hull, of Oxford, May 23, 1860. She died at Huntington June 4, 1864, childless.

Mr. and Mrs. Perry were buried at the White Hills, but their daughter and only child, Mrs. Jane P. Shelton, purposes soon (1873) to remove their remains to Birmingham.

Mrs. Shelton still resides at the hospitable mansion of her late husband, about a mile west of the village of Shelton, and almost midway between the Housatonic and the center of the town of Huntington. She is still the owner of a large part of the farm taken up about 1721, by her great-great-grandfather, Deacon Thomas Leavenworth, the son of the immigrant. She has taken great interest in this work, and has been indefatigable in her efforts to procure every species of valuable information within her reach. Her son-in-law, Mr. Wooster, is still a member of her family.

208. DELILAH LEAVENWORTH.[5]—EDMUND,[4] EDMUND[3], THOMAS,[2] THOMAS.[1]

Born January 1, 1792, at Huntington.

Married April 6, 1823, Joseph Hull Smith, of Derby, who was born in March, 1793, son of Isaac Smith and Elizabeth Hull, the sister of Gen. William Hull, and aunt of Commodore Isaac Hull.

He was first a merchant, then a hotel keeper, and finally retired a farmer—all at Derby. He died in September, 1854. at Derby. Delilah lives, 1872, at Huntington, mostly with her niece, Mrs. Shelton.

CHILDREN.

1. SYLVESTER PERRY, b. September 11, 1826, at Derby, and d. there August 15, 1855. He m. Sarah Bassett, of Seymour, and had two children.
   1. ELIZABETH HULL, b. June 23, 1846, at Derby, m. November 3, 1869, Mansfield J. French, at Seymour, but of New York. Revenue officer, lives at Harlem. She has two sons—1. Edward Leavenworth, b. October 12, 1870, at New York. 2. Mansfield Joseph, b. Feb. 13, 1872.
   2. JOSEPH HULL, b. November 24, 1851, at Seymour. Lives mostly at Huntington, unmarried.

209. MARIA LEAVENWORTH.[5] — EDMUND,[4] EDMUND[3], THOMAS,[2] THOMAS.

Born March 13, 1794, at Huntington.

Married December 30, 1813, David Durand, of Derby; a farmer. Son of Noah Durand and Abigail Tomlinson. David Durand was born May 1, 1790.

CHILDREN,

1. WILLIAM LEAVENWORTH, b. September 2, 1814. He m. Ruth Coe and had four children.
   1. MARY, who d. young.
   2. DAVID, who lives at Waterbury, m., no children.
   3. CYNTHIA, who d. young.
   4. WILLIAM.
2. ELIZABETH MARY, b. March 9, 1816, m. Nelson Beach, of Woodbridge and has seven sons.
   1. EDMUND LEAVENWORTH, now in the Treasury Department at Washington, unmarried.
   2. JOSEPH SMITH, m. Grace Beach, of New Haven; has one child and lives at Harlem.
   3. HENY CLAY, m. Elizabeth Searls, of New York, lives at Bridgeport and has no children.
   4. FREDERICK, unmarried, lives at Derby.
   5. HERMAN, unmarried, engaged in a bank at Bridgeport.
   6. WILLIAM, unmarried, in a telegraph office at New Haven.
   7. NELSON, is at Bridgeport.

Beach was from Derby; lives there, and Mrs. B. also. Children all born there.

3. LAURA ANN, b. July 24, 1820, d. September 2, 1827, at Derby.
4. FREDERICK, b. December 19, 1824; m. first Esther Merwin, who had one daughter, Mary. Esther M. d. about 1866. Married, second, Amorette Wilson, of Winsted, about 1870. No children. Mary is with her father at Derby.
5. MARTHA ANN, b. July 23, 1827, m. Ely T. Nichols in January, 1857, and now lives in Bridgeport, a widow and no children.
6. ALBERT, b. August 29, 1834, and d. in 1836.

All born in Derby, where Maria Durand now lives, a widow. Her husband, a farmer, died there May, 1868.

210. LAURA LEAVENWORTH.[5] — EDMUND,[4] EDMUND[3], THOMAS,[2] THOMAS.[1]

Born September 29, 1796, at Huntington. Died unmarried at Derby, January 22, 1865.

She and Hepsey, her sister, lived with Delilah for many of the last years of their lives, during all of Delilah's married life, and died within four days of each other.

213. BETSEY LEAVENWORTH.[6] — ANDREW,[5] DANIEL,[4] JAMES[3], THOMAS[2], THOMAS.[1]

Born January 19, 1795.

Married John Benedict, of Bethel (set off from Danbury) February 17, 1819. He was born June 10, 1790, and died July 28,1858. He was a cloth manufacturer and afterward a successful farmer. She was living in 1865. He was justice of the peace in 1844-5-7.

CHILDREN.

1. ELIZA, b. April 11, 1820.

2. ANDREW LEAVENWORTH, b. August 13, 1822, m. Ruth A. Allen, daughter of Jared A, of Woodbury, September 22, 1847.

Children.

1. ARTHUR T. 2. JOHN M. 3. URSULA E. 4. FRANK A.

His business has been teaching and farming, trades etc. Now keeps a coal yard in N. Y. city.

3. GEORGE, b. December 26, 1824, m. Ann Grace Colbreath, April 17, 1852.

GEORGE B. a son of George, graduated at Yale Medical School and went with 73d Conn. volunteers as surgeon.

214. Daniel Leavenworth.[6]—ANDREW,[5] DANIEL,[4] JAMES[3], THOMAS,[2] THOMAS.[1]

Born July 18, 1797, at Monroe. He was a hatter and is now a farmer.

Married FLORILLA FAIRCHILD, at Newtown, daughter of Adoniram F.

CHILDREN.

435. SUSAN, b. ——, d. young.
436. GEORGE, b. October 15, 1828, at Monroe, d. November 3, 1859, at Danbury, Conn.
437. ABBEY JANE, b. October 15, 1832, d. December 16, 1863, in Monroe.

Daniel died August 2, 1868.

216. POLLY LEAVENWORTH.[6]—ANDREW,[5] DANIEL[4], JAMES,[3] THOMAS,[2] THOMAS.[1]

Born September 13, 1801, at Monroe.

Married John Edwards, Esq., of Weston, now Easton; a farmer. She died February 9, 1838.

CHILDREN.

1. LEWIS, b. December 14, 1823, m. Lovintha Gregory, of Trumbull. He has three children,—Charles, John and Eva. He is now a farmer.
2. DAVID, b. April 22, 1829, m. Julia Turney, of Easton. Has two children—Lillian and Ella.

Was a merchant, then a farmer. Enlisted in the 23d Conn. Volunteers, and died at New Orleans December 19, 1863. Buried at Easton.

218. Eli Leavenworth.[6]—ANDREW,[5] DANIEL,[4] JAMES[3], THOMAS[2], THOMAS.[1]

Born March 23, 1809, at Monroe.

Married SARAH A. LORD November 24, 1833, at Monroe. She was born in Lyme, Conn., February 15, 1816, but at the time of their marriage lived in Easton. Resides near Stepney, Conn.; farmer and school teacher.

CHILDREN.

438. MARY, b. May 1, 1838.
439. ANDREW, b. August 12, 1840.
440. SYLVIA, b. July 11, 1843, d. September 18, 1865, of typhoid fever. She was teaching when taken with her last sickness.
441. NATHAN, b. June 20, 1849, student, preparing for College.
442. EMMA E., b. December 28, 1851. All born in Monroe.

219. ABBY BETSEY LEAVENWORTH.[6] — EBENEZER[5], JAMES,[4] JAMES[3], THOMAS,[2] THOMAS.[1]

Born September 23, 1780, in Stratford, Conn.

Married Elias Smith, at Kingsboro, N. Y. farmer. Removed to Wisconsin, and afterward to California, where both died.

CHILDREN.

1. SIDNEY, b. —— lost his eyesight when a week old.
2. TREAT, b. —— entered the service of U. S. and died in Florida.
3. JULIA ANN, b. ———m. Jacob VanAlter, farmer.
4. ELIZABETH, b. ——m. ———Williams, a farmer.

220. SALLY PAMELIA LEAVENWORTH.[6] — EBENEZER[5], JAMES,[4] JAMES,[3] THOMAS,[2] THOMAS.[1]

Born May 20, 1783, in Stratford, Conn,

Married Gurdon Parsons March 11, 1801. He died at Kingsboro, N. Y., where they were married October 5, 1848.

CHILDREN.

1. SON, b. March 11, 1802, d. March 11, 1802.
2. MARY ANN, b. August 29, 1806, m. Joseph Wood, February 23, 1826. He was a farmer, then of Greenfield, N. Y., now of Kingsboro, N. Y. He was b. May 13, 1800. They had four children, all now dead, viz:—
   1. JOEL, b. June 4, 1827, d. Aug. 2, 1851; was a partner in a mercantile house in Saratoga at the time of his death.
   2. SAMUEL GURDON, b. September 5, 1834, d. February 28, 1835.
   3. HARLAN PAGE, b. October 21, 1836, d. May 10, 1839.
   4. JOHN HARLAN, b. May 7, 1839, d. May 23, 1860, at Galesburg, Ill., having just entered upon the profession of law. None of these children were married.
3. GURDON LESTER, b. August 28, 1810, d. September 17, 1840. He was a physician.
4. TALMADGE LEAVENWORTH, b. January 13, 1813, m. Jane McGregor September 21, 1841. She was b. August 8, 1814. He d. January 13, 1847. Had one child, Talmadge Lester, b. July 2, 1843, now living and a farmer as was also his father.
5. CAROLINE, b. March 25, 1815, m. Edward Parsons September 3, 1855. He resides in Chicago, and is a merchant.

6. JOHN RANDOLPH, b. May 10, 1817, m. Caroline Mead February 22, 1843, at Kingsboro, N. Y. Resides in Chicago in trade.
7. JANE ALMIRA, b. August 15, 1819, m. David Wilson, of Kingsboro, N. Y., March 22, 1849, and d. October 28, 1849.
8. LEVI, b. July 1, 1822, m. Mary Jane Cuyler September 5, 1861. She was of Fort Plain, N. Y., and was b. December 15, 1834. They reside in California, where he is a lawyer; was one of the first State Judges, and has been engaged in public works in San Francisco.

221. MARY ANN LEAVENWORTH.[6]—EBENEZER,[5] JAMES[4], JAMES,[3] THOMAS[2], THOMAS.[1]

Born July 23, 1786, in Stratford, Conn.

Married Sylvester Judson October 30, 1809, at Kingsboro, N. Y. He was b. March 9, 1788, in ——— Conn., was a farmer.

CHILDREN.

1. LEBBEUS, b. April 9, 1811, d. May 29, 1811, at Kingsboro, N. Y.
2. EBENEZER, b. May 18, 1812. d. September 14, 1834; was a student.
3. GURDON C., b. November 4, 1814, m. Catharine Hardie, February, 1838, Had three daughters and one son. Two are dead. Reside in Boston. Mass., where he is a merchant.
4. SYLVANUS M., b. March 9, 1817, m. Harriet Ann Judson, of Oberlin, O., January 1, 1855. Have a son and a daughter. He is a Congregational minister, and resides in ——, Ohio.
5. MARY ANN L., b. September 15, 1820, m. E. Williams September 15, 1859, who is employed in the Springfield armory.
6. TIRZAH Y., b. October 12, 1821, m. T. Phillips, February, 1839, a manufacturer. Has had three children, two d. young, one son living. She d. January 22, 1851.
7. LUCY, b. July 20, 1824, m. N. Haskins May, 1850, of Simsbury, Conn., a farmer; have three sons and two daughters, oldest aged 19, (1866.)

223. SOPHIA LEAVENWORTH.[6] — EBENEZER,[5] JAMES[4], JAMES,[3] THOMAS[2], THOMAS.[1]

Born December 3, 1790, at Easton, Washington Co., N. Y.

Married Lemuel Heacock May 28, 1817, at Kingsboro, N. Y. He was born October 8, 1786, and was a son of Job Heacock; farmer.

CHILDREN.

1. ABIGAIL, b. February 22, 1818, m. Daniel S. Tarr, of Gloversville, N. Y., manufacturer. Has two sons,—David Henry and Edward.
2. MARGARET, b. January 26, 1820, m. Clinton Leonard, glove manufacturer. Has no children.
3. LEMUEL, b. August 1, 1821, d. December 28, 1821.
4. PHILANDER C., b. December 11, 1823, m. Jennett Thomas. Has a son Lemuel Albert; and a daughter Jennett. He is a glove manufacturer.
5. ROSWELL, b. August 1, 1826, d. December 28, 1821.
6. DAVID G., b. July 14, 1827, m. Jane Ann Van Wycke. Has a son, Eugene, and daughter, Helena. Glove manufacturer.
7. CATHARINE SARAH, b. January 10, 1832, m. C. R. Bellows, cabinet maker. Has an infant son, (1866.)

224. Treat Mills Leavenworth.[6]—EBENEZER,[5] JAMES,[4] JAMES[3], THOMAS[2], THOMAS.[1]

Born August 10, 1793, at Easton, Washington Co., N. Y.

Married CATHARINE ROBERTSON, September 30, 1822. She was b. in Perth, N. Y., in 1791, and was daughter of Robert Robertson, native of Perthshire, Scotland. They were married at Kingsboro. All their children were born in Johnstown, to which place he removed with his parents when an infant. Residence, 1874, Galway, Saratoga Co., N. Y. He inherits the strict Puritan faith and principles of his grandfather, and the hospitality, kindness and benevolence of his father.

CHILDREN.

443. LOUISA JANE, b. August 20, 1823.
444. ANN MERCY, b. January 12, 1825. d. September 15, 1839, in Galway.
445. MARGARET, b. August 28, 1826, d. unmarried, at Amsterdam, at her brother's, Edwin T., July 9, 1872.
446. ELIZABETH. b. December 28, 1828, teacher in a seminary, unmarried.
447. EDWIN TREAT, b. February 21, 1831.
448. SOPHIA JENNETT, b. April 16, 1833, m. Alexander Hegeman.
449. MIRIAM, b. September 16, 1835, d. July 3, 1840, in Galway

225. Eli Leavenworth.[6]—EBENEZER[5], JAMES[4], JAMES,[3] THOMAS[2], THOMAS.[1]

Born April 21, 1796, in Johnstown, (Kingsboro), N. Y.

Married SARAH CLIFTON, November 27, 1817, at Kingsboro. N. Y. She was born of Irish parents, who emigrated to America a short time before her birth, Cctober 24, 1794. Their children were all born in Kingsboro. He died September 28, 1866. He followed in the footsteps of his grandfather, and was most exemplary in his religious life.

CHILDREN.

450. ELEANOR, b. September 23, 1818.
451. EBENEZER, b. March 9, 1820, d. November 11, 1869.
452. WILLIAM CLIFTON, b. December 1, 1825, d. January 7, 1855, unmarried.

226. POLLY LEAVENWORTH.[6] — EBENEZER,[5] JAMES[4], JAMES[3], THOMAS,[2] THOMAS.[1]

Born May 25, 1797, near Kingsboro, N. Y.

Married Daniel McKinlay, at Kingsboro, May, 1, 1833, farmer. He was born February 4, 1794, and was son of John McKinlay, a native of Scotland who emigrated to U. S. before marriage.

CHILDREN.

1, ELIZABETH MCDOUGAL, b. June 25, 1835, in Canada West. m. Jonathan Worden, a miller. They reside at Flamboro, C. W. and have a family of children.
2. JOHN, b. December,14, 1837, d. January 31, 1839.

227. ORILLA LEAVENWORTH.[6] — EBENEZER[5], JAMES[4], JAMES,[3] THOMAS,[2] THOMAS.[1]

Born August 4, 1799, near Kingsboro, N. Y.

Married David Hagadorn, at Kingsboro, N. Y., October 11, 1827. He was son of Harman Hagadorn, of Dutch descent and was born five miles north west of Schenectady August 4, 1800. He was formerly a glove manufacturer and is now a farmer. She died near Beloit, Wis. September 11, 1858.

CHILDREN.

1. HENRY MARTIN, b. October 7, 1829, m. Eliza T. Palmer, October 4, 1855, at house of her father, seven miles north west from Beloit Wis. They reside at Beloit and have one daughter.
2. MARY FRANCES, b. January 7, 1833, m. (1) HenryCochran, (farmer, native of western N. Y.) March 19, 1865. Had a child that d. aged two years. Her husband d. in 1857. She m. second, Israel S. Knowlson, of Byron, Ogle Co., Ill., July 7, 1864. He is a nurseryman, dealing in fruit and shade trees.
3, ELI LEAVENWORTH, b. January 19, 1833.
4. ANN ORRILLA, b. December 2, 1838, m. Orville S. Harmon, January 1, 1862, at Kingsboro, N. Y. He is a glove manufacturer. They have one son, Willard.
5. DAVID TALMAGE, b. October 20, 1839.
6. MIRIAM LEAVENWORTH, b. December 26, 1841. unmarried.

229. HULDAH LEAVENWORTH.[6] — EBENEZER,[5] JAMES,[4] JAMES,[3] THOMAS,[2] THOMAS.[1]

Born April 17, 1805, at the home of her father, two miles north of Kingsboro N. Y.

Married Peter Cough at Kingsboro, April 20, 1826. He was a farmer, and a son of Christopher Cough, and died at or near Kingsboro November 7, 1858. She resides at Kingsboro with her daughter.

CHILDREN.

1. ORILLA, b. about 1826.
2. LOUISA FRANCES, b. about 1829.
3. ABIGAIL ELIZABETH, b. about 1833.

Two of the daughters are very deaf, and the other has long been an invalid.

230. HESTER LEAVENWORTH.[6]—NATHAN,[5] NATHAN[4], DAVID,[3] THOMAS,[2] THOMAS.[1]

Born August 4, 1796, at Hinesburg, Vt.

Married Henry Miller, of Williston, Vt. He was a farmer. She died at Williston, aged sixty-two years, leaving no issue, February 27, 1864. He was a member of the Senate of the State in 1836, and 1837.

His father, Solomon Miller, was a member of the Governor's Council in 1799, 1800-1-2-8-13 and 14. Representative in 1797 ; Clerk of the Courts from 1793, to 1807 inclusive ; Register of Probate from 1801 to 1805 inclusive ; Judge of Probate from 1796 to 1808 inclusive and in 1814.

231. Henry Leavenworth.[6]—Nathan[5], Nathan,[4] David,[3] Thomas[2], Thomas.[1]

Born August 1, 1799, at Hinesburg, Vt. Graduated at the University of Vermont, in 1821, and took his second degree in 1824.

Married Jane Ann Hickok, September 29, 1830. Resided at Burlington, Vt. He was States Attorney for Chittenden Co. in 1842-3; was a member of the State Legislature from Burlington, in 1851, and several years a Director in the Farmers' and Mechanic's Bank at Burlington. He died there May 10, 1854. He had one son who died before being named, and was buried with his mother.

He was a lawyer, a gentleman of high character for intelligence and integrity, but of delicate health. He owned and occupied the fine residence at Burlington, formerly the property of the late Gov. Van Ness.

At a meeting of the Bar of Chittenden county, held the day following his death, the following resolutions, with others, were passed on the report of a committee :—

Resolved, That we learn with deep sorrow, that our friend and brother, Henry Leavenworth, Esq., a member of this Bar, passed from this life yesterday afternoon, at five o'clock.

Resolved, That in his life, as an attorney and counselor, as a neighbor, citizen and friend, he manifested constantly the utmost integrity, and enlarged benevolence, and public spirit, and a devotion to the principles of christianity, which, from early life, he professed, and ever afterwards eminently adorned; and that he has left behind him a life and character marked by as much of good and as little of evil as falls to the lot of man.

Resolved, That we will cherish the memory of his many excellences and virtues, by seeking to reproduce them in our own characters and lives.

He was buried at Burlington, from the Congregational church of which he was an honored member, on the 12th day of May, 1854.

232. Nathan B. Leavenworth.[6]—NATHAN,[5] NATHAN,[4] DAVID[3], THOMAS,[2] THOMAS.[1]

Born July 7, 1801, at Hinesburg, Vt.

Married SAPHINA BURNAM, July 5, 1853. Resides in Hinesburg, Vt. Has no children. He is a farmer.

234. RACHEL LUCRETIA LEAVENWORTH.[6]—NATHAN[5] NATHAN,[4] DAVID,[3] THOMAS.[2] THOMAS.[1]

Born May 14, 1810, at Hinesburg, Vt.

Married Francis Willson December 29, 1831. He was a merchant at Hinesburg, and died September 27, 1864. She is still living, (1874) at Hinesburg, at the old homestead, first occupied by her grandfather, about one mile west of the village. Her mother lives with her.

CHILDREN.

1. LUCRETIA, b. November 9, 1832, m. March 5, 1856, Rev. John B. Perry, A Congregational minister, then of Swanton, now (1870) of the Depart ment of Zoology at Harvard College, Mass.; d. March 28, 1858, leaving one child, Francis Willson Perry, b. February 8, 1857. Rev. John B, Perry d. October 3, 1872, at Cambridge, Mass.
2. HENRY MILLER, b. May 30, 1835, m. Sarah Gregg, of Corning, Steuben Co., N. Y., September 3, 1857. Has a son, Robert Howland, b. at Hinesburg December 26, 1862; and a daughter Mary Lucretia, b. February 7, 1869. His wife died in 1873; he m. second Isadore Hickok, January 28, 1874.

Francis Willson was an Assistant Justice of the County Court, (now called County Judge), in 1840-1. He was for two years a member of the State Senate. He was born at Lancaster, N. H., on the 9th day of October, 1803, and was the son of Francis Willson, a respected physician of that town, and of Temperance Giddings. He died at Hinesburg on the 27th of September, 1864. He was a christian gentleman, and an exemplary and valuable citizen.

John Buckley Perry, was born at Richmond, Berkshire Co., Mass., December 12, 1825. He was the eldest son of Daniel, who was the youngest and eleventh child of the Rev. David Perry, of Richmond, who was the pastor of the Congregational church there for nearly forty years. His mother was Catharine the youngest daughter of Mr. Aylesworth, of Canaan, Columbia Co., N. Y. He was the great-grandson of Joshua Perry and Mary Leavenworth, of Stratford (Ripton parish) Connecticut. See No. 13.

At six years of age his father removed to Burlington, Vt., where he fitted for college at the old Burlington Academy. In 1843, he entered the University of Vermont and was graduated there in 1847, and the same year united with the first Congregational church there.

After spending about three years at the south, teaching and for his health, he entered the Theological Seminary at Andover in 1850, and was graduated there in September 1853.

In 1854, he became the stated supply of the Presbyterian church at Sandlake N. Y., remaining there some seven months, declining to become their pastor. He was then the stated supply at Hinesburg for a few months. In 1855, he accepted a call from the Congregational church at Swanton, Vt. and was ordained and installed there December 12, 1855, over which church he remained eleven years. At the close of his pastorate at S. supplied the church at Wilmington, Vt. for one year, but he declined a call there.

During the later part of the great conflict, he spent some time in the army, first as a delegate in the service of the Christian Commission and afterward as a chaplain of the 10th Vermont regiment. He was present at the taking of Petersburg and also at the surrender of Gen. Lee at Appomattox.

In June 1867, having a desire to continue his studies, he went to Boston, occupying different pulpits until the next autumn. Toward the close of that year, he received through Professor Agassiz, an invitation to a position in the museum of comparative zoology at Harvard College, Cambridge, of which he is the director. Having accepted the situation, he took charge under Professor Agassiz of the department of Paleontology.

During the year 1871, he accepted his appointment as Professor of Sciences and Theology in Oberlin College of Ohio, devoting five months to the duties of his Professorship, still holding his position at Cambridge and giving the rest of the year to the duties growing out of his connection with the museum.

Mr. Perry was joined in marriage to Lucretia Leavenworth Willson, only daughter of the Hon. Francis and Mrs. Rachel (Leavenworth) Willson, of Hinesburg, Vt., March 5, 1856. Mrs. P. died March 28, 1858, leaving an infant son, who is yet living—Francis Willson Perry.

He married as his second wife, Mrs. Sophia Harmon Wright, at South Bend, Ind., May 27, 1867. She was the daughter of Dr. Ezekiel and of Sophia Smith Harmon, of Clarkson, N. Y., and survives him.

Two extracts from his diary will, perhaps, give as clear an insight into his character, as anything which could be written. On his 23d birthday he writes thus :—

"If my life is spared, I trust I may some day be able to reconcile the sciences with each other, and especially with religion. I am beginning to look upon that as the great work of my life. It is more than yet has been fairly accomplished, so far as I know, and more than I can hope to do satisfactorily. I would direct all my efforts to the unfolding of my own powers, so as to be able to understand the scriptures, and be able to justify the ways of God to man. I have for a long time felt in this way, and O, that I may have strength to accomplish it, if it will tend at all to the advancement of the Redeemer's kingdom."

Towards the close of his diary, he penned the following ;—

"The foregoing meagre summary indicates that I have lived a very quiet, uneventful life, as that of a student, be it of Nature or of books, usually is. What I have aimed at has been a simple, faithful discharge of duty, wherever I have happened to be. The little I have done has been in a silent unobtrusive way, and without ostentation. Thus, as I fain would believe, seeds of truth have been sown in many hearts, and gentle influences constantly infused into the lives of those in whose society I have moved, which, as we may well trust, have been silently working as good elements for the elevation of my fellows, and so to the glory of God."

The great work of his life, as indicated in the first of the above extracts, made him a devout stndent of the *word of God*, and not only an enthusiastic, but also a devout student of the *works of God*.

The idea of his youth he carried out. All through his ministry he recreated where he might find the most nature. The first place of his ministry, Swanton, Vt., was washed by the waters of Lake Champlain. Always faithful to his people, he yet found time to explore most fully the geologic formation of the region. His thorough knowledge on this subject made him acquainted in the year 1860, with the celebrated geologist, Prof. Jules Morron, of Zurich, Switzerland, now a resident of Cambridge. And a paper which he read in 1867, before the Boston Society of Natural History, (Prof. Agassiz being present), entitled, Queries on the Red Sandstone of Vermont, led to his immediate acquaintance, at the close of the reading, with that world-renowned naturalist—to an invitation to meet him at the museum on a certain day, and to an offer on that occasion of the place which he occupied till his death.

"The only fault I have ever seen in him," says the great naturalist, "was his

H.W. Smith

John B. Perry.

propensity to overwork. I sent him South, thinking the excursion would give him recreation, but he worked the more, and when his call came to accept the Professorship at Oberlin, I said,go ! it will be a means of rest. But the recreation brought only a large amount of labor. While in the Seminary he devoted much time to the study of languages, and was very conversant with twelve. "I have hardly known which to admire most," says Prof. Agassiz, "his thorough understanding of his profession, or his broad culture. He seemed at home in every department of literature."

"There are four things," writes another, (the Rev. Walter Forsyth, of Englewood, Ill.,) "which impressed me the more, the more I knew him: these were, his sincere goodness, his intellectual ability and culture, his great devotion to the cause of science and religion, and his remarkable modesty."

The above seems a clear analysis of his character.

Various suggestions have been made relative to the preservation of his writings in some permanent form. As one incentive to such a result, Prof. Agassiz has given the following order in which his collected writings should be arranged.

1. Theological Geology.
2. Tertiaries.
3. The Lake Champlain Series.
4. Massachusetts Geology.
5. Glacial Phenomena.
6. Paleozoic Corals.
7. Foliated Rocks.
8. Change of Level of Continents.

He was a faithful minister, he was an honored scientist, but he will always be remembered as an expounder of the relations between the two, an interpreter of the word and works of God.

I have taken the foregoing sketch of Prof. Perry, almost literally from a sketch of him published in the Congregational Quarterly for April 1873. But it embraces but a small part of the sketch. He was a rare scholar and an accomplished christian gentleman.

235. Whitman Leavenworth.[6]—David,[5] Ebenezer,[4] David[3], Thomas,[2] Thomas.[1]

Born November 22, 1777, in New Milford, Conn.,—(in Woodbury, his son Russell says.)

Married Sarah Sweet, of Stephentown February 1, 1797. Lived several years in New Milford, then in Stephentown, Rensselaer Co., and in 1818 removed to Vermont; in 1821 to Kingsbury, Washington Co., and in 1822 to Sandy Hill, and died there August 14, 1823. He was a farmer and carpenter, and taught school. Sarah Sweet was born in New Milford, September 10, 1783. She died in Montour, Schuyler Co., January 25, 1869. She lived with her son, Russell, and was a widow over forty-six years. The parents of Whitman and wife lived a mile apart, one in Popham and one in Stephentown.

CHILDREN.

453. Mary Downs, b. August 24, 1801, m. Truman Tucker.
454. Juda, b. October 27, 1803.
455. Lydia, b. December 27, 1806.

456. RUSSELL, b. December 19, 1809. All in Nassau, Mrs. Boughton says; but Russell says they were born in Stephentown.

236. MARY LEAVENWORTH.[6]—DAVID,[5] EBENEZER,[4] DAVID,[3] THOMAS,[2] THOMAS.[1]

Born March 16, 1780, at New Milford, Conn.
Married Jeremiah Boughton, of Nassau, N. Y., farmer, January 14, 1800.
Lives upon the farm owned by her father, and where he died and her mother also, two years afterwards and was buried by his side.

CHILDREN.

1. HARRIET, b. August 8, 1801, m. Isaac Woodward of Nassau, farmer, June 5, 1825. Lived mostly in Nassau and now, (1867) in Stephentown, N. Y. She had eight children, viz.;—
   1. CURTIS, b. October 29, 1824, was a mason, m. Mary Holmes, of Lee, Mass. and lived there until 1865, and then moved to Nassau, where he now resides. Has three children.—1. Sophia, b. 1852, 2. William, b. 1857, 3. Agnes, b. 1861.
   2. JAMES, b. February 6, 1826, m. Electa Woodward, of North Lee, Mass., July 4, 1855, and has always lived there. Has two children, born in 1857, and 1859.
   3. STEPHEN E. b. October —, 1834, m. Lucy Gardner, of Stephentown, and removed to Columbia Co., Wis. and lives there, a farmer. Has two children born in 1859, and 1862.
   4. LEWIS N. b. October —. 1836, a mason, lives at Springfield, Mass. single, (1867).
   5. NELSON N. b. February 1840, m. Sarah Saunders, of Stephentown, June 1856, and lives in West Meriden, Conn.
   6. LEVI M. b. October 1838, m. Addie Streeter, of Pittsfield, Mass. September 25, 1865, was a farmer and left no children.
   7. HIRAM B. b. February, 1842, and enlisted in the 125th, N. Y. volunteers, as a private, was promoted to sergeant, was with the regiment through nearly all its service and d. at Philadelphia, in hospital, of disease, January 1865. Single. He was a farmer.
   8. MARY, b. April —, 1830, m. Orry S. Strait, of Stephentown, (a farmer) about 1850-1, and resides there, (1867). She has two children. 1. Eugene b. 1853, and Josephine, b. 1855.
2. HIRAM, b. March 17, 1803, at Nassau, N. Y., m. Lydia Leavenworth, (his cousin) dau. of Whitman L.; lived in Nassau, until 1860, and then removed to Clifon Park, N. Y., where they now reside. Has three children—

   1. GEORGE, 2. JOHN, 3. SARAH.

All of whom are married and reside in Clifton Park, N. Y. He is a farmer.

3. Lucinda, b. February 2, 1806, m. Elias Richmond, of New Lebanon, N. Y., a cooper. He has always resided there and has eight children, viz. :—
   1. JEREMIAH, m. Clara Penoyer, of Valatie, N. Y., and has one child. Lives in Valatie, and is a merchant.
   2. SIMEON, m. Adeline Hicks, of New Lebanon ; have two young children, and lives in New Lebanon, where he is a dealer in tin and hardware.
   3. LESTER, unmarried, a tinsmith, and with his brother Simeon in New Lebanon.
   4. CORNELIUS, unmarried, a harness maker at New Lebanon.
   5. OPHELIA, m. Jeremiah Chandler, of New Lebanon, a carpenter and joiner.
   6. MARY, m. Darius Leonard, a farmer in New Lebanon.

7. ANN ELIZA, unmarried and living at home.
8. FRANCIS, unmarried, living at home with her parents.

4. LAURA, b. January 19, 1808, m. William Sandford, of Stephentown, a carpenter. Lived there ten or twelve years, and then moved to the Genesee country, and two or three years after to Allegany county, where she d. March 7, 1842. He d. there about 1862-3, leaving five children,—

1. ORELIA. 2. EPHRAIM. 3. LUCENIA. 4. ORLANDO. 5. HARRIET.

Orelia m. Coke, a grocer, and now resides in Ohio, with one child. Ephraim, unmarried. Was, when last heard from by his family, in the lumber business in western Michigan. Lucenia m. Victor Austin, farmer, and lives in Allegan, Mich.; has five children. Orlando, m. and lives in Allegany county. He was in the army in the late war. Harriet, m. and lives in New Albany, Ind.

5. CORNELIUS, b. December 10, 1810, m. Mary Sanford, of Stephentown; is a farmer, and about 1865-6 moved from Nassau to Painted Post, N. Y., where he lost his wife, who had three children,—1. HENRY, 2. EPHRAIM, 3. JEREMIAH. All married. The first two live near there, and the last at Springfield, Mass. He again married a widow —— and had three more children, and a few years ago removed to Blossburg, Pa., where he now resides. His second wife was Catharine Landis Wygant.
6. MARIA, b. January 31, 1812, m. Major L. Woodward, of Nassau, November 17, 1835, and has resided there, excepting eighteen years that they lived in Lee, Mass. He is a mason and farmer. They have no children.
7. STEPHEN, b. March 22, 1814, m. Ann Boughton, of Stephentown. Is a farmer; lived in New Lebanon three or four years, and then removed to Monroe county, N. Y., where he resided until his death, October 28, 1865, leaving two children:—

1. SILAS, b. ——, 1843. 2. LAURA, b. ——, 1849.

8, LESTER, b. July 8, 1816. Was a farmer, and d. October 9, 1840, from the effects of a wound received from an accidental shot from a gun in the hands of a friend, who was shooting birds from a canal boat near Syracuse, N. Y.
9. GRACIA, b. September 12, 1818, m. Henry Hopon, a farmer of Nassau, N. Y., and usually lived in that town, but now resides in Hancock, Mass. She has five children.
10. ENOS, b. March 31, 1820, m. Ruth Gale, of New Lebanon, and resided there until his death, October 28, 1861. He was a farmer, and left a child HERBERT, b. 1853.
11. JARED, b. April 17, 1822. Farmer, m. Matilda Huntington, of Stephentown, N. Y., and moved to Painted Post, N. Y., where he lived three years; he then removed to Reedsburg, Wis., where he now resides. He has three children.
12. SARAH, b. August 29, 1826, m. Cyrus Tooley, a farmer of New Lebanon. Went West, and after nine years residence there returned to New Lebanon. They have two children aged seven and nine years.

237. David Downs Leavenworth.[6] — DAVID,[5] EBENEZER[4], DAVID,[3] THOMAS,[2] THOMAS.[1]

Born May 3, 1783, in Sandgate, Vt.

Married REBECCA ROOT, July 6, 1806, at Sandlake. N. Y., by Rev. Justice Gregory. She was a daughter of John and Avis Root, farmer of Sandlake, and was born November 15, 1788. She died February 12, 1844, at Schodac, N. Y., a most excellent benevolent, and religious lady. He lived most of his life at Nassau, N. Y., and died November 8, 1861, at Nassau; a millwright. Mrs. Avis Root was a Hunt.

CHILDREN.

457. JOHN S., b. July 25, 1807.
458. AVIS, b. June 6, 1809, d. June 26, 1810; drowned.
459. MARY ANNA, b. August 11, 1810.
460. DAVID WATERBURY, b. September 30, 1812.
461. WILLIAM, b. April 23, 1815.
462. BURZINAH, b. July 3, 1817.
463. JOSIAH BURTON, b. June 5, 1820.
464. IRA HURD, b. September 1, 1822.
465. DENNIS ROOT, b. December 25, 1825, d. March 24, 1826.

First five born at Sandlake, N,Y., the last four at Sandgate, Bennington Co., Vt.

238. ANNA LEAVENWORTH.[6]—DAVID,[5] EBENEZER[4], DAVID,[3] THOMAS,[2] THOMAS.[1]

Born February 7, 1785, ia Nassau, N. Y.

Married Noah Ashley, farmer, of Nassau, about 1807. Lived in that town. She died at Mrs. Boughton's September —, 1857.

CHILDREN.

1. RANSOM, b. ——, d. a young man.
2. FANNY, b. ——, m. Michael Rona, who d. some years ago. She lives at Pittsfield, Mass.; is a widow and has three children.
3. JOANNA, b. ——, m. Greenleaf Richmond, a cooper, of New Lebanon. Removeb to Michigan.
4. EMELINE, b. ——

239. SARAH LEAVENWORTH.[6]—DAVID,[5] EBENEZER,[4] DAVID,[3] THOMAS[2], THOMAS[1]

Born February 11, 1788, in Nassau, N. Y.

Married Calvin Reed, a farmer of Taghkannic, Columbia Co., N. Y. Removed to Painted Post, N. Y., and from thence to New Albany, Ind., where he was living a few years since, but both are now, 1870, dead.

CHILDREN.

1. ROYAL A., is a farmer at or near Sauk Rapids, Minn.
2. WILLIAM P., b. ——, m. Esther Bailey, aud resided in Campbell, Steuben Co., d. at Plymouth, Marshall Co., Iowa.
3. JAMES W., lives near Plymouth.
4. MARY ANN, b. ——, m. David Miller.
5. ANN.
6. LAURA O., b. ——, m. Harvey P. Chaffee, Plymouth, Marshall Co., Iowa, d.
7. CHLOE W., b. ——, d. ——

240. Isaac Leavenworth.[6] — DAVID,[5] EBENEZER,[4] DAVID,[3] THOMAS,[2] THOMAS.[1]

Bosn September 22, 1790, in Nassau, N. Y.

Married SARAH SEYMOUR, 1814.

He was a carpenter, poor and unthrifty. His family was living in Troy, near the corner of Washington and Fifth streets, First Ward, when, on the evening of January 1, 1837, an avalanche of clay broke from the summit of a hill, Mt. Ida, five hundred feet above, and followed by a torrent of water and sand glided swiftly to the plain below, overwhelming three dwellings and instantly killing three of the children of Isaac Leavenworth. One, Emma, was taken out of the ruins alive, and Mrs. L. was rescued alive, but shockingly bruised and injured. Two of the houses were occupied, one of them by John Grace, who was killed, as was also his wife.

The land-slide also swept away two stables, containing twenty-two horses, of which sixteen were killed, and a burning brick kiln, owned by a Mr. Cone. In the summer previous, a slide had occurred near the same place, doing but little damage at the time. At the scene of the disaster on New Year's evening, the clay covered several acres, and was from ten to forty feet deep.

CHILDREN.

466. REUBEN, b. July 22, 1817.
467. ADELINE, b. ——, 18—.
468. SARAH, b. ——, 18—.
469. EMMA, b. ——, 18—.
470. MARIETTE, b. ——, 18—.
471. AMATUS, b. ——, 1827, d.
472. ISAAC, b. ——, 1829.
473. SEAMAN, b. ———, 1833.

The last three d. by the landslide at Troy.

241. Ebenezer Leavenworth.[6]—DAVID,[5] EBENEZER,[4] DAVID[3], THOMAS[2], THOMAS.[1]

Born May 28, 1793, in Nassau, N. Y.

Married, first, MATILDA CURTIS, March 6, 1814, of Nassau. She was born September 6, 1794, and died June 14, 1835.

Second, JULIA ROBBINS, March 6, 1836. She was born February 1, 1809, married at Hornby, N. Y. and died at Campbell, N. Y. November 20, 1846.

Third, BETSEY SMITH, (formerly Holly) widow of Luman Smith March 6, 1847, at North Urbana, N. Y.

He was a farmer, removed to Painted Post, N. Y., about 1822. After going to Western N. Y., he lived in Wayne, then at Mead Creek, where he cleared another farm, then three miles above Cooper's Plains, on Mead Creek, in Campbell, where he lived nine years. In February 1843, he bought a farm on Oak Hill, in Campbell. In the winter of 1853-4, he traded the farm for a grist mill five miles west of the head of Seneca Lake and lived there four years. He then bought a farm in Hornby, where he died October 18, 1863. He was a farmer.

CHILDREN.

474. PHILO CURTIS, b. November 8, 1814.
475. LORENZO DOWNS, b. January 15, 1816, d. February 18, 1818.
476. ALMON TICKNOR, b. April 27, 1818, d. May 2, 1819.
477. MITTIE ANN, b. August 20, 1819, d. November 2, 1848.
478. LOREN MILLS, b. September 30, 1821, d. August 1823.
479. SILVAN EBENEZER, b. June 28, 1824.
480. MATILDA JANE, b. April 15, 1825, d. young.
481. MARY MATILDA, b. September 14, 1826, d. November 3, 1827.
482 JOHN ROBBINS, b. January 22, 1837.
483. ISAAC HILL, b. September 22, 1838.
484. MATILDA ELIZABETH, b. May 1, 1841.
485. DAVID DOWNS, b. January 21, 1844.
486. LYMAN BIXBY, b. November 1, 1846.

242. Lorenzo W. Leavenworth.[6]—EBENEZER ISAAC,[5] EBENEZER,[4] DAVID,[3] THOMAS[2], THOMAS.[1]

Born July 17, 1809, at Watertown, N. Y.
Died October 16, 1830, at Brownhelm, Ohio.

243. Eboni Leavenworth.[6]—EBENEZER ISAAC[5], EBENEZER,[4] DAVID[3], THOMAS[2], THOMAS.[1]

Born October 16, 1811, at Camden, N. Y.

Married, first, ELIZA S. HENDERSON, June 2, 1847. She was daughter of John Henderson, a carpenter, now of Randolph Co., Ill. She died at Chester in said county, December 21, 1850.

Married, second, ALICE M. LITTLE, Jan. 21, 1856, daughter of Ebenezer Little, farmer in Lasalle Co., Ill.; once a member of N. H. Legislature. She died at Dongola July 4, 1865.

Married, third, S. JANE GALBRAITH, of Belleville, Ill., August 2, 1866.

Ebeni Leavenworth went to southern Illinois in 1841, and has been there ever since. Resides in Dongola, Union Co., Ill., where he is engaged in trade and manufactures, milling, etc. Has had four children, of whom one only is now alive. He was the founder of Dongola; is a man of character, enterprise and wealth, and the architect of his own fortune. Post master, express agent, etc.

CHILDREN.

487. CHARLES, b. November 2, 1848, in Sparta. Ill.
488. DAUGHTER, b. October 8, 1857, at Dongola, d. Oct. 8, 1857.
489. DAUGHTER, b. July 26, 1859, " d. Aug. 7, 1859.
490. SON, b. June 3, 1865, at Dongola, d. June 23, 1865.

244. SARAH ELIZABETH LEAVENWORTH.[6]—EBENEZER ISAAC,[5] EBENEZER,[4] DAVID,[3] THOMAS[2], THOMAS.[1]

Born November 6, 1813, at Rome, N. Y.
Lives at Dongola, Ill., with her brother Ebeni, unmarried.

245. Charles Leavenworth.[6]—EBENEZER ISAAC,[5] EBENEZER[4], DAVID,[3] THOMAS,[2] THOMAS[1].

Born March 25, 1816, at Pompey, N. Y.

Married SOPHIA GIBSON, March —, 1846, at Brownhelm, Ohio. He died at St. Johns, Perry Co., Ill., April 11, 1858, where the family reside. He was a mechanic, and at the time of his death was a third owner in a grist-mill.

CHILDREN.

491. MARY J., b. September 22, 1847, at Erie Co., Pa., unmarried, 1866.
492. HARRIET M., b. October 6, 1849, d. November 26, 1849, at Erie, Pa.

493. Eliza S., b. October 9, 1850, at Hudson, Mich., unmarried, 1866.

494. Sarah Josephine, b. October 29, 1852, d. November 1, 1854, at Ullin, Ill.

495. George J., b. September 7, 1855, at St. Johns, Ill.

246. Heman E. Leavenworth.[6]—Ebenezer Isaac,[5] Ebenezer,[4] David,[3] Thomas,[2] Thomas.[1]

Born October 7, 1820, at Onondaga N. Y., two and one half miles south-east from Syracnse.

Married ——— in Wisconsin. Died 18—, in Wisconsin.

He left home before he was of age, lived a few years in northern Illinois. Then moved to Wisconsin, married and soon after died. His widow married again and moved west.

496. Son.

247. MARY LEAVENWORTH.[6]—Ebenezer Isaac[5], Ebenezer,[4] David[3], Thomas,[2] Thomas.[1]

Born September 16, 1822, at Onondaga, near Syracuse.

Married, first Israel P. Frink, April 14, 1856, at Brownhelm, O. He was a mason by trade, but became a farmer. He died, 18—, leaving all his estate to his wife.

Second, Henry B. Goucher, M. D., at Pecatonica, Ill., September 12, 1861. Resides at Pecatonica, Ill. No heirs.

248. MARTHA LEAVENWORTH.[6]—Ebenezer Isaac,[5] Ebenezer,[4] David,[3] Thomas,[2] Thomas.[1]

Born November 16, 1826, at Linclaen, Madison Co., N. Y.

Married Franklin G. Smith, April 14, 1856, at Pecatonica, Ill. at which place she died December 20, 1862, without issue.

250. CHARLOTTE LOIS LEAVENWORTH.[6] —Gideon[5], David,[4] John[3], Thomas[2], Thomas.[1]

Born November 28, 1778, at Roxbury.

Married June 20, 1796, Judson Hurd. He was a farmer. She died April 14, 1858.

CHILDREN.

1. Cyrus C., b. April 23, 1797, d, September 25, 1823, unmarried.
2. Nelson L., b. January 14, 1799, m, Hannah Cornwall. Had two children, Sarah and Charlotte. d, at Brooklyn, February 14, 1834.
3. Maria, b. June 25, 1801, m. Wakeman Lyon. Lives at Lodi, Ill. No children.
4. Almira, b. October 4, 1803. m. David Brothwell. Has two boys, William and Joseph.

5. SOPHIA LEAVENWORTH, b. April 20, 1806. m. Thomas J. Keeler, of Syracuse. Had three children, one dead and two living, Nelson R. and James M. She d. at Syracuse, December, 1871.
6. CAROLINE, b. September 24, 1808, m., first, Tuttle Dayton, he d. 1843; married, second, Edward Young, at Woodbury. He lived at Liberty, Sullivan Co. He d. in 1871, and now 1872, she lives at Woodbury.
7. FREDERICK W., b. January 2, 1812, m., first, Mary Coles, one child. She d. about 1845, and he m. Harriet Coles.
8, CATHARINE, b. July 29, 1814, m. George Wells, no children.
9. JAMES M., b. September 19, 1817, m. Augusta Griswold, December 22, 1851, One child, Clarence W.
10. CHARLOTTE, L., b. April 2, 1822, m. George Lewis, of Roxbury.

251. Russell Leavenworth.[6] — GIDEON,[5] DAVID,[4] JOHN,[3] THOMAS[2], THOMAS.[1]

Born October 16, 1781.

Married EVELINE STONE, March 27, 1816, at Litchfield. She was born in 1800. He resides at Northampton, Mass. He died there March 12, 1866, aged eighty-five. She died at New Haven at her son's, May 14, 1870, aged seventy; her son, Daniel C. says seventy-four.

CHILDREN.

497. OSCAR, b. November 27, 1818.
498. REBECCA, b. December 9, 1820.
499. BOARDMAN H., b. January 16, 1826.
500. DANIEL C., b. April 29, 1828.
501. CLINTON, b. November 6, 1830.

All born in Woodbury.

252. LOVINA LEAVENWORTH.[6]—GIDEON,[5] DAVID[4], JOHN[3] THOMAS,[2] THOMAS.[1]

Born in December, 1784, at Roxbury.

Married, first, Dr. Samuel S. Masters. She separated from him and procured a divorce before 1828, as her mother, by her will, proved October 6, 1828, calls her "Judson."

Married, second, Oliver Judson. He died in a few years.

Married, third, Elijah Andrus, some twenty-five or thirty years since. Andrus died in 1854-5. She died at Plymouth, Conn., about 1861.

CHILDREN.

1. HELEN MASTERS, b. ——, m. Eber Thomas, of Roxbury, d.
2. PHILO JUDSON, b. ——
3. MARY JUDSON, b. ——
4. MARIA JUDSON, b. ——
5. JAMES ANDRUS, b. —— All born in Roxbury.

253. ANNA LEAVENWORTH.[6]—GIDEON,[5] DAVID[4], JOHN[3], THOMAS,[2] THOMAS.[1]

Born May 23, 1789, at Roxbury, Conn.

Married Ralph Revillo Keeler, He was born April 19, 1782. They were married in Connecticut. He was a farmer, and early in life moved to Pompey, N. Y. He moved to Syracuse some thirty years since, (1830 to 1840,) and was a hotel keeper, owning a valuable property near the center of the city, opposite (west) of the First Church, on which was his hotel.

CHILDREN.

1. THOMAS J., b. July 8, 1808, m. his cousin Sophia Hurd, June 25, 1835, at Roxbury, and had three children. Early in life a hotel keeper; then lived on his rents; d. at Syracuse August 6, 1867.

Children.

1. NELSON R. KEELER, b. December 31, 1837.
2. GEORGE KEELER, b. May 1, 1841, d. September 1, 1841.
3. JAMES M. KEELER, b. June 2, 1845.

Nelson R. married at Albany, December 30, 1867, Ada M. B. Alvord, of Salina. She was born November 21, 1837. *Children*—Thomas Alvord, b. October 12, 1868. Ella Alvord, b. November 30, 1872, d. February 2, 1874. Nelson R. resides at Syracuse.

2. JULIA ANN, b. June 2, 1811, m. Milton Worden and had one son. She d. November 8, 1839.
3. MARY P., b. September 14, 1819, m. Barney Lincoln, of Onondaga, and had two children, Mary and Edward.
4. SARAH, b. January 2, 1824, m. Frank Chapin and had one child, Ella. Sarah d. January 7, 1864. Ella was adopted by Mr. Stone, of Syracuse, whose son she married.
5. CHARLES S., b, July 5, 1829, d. May 9, 1867, at Syracuse.

Probably the children were all born at Pompey.

254. Sheldon Leavenworth.[6]—GIDEON,[5] DAVID,[4] JOHN[3], THOMAS,[2] THOMAS.[1]

Born January 27, 1801, at Roxbury, Conn.

Married SARAH J. WOOSTER May 1, 1830. Residence Roxbury, Conn.; was a farmer. Died at Roxbury June 17, 1868, aged sixty-seven.

CHILDREN.

502. JULIA A., b. June 2, 1831, m. Henry A. Warner, June 2, 1850.

503. CHARLOTTE S., b. August 27, 1833, m. Henry M. Beach, March 17, 1851, has two children, 1870.

504. LOISA M., b. August 27, 1835, m. Wm. Henry Cooper, December, 1856. Resides at New Haven and is a coachmaker.

504½. GEORGE F., b. June 15, 1839.

All born at Roxbury, Conn.

255. Martin Leavenworth.[6]—MORSE,[5] DAVID,[4] JOHN[3], THOMAS[2], THOMAS.[1]

Born in Roxbury, January 12, 1785.

Married January 1, 1809, CLARA SHERMAN. She joined the first Congregational church at Woodbury, July 5, 1835. He died in Roxbury February 16, 1813, aged twenty-eight years. Was universally esteemed and respected.

CHILDREN.

505. JEANETTE, b. September 30, 1809, at Woodbury.

506. ELIZABETH, b. August 7, 1812.

March 8, 1813, Administration granted to the widow and his brother Truman, 12th Probate vol., p. 19. March 7, 1814, Mrs. L. was appointed guardian for the two children—10th Probate vol., p. 347.

256. Truman Leavenworth.[6]—MORSE,[5] DAVID,[4] JOHN[3], THOMAS,[2] THOMAS.[1]

Born August 18, 1786, at Roxbury; a farmer.

Married, first, PHEBE GRAHAM, Nov. 4, 1807, daughter of Geo. and Nancy A. Graham, who was b. April 22, 1790, d. April 23, 1841, in Washington, Conn. He d. in Roxbury March 26, 1852. Lived in the west part of Roxbury.

Married, second, LUCRETIA FROST, July 7, 1842, daughter of Joseph and Marian Frost. She died July 29, 1857, in Litchfield, aged sixty-four.

CHILDREN.

507. SALLY, b. October 9, 1809, m. William Hartwell, a farmer, January 17, 1828. *Children*—Oliver S., Rachel M., Frederick W., Henry H., Minot, and Roger T.

508. ALMIRA, b. June 23, 1811, d. March 3, 1852, in Litchfield.

509. NANCY A., b. April 23, 1814, m. Harvey P. Smith, farmer, November 23, 1836. They lived in Washington fourteen years, and in Monroe fourteen years. *Children*—Catharine A., Daniel A., Julia M.

510. EVELYN M., b. September 17, 1815, lives in Litchfield.

511. MARIA D., b. July 29, 1817, d. March 19, 1852, "

512. ROYAL, b. January 7, 1825, d. Jan. 11, 1825, in Roxbury.

All born in Roxbury.

Truman moved from Roxbury to Bethlehem in 1835; from

Bethlehem to Washington in 1837, and from Washington to Litchfield in 1846. He and his daughters, Almira and Maria, were buried at Bantam grave yard in Litchfield.

257. Philo Leavenworth.[6]—MORSE[5], DAVID,[4] JOHN,[3] THOMAS[2], THOMAS.[1]

Born October 3, 1789, in Roxbury.

Married April 12, 1814, ANNA OSBORN, of Roxbury, daughter of John Osborn, of Goshen, Ct. She died October 13, 1865, at Nobles' house in Herrick, Bradford Co., Penn.

He died in Roxbury, February 11, 1835. Had four sons, all born in Roxbury. He served in the war of 1812,—Cothren, p. 788. She then married, ——— Roberts, and moved to Goshen, Ct., and took her children and had a family by him.

CHILDREN.

513. EDWARD B., b. August 13, 1816.
514. CHARLES J., b. September 22, 1818.
515. THEODORE, b. July 10, 1821.
516. NOBLE, b. May 5, 1824.

Philo L. and his father-in-law, John Osborn, were farmers.

258. Wait Leavenworth.[6]—MORSE,[5] DAVID,[4] JOHN[3], THOMAS[2], THOMAS.[1]

Born in Roxbury, September 12, 1792.

Married AMORETTA PATTERSON, of Roxbury, daughter of James and Clara Patterson, of Roxbury, March 30, 1812. He is still living; is a farmer and resides in Roxbury; a good citizen, universally esteemed; a large man weighing two hundred lbs.

CHILDREN.

517. JAMES MARTIN, b. February 26, 1813, d. Jan. 26, 1814.
518. A. JAMES MARTIN, b. September 28, 1815.
519. WILLIAM, b. July 23, 1816.
520. GEORGE, b. September 15, 1820.
521. WAIT, b. May 9, 1827.
522. EDWIN, b. April 21, 1831.
523. CHARLES ROYAL, b. December 14, 1834.
524. ——— ———
525. ——— ———

All born in Roxbury.

He was a member of the Legislature in the year 1838, has been Selectman of Roxbury, etc., and is a gentleman worthy of the respect he enjoys.

259. HARRIET LEAVENWORTH.[6] — MORSE,[5] DAVID[4], JOHN,[3] THOMAS,[2] THOMAS.[1]

Born Octobr 30, 1796, at Roxbury.
Married Charles Patterson, of Roxbury, Conn., May 6, 1812,
They had six children and she is now (1870) living in Bridgeport, Conn.

CHILDREN.

1. SARAH, b. in 1815.
2. SUSAN, b. in 1819.
3. ANN MARIA b. in 1821, d.
4. JAMES, b. in 1824. Disappeared when six-teen years old, never since been heard from; supposed murdered, as he had money with him.
5. CLARA, b. in 1828.
6. CELESTE, b. in 1833. They were all born in Roxbury.

He was a farmer at Naugatuc, (where he died), the latter part of his life. Before that a blacksmith at Roxbury.

260. Morse Leavenworth.[6]—MORSE[5], DAVID,[4] JOHN,[3] THOMAS[2], THOMAS.[1]

Born July 27, 1805, at Roxbury, died there November 23, 1852, at the homestead of his father.

Married AMARILLA BEECHER, December 25, 1827, daughter of Deacon John Beecher, of New Milford, Conn. He was a farmer lived near his brother Wait, in Roxbury, on the old homestead.

She married for her second husband, O. B. Seward Esq., of Roxbury.

CHILDREN.

526. JOHN HENRY, b. August 13, 1830.
527. JEROME BEECHER, b. Cctober 9, 1832.
528. BURNET MORSE, b. February 13, 1838.

His remains were buried in the new cemetery at Roxbury.

261. EMELINE LEAVENWORTH.[6] — DAVID,[5] DAVID[4], JOHN,[3] THOMAS,[2] THOMAS.[1]

Born September 15, 1804, at Woodbury.
Married October 13, 1824, at Woodbury, Horace G. Miner. She died June 24, 1851. He was born in Woodbury August 24, 1804, and lives now at Waterville. The children were all born in Woodbury.

CHILDREN.

1. SARAH, b. June 14, 1826, m. Wait Leavenworth, of Roxbury. See 521.
2. OLIVE, b. January 18, 1830, d. April 22, 1833.
3. SAMUEL, b. June 17, 1833, m. January 17, 1863, Laura E. Decker, daughter of Edington E. Decker, of New York. They live in Waterville, no children.
4. CORNELIA, b. April 25, 1835, m. James M. Colby. July 6, 1853. Live in Waterbury and have a son.
5. EMILY, b. September 5, 1839, m. William Beebe May 14, 1859. She obtained a divorce from him and now, 1870, resides in New Haven, Conn.

262. ELIZA LEAVENWORTH.[6]— MORSE,[5] DAVID,[4] JOHN[3], THOMAS[2], THOMAS[1]

Born March 22, 1806, at Roxbury.

Married David Beard April 7, 1824. Removed to Huntington and settled on a farm. Removed from Connecticut to New York, and bought a farm in Pompey in 1839. Removed to Manlius in 1865, and now resides there—1874.

CHILDREN.

1. SPENCER, b. February 4, 1830, m. Mary Cornelia Kershaw, of Earlville, January 5, 1850. Resides near Syracuse, and has had three children, one of whom is dead. Now, 1870, a merchant and farmer and lives just outside of Syracuse, in Onondaga.

Children.

1. CLARA CORNELIA, b. at Pompey March 24, 1851, m. H. L. Curtiss, son of Palmer Curtiss, of Syracuse, December 9, 1869. Child b. October 23, 1870. Mr. C. d. in 1870.
2. AMELIA, b. at Pompey September 22, 1857, d. there March 26, 1862.
3. EDWIN SPENCER, b. at Pompey February 20, 1863.

Mrs. Spencer Beard is the daughter of Thomas Kershaw and Finette Sears.

263. David Birdseye Leavenworth.[6]—DAVID,[5] DAVID[4], JOHN[3], THOMAS,[2] THOMAS.[1]

Born about 1810, at Roxbury.

Married first, ALMIRA STREW, of Smyrna, N. Y., September 22, 1844. She died last of September, 1851, in Illinois.

Married, second, AMELIA PARMETER, August 25, 1853, in Illinois. He was in trade at Smyrna. Is again in trade or farming, in Illinois. Lived at Chatham, Ill.; at Bloomington, Ill. in 1870, with his daughter Ella, wife of John Van Syse.

CHILDREN.

529. ELLA, b. May, 1846, at Ithaca, N. Y., m. John Van Syse, of Hamilton. N. Y.

530. WILLIAM, b. in 1848, at Smyrna, N. Y.

264. SARAH LEAVENWORTH.[6]—DAVID,[5] DAVID,[4] JOHN[3], THOMAS[2], THOMAS.[1]

Born about 1814 or '15, at Roxbury or Woodbury.

Married Charles N. Ryan October, 1838, at Pompey. Resides in Sandusky, O.; no children.

265. Edwin Alonzo Leavenworth.[6]—DAVID[5], DAVID[4], JOHN[3], THOMAS,[2] THOMAS.[1]

Born in 1818-19, at Roxbury or Woodbury.

Went South and died on his way to New Orleans, on board of vessel, of yellow fever; unmarried.

266. Wolcott Leavenworth.[6] — DAVID,[5] DAVID,[4] JOHN,[3] THOMAS,[2] THOMAS.[1]

Born October 20, 1821, at Woodbury.

Married August 25, 1845, at Earlville, Madison Co., N. Y., MARY E. CALKINS, born at Earlville June 20, 1820. She was the daughter of Daniel C. and Mary Carrier. He was born in Washington Co., N. Y., in 1782, and married July 4, 1805. She was born in the same county in 1782, married in Chenango Co. He died December 20, 1840. She died November 10, 1847; was a farmer.

Wolcott Leavenworth was a merchant at Earlville, and died at Chatham, Ill., on his return from Kansas, June 20, 1857, and was buried at Huron, O., by the side of his mother. His widow remained some years at Earlville, till 1868, and is now at Edgerton, Kent Co., Mich., with her children.

CHILDREN.

531. ALONZO D., b. August 2, 1846, at Earlville.

532. FREDERICK M., b. December 14, 1848, at Earlville, and is now, 1870, on the farm with his brother, near Rockford, Kent Co., Mich.

267. Beard Leavenworth.[6]—DAVID,[5] DAVID,[4] JOHN[3], THOMAS[2], THOMAS.[1]

Born August 6, 1824, at Woodbury.

Married CATHARINE E. COMAN, November 11, 1857, at Eaton, N. Y. In trade at Eaton with his father-in-law, who has been a merchant there for the last thirty or forty years. In 1871 removed to Syracuse, N. Y., but continued his business at Eaton.

CHILDREN.

533. LUCIEN COMAN, b. September 21, 1859, at Eaton.
534. ELLIS BEARD, b. April 19, 1865, "

268. CHARLOTTE LEAVENWORTH.[6] — JOHN PECK,[5] JOHN[4], JOHN,[3] THOMAS[2], THOMAS.[1]

Born January 28, 1798, in Woodbury, Conn.

Married, first, Daniel Hurlbert, March 15, 1824. He was a farmer, of Woodbury, and died there May 9, 1828. Son of Capt. Freeman Hurlbert, of Woodbury. Removed to Rush October, 1828.

Married, second, Thomas H. Brown, of Avon, September 3, 1834. Resides in Avon, N. Y. Daniel Hurlbert was born October 10, 1787. Thomas Brown died May 9, 1864, at Avon.

CHILDREN.

1 MARY LOIS, b. October 15, 1825, m. Heman Brown, of Rush, a farmer, June 8, 1851. Still lives there.
2. INFANT, b. May 12, 1828, d. young.
3. GEORGE B., b. at Avon Livingston Co., N. Y., February 7, 1837, d. young.
4. HENRY B., " " " "
5. INFANT SON, b. " " August 12, 1838, "

Mrs Brown still resides at Honeoye Falls, in Monroe Co., has taken a deep interest in this work and furnished me with the genealogy of her father's large family.

269. William Curtiss Leavenworth.[6]—JOHN PECK,[5] JOHN,[4] JOHN[3], THOMAS,[2] THOMAS.[1]

Born March 23, 1799, in Woodbury, Conn.

Married, first, MARY SPAYDE, August 17, 1824, in Reading, Pa. She died July 5, 1825, leaving no issue. Her father was Attorney-General of Penn.

Married, second, SUSAN DEYSHER, November 24, 1826, of Reading, Pa. She was born June 17, 1811; daughter of John and Catharine Deysher, of Berks Co.

He studied law in Woodbury with Frederick Smith. Went in April, 1821, to Reading, Pa., and practiced his profession until February 1, 1844, when he left for California, where he has since resided. 1869, has returned and lives in Philadelphia with Mr. Dreer.

CHILDREN.

535. MARY, b. September 24, 1827, m. Henry A. Dreer, of Philadelphia, June 22, 1847.

270. SARAH LEAVENWORTH.[6] — JOHN PECK,[5] JOHN[4], JOHN[3], THOMAS,[2] THOMAS.[1]

Born July 15, 1801, in Woodbury, Conn., d, July 3, 1865.

Married Alfred Beecher, at Avon, October 6, 1829. He is a farmer and resides in Livonia, Livingston Co., N. Y., where all her children were born on the farm they took the day after marriage. She died July 3, 1865, at Oberlin, O., while on a visit to her son Edward at Memphis, Tenn. Alfred B. b. at Bethlehem Ct., December 13,1795, is a farmer and was a teacher to the Seneca Indians and also to Americans.

CHILDREN,

1. SAMUEL BEECHER, b. September 8, 1830.
2. DAUGHTER, b. December 13, 1831, d. December 20, 1831.
3. EDWARD A., b. September 29, 1833.
4. DAVID S., b. June 13, 1835, m. Anna —— 1858.
5. SARAH b. April 16, 1837, d. September 7. 1838.
6. CHARLES H., b. January 26, 1840.
7. JULIA ANN, b. August 9, 1842.

3. EDWARD A. BEECHER, b. September 29, 1833, at Livonia, Livingston Co., N.Y., m. June 25, 1864, to Mary L. Bayliss of Memphis, Tenn., where he lives and is a lawyer. Three children.
4. DAVID S. BEECHER, b. at Livonia, Livingston Co., June 13, 1835, m. Anna ——, in 1858. He is a farmer and teacher. After marriage, lived in Ill. where he had two children and one died. Then moved to Missouri.
6. CHARLES H. BEECHER, b. at Livonia, Livingston Co., January 26, 1840. Lives in Mo., with his brother David, who is a farmer.
7. JULIA ANN BEECHER, b. August 9, 1842 at Livonia, Livingston Co., m. November 24, 1868, Alvah Kellogg, at her father's, at Oberlin. Resides in Cleveland.

271. Thaddeus Miner Leavenworth.[6]—JOHN PECK,[5] JOHN[4], JOHN,[3] THOMAS,[2] THOMAS.[1]

Born April 15, 1803, in Woodbury, Conn.

Married CORNELIA TERENTIA CARDELL, daughter of William Samuel Cardell, of Bennington, Vt., and of Clementine Rogers, his wife, November 13, 1831, in Philadelphia, Pa. She was born at Bennington, June 4, 1814. He received the honorary degree of A. M., from Union College in 1841. Was a lawyer, then an Episcopal clergyman and physician. Went to California in the first expedition, as surgeon in Col. Stevenson's regiment, and resided in San Francisco. No issue.

He was in 1848-9, Alcalde of San Francisco, and now lives on a ranche across the bay, at Sonoma, which is his post office.

While officiating as a clergyman, between 1840 and 1850, he lived for a year or two at Syracuse, and had care of a church at Liverpool, Onondaga Co., and in 1830 was settled over an Episcopal church in Troy, Miami Co., O., and at other times officiated in other places.

272. KEZIAH LEAVENWORTH.[6]—JOHN PECK[5], JOHN,[4] JOHN,[3] THOMAS,[2] THOMAS.[1]

Born February 3, 1805, in Woodbury. Conn.

Married Eralziman Gilbert October 17, 1827, of Lima, N. Y. He is a tanner and currier, and shoemaker, and lives at Fowlerville, Livingston Co., N. Y. Was married at Rush.

CHILDREN.

1. CHARLES J., b. April 15, 1829, lives in Chicago; is a commission merchant; b. in Lima, Livingston Co., and has a family; m. Jenny Goodrich in Washington, D. C.
2. DANIEL H., b. December 19, 1833, in Lima. Lives at Baxter Springs, Kansas; is a farmer.
3. WILLIAM, b, at Fowlersville July 4, 1835, d. young.
4. WILLIAM CURTISS, b. at Fowlersville November 13. 1843, lives in Chicago, and is a commission merchant. Now, 1870, has joined his brother at Baxter Springs, Ks.
5. MARY JANE, b. July 24, 1845, in Fowlersville, Livingston Co., N. Y.

274. Rev. Chauncey Leavenworth.[6]—JOHN PECK,[5] JOHN,[4] JOHN,[3] THOMAS.[2] THOMAS.[1]

Born November 6, 1808, in Woodbury, Conn.

Married CATHARINE CRAIG May 19, 1841, of Princeton, N. J. Came to Rush, N. Y., with his father's family in 1822. Graduated at Union College in 1837. Entered Princeton Seminary, in 1837, was graduated and licensed as a Presbyterian clergyman in 1840. Settled first at Mt. Vernon, O., 1841; second, at Madison, Ind., 1844; third, at Richmond, Ind., 1852; moved to Henry Co., Ill., in 1856, and thence (a little indirectly) to Galesburg, Ill. Died September 13, 1870, at Galesburg.

CHILDREN.

536. CAROLINE CRAIG, b. June 3, 1842, at Mt. Vernon, O., d.
537. MARY, b. December 4, 1844, at Madison, Ind.
538. JOHN CHAUNCEY, b. June 5, 1848, at Madison, Ind., d. December 27, 1866, at Galesburg, Ill.
539. WILLIAM B. b. February 12, 1855, at Richmond, Ind. and d. August 27, 1857, at Geneseo, Henry Co., Ill.

275. RUTH LEAVENWORTH.[6]—JOHN PECK,[5] JOHN,[4] JOHN[3], THOMAS,[2] THOMAS.[1]

Born September 5, 1811, at Woodbury. In 1822, moved to Rush. Went to Chicago to teach in 1835.

Married Joseph L. Hanson, October 27, 1836; grocer in Chicago; b. in London May 23, 1808.

CHILDREN.

1. LEAVENWORTH, b. October 30, 1837, at Chicago, enlisted and served three years; now at Memphis.
2. ELIZA JANET, } Twins. b. August 7, 1839, d. August 7, 1841.
3. SARAH MARY, } m. Newton S. Otis April 18, 1860, at Dunklin's Grove, Ill. Lived in Aurora, Ill., now in Memphis, Tenn.
4. VINCENT, b. April 26, 1841, d. July 20, 1841.
5. WILLIAM JUDSON, b. January 10, 1844, served three years in the army, and fifteen months as a veteran. Was at Pea Ridge. Was in the Army of the Cumberland. Is now 1870, a student of medicine with Dr. Austin, of Norwalk, O.
6. NELLIE FRANCES, b. February 1, 1847, is with Mrs. O. at Memphis.

In 1849, procured a divorce from Hanson in Missouri, returned to Chicago with four children, and taught four years. September 6, 1854, married Ebenezer Dunklin, at Chicago, who died July 24, 1864. June 21, 1866, married Alfred Beecher, of Oberlin, Ohio, at Rush, Monroe Co.

3. SARAH MARY HANSON, b. April 18, 1840, at Chicago, m. Newton S. Otis, April 18, 1860, at Dunklin's Grove, eighteen miles west of Chicago. Lived five years in Aurora, and then moved to Memphis, Tenn. Otis is an insurance agent.

Children.

1. Fanny G., b. in 1862. 2. Maria, b. in 1864. 3. An infant.

277. Rev. Hobart Leavenworth.[6]—JOHN PECK,[5] JOHN[4], JOHN,[3] THOMAS[2], THOMAS.[1]

Born April 4, 1815, at Woodbury, Conn.

Married NANCY K. GRIDLEY, March 29, 1837, at Rush. Lives on his father's homestead in Rush, N. Y., (P. O. Honeoye Falls) and is a Baptist clergyman and farmer.

CHILDREN.

540. SARAH CORNELIA, b. in Chili, September 26, 1838, d. September 1, 1864, while on a visit to relatives.
541. FRANCES, b. May 23, 1840, at Rush, m. in 1871.
542. HENRY, H. b. November 6, 1845, at Honeoye Falls.
543. WILLIAM WALTER, b. December 6, 1855, at Darien, Censee Co.
544. EDWARD. b. September 3. 1857, at Pembroke, Genesee, Co.

278. MARY JANE LEAVENWORTH.[6] — JOHN PECK,[5] JOHN,[4] JOHN,[3] THOMAS,[2] THOMAS.[1]

Born July 2, 1820, at Woodbury, Conn.

Married Samuel Lee Seeley, of East Henrietta, Monroe Co., N. Y., April 17, 1845; farmer at Rush, N. Y. He died July 3, 1865. She lives in Henrietta, N. Y.

CHILDREN.

1. JOHN LEAVENWORTH, b June 2, 1846.
2. SAMUEL LEE, b. March 3, 1848.
3. ISAAC JUDSON, b. February 9, 1850. All born in Henrietta.

279. Benjamin Judson Leavenworth[6]—JOHN PECK,[5] JOHN[4]. JOHN,[3] THOMAS,[2] THOMAS.[1]

Born July 1, 1822, at Woodbury, Conn.

Married CHARLOTTE H. DUBOIS, March 1, 1848, at East Avon, Livingston Co., N. Y. She was born at Cohocton, Steuben Co., N. Y., June 7, 1824. Her father was Abraham Dubois, her mother Sarah Van Voorhees. He died June 4, 1853, on the homestead in Rush, Monroe Co., N. Y. He was a farmer. His widow lives in Albion, Mich.

CHILDREN.

545. CORNELIA HENRIETTA, b. August 13 or 18, 1849, at Rush. She was, in 1870, a graduate and teacher in a high school in Michigan, where she and her mother resided.

280. John D. Leavenworth.[6]—RUSSELL,[5] JOHN,[4] JOHN,[3], THOMAS,[2] THOMAS.[1]

Born January 2, 1803, in Woodbury, Conn.

Married MARIA BEECHER, of Southbury, daughter of David Beecher, September 11, 1825. Was in 1830 with his brother Mark, a merchant at Monroe, Conn. He is a tailor and lives at Bridgeport.

CHILDREN.

546. SARAH MARIA, b. June 10, 1826, d. June 14, 1848, at Stepney, Conn.

547. CHARLES DEFOREST, b. May 18, 1828.

548. JOHN MERRITT, b. June 2, 1839, m. and died about 1867, without children.

281. ABIGAIL LEAVENWORTH.[6] — RUSSELL,[5] JOHN[4], JOHN,[3] THOMAS,[2] THOMAS.[1]

Born June 4, 1804, in Woodbury, Conn.

Married Judson Warner, nephew of Polly Warner, wife of Russell L., September 27, 1826. He was a merchant in Bethlehem, Conn. Moved to Newtown in 1839. The sons all farmers, excepting Mark. She died in March, 1867.

CHILDREN.

1. MARK, b. October 18, 1827, d. July 15, 1828.
2. JOHN, b. July 23, 1829, m. December 4, 1862.
3. CHARLES, b. February 17, 1831, m. December, 1856. Has one child, lives in Southbury.
4. JANE. b. March 10, 1833, m. May, 1855, has four children.
5. MARK LEAVENWORTH, } Twins, b. Mar. 25, 1835. Mark L. lives in Unionville, Lake Co., O.,
6. MARGARET, } and is a merchant; m. April, 1860, and has one child.
7. NETTIE, b. July 14, 1837, m. January, 1866, lives in Bridgeport, Conn.
8. RUSSELL L.. b. March 10, 1840, m. 1861, has one child.
9. POLLY L., b. July 22, 1842, d. September 11, 1855.
10. HARVEY DEFOREST, b. November 20, 1846.

The first three born in Bethlehem, Conn.; next three in Southbury, and last three in Newtown.

282. EMELINE LEAVENWORTH.[6] — RUSSELL[5], JOHN,[4] JOHN,[3] THOMAS[2], THOMAS.[1]

Born August 14, 1807, in Woodbury, Conn.

Married William Baldwin, after 1827. He was born November 28, 1803, and died January 11, 1847. She is a widow and resides in Newtown, Conn.

CHILDREN.

1. JAMES D., b. February 21, 1832. He was a member of the Connecticut Legislature in 1867. Was in Hawleyville. Removed to Bethel, Conn. Is a merchant.

283. Mark Leavenworth.[6]—RUSSELL,[5] JOHN,[4] JOHN[3], THOMAS,[2] THOMAS.[1]

Born March 25, 1809, at Woodbury.

Married July 31, 1830, EMELINE PECK, daughter of Truman Peck, of Monroe. She died at San Jose, Cal., March 23, 1856. Resides at San Jose, where he was Recorder for over six years, and Mayor for the city for the years 1868-9.

May, 1859, he married, second, SARAH MCKEE, *nee* Sarah Sage, widow of Henry McKee, a sea captain, of Middletown, born at Middletown, Conn., daughter of Allen Sage and Sarah Stocking.

CHILDREN.

549. DELIA, b. September 2, 1831, in Monroe, Conn., d. in New York city February 22, 1862.

550. JOHN RANDOLPH, } Twins, b. in Monroe, Sept. 6, 1836.
551. ROYAL RALPH, }

552. FRANCES AMELIA, b. December 2, 1846, in Monroe, d. at San Jose, Cal., January 15, 1859.

553. SARAH, b.———, d. January 22, 1859, at San Jose, Cal.

He represented the town of Monroe in the Legislature of Connecticut 1839.

284. Lorenzo W. Leavenworth.[6] — RUSSELL,[5] JOHN,[4] JOHN[3], THOMAS[2], THOMAS.[1]

Born July 2, 1821, in Woodbury, Conn,

Married SARAH E. TYRREL, b. April 28, 1821, in Monroe, daughter of Squire Tyrrel, a blacksmith, m. January 18, 1843, in Monroe, Conn.

Resided at New Milford, Conn., and engaged in the wool hat factory of Sanford and Sons, Bridgewater. He was formerly a teacher; now resides at Bridgeport, engaged in merchandise.

CHILDREN.

554. MARK R. b. January 19, 1846, in Monroe. In the stove and tin business at Bridgeport.

555. THEODORE D., b. March 19, 1850, Bookeeper at Bridgeport.

556. LEROY W., b. September 15, 1851. Same business as Mark R.

557. ELIZA JANE, b. May 8, 1856, in New Milford.

286. LUCY PARKER LEAVENWORTH.[6]—LEMUEL,[5] LEMUEL[4], JOHN[3], THOMAS,[2] THOMAS.[1]

Born August 25, 1803, in Whitestown, N. Y.

Married Ziba Knox, February 15, 1854. He was the eldest son of Sylvanus Knox, and was born at Cavendish, Vt., September 22, 1797. Taught school in early life. Studied law with Charles Dayan, at Lowville, was admitted to practice in Supreme Court, August, 1826, and remained through life a practicing attorney and magistrate at Lowville, where he held town offices thirty-four years, and died there September 6, 1868.

CHILDREN.

1. ELIZABETH, b. November 27, 1824, at Lowville, m. George Wells Fowler September 19, 1848. He was born November 21, 1820, at Trenton, N.Y., son of Edward Fowler, a lawyer. G. W. Fowler is a hardware merchant at Lowville, N. Y.

Children.

1. MARIA KNOX, b. July 25, 1849, d. October 1, 1851.
2. ELIZABETH, b. August 19, 1851, d. December 31, 1868.

3. Edward, b. July 1, 1853.
4. Philip, b. July 1, 1855.
5. Thomas, b. October 6, 1859.

2. Maria Augusta, b. February 1, 1827, at Lowville, N. Y., m. John Doig, May 2, 1848. He was born May 15, 1819, and died November 15, 1867. He was a druggist at Lowville and left two children :—

1. Frank Collins, b. August 19, 1851.
2. Charles Knox, b. November 28, 1853.

3. John Jay, b. June 13, 1831, at Lowville, and d. there December 19, 1867.
4. Mary Jane, b. July 28, 1834, m. first, Samuel P. Mills, December, 1851 ; was divorced May 28, 1861 ; m., second, William Doig January, 1864. She resides in New York. Child by first marriage—Maria Knox, b. September 29, 1855.
5. Charles, b. September 24, 1836 ; single, lived fourteen years in Utica, and now resides in New York city, in mercantile business.
6. Julia Emma, b. March 31, 1839, resides in Lowville, N. Y.
7. James Leonard, b. August 26, 1845. Resides in Lowville, and is employed as clerk in a hardware store.

287. Amos Warner Leavenworth.[6]—Ralph,[5] Amos,[4] John[3], Thomas,[2] Thomas.[1]

Born September 21, 1820, in St. Genevieve Co., Mo., twenty miles from the town of St. G.

Married Pernetta Ann Perkins, April 20, 1848. She was born May 30, 1817, in Buckingham Co., Va., afterwards lived in Shelby Co., Ky., daughter of Joseph Perkins. Resides in St. Louis, and is a millwright and steamboat engineer.

CHILDREN.

558. John Ralph, b. February 6, 1849, at St. Genevieve city, d. March 13, 1850.
559. Mary Edna, b. January 6, 1852, at St. Genevieve Co. Mo.
560. Martha Jane, b. September 13, 1853, at St. Louis, Mo.

288. Ralph Baptist Leavenworth.[6]—Ralph,[5] Amos,[4] John[3], Thomas[2], Thomas.[1]

Born December 3, 1822, in St. Genevieve Co. Mo.

Married Sarah Ann Ousley, October 31, 1849, at St. Genevieve. She was born in Kentucky, July 22, 1832 ; was daughter of Willis G. Ousley, nephew of Gov. Ousley, of Kentucky, and of Scotch descent.

He was a millwright and engineer, and died June 18, 1865, at St. Louis. She married Thomas Moore, of St. Louis, early in 1867, and he died in 1868, as Mrs. L. supposes—he went west and was never after heard from.

CHILDREN.

561. EMILY CHRISTIAN, b. September 12, 1850, at St. G., Mo.
562. LAURA, b. April 15, 1854. " "
563. EUNICE OUSLEY, b. February 25, 1858, at St. Louis, Mo.
564. ELENORA, b. October 7, 1860, at St. Genevieve, Mo.

Mrs. Moore had a daughter by her second husband, named Daisy, b. at St. Louis January 8, 1868, and in May, 1870, the family moved to New York.

289. MARY ANN LEAVENWORTH.[6]—RALPH[5], AMOS,[4] JOHN,[3] THOMAS,[2] THOMAS.[1]

Born December 27, 1824, in St. Genevieve Co., Mo.

Married James C. Cozens, September 19, 1848. He is a farmer and resides in St. Genevieve Co., Mo. He was born in that county April 1, 1820. His father was from Ireland.

CHILDREN.

1. MARY ANN, b. July 8, 1849.
2. FRANKLIN LEAVENWORTH, b. October 14, 1850.
3. SARAH PERNETTA, b. February 19, 1852.
4. NOAH WILLIAM, b. February 21, 1853.
5. JAMES, b. November 19, 1855.
6. JOHN COFFMAN, b. September 29, 1857.
7. EDWARD, b. September 21, 1859.
8. JANE LANE, b. October 27, 1861.
9. JOSEPH F., b. November 23, 1863, d. April 1, 1864.

290. Noah Hunt Leavenworth.[6] — RALPH,[5] AMOS,[4] JOHN[3], THOMAS[2], THOMAS.[1]

Born October 7, 1826, in St. Genevieve, Co., Mo.

Married 1865. Was a steamboat captain. His home is in St. Louis.

291. Franklin Leavenworth.[6]—RALPH[5], AMOS,[4] JOHN,[3] THOMAS[2], THOMAS.[1]

Born September 13, 1828, in St. Genevieve Co., Mo.

Married ANN D. JONES, October 7, 1855. She was from Ky. and was born June 22, 1836.

Resides in St. Louis, Mo., and is an engineer. In 1855, he was in the lime business. His children were born in St. Genevieve Co., Mo.

CHILDREN.

565. AUGUSTA W., b. May 1, 1857, d. December 15, 1860.

566. CHARLES J. b. August 29, 1859, d. October 19, 1860.
567. WILLIE, b. August 8, 1861.
568. GEORGE, b. March 15, 1863, d. November 27, 1863.
569. FRANKLIN, b. April 29, 1864.

295. Joseph Harrison Leavenworth.[6] — RALPH,[5] AMOS,[4] JOHN,[3] THOMAS,[2] THOMAS.[1]

Born April 27, 1841, in St. Geneveive Co., Mo.
In 1865 was a steamboat clerk.

296. Elihu Leavenworth.[6]—JEHIEL,[5] ELIHU,[4] JOHN,[3] THOMAS,[2] THOMAS.[1]

Born in 1805, at Woodbury, Conn.

Married, first, MARIE SHAVER, in 1824. She died in 1827, at Hillsdale, N. Y.

Married, second, MARIA LUCINDA BURLISON before 1832, in Clarence, Erie Co., N. Y. She was born January 11, 1806, in Vermont. She died January 14, 1863 or '64, aged fifty-seven, having married again. He was a clothier. Went to Michigan in 1844, and died in the fall of 1849. His children were born in Hillsdale, N. Y., except the youngest by his second wife.

CHILDREN.

570. JOHN JEHIEL, b. in Spring of 1824, d. in 1846. Enlisted and died in Mexican war.
571. MARIA, b. in Spring of 1827, d. in 1858.
572. WILLIAM H., b. March 7, 1832.

Elihu was at his brother LeGrand's, in Canaan, in the Fall of the year 1849, and left there to return to his family in Michigan and died in Bruce, Mich., Dec. 1, 1849.

297. Le Grand Leavenworth.[6] — JEHIEL,[5] ELIHU,[4] JOHN[3], THOMAS[2], THOMAS.[1]

Born April 28, 1807, in Woodbury.

Married REBECCA MANSFIELD, of Canaan, Conn., May 12, 1834. She was born May 4, 1810. He resided in Canaan, Conn. Was a miller, and died there May 25, 1864. In 1837 he removed to

Johnsonville, Trumbull Co., Ohio, but returned. Was a farmer She is now, 1870, living at Bridgeport.

CHILDREN.

573. WILLIAM, b. March 27, 1835, d. June 2, 1857.
574. PHINEAS, b. March 10, 1837, d. January 1, 1866.
575. LAURA A., b. July 13, 1839.
576. CARRIE, b. July 13, 1843.
577. MARY, b. May 12, 1844, now, 1870, at Bridgeport.
578. IRA, b. March 30, 1847, d. July 12, 1862, at Canaan.
579. ELISHA M., b. November 16, 1849, now, 1870, at Bridgeport.
580. GEORGE, b. August 9. 1852, now, 1870, at Bridgeport. A car-painter.

The first three children born at Johnsonville, O. Carrie at Salisbury, Conn. The others in Canaan, Conn., where he resided all the latter part of his life.

298. William C. Leavenworth.[6] — JEHIEL,[5] ELIHU,[4] JOHN,[3] THOMAS[2], THOMAS.[1]

Born ——— 1809, in Woodbury.

Was clerk in a store and died at Cannaan 1826.

299. SALLY M. LEAVENWORTH.[6]—JEHIEL,[5] ELIHU,[4] JOHN[3], THOMAS,[2] THOMAS.[1]

Born December 8, 1811, in Woodbury.

Married Luther Langdon, of Salisbury, May 28, 1831, at Canaan Falls, Litchfield Co., Conn. In 1834, moved to Johnson, Trumbull Co., O. In 1840 to Union Vale, Duchess Co., N. Y., and engaged in mining. In 1841 to Amenia Duchess Co., and engaged as above. In 1843 returned to Ohio, and in 1845 removed to Solon, Iowa, where they now live. They are farmers.

CHILDREN.

1. CAROLINE E., b. August 23, 1832, at Salisbury, Conn., m. Harvey S. Sutliff, at Cedar Township, Johnson Co., Iowa, June 8, 1856. He is a farmer and stock dealer.

Children.

1. CLARA A., b. in Big Grove, Johnson Co., Iowa, October 13, 1856, d. in Cedar Township, October 5, 1865.
2, JESSE B., b. in Cedar Township March 31, 1858, d. there Feb. 22, 1859.
3. FLORA V., b. in Cedar Township, June 14, 1859.
4. NANNIE M., b. in Cedar Township November 27, 1861, and d. October 21, 1865.
5. SON, b. in Cedar Township March 3, 1864, d. March 12, 1864.
6. MINNIE, b. in Cedar August 26, 1865.
7. HARVEY S., b. in Cedar, January 18, 1868.
8. CAROLINE, b. in Cedar March 21, 1870.

2. ELIZA A., b. December 15, 1834, at Johnsonville, Ohio.
3. HANNAH E., b. July 28, 1839, at Salisbury, Conn., m. George L. Griggs November 10, 1860, at Big Grove, Iowa. He is a lawyer.

Children.

1. EMMA M., b. July 17, 1861, at Big Grove.
2. BERKLEY L., b. October 24, 1862, at Big Grove, d. there Nov. 9, 1865.
3. LIZZIE D., b. at Iowa Falls, Harden Co., Iowa, September 1, 1866.
4, GEORGE LUTHER, b. at Iowa Falls December 18, 1870.

4. THOMAS E., b. November 2, 1840, at Union Vale, Duchess Co , N. Y. Enlisted in the 24th Iowa Infantry August 11, 1862, and was killed at the battle of Champion Hills, Miss., May 16, 1863.
5. DAVID M., b. March 21, 1844, at Johnsonville, Ohio, m. Mary A .Stream in Cedar Rapids, Linn Co., Iowa, January 29, 1868. He is a farmer.
6. ANNIE G., b. June 7, 1845, at Johnsonville, O., m. Perry C. Stream, at Cedar Rapids, Iowa, December 18, 1866.

Children.

1. THOMAS L., b. in Putnam Township, Linn Co., Iowa, June 11, 1869.
2. CHARLES ELIAS, b. at Grand River, Madison Co,, Iowa, Sept. 4, 1871.

Mrs. Langdon has been one of my most valued assistants in obtaining information in regard to her branch of the family.

300. CAROLINE D. LEAVENWORTH[6]—JEHIEL,[5] ELIHU[4], JOHN[3], THOMAS[2], THOMAS.[1]

Born in 1813, in Woodbury, Conn.

Married Herman Jackson, of Johnsonville, O., in 1835. She died —— 1837, at Johnsonville. She was born with but one hand; one arm terminated below the elbow, but she was still very able to do any common domestic work as readily as ladies generally.

CHILDREN.

1. JAMES, b. in Johnsonville, ——, 1837, d. ——, 1860.

302. MARGARET LEAVENWORTH.[6] — JOHN,[5] ELIHU,[4] JOHN,[3] THOMAS,[2] THOMAS.[1]

Born —— ——

Married, first, J. C. Booth, of New York city; a clothing merchant. He went to California, and died there.

Married, second, Judge Leonard Ferris, a former partner of her first husband and still resides in San Francisco, Cal. Now, 1872, at Virginia City, Nevada.

CHILDREN.

1. ELLA BOOTH, b. —— ——. She is with her mother.

304. Alson E. Leavenworth.[6] — ALSON,[5] ELIHU,[4] JOHN,[3] THOMAS,[2] THOMAS.[1]

Born May 17, 1831, in Little Valley, Cattaraugus Co., N. Y.

Married HANNAH M. EGERT, of Randolph, N. Y., October 7, 1857.

Studied law and was admitted to practice in the State of New York. Removed to Chicago in 1867, and is engaged in trade. Is a hardware merchant.

CHILDREN.

581. EDMUND FREDERICK, b. May 14, 1870, at Chicago.

305. Seth M. Leavenworth.[1]—SETH MARSHALL,[5] ZEBULON[4] ZEBULON,[3] THOMAS,[2] THOMAS.[1]

Born July 30, 1821, at Milltown, Harrison Co., Ind.

Married SARAH NETTLETON November 24, 1844, daughter of Joseph N. and Nancy Lowry, of Mt. Vernon.

He graduated at Indiana Universlty, at Bloomington, in the year 1841. Studied law with Mr. Edson, of Mt. Vernon, Ind., and settled there in 1840. Was many years in trade, after having practiced law at Mt. Vernon some years, but since 1857 has been Cashier of the Mt. Vernon Bank, (now the First National Bank of Mt. Vernon.) Died at Mt. Vernon November 21, 1868 after organizing the Mt. Vernon Banking Co. He was a very successful banker.

CHILDREN.

582. MARY L., b. November 26, 1845.
583. ESTHER, b. February 2, 1848.
584. NANNIE, b. March 18, 1850.
585. RICHARD H., b. February 2, 1852, d. April 16, 1855.
586. SETH MARSHALL, b. May 1, 1856.
587. FRANCIS P., b. September 3, 1858.
588. HUDSON P., b. May 24, 1861.

The oldest child was born at Leavenworth, Ind. The remainder at Mt. Vernon, Ind.

303. Francis P. Leavenworth.[6]—SETH MARSHALL,[5] ZEBULON,[4] ZEBULON,[3] THOMAS,[2] THOMAS[1].

Born January 27, 1824, at Milltown, Ind.

Went to St. Louis, Mo., in 1845. Was educated there, at the St. Louis University, and was afterwards graduated at the medical college in Philadelphia 1852. He was seven years quarantine physician at St. Louis, and died there May 17, 1857.

He was a man of fine attainments and great promise in his profession, but cut off in the midst of his usefulness.

307. Mark Leavenworth.[6]—SETH MARSHALL,[5] ZEBULON,[4] ZEBULON,[3] THOMAS.[2] THOMAS.[1]

Born December 6, 1825, at Leavenworth, Ind. Removed to St. Louis, Mo., in 1847. Was engaged in the steamboat business for twenty years and was in the banking business from the breaking out of the Rebellion. He died February 17, 1866, at St. Louis. At the time of his death, he belonged to the firm of "Gaylord, Leavenworth and Co.," Bankers. He was unmarried.

He commenced life as a clerk on a steamboat; soon rose to be captain and commanded at different times various fine boats on the Missisippi. He was a man of energy and activity and a successful banker.

308. HELEN LEAVENWORTH.[6]—SETH MARSHALL[5], ZEBULON,[4] ZEBULON,[3] THOMAS,[2] THOMAS.[1]

Born March 6, 1828, at Leavenworth, Ind.

Married Samuel Pepper, August 26, 1845, at Leavenworth, Ind. Removed to St. Louis, Mo., in 1857, is a lawyer and banker.

CHILDREN.

1. FRANCIS, b. February 8, 1847, at Leavenworth, Ind. d. August 6, 1855, at same place.
2. ESSIE B. b. May 30, 1849, at Leavenworth, Ind.
3. SAMUEL E., b. November 13, 1851, at Leavenworth, Ind.
4. FANNIE L., b. December 11, 1859, at St. Louis, Mo.

309. Zebulon Leavenworth.[6]—SETH MARSHALL,[5] ZEBULON[4], ZEBULON,[3] THOMAS,[2] THOMAS.[1]

Born June 2, 1830, at Leavenworth, Ind.

Removed to St. Louis, Mo., in 1849. Engaged in steamboating. Never married, and is still on the river engaged in steamboating, but resides at St. Louis.

310. John M. Leavenworth.[6]—SETH MARSHALL,[5] ZEBULON[4], ZEBULON,[3] THOMAS[2], THOMAS.[1]

Born March 26, 1835, at Leavenworth, Ind.

Married FANNIE M. SPARHAWK, June 5, 1852, daughter of George W. and Martha D. Sparhawk, of St. Louis. She was born there October 23, 1841. Removed to St. Louis in July, 1851. Engaged first in mercantile business, and then in steamboating. He was two years at the St. Louis University, then seven years with W. L. Ewing & Co., St. Louis grocers, then went on to the river, and has since been engaged in commanding various steamers on the Mississippi, commencing as a clerk. He died at St. Louis on the 3d day of June, 1873, of apoplexy.

CHILDREN.

589. GRACE, b. August 25, 1865, at St. Louis.
590. MARK, b. September 28, 1867. "

312. MARY JANE LEAVENWORTH.[6] — ZEBULON,[5] ZEBULON,[4] ZEBULON[3], THOMAS,[2] THOMAS.[1]

Born November 9, 1822, at Leavenworth, Ind.
Married John A. McKoon, at Leavenworth, July 30, 1840. Resides at Stanton, Kansas, where he is a farmer and merchant.

CHILDREN.

1. MAGGIE S., b. at Leavenworth, April 13,1841, m. Tollie Fowler at LaGrange Mo., December 3, 1858.

Children.

1. LINN F., b. March 9, 1861.
2. LEAVENWORTH F., b. August 10, 1863.
3. HENRY F., b. June 11, 1866. All at LaGrange.
4. CARTER F., b. at Stanton, Ks., February 5, 1869.

2. MARY JANE, b. June 24, 1843, d. at Leavenworth, April 22, 1847.
3. SARAH, b. at Leavenworth, August 22, 1846.
4. JOSEPH Z., b. at Leavenworth, September 1, 1849.
5. JOHN L., b. at LaGrange, Mo., October 1. 1854.
6. CHARLES M., b. " " February 11, 1858
7. OLIVER P., b.at Leavenworth, Kansas, April 19, 1860, d. at Stanton, Kansas, November 3, 1864.

314. LYDIA ISABEL LEAVENWORTH.[6] — ZEBULON,[5] ZEBULON,[4] ZEBULON,[3] THOMAS,[2] THOMAS.[1]

Born September 10, 1830, at Leavenworth, Ind.
Married Joseph Henry Thornton, at Leavenworth, April 5, 1849. He was Lient. Colonel of 49th Indiana Infantry, (Vols.) in the late war. Resigned July 27, 1863, on account of sickness. Resides in Cincinnati, where he is an accountant in a mercantile house. Was born at Madison, Ind., July 28, 1818, and is a son of Henry P. Thornton, lawyer, of Bedford, Ind.

CHILDREN.

1. MATTIE M., b. at Leavenworth, December 28, 1849.
2. HENRY L., b. " " March 6, 1853.
3. MARY BELLE, b. " February 10, 1857, d. at Leavenworth, December 29, 1859.
4. ALICE CAROLINE, b. at Cincinnati, O., October 5, 1867.

316. MAGGIE LEAVENWORTH.[6]—ZEBULON,[5] ZEBULON[4], ZEBULON,[3] THOMAS,[2] THOMAS.[1]

Born January 24, 1836, at Leavenworth,
Married, first, Allen D. Thorn, at Leavenworth, April 10, 1855. Allen D. Thorn was born at Fredonia, Ind., September 21, 1831. He died at Leavenworth November 23, 1855.

Married, second, Edward T. Sullivan, November 20, 1862, at Leavenworth, Ind. He is a produce dealer and has been a member of the State Legislature, and is now, 1870, a banker. Was born at Mt. Vernon, March 15, 1827. He is a gentleman of large and successful business.

CHILDREN.

1. ZEBULON LEAVENWORTH, b. at Mt. Vernon, January 6, 1864.
2. HARRIET E., b. at Leavenworth, May 1, 1866.

317. Oliver S. Leavenworth[6]—ZEBULON,[5] ZEBULON,[4] ZEBULON,[3] THOMAS,[2] THOMAS.[1]

Born September 2, 1838, at Leavenworth, Ind.

Married MARGARET L. BATES, September 3, 1861, near LaGrange Mo., daughter of James B. Bates, a farmer near La Grange.

Oliver L. is a farmer and resides at Leavenworth, Ind.

CHILDREN.

591. JAMES Z., } Twins, b. Aug. 3, 1862, near Leavenworth.
592. LIZZIE M., }

James Z. d. at Leavenworth, February 18, 1863. Lizzie d. October 16, 1868, at that place.

318. SARAH JENETTE LEAVENWORTH.[6] — ZEBULON,[5] ZEBULON,[4] ZEBULON,[3] THOMAS,[2] THOMAS.[1]

Born February 12, 1842, at Leavenworth, Ind.

Married Joel Alonzo Lyon, at Leavenworth, April 22, 1861. He is the son of Joel L., a farmer. He is a merchant and farmer at Leavenworth.

CHILDREN.

1. FANNIE M., b. at Leavenworth, October 1, 1864.

319. Elias P. Leavenworth.[6]—ZEBULON[5], ZEBULON,[4] ZEBULON,[3] THOMAS[2], THOMAS.[1]

Born June 12, 1845, at Leavenworth, Ind.

Married MASSIE E. BATES, near La Grange, Mo., February 2, 1869, daughter of James B. Bates, farmer near La Grange.

Elias P. is a farmer near Leavenworth. Massie E. Bates was born near La Grange, March 15, 1850,

321. LUCIA LEAVENWORTH.[6] — FREDERICK,[5] JESSE,[4] MARK,[3] THOMAS,[2] THOMAS.[1]

Born March 24, 1797, at West Stockbridge, Mass.

Married Rev. Asa M. Train, of Milford, Conn., November 2, 1826. He died June 14, 1863. Mrs. Train died at New Haven April 10, 1873.

CHILDREN.

1. AUGUSTUS L., b. February 18, 1828, at Waterbury, d. there Oct. 2, 1828.
2. ABNER L., b. September 16, 1830. Now edits Daily Palladium at New Haven.
3. ANN ELIZA, b. May 17, 1833, d. October 24, 1857.
4. FRANCES REBECCA, b. October 27, 1835, d. June 28, 1836.

The last three born at Milford, Conn.

2. ABNER L. TRAIN, b. September 16, 1830, at Milford, Conn., graduated at Yale College in 1853. Chief clerk in Prize Bureau, Naval Dep. in 1863-4. Married Susan A. Bull, of Milford, March 17, 1863. She died July 22, 1870.

Children.

1. —— ——, b. January 12, 1864, d. soon after.
2. ANNIE L., b. March 31, 1865.
3. WILLIAM A., b. June 12, 1866, d. August 12, 1866.

The following notice of Mrs. Train was sent to her relatives and friends on the occasion of her death :—

IN MEMORY.

Fell asleep in Jesus, on Thursday, April 10, at the ripe age of 76, MRS. LUCIA LEAVEAWORTH TRAIN, widow of the late Rev. Asa M. Train, for twenty-two years pastor of Plymouth Church in Milford, Connecticut.

The aged pilgrim has found rest at last in the home which knows no change. For many years suffering from those bodily ailments which are incidental to advancing age, and in her last illness enduring intense pain, she was glad "to depart and be with Christ, which is far better." Mrs. Train was a woman of strong character, with a clear intellect, a discriminating judgment, a generous heart, and unselfish devotion to the good of others.

What she was as a true helpmeet of one who, during so long a pastorate, served his generation as a faithful minister of Jesus Christ, how she abounded in good works, and illustrated the beauty of a symmetrical christian character, those who labored with her and enjoyed her companionship, can bear witness.

Being called, in the sad Providence of God, to part with three children, two in early life, and the third in the loveliness of budding womanhood, and finally closing the eyes of her dear husband in death, she has walked these many years past in life's journey almost alone, yet not alone, for Christ has been with her.

Mrs. Train left no dying words for her friends to cherish and enshrine in memory; but she did leave what is better, the legacy of a good name—the record of a life well spent. Having let her light so shine on earth, she has gone to shine among those who have turned many to righteousness, even as the stars forever and ever.

The funeral obsequies were observed at the residence of Dr. Beardsley, Milford, whither the remains were brought from New Haven, the place of our friend's decease. Tender hands bore the body to its burial, in the old family ground, there to lie with the dust of her kindred till the Resurrection.

322. ELIZA LEAVENWORTH.[6]—FREDERICK,[5] JESSE,[4] MARK[3] THOMAS[2], THOMAS[1]

Born December 17, 1798.

Married Charles Denison Kingsbury, March 5, 1821. She died November 16, 1852. Charles D. Kingsbury, son of John Kingsbury, (Yale College 1786),

Eng.d by G. E. Perine N.Y.

A. L. Leavenworth

and Marcia Bronson, b. at Waterbury, November 7, 1795. Engaged in mercantile business early in life. Read medicine for a short time, but remained in mercantile business till 1838. His health not being good, he then retired from business, and has since occupied himself in farming, and with his real estate.

CHILDREN.

1. FREDERICK JOHN, b. January 1, 1823, m. by D. J. S. Clark, of Waterbury, Alathea Ruth Scovill, daughter of William H. Scovill of Waterbury, May 29, 1851. She was born March 21, 1828.

Children.

1. WILLIAM CHARLES, b. July 2, 1853, d. March 2, 1864.
2. MARY EUNICE, b. June 9, 1856.
3. ALICE ELIZA, b. May 4, 1858.
4. EDITH DAVIS, b. February 6, 1860.
5. FREDERICK J. Jr., b. July 7, 1863.

Frederick J. Kingsbury, son of preceding b. at Waterbury, Jan. 1, 1823. Graduated Yale College, 1846 ; studied law at Y. Coll. law school and in office of Hon. Charles G. Loring of Boston. Admitted to Suffolk Co., (Boston) Bar, March 10, 1848. Afterward spent some months in the office of Hon. Thomas C. Perkins, Hartford, Conn. Opened an office in Waterbury, in the spring of 1849. Represented the town in the State Legislature in 1850, and obtained a charter for a Savings Bank, which he has continued to manage since that time and which probably influenced the future business of his life. In 1853, in connection with the late Abram Ives he established the Citizens' Bank, now the Citizens' National Bank of Waterbury, of which he still holds the presidency and retired from the practice of law. Banking was his principal business until 1868, when he became president of the Scovill Manufacturing Co. and has since devoted a large part of his time to that business. He is also treasurer of the Bronson Library, which has a permanent fund of $200.000 and is director and trustee in various other business, charitable, religious and public corporations.

He was a member of the State Legislature in 1850, 1858, and 1865. Serving the last two years as chairman of the committee on banks ; also in 1865, as a member of the committee on the revision of the statutes.

He has been much interested in the prosperity of his native town and taken an active part in the construction of public water works, in organizing and conducting the Bronson Library, in establishing a rural cemetery and in various other public improvements. His name has frequently been mentioned in connection with some of the highest offices in the State, but he has no inclination for political life and seeks relaxation from business in literary occupations and affairs of local public interest.

2. SARAH LEAVENWORTH, b. April 1, 1840, at Waterbury, m. February 24, 1863, Franklin Carter, Professor of Latin in William's College.

Children.

1. CHARLES FREDERICK, b. at Paris, August 10, 1864.
2. ALICE RUTH, b. September 17, 1865.
3. EDWARD PERKINS, b. April 13, 1870. The last two b. at Williamstown.

324. Rev. Abner Johnson Leavenworth.[6]—FREDERICK,[5] JESSE[4], MARK,[3] THOMAS,[2] THOMAS.[1]

Born July 12, 1803, at Waterbury, Conn. Graduated at Amherst College in 1825. Studied theology at Andover, and was licensed to preach April 22, 1828.

Married Elizabeth Manning Peabody, of Salem, Mass., June 14, 1831. She died June 25, 1841.

CHILDREN.

593. FREDERICK P., b. June 13, 1833.

594. HELEN E., b. June 11, 1836, m. John McGill.

595. ABNER AUGUSTUS, b. March 30, 1838, d. Dec. 2, 1841.

596. MARY FRANCES VIRGINIA, b. April 25, 1841, d. July 5, 1842.

The following notice of him was prepared by the Hon. Frederick J. Kingsbury, his nephew, to whom, as will be seen, I have in the course of this work been greatly indebted :—

"He began fitting for college at Waterbury, with Rev. Daniel A. Clark, and went with him to Amherst Academy, entered Amherst College and was graduated in the Class of 1825. He was at one time a student in the family of Rev. J. Hallock, of Canton, Conn., but I have not been able to ascertain the date. He was also at one time a student and assistant at the Rensselaer Institute, Troy. After graduating, he was principal, for a year, of an academy at Boxford, Mass., and completed his theological studies at Andover Seminary in 1827. He had intended to enter the Turkish missionary field with Dwight and Schaufler, but his plans were changed by the death of the lady whom he was to marry.

He supplied the Congregational church at Orange, Conn., one year, and was ordained pastor at Bristol, Conn., December 16, 1829. In June, 1831, he married Miss Elizabeth Manning Peabody, of Salem, Mass., a lady of great loveliness of character and highly accomplished. During her life she assisted him in his school enterprises, into which she entered with great zeal, and for which she evinced peculiar aptness. He was dismissed from Bristol in September, 1831, and removed to Charlotte, N. Carolina, where he became pastor of the Presbyterian church, and Principal of a Young Ladies' School. He also took a very active interest in the general educational affairs of the State. He delivered lectures, wrote articles for the papers, published pamphlets, and edited almanacs, endeavoring in every way to wake up the people to the importance of public education. In the Summers he traveled among the mountains, hunting with the pioneers, talking with influential men on his favorite topic, and preaching to such scattered people as he could bring together on Sundays. In 1838, on account of the health of his family, he removed to Warrenton, Virginia, where he established a school.

In 1839 having been called to the new High St. church in Petersburg, he left his school temporarily iu charge of his wife and went at once to Petersburg. At this time the trouble in the Presbyterian church was at its height, and he took an active part in the controversy. The church to which he was called, grew out of this difficulty, and was a new organization and without a building. Under his energetic management they soon had a handsome church provided with organ and bell. After the quarrel was adjusted, or had lost its force, the new church was absorbed again in the old one. After this, though he continued to preach frequently to destitute churches in various parts of the State, he assumed no regular charge, but devoted his energies chiefly to his school, which he had, in the meantime, re-established at Petersburg. He was pastor of the High St. church about four years. His school soon rose to great importance, and drew scholars from a long distance. He continued it with success until the breaking out of the war. He sympathized with the South in this unfortunate struggle, and entered into the contest with the same energy that marked all his undertakings. When the war was over he again turned his attention to educational matters, and at the time of his death was Corresponding Secretary of the Virginia Educational Association, an organization which owed its existence largely to his efforts, and through which he hoped to develop some broad plans in educational interests.

Mr. L. was a man of medium hight, rather slender, having thin, light hair, and bright blue eyes. He was very erect and dignified in his carriage, having great energy, physical activity and personal courage. He was a bold and vigorous writer, a ready and eloquent speaker, and accomplished scholar, both in literature and the sciences. He possessed rare administrative capacity and business talent. Whatever he put his hand to was very apt to prosper. As a teacher his talent amounted to genius. He combined a remarkable power of exciting enthusiasm in the minds of his pupils, with great facility for communicating knowledge, and a dignity of manner which enabled him to maintain discipline with little apparent effort. The resolutions passed at the time of his death, by the various bodies to which he belonged, speak in the highest terms of his ability and usefulness.

325. FRANCES AUGUSTA LEAVENWORTH.[6]— FREDERICK,[5] JESSE,[4] MARK,[3] THOMAS,[2] THOMAS.[1]

Born at Waterbury June 1, 1812.

Married Nathaniel S. Wordin, of Bridgeport, Conn., May 29, 1839. Nathaniel S. Worden, son of Thomas C. Wordin was born at Bridgeport, and bred to the business of an apothecary, which he followed for some years, but gave up business on account of failing health, about 1850. Is in comfortable circumstances, and has since devoted himself to the care of his property.

CHILDREN.

1. FREDERICK A., b. April 19, 1840, d. June 9, 1843.

2. HELEN CAROLINE, b. November 17, 1842.
3. NATHANIEL EUGENE, b. May 26, 1844, served three years in the army. Yale College, class of 1871.
4. FANNY L., b. August 19, 1848.
5. THOMAS COOKE, b. October 15, 1853. All born at Bridgeport.

326. Elisha Leavenworth.[6] — FREDERICK,[5] JESSE,[4] MARK,[3] THOMAS,[2] THOMAS.[1]

Born March 15, 1814, at Waterbury.

Married CYNTHIA C. FULLER, daughter of Benjamin Fuller, then of Waterbury, September 17, 1845. She died December 5, 1854.

CHILDREN.

597. MARY E., b. October ——, d. November 7, 1854.

He lives at Waterbury, Conn., and is the President of the Dime Savings Bank, of Waterbury. He was bred to the business of an apothecary with Dr. Lewis Hotchkiss, of New Haven; was in business at Milford for two years before reaching his majority, and afterwards with his father in Waterbury, till his father's death in 1840. He still retains an interest in the business, but has not been actively occupied in it for the last twenty years. He was for many years Postmaster at Waterbury, after the death of his father, and has been engaged to some extent in public business. He has several times represented Waterbury in the Legislature of Connecticut.

327. CATHARINE LEAVENWORTH[6] — JESSE,[5] JESSE,[4] MARK[3], THOMAS[2], THOMAS.[1]

Born May 1, 1792, at Danville, Vt.

Married, November 3, 1812, Enoch Hazeltine, cabinet maker then of Danville Vt. He subsequently removed to Littleton, N. H., then with his son Charles, to New Bedford, Mass., where he now resides (August 1870). He was born January 29, 1788 and died at New Bedford, February 1, 1873.

The following letters from Wm. Lloyd Garrison and Wendell Phillips illustrate the character of Enoch Hazeltine.

Boston, Feb. 9, 1873.

DEAR MR. HAZELTINE,—I see that your venerable father has at last succumbed to that law of mortality which, sooner or later, reduces the whole human race to dust, so far as these "fleshly tabernacles" are concerned; for over the spirit it has no power, except to change its sphere of activity and remove what would otherwise prove an insurmountable obstacle to development and progress. The translation must have been to him a joyous one, not only in the deliverance thereby secured from all bodily suffering, but in the advantages derived from being "clothed upon" for a higher state of existence. His was no untimely exit. The term of his earthly sojourn extended to that of two generations, and his birth was coeval with the constitutional organization of our republic. There has been no President of the United States, from Washington to Grant, no changes of the administration, no rise and fall of parties, outside of his personal knowledge. Though at no time conspicuous to the public eye, he was no ordinary man, acting well his part in all the relations of life. Eminently disposed to "prove all things," and equally inclined to "hold fast that which is good," he kept step with the foremost in the march of reform, eschewing all considerations of worldly expediency in a tenacious adherence to immutable principle, fearing no obloquy or persecution, and ever seeking to leave the world better than he found it. Hence his prompt and zealous espousal of all the marked reformatory movements of the present century—not at the eleventh hour,but among the earliest in the field; never waiting for reinforcements, or for that partial success which seems to be prophetic of ultimate triumph, but standing alone if need be, never doubting how the conflict would end. Such qualities of head and heart are too rarely found ; for there are few independent seekers after truth and duty , the great mass of society being controlled by traditon and custom, ever raising the old inquiry, "Have any of the rulers believed on him?"

To the present generation—especially the younger portion—it may now seem a small matter, requiring no moral courage or self denial, to have signed the total abstinence pledge and given an uncompromising support to the temperance cause more than forty years ago ; for that cause has attained the highest respectability, and gathered to itself the strongest moral forces in the land, enacting laws and shaping legislation for the futherance of its beneficent object. So far as relates to this part of the country, the "offence of the cross" has long since ceased in regard to the temperance question. But in its early stage, and for a considerable period, it had to encounter popular ridicule, censure, opprobrium, hostility, to an extreme degree. It was, therefore, a time that demanded exceptional conscientiousness, firmness, persistency, courage and fidelity:

"Possesions vanish, and opinions change,
And passions hold a fluctuating seat;
But. by the storms of circumstance unshaken,
And subject neither to eclipse nor wane,
Duty exists—immutably survives!

So reasoned and so acted your stalwart sire. Hence, no sooner was the antislavery flag unfurled than he enlisted for the war, and never laid down his weapons until victory was achieved, and every bondman set free.

An octogenarian, he was wholly exempt from the conservatism of old age. With deep conviction he united a teachable spirit, conforming his views to the light vouchsafed to him, and aiming always to be right. Blessed be his memory.

Very truly yours, WM. LLOYD GARRISON.

Charles Hazeltine.

9th February, 1873.

DEAR SIR:—Your letter I opened on my return from a lecture tour—too late to be of any service in the respects you were to pay to your father's memory. I regret this, for my heart warms at every recollection of the hardy few who bore the brunt and toil of that day of trial. I remember your father's name as often on tbe lips of those early laborers, though I seldom, if ever, enjoyed his society more than a few minutes at a convention. These are precious memories. He has left you the best of legacies—such a name and such an example. I am with you in earnest sympathy. Cordially, WENDELL PHILLIPS.

Mr. Hazeltine.

She died February 28, 1855. They had lost three infant children before birth of Frederick.

CHILDREN.

1. FREDERICK, b. September 28, 1817, d. September 29, 1865, at Littleton, N.

H.; was killed by overturning of a load of machinery which he was moving. He was a man of great energy and enterprise. He married widow Ellen Fuller, of Barton, Vt., in 1849, left one son Frederick. His widow has since married his cousin, Charles Hazletine.

2. NANCY, b. January 16, 1820, m. May, 1840, John S. Roby, a lawyer of Littleton, N. H., d. January 5, 1870. Her husband had previously died. Left two sons—Curtis and John Roby.
3. ROSWELL, b. October 20, 1822, d. September, 1823.
4. CHARLES, b. April 8, 1826, m. first, Lillias Clough, July, 1852. She d. 1860. Married, second, Abby D. Ottiwell, July 12, 1865. Lives at New Bedford, Mass. Musician and music dealer.
5. ROSWELL CURTIS, b. October 16, 1829, d. March 1, 1832.
6. ENOCH CARROL, b. August 9, 1833, d. March 7, 1848.
7. ANDREW ARTHUR, b. April 4, 1836, m. Maria Weller May, 1864. Profession a dentist, formerly of Littleton, N. H.

328. Dr. Frederick Leavenworth.[6]—JESSE,[5] JESSE,[4] MARK,[3] THOMAS,[2] THOMAS.[1]

Born May 11, 1794, at Danville, Vt.

Married SARAH WHITTAKER, of Danville, Vt., in 1817. He studied medicine with Dr. Samuel Collins, of Danville, his mother's relative; admitted to practice in 1816 or '17, and located at Wheelock, where he remained many years in full practice. In 1845 he removed to Dorchester, Mass., and settled in Neponset village, as a merchant, physician and agriculturist. He died there December 12, 1855. His wife died November 3, 1857, at Springfield, Mass., aged sixty-three, then living with her eldest daughter.

CHILDREN.

598. CYNTHIA MARIA, b. January 8, 1819.
599. MELINA, b. June 22, 1822.
600. HARRIET FRANCES, b. August 3, 1830.

All born at Wheelock, Vt.

He had a thorough knowledge of his profession, a fine person and prepossessing manner and address, which enabled him at an early day, to command an extensive practice, almost without a rival, in the towns of Wheelock and Sheffield, and extending also into neighboring towns. He finally left Wheelock in consequence of ill health, brought on by his arduous and unceasing labors. Dr. L. was a christian gentleman, proverbial for his kindness and benevolence, answering the calls of the poor, where he expected no return, with the same promptness and fidelity as those of the rich.

329. NANCY LEAVENWORTH.[6]—JESSE,[5] JESSE,[4] MARK[3], THOMAS[2], THOMAS.[1]

Born September 27, 1797, at Danville, Vt.
Died February 10, 1820, unmarried, at Danville.

330. FANNY POPE LEAVENWORTH.[6] — JESSE,[5] JESSE,[4] MARK,[3] THOMAS,[2] THOMAS.[1]

Born November 27, 1800, at Danville, Vt.

Married Edward N. Darling, October 4, 1826; a farmer for several years, then engaged in mercantile business. Formerly lived in Lindon, then in Albany, Vt. Afterwards in Dorchester, Mass., and now, 1870, at Hudson, Wisconsin. She died at Hudson, Wis., August 24, 1872.

CHILDREN.

1. HENRY FRANKLIN, b. August 17, 1827, at Lyndon, m. Lydia A. Parker, at South Boston. Was killed June 19, 1860, by being thrown from a hand car, while in charge of a section of the Eastern Railroad. Died at Massachusetts Gen. Hospital, Boston.
2. NANCY MARIA DARLING, b. July 22, 1829, at Albany. Vt., d. ——
3. FREDERICK LEAVENWORTH, b. June 26, 1831, " " m. Abbie Maria Capen, at Neponset village, December 8, 1859.

Children.

1. FANNY MARIA, b. at River Falls, Wis., December 30, 1864.
2. CHARLES HENRY, b. at Hudson, Wis., August 11, 1866.
3. MINNIE JUDITH, b. at Hudson June 23, 1868.

4. CHARLES EDWARD, b. March 27, 1834, at Albany, Vt., m., first, Euphemia Stark, of Fox Lake, Dodge Co., Wis., September 27, 1856. She d. at Hudson, Wis., March 21, 1862; m., second, Loomia L, Lacy, September 7, 1863, at Hudson.

Children.

1. EDWARD LACY, b. at Hudson, Wis., August 1, 1868.

5. EMILY MELINA, b. October 2, 1837, at Albany, Vt., m. August 13, 1859, T. W. Pillsbury, Neponset village, Dorchester, (now Boston) Mass.

Frederick Leavenworth Darling and Charles Edward, his brother, are merchants at Hudson, Wis.

331. MARIA LEAVENWORTH.[6]—JESSE,[5] JESSE,[4] MARK,[3] THOMAS,[2] THOMAS.[1]

Born February 17, 1803, at Danville, Vt. Died March 13, 1823, unmarried.

332. MELINA LEAVENWORTH.[6]—JESSE[5], JESSE,[4] MARK,[3] THOMAS[2], THOMAS.[1]

Born June 19, 1805, at Danville, Vt. Died September 2, 1830, unmarried.

333. MARY JANE LEAVENWORTH.[6] — JESSE[5], JESSE,[4] MARK,[3] THOMAS,[2] THOMAS.[1]

Born ———, 1817.

Married Orrin Cutler. He is a farmer and cattle broker for the Massachusetts markets. Resides in Barton, Vt., (1867.)

CHILDREN.

1, AUGUSTA J., b. ——. Has a miliner store in Barton, Vt.

2. HARRIET H., b. ——. Teacher in Ladies' Seminary.
3. MILO C., b. ——. Druggist at Barton, Vt.
4. ANNETTE, b. ——
5. HARRY LEAVENWORTH, b. ——
6. AI, b. ——, 1860.

All facts in regard to the family were refused.

334. Mark Jesse Leavenworth.[6] — JESSE,[5] JESSE,[4] MARK[3], THOMAS[2], THOMAS.[1]

Born December 11, 1828, at Wheelock, Vt.

Married July 15, 1848, LYDIA C. DOWNES, of Byron. Resides at Andover, N. H., 1867; at Danbury, N. H., 1870. Farmer. Was in the army in 1864.

CHILDREN.

601. MELINES, b. August 5, 1849.
602. STELLA MARIA, b. August 17, 1852, d. July 16, 1853.
603. MARK HENRY, b. February 9, 1860, d. April 4, 1862.

335. Dr. Melines Conkling Leavenworth.[6]—MARK[5], JESSE,[4] MARK,[3] THOMAS[2], THOMAS.[1]

Born January 15, 1796, at Waterbury, Conn.

Died unmarried November 20, 1862, at New Orleans. Graduated at the Yale Medical School in 1817. Was Assistant-Surgeon in the U. S. army from 1833 until he resigned September 30, 1840. He never married. At fourteen he was sent to the Cheshire Academy, then under the care of the Rev. Tillotson Bronson, and then to the Ellsworth Academy, under the Rev. Daniel Parker, father of Hon. Amasa J. Parker. Here he remained three years.

At eighteen he began the study of medicine with Dr. Edward Field, of Waterbury; but soon went to study with Dr. Isaac Baldwin, of Great Barrington, Mass. He also studied under Dr. Jonathan Knight, and Dr. Eli Ives, of New Haven; and after attending two courses of lectures, was graduated in 1817, with high honors. He devoted himself largely to botany, and was placed in charge of the Botanical Garden attached to the Medical College at New Haven. He studied French at Augusta, and settled at Cahawba, Alabama; but his health suffering, he removed to Augusta, and became a druggist, and remained four years.

Melines C. Leavenworth

WATERBURY, CONN.

See Page 375 for the first part of sketch,
omitted by mistake.

He then entered the army as Assistant-Surgeon, and was stationed at Forts King, Jessup, Huron and Leavenworth, Black Creek and Camp Sabine, and finally at Fort Gratiot, Mich.

He served through the Florida war with Gen. Taylor, and remained eleven years in the army, constantly pursuing his favorite study of botany.

His knowledge of botany was very extensive, and his contributions numerous, and often acknowledged by Drs. Young and Gray, and very handsomely, in their large work; in Silliman's Journal, and by others. He made large additions to botanical science.

He resigned in 1842. He was with Gen. Henry Leavenworth at his death near the False Washita, on the 21st day of July, 1834. At the age of twenty he united with the Congregational church at Waterbury, and was ever a consistent member.

The following sketch of him was published in one of the Waterbury papers soon after his death:—

"The deceased was the eldest son of the late Mark Leavenworth, and after receiving an academical education, graduated at the Yale Medical College, about the year 1818, with high honors. Having a passion for the study of Botany, he was selected by the Faculty, with the late Dr. Percival, the poet, to make a tour South to obtain specimens, and develop the rich floral and herbal treasures of that sunny clime. Having discharged his mission, the doctor concluded to remain south, and entered into practice in Alabama, and afterwards, in Ga., but ultimately having a desire to enter the army, he obtained the appointment of Ass't-Surgeon in the U. S service, where he continued for ten years, and was with Gen. Taylor in the Florida war. Desirous of coming north, he at length resigned his appointment, and for the last 25 years has resided in his native place honored, and respected by all who enjoyed his acquaintance. He was one of the best read men in the place—a sort of walking library—never at fault for reference. Had he devoted his whole energies to botanical science, he would have had no superior in that branch. As a practitioner he was respectable and trustworthy, and hundreds of patients will never cease to remember his kindness and care.

The Doctor possessed an evenly balanced mind, the kindly traits predominating. He was free from all affectation, modest, though of an independent spirit courting no man's wealth or honors, and would cut his right hand off before being guilty of a mean action to advance his own reputation or interests. He had suffered from the imprudence of others, but he never repined, and took the world in the spirit of a philospher and Christian, always looking on the bright side. Generous to a fault, he was more mindful of others than of himself, a trait rare in these degenerate days. His integrity was without a stain, and in all the various walks of life he leaves an enviable record. The writer, who knew him well from childhood, and loved him like a brother—can bear testimony to the uniform excellence of his character and manly virtues. As one of our old citizens, his death will strike home to his early associates, few of whom now remain. He was, however, engaged in a noble cause, that stood near to his heart, and having devoted his last days to the service of his country, he leaves behind him an honored memory as a legacy to his many friends.

The remains of the deceased were intered in the Regimental Burying-ground but we trust, at no distant day, will be transferred to the family tomb at Riverside."

336. ANNA MARIA LEAVENWORTH.[6]—MARK,[5] JESSE,[4] MARK,[3] THOMAS,[2] THOMAS.[1]

Born February 10, 1798, at Waterbury.

Married Green Kendrick, June 12, 1823, at Augusta Georgia. He was then of Charlotte, North Carolina; afterwards removed to Waterbury Conn., and has since resided there. Died May 6, 1870.

CHILDREN.

1. JOHN, b. May 27, 1825. Yale College 1843. Yale Law School 1847; m. Marion Marr, 1849.

Children.

1. JOHN, b. February 13, 1850.
2. GREEN, b. May 31, 1851, both Yale College. Class 1872.
3. KITTY, b. September 6, 1852, d. April 17, 1861.

He is a manufacturer at Waterbury. John, the son of John, m. at New York November 19, 1870, Ella, daughter of R. H. Goldsmith, of New Haven, Ct.

2. KATHARINE, b. August 13, 1827, m. Frederick Gridley Wheeler December 12, 1849. Reside at Stamford, Conn. His business is in New York.

Children.

1. KENDRICK, b. February 8, 1852
2. LAURA W., b. May 11, 1853.
3. FRED G., b. May 27, 1855.
4. HOWARD, b. July 30, 1859.
5. LEAVENWORTH, b. June 30, 1860.
6. KITTY, b. August 5, 1865.

3. MARTHA, b. September 21, 1829, unmarried, lives with her father at Waterbury.

The following notice of Mrs. Kendrick is taken from the Waterbury American of May 9, 1870, and was written by E. B. Cooke, Esq., the senior editor, who had been a neighbor and friend throughout the greater portion of a long life:—

"Mrs. Kendrick was the daughter of the late Mark Leavenworth, a prominent man in his day, who favored her with an education superior to that of most young ladies of the time. With a superior mind, sound practical sense, quiet and unassuming manners, her genial influence was perceptible in all things relating to the family or society Amiable in disposition, with the kindest of hearts, her friendships were sincere and lasting. She was beloved and honored by all who knew her. An invalid for many years, she, so far as health permitted, shared in the various duties of society, an ornament to the circle in which she moved. Notwithstanding these manifold demands upon her time, it was at her home, and at the fireside in the bosom of her family, that her influence was pre-eminent. She was the center of a charming circle, which is now broken by the relentless hand of the king of terrors. She was fully resigned and prepared to meet the inevitable destiny. The deceased early embraced the religion of the Savior, and was a bright and shining example of christian character. She was a communicant for fifty years in the First Congregational church in this city. Few women have been more faithful and more beloved. Few have exerted a better and purer influence. She leaves one of the most fragrant of memories. She will long be missed by her friends, and by the community.

Thus another name is stricken from the roll of our older townsfolk, who are fast disappearing from the stage of life. The surviving relatives of the lamented dead can obtain comfort alone from above. God doeth all things well, though it may be hard to bear so sad a dispensation."

The following sketch of Governor Kendrick is taken from Bronson's History of Waterbury:—

"John, the grandfather of Green Kendrick, was a Virginian, supposed to be the second or third generation, from the original ancestor from Massachusetts. He was a tobacco planter, and had four sons, John, William, James and Benjamin, and four or five daughters. He was born about the year 1735, and died 1810. John, his eldest son, father of Green, removed to North Carolina about the year 1786, and was a tobacco planter, until the invention of the cotton gin by Whitney, when he became a cotton planter. He was a man of ability, integrity, and eminent usefulness in all matters pertaining to the church, the State, and society. He was a deacon of the Baptist church, was born in 1764, and died in 1823. The wife of the above John Kendrick was Martha Dinkins, daughter of John Dinkins, a wealthy planter, believed to have been of Welch descent. She was born in 1765, and died in 1825. Was a woman of many virtues, fulfilling the duties of life with a scrupulous regard to the precepts of the bible. She was the mother of eleven children, nine of whom became heads of families. There were eight sons and three daughters. Green was the seventh child, and is the only survivor.

Green Kendrick was born in Mecklenburg county, North Carolina, April 1, 1798, from seven to ten years of age, attended a common country school, to and from which he walked more than three miles night and morning. From ten to nineteen, he labored on the plantation, attending school at such brief intervals as his duties would allow. For two years during the latter part of the time he enjoyed somewhat better educational advantages than was common for the sons of planters at that time. He was very ambitious, both in his labors in the field and in his studies, and thus accomplished more than most others with whom he was associated. His father taught him industry and necessity made him frugal. At the age of nineteen after teaching a common school nine months he obtained a place in a country store where he remained about a year, when he procured a more desirable position as salesman in a store in Charlotte, the county town. In a little more than a year he purchased the stock of his employer on credit and commenced business on his own account. In 1823, he married Anna Maria, daughter of Mark Leavenworth, of Waterbury. The death of his father which occurred about this time, put him in possession of additional means. He continued the mercantile business at Charlotte, until the spring of 1829, when he closed it and removed to Waterbury where he engaged in the manufacture of clocks under the name of Mark Leavenworth & Co., and in that of gilt buttons, under the name of Leavenworth and Kendrick; since then he has continued to be interested to some extent in the manufacture of the various articles for which Waterbury is somewhat distinguished. In 1845, 1847, and 1858, Mr. Kendrick was a member of the House of Representatives, of Connecticut. In 1846, he was elected to the Senate and was chosen Lieut. Governor in 1851. In 1854, he was again a member of the house and Speaker, after the resignation of L. F. S. Foster, who was elected to the United States Senate and throughout the session of 1856, he was the Speaker of the House of Representatives.

In addition to the foregoing account of Governor Kendrick, it should be stated that since the publication of Dr. Bronson's History, he has been often in the upper or lower house of the Legislature of Connecticut, and in all three years in the Senate, and in all, eight in the Houses.

He has at different times presided over three of the manufacturing corporations of the city of Waterbury and has been for many years, and is now (1873) Chairman of the Board of Education. He was elected President of the Bronson Library (a splendid institution, with a capital of $200.000) for ten years from the fourth day of July 1868, and still holds that position.

For two years, he was County Commissioner. From his first residence at Waterbury, he has been one of the most liberal and active members of the first Congregational society. He was Chairman of the Building Committee, which erected the present church in 1840, and is now Chairman of another Building Committee elected to erect another church ubon the same ground, and has subscribed ten thousand dollars towards the fund for its erection.

The city of Waterbury is mainly indebted to him and two other gentlemen, now deceased, for the beautiful park which so elegantly adorns its center. Indeed, for forty years past he has taken a very active and conspicuous part in all matters pertaining to the interests and prosperity of the city, county and State of his adoption. His enterprise and public spirit have contributed greatly to the beauty and growth of the city of Waterbury, and advancing years have not dampened his ardor or his anxiety still to be useful.

It must be to him a source of great satisfaction, that his fellow citizens have fully appreciated the value of his services, and have at all times been ready to make it manifest both by word and deed.

Before handing the above to the printer, I learn from the public papers that Mr. K. died at Waterbury, of paralysis, on the 25th day of August, 1873.

The Waterbury Daily American of the 26th inst. thus announces his death :—

"DEATH OF HON. GREEN KENDRICK.

"We announce to-day, with feelings of deep grief and sadness, the death of the Hon. Green Kendrick, one of the oldest and most esteemed citizens of Waterbury. Mr. Kendrick has been suffering for the past ten days from a severe attack of rheumatism, which confined him to his house and part of the time to his bed. Yesterday afternoon about half past three, he was stricken with paralys s, from which he died at half past ten in the evening, never having shown thei least sign of consciousness from the time of the fatal attack until death relieved him from his sufferings, and took from our midst a man honored for his liberality, kindness of heart and sterling integrity. He was a native of Charlotte, N. C., but has resided in Waterbury for over forty years, and was one of those noble pioneers who aided in laying the foundation of the future greatness and prosperity of our city, and as a business man contemporaneous with the Scoville Brothers, J. P. Elton, and Aaron Benedict,—names including Green Kendrick, which Waterbury can not too much honor. Mr Kendrick has repeatedly, and without solicitation on his part, received places of trust at the hands of his fellow-townsmen. We defer a more extended obituary until to-morrow. This sudden and unexpected event has cast a gloom over the whole community."

The same paper of the 28th of August, contains the following editorial notice of Gov. K., omitting some facts in his life, contained above :—

"A PROMINENT CITIZEN GONE.

It is not often that our community is so deeply moved as it was on Wednesday by the news of the death of Hon. Green Kendrick. It was known to a few of his friends that he was confined to his house by illness ; but the sudden stroke by which he was cut down could not have been foreseen and when the fact was communicated to the public that he was dead, surprise and sadness were mingled in all hearts. There is scarcely another citizen in Waterbury who has filled so large a space in it for many years past, or who has done so much to develop the resources of the city, to harmonize and elevate its various classes, and thus to secure a lasting place in the remembrance of the people. He had resided in this town forty-four years, and almost from the first, had exerted a marked influence in business, in politics, and in the social life of the community. But his influence was not confined to Waterbury ; he was known throughout the State, and fn former years had held some of the highest offices in the gift of the people.

Amidst the cares of a busy life Mr. Kendrick found opportunity to interest himself in the great public questions of the times, both within the limits of the town, and in the State at large. He was an active member of the Whig party so long as it remained in existence, and frequently represented his doctrines as well as the general interests of his adopted town, in the State Legislature. He was repeatedly chosen to the House of Representatives, and more than once to the Senate. In 1851 he was elected Lieutenant-Governor of the State,

Green Kendrick

WATERBURY CONN

the late Thomas H. Seymour being Governor, and subsequently in an election by the legislature came within one vote of being chosen Governor. In 1854, after the resignation of the Hon. LaFayette S. Foster, he was made Speaker of the House, and was again chosen speaker in 1856. In the breaking up and reconstruction of parties in 1856, he cast in his lot for a time, with the Fillmore men, but ere long, in view of the attitude of the Republican party towards the South and its "institutions," he became a Democrat, and so continued to the end of his life. By nature a broad and kindly man, he largely out-grew in his later years the bondage of party, and exhibited a large liberality and a constant desire for conciliation and the spread of good feeling.

Mr. Kendrick's influence in his own town was very marked, and was always exerted in favor of progress and right. He did much to develop and beautify the city, and to the very last was interested in the various public enterprises of the place, and anxious in regard to its future growth. For many years he was a member of the Board of Education, and at the time of his death was its president. He was also president of the Board of Agents of the Bronson Library, and was deeply interested in the progress of education and good taste among the people. He was an active member of the Congregational Society, and next to the late Aaron Benedict, was the largest contributor to the building fund for the new church now in process of erection. He was chairman of the building committee, and until within two or three days of his death watched the progress of the new edifice with deep interest.

Educated a Baptist, Mr. Kendrick never saw his way clear to uniting with the Congregational church; but his interest in religion was deep and constant and his desire to live a Christian life, frequently found distinct expression in his converse with intimate friends. Amid the sorrows of his later life, he bore himself with Christian resignation and courage. It was only to those who knew him best, that the seriousness of his purpose, the depth and vigor of his thinking, and the kindness of his heart were fully known. He found his chief joy not in his own comfort but in the happiness of others, and died admidst the sympathies and affections of the entire community. When the people of Waterbury assemble on the morrow to follow his remains to their burial, they will mourn a leader and a father,—a citizen who deserves to be honored, a true and noble man whose decease will long be regretted.

337. Mark M. Leavenworth.[6]—MARK,[5] JESSE,[4] MARK[3], THOMAS[2], THOMAS.[1]

Born May 13, 1800, at Waterbury, Conn.

Died July 22, 1825, of fever, at Middletown, Conn., after an illness of ten days, unmarried.

He was the son of Mark, and the great-grandson of Rev. Mark Leavenworth, both of Waterbury, and was born May 13, 1800. His mother was Anna, a daughter of Moses Cook, also of Waterbury, a woman of excellent sense, and greatly esteemed. His earliest education was obtained in the common schools of his native village. Resolved to go to college, he began to fit himself by classical study, but when he was nearly prepared, owing partly to excessive application, his eyes failed and he was obliged reluctantly to change his plans.

In the fall of 1823, he joined the medical class of Yale College, and for one term attended the lectures of Drs. Smith, Ives and Knight. Subsequently, he became the student of Dr. Edward S. Cone, of Middletown, the intimate friend of Drs. Miner and Tully, prosecuting diligently his chosen profession. The last two had just become famous as the authors of a volume containing peculiar views of practice, entitled "Essays on Fevers and other Medical Subjects." Dr. Cone sympathized with these views, while his pupil, naturally enough, became an earnest convert. Dr. Tully had recently been appointed to a chair in the Vermont Academy of Medicine, in Castleton, and there young Leavenworth repaired in the fall of 1824, to hear the great man lecture. He returned an enthusiastic admirer of the Professor and of his teachings.

In the summer of 1825, the spotted fever, or "sinking typhus" had made its appearance in Middletown, and Mr. Leavenworth, (at that time in Waterbury), was sent for by Dr. Cone, to assist them in their business. Though discouraged by his father, he accepted the invitation, unwilling to lose so good an opportunity to test the practice of his instructors, and to gain important knowledge. Worn down with incessant attendance on the sick, and disheartened, probably, by the unyielding character of the disease, he was himself at length attacked, and in spite of the best skill of his physicians, died July 22, 1825, aged twenty-five.

Dr. Miner published in pamphlet form an interesting history of the fever, (which he styled *typhus syncopalis*), in which he gave a detailed account of the unfortunate case before us.

Thus was cut down when he had nearly completed his professional studies, and when engaged in the discharge of imperious duty, a young man of rare accomplishments and great promise. His death was mourned by a large circle of medical friends, and by the whole community in which he had lived, while his father's susceptible heart was nearly broken by the loss of his favorite son.

Dr. Miner says in regard to him :—

"It is rare that an instance of mortality is attended with a combination of circumstances equally afflicting, and at the same time equally consoling to his sorrowing relatives, friends and acquaintances. The death of such a young man is as much a public as a private loss.

"From his classical education, from his close application to the study of physic and the auxiliary sciences, from his accurate discrimination at the bedside of the sick, he promised fairer to arrive at high eminence and usefulness than most of the candidates of the profession.

"To an uncommonly amiable disposition, was added the all-important qualification of being a man of hopeful piety. He was not ashamed of the gospel of Christ, but several years since made a profession of religion, and was a member in full communion, with the First Congregational church in his native town."

He was a young gentleman of remarkably fine personal appearance, of agreeable address, polished manners, unblemished character and high promise. Of all the young men who bore the name fifty years since, no one was more generally beloved and admired, or entered upon the duties of life with brighter promise.

The author made his acquaintance while at Yale in the winter of 1823-4, and became at once one of his warm friends and admirers.

338. Benjamin Franklin Leavenworth.[6]—MARK,[5] JESSE[4], MARK,[3] THOMAS,[2] THOMAS.[1]

Born July 27, 1803.

Married, JANE BARTHOLOMEW, November 12, 1833, She now lives in New Haven. Was murdered in Calaveras Co., Cal., 1851. Left no children.

341. CATHARINE E. LEAVENWORTH.[6]—MARK,[5] JESSE,[4] MARK,[3] THOMAS[2], THOMAS.[1]

Born August 1, 1816.

Married Corydon S. Sperry, June, 1835. He died February 10, 1856. She died February 9, 1855.

CHILDREN.

1. HARRIET L., b. May 3, 1836, m. August 6, 1860, Edward H. Twining, Professor of Chemistry in the University of Minnesota.

Children.

1. DAUGHTER, b. August 4, 1861, d. August 4, 1861.
2. MARGARET JOHNSON, b. October 5, 1864, d. June 14, 1865.
3. JANE LEAVENWORTH b, February 5, 1866.
4. ALMIRA CATLIN, b. November 13, 1867.
5. A SON, b. January 6, 1870, d. January 6, 1870.

2. MARY M. b. February 24, 1839, m. December 20, 1864, Ransom Holly, Wolcottville, Ct.
3. MARK L., b. October 23, 1842, lives at Waterbury, Sec'y Scovill M'f'g Co.
4. CHARLES S., b. September 3, 1847, Lieutenant in U. S. Navy.
5. CATHARINE E., b. March 4, 1850.
6. HELEN, b. May 8, 1853.

342. Jesse Henry Leavenworth.[6]—HENRY,[5] JESSE,[4] MARK[3], THOMAS[2] THOMAS.[1]

Born March 29, 1807, at Danville, Vt.

Married ELVIRA CAROLINE CLARK, daughter of Festus Clark, of Sacketts Harbor, June 12, 1832, b. in Sherburne Chenango Co., N. Y., January 3, 1813.

He received an appointment as Cadet at West Point, through the influence of Governor Palmer, of Vt., in 1826. Was commissioned as Brevet Second Lieutenant 4th U. S. Infantry July 1, 1830; in 2d Infantry 1831. Resigned October 31, 1836; civil engineer. Was stationed at Chicago some years and superintended the erection of the piers etc., to the harbor. In 1862, was commissioned as a Colonel by Stanton while secretary of war with full power to select his own officers. Raised one thousand men at Denver, Col.,—the "Rocky Mountain Rangers." They were furnished with mountain howitzers for fighting Indians, who were then very troublesome, being continually incited by Gen. Albert Pike and his agents. He defended a thousand miles of frontier against the Indians during the war, and is now and has been since 1865, employed by Government negotiating with the Indians on the Plains.

CHILDREN.

604. HENRY CLARK, b. August 1, 1833, at Mackinac, d. November 2, 1856, at Peshtigo, Green Bay.

605. MARY ELIZABETH, b. May 21, 1836, at Mackinac.

606. ALIDA CAROLINE, b. April 2, 1841, at Chicago.

607. JESSE ELVIRA, b. November 16, 1843.

608. FRANKLIN. b. July 28, 1846, d. August 18, 1846.

609. FESTUS AKERLY, b. June 6, 1848, d. September 6, 1849.

610. HARRIET MAY, b. March 9, 1851.

611. KATE, b. September 17, 1853, d. June 17, 1868, in Milwaukee.

The last five born in Milwaukee.

One of the high mountains above Georgetown, in Colorado, is called Mount Leavenworth, in honor of the Colonel and his services, in protecting that Territory during the Rebellion.

343. EUNICE ELIZA LEAVENWORTH.[6]—HENRY,[5] JESSE[4], MARK[3], THOMAS,[2] THOMAS.[1]

Born in 1806 at Danville, Vt.

Married Duncan McNab, 1825. She resided there till her marriage, and then removed, first to Canada, with her husband and his mother and then moved to Illinois. He died while on a visit at Toronto about 1867-8. She died in April 1872, on her farm at Half Day near Dunton, Ill.

CHILDREN.

1. JESSE L,, b. — 1827, m. Rebecca ——, has five children and lives at Dunton.
2. HENRY, b. — 1829, m., was drowned near Dunton before 1861, and left one child.
3. DUNCAN, b. — 1831, m. in 1861 and has two children.
4. GEORGE, b. — 1833. and lives at Half Day, on the homestead, is unmarried.
5. MARY b. — 1835, to 1840, and d. at Dunton, about 1860, aged 21, about.
6. ATLANTA, b. — 1841-2, d. at Dunton, about 1858, aged 17.

344. ALIDA YATES LEAVENWORTH.[6]—HENRY,[5] JESSE,[4] MARK,[3] THOMAS,[2] THOMAS.[1]

Born about 1820, probably at some Fort west of the Missisippi, died at Newburgh, January 21, 1839.

She and her mother are buried on the lot of the late Gen. Belknap, near the First Presbyterian church in Newburg. One monument serves for both. She is supposed to have been engaged to Gen, B.'s son at the time of her death.

The inscription upon the monument, which is of white marble is as follows,

ALIDA YATES,

DAUGHTER OF GEN. LEAVENWORTH, U. S. ARMY,

DIED

At Newburgh, January 21, 1839.

She was a young lady of rare accomplishments and a most lovely character and was universally admired and beloved in the village of Newburgh.

346. SARAH HANNAH LEAVENWORTH[6] — WILLIAM,[5] WILLIAM,[4] MARK,[3] THOMAS[2], THOMAS.[1]

Born at Albany June 16, 1818.

Married, first, Benjamin Pierson Watrous, merchant of Albany, at Waterbury, Conn., October 6, 1839, by Rev. Dr. J. L. Clark, in St. Johns church. He died in Brooklyn April 9, 1853, buried at Waterbury.

Married, seeond, Frederick A. Nash, lawyer of Akron, Ohio, October 1, 1855 They now reside at Brattleboro, Vt.,—*(1870.)*

CHILDREN.

1. SARAH FRANCES, b. October 23, 1840, at Albany, d. November 30, 1842.
2. WILLIAM EDWARD, b. August 18, 1844, at Hartford, d, Nov. 14, 1862, at Akron, O.
3. JOHN PIERSON, b. April 29, 1846, at Brooklyn.
4. CHARLES BENEDICT, b. May 17, 1849, " d. Aug. 31, 1850.
5. MARY TOTTEN, b. January 11, 1853, "
6. SARAH LEAVENWORTH *(NASH)*, b. September 24, 1757, at Akron, O.

347. Edward Leavenworth.[6]—NATHAN,[5] ELISHA,[4] MA THOMAS,[2] THOMAS.[1]

Born January 16, 1829, in New York city. Graduated at lumbia College in 1848. Was appointed Consul to Sydney, A tralia, just before the war, and remained there until the pe was proclaimed. He lives in New York city and on Staten Island.

348. Capt. Mark Frederick Leavenworth.[6]— NATHAN[5], ELISHA,[4] MARK,[3] THOMAS,[2] THOMAS.[1]

Born, October 17, 1832, at Bennington Iron Works, Vt.

Married, MARY ADELAIDE BOUCKER, of New York, March 6, 1861.

Died March 18, 1864, of disease contracted in the swamps of Tennessee, as Captain in U. S. army,

Left no children. Married by the Rev. Dr. Taylor, at Grace church, N. Y.

349. George Henry Leavenworth.[6]— NATHAN,[5] ELISHA,[4] MARK,[3] THOMAS,[2] THOMAS[1].

Born September 12, 1835, at the Bennington Iron Works, Vt. Was appointed U. S. Consul at the Bay of Islands, New Zealand. Returned after a four years residence there, and died a year afterwards, (July 9, 1865), of congestion of the lungs, unmarried. In 1854-5, etc., he was an engineer on the Eriè canal enlargement.

350. John Johnstone Leavenworth.[6]— NATHAN,[5] ELISHA[4], MARK,[3] THOMAS,[2] THOMAS.[1]

Born August 16, 1837, at Bennington Iron Works, Vt.

Died February 18, 1868, at Hartford, Conn., unmarried.

351. ANNE FLEMING LEAVENWORTH.[6]—NATHAN,[5] ELISHA,[4] MARK,[3] THOMAS,[2] THOMAS.[1]

Born March 4, 1839, at Elizabethtown, N. J.

Married Roderick William Cameron, February 12, 1861· He was from Glen Nevis, Scotland, and resides on Staten Island. N. Y. Married by the Rev. Edward Anthon of St. Mark's Church, N. Y. He is an importing merchant in the city of New York.

CHILDREN.

1. ALICE LEAVENWORTH, b. at New York, or Staten Island, 1861-2.
2. MARGARET SELINA EME, b. " " " 1862-3.
3. DUNCAN EWEN CHARLES, b. " " " about 1865-6.
4. RODERICK MCLEOD, b. on Staten Island in 1868.
5. KATHARINE, b. on Staten Island September, 1870.

352. Charles Leavenworth.[6] — DAVID,[5] ASA,[4] THOMAS,[3] THOMAS[2], THOMAS.[1]

Born January 26, 1796, at Canaan, Columbia Co., N. Y.

Married ELBERTINE KELSEY, at Green River, Columbia Co., N. Y., April 2, 1825. She was the sixth child of Calvin Kelsey and Mary Hogeboom, and was born at Alford, Mass., September 25, 1808. He died at Egremont, Mass., January 19, 1829, aged thirty-three. Yale College, 1815. He studied law with Robert F. Barnard, of Sheffield, Mass., brother of Dr. Frederick P. Barnard, President of Columbia College, and of Gen. John Gross Barnard, U. S. A., and of Mrs. Augustus Porter, of Niagara Falls. Settled at Egremont, Mass., and for many years did a very large business. But his constitution was feeble and he died of consumption at the time above stated. He was a constant reader, a good lawyer, and of strict integrity, had few friends, and with them was genial and entertaining, and a great favorite.

CHILDREN.

612. HENRY CHARLES, b. August 6, 1826, at Egremont.

He was devoted to books, but fond of fishing for trout in the pure sparkling waters of Green River, which passes through Egremont, and spent many of his leisure hours along its banks.

He was intimately acquainted with Wm. C. Bryant, and while he practiced at Great Barrington, Charles L. did the same at Egremont, an adjoining town. He was very fond of his violin and it was his constant companion not only at college, but till the very close of his life. Mrs L. subsequently married Mr. WARHAM BURT, of Southampton, Mass., brother of the Rev. Sylvester Burt, late of Great Barrington, and the Rev. Jairus Burt, late of ——, Conn. She is now, 1874, a widow living at East Hampton, Mass.

353. William Leavenworth.[6] — DAVID,[5] ASA,[4] THOMAS[3], THOMAS[2], THOMAS.[1]

Born November 10, 1799, at Canaan, Columbia Co., N. Y.

Married MARY DEBOW, August 11, 1830, at Allentown, N. J. She was the youngest child of John DeBow and Sarah Montgomery, daughter of General Robert Montgomery, of Allentown, and was born at Allentown, N. J., September 9, 1810. He died May 6, 1860, at Allentown, N. J.

William L. was in early life in trade with his father at Great Barrington, Mass., then at West Stockbridge; then lived in New York, Astoria, and on Long Branch. He was a man of great ingenuity, of fine mechanical genius, a splendid penman, a fine engraver, and, indeed, could do anything requiring ingenuity, mechanical skill or taste. He abounded in enterprise, enthusiasm and genius. He was over sanguine and hopeful, more intent on the object to be accomplished, than on its pecuniary results. He was at different periods of his life engaged extensively in business, and after a life of great activity he died of consumption, leaving his wife still living, and now, 1874, residing at Allentown, N. J.

CHILDREN.

613. James DeBow, b. July 5, 1831, at Allentown, d. April 1, 1856, at Sonoma Valley, California, at the ranche of Rev. Thaddeus M. Leavenworth. He was unmarried. He was a young man of most excellent character, and great promise.

354. Elias Warner Leavenworth.[6] — David,[5] Asa,[4] Thomas,[3] Thomas,[2] Thomas.[1]

Born December 20, 1803, at Canaan, Columbia Co., N. Y.

Married Mary Elizabeth Forman, at Syracuse, N. Y., June 21, 1833. She is the third child of Joshua Forman, and Margaret P. Alexander, and was born at Onondaga Hollow, N. Y., May 27, 1807. Resides at Syracuse, N. Y.

My father removed from Canaan, Columbia Co., N. Y., to Great Barrington, Mass., in the Spring of 1806.

I spent my early life at Great Barrington, among the beautiful hills and valleys of Berkshire. I spent the year 1819, at the Hudson Academy, under the care then of the Rev. Mr. Parker, father of the present Judge Amasa J. Parker, of Albany. I also pursued my preparatory studies in part under Erastus C. Benedict, Esq., at Great Barrington, now, 1873, one of the State Senators from the city of New York, and formerly President of the Board of Education there. I entered Williams College as a Sophomore, in the Fall of 1820, and remained there one year.

My father was persuaded to send me one year to Williams, in consequence of President Moore's going to Amherst, and of

E W Leavenworth

SYRACUSE, N.Y.

the effort made in Berkshire to sustain the College at Williamstown at that very trying period in its history.

I entered Yale as a Sophomore in the Fall of 1821; was elected a member of the Phi Beta Kappa Society in 1823; was graduated in 1824, and took my second degree in 1827. My room-mate the last two years was Willis Hall, Valedictorian of the Class, and late Attorney-General of the State of New York. When I entered Williams as a Sophomore, I was prepared to enter Yale as a Freshman, and had intended to do so.

On the 20th day of December, 1824, I began the study of law with Wm. Cullen Bryant, then practicing at Great Barrington, and on the 16th day of May, 1825, entered the Law School at Litchfield, Conn., then under the care of the Hon. James Gould, assisted sometimes by the Hon. Jabez Huntington. I remained there till January, 1827, living in the family of Judge Gould, and rooming with his son James, my classmate in college at Yale. In January, 1827, I was admitted to practice in all the Courts of Connecticut. The Spring, Summer and most of the Fall of that year was spent at Great Barrington, on account of the weakness of my eyes, but in the law office of the late Increase Sumner. On Monday, the 12th day of November, 1827, I left Great Barrington for Syracuse, reaching there, by great diligence, at sunset on the following Saturday. I selected Syracuse under the advice of the Hon. Joshua A. Spencer, late of Utica, who, in the Fall or Summer of 1827, was on a visit at my father's, in Great Barrington, which was the residence of himself and his father's family in his early life.

I was admitted in the Common Pleas as an attorney and counselor, at the February Term, 1828, on the motion of Gen. James R. Lawrence, and in the Supreme Court nearly two years later, at Albany at the October Term, 1829, as an attorney, and as counselor in 1833.

On reaching Syracuse, I studied and practiced with Alfred Northram, Esq., until February, 1829, when the late B. Davis Noxon, Esq., removed to Syracuse, in consequence of the removal of the Courts from Onondaga Hill. We at once formed a partnership, which continued with various members of the family until 1850; first under the names of Noxon & Leavenworth; then of Noxons, Leavenworth & Comstock, having taken in George F. Comstock and George W. Noxon; then of Noxon, Leavenworth & Comstock, George Noxon having died, and his father having retired, and James Noxon having come into the firm; and finally of Noxon & Leavenworth again, including James Noxon and myself.

I abandoned my profession in the year 1850, entirely on account of the state of my health. In the great campaign of 1840, I contracted the bronchitis by constant public speaking to large audiences, often for hours at a time, and continued for weeks.

It grew more severe from year to year, and was greatly aggravated by public speaking at Court. In 1850 my condition became somewhat critical, and though enjoying probably the largest and most lucrative practice in the center of the State, I felt constrained to retire from the profession and turn my attention to other pursuits.

While engaged in the practice of law, I uniformly remained in my office to eleven o'clock at night, and allowed nothing to divert me from my profession. Rest and care for two or three years, and abstaining from public speaking, fully restored my health, and other pursuits having engaged my attention, I never returned to the practice of law.

In January, 1832, I was appointed a Lieutenant of Artillery in the 147th Regiment of Infantry, commission signed by Enos T. Throop, Commander-in-Chief and John L. Dix, Adjutant-General. In 1832, I was appointed a Captain of the Artillery in the 147th Regiment of Infantry, commission signed as above.

In 1834, I was appointed Lieutenant Colonel of the 29th Regiment of Artillery, commission signed by Wm. L. Marcy, Commander-in-Chief, and Levi Hubbell, Adjutant-General. In 1835 was appointed Colonel of the same regiment, commission signed as above. In the Fall of this year I was nominated at the Whig County Convention, as one of the four Members of Assembly from Onondaga. But the county was hopelessly Democratic, or I should not have consented to be a candidate.

In 1836 was appointed Brigadier-General of the 7th Brigade of Artillery, commission signed by William L. Marcy, and by Thomas W. Harman as Adjutant-General.

In 1837 was appointed a Trustee of the Village in the room of Elihu L. Phillips, elected Sheriff of the County. In 1838-9 and 1840 was President of the village, going out in the Spring of 1841. In 1839 was elected Supervisor of the old town of Salina, then the largest town in the State, having in it four incorporated villages—Geddes, Liverpool, Salina and Syracuse. It was the first election at which the Democrats had been beaten for twelve or fifteen years at least. Re-elected in 1840.

In 1841 my resignation of the office of Brigadier-General was accepted, Rufus King, Adjutant-General. In 1846 and '47 was again President of the village. While President of the village from 1838 to 1841, the Board opened or extended many of the streets, which are now among the most important in the city. Among them was Warren street, opened from Jefferson south to Salina, and we built in it quite a substantial bridge over the Yellow Brook, at the point where Warren is intersected by Madison street.

During the year 1838, the Syracuse and Utica Railroad Company, applied for leave to locate their depot on Washington street, between Salina and Warren, with a width of forty-nine feet. The Board declined to grant the request, though favorable to it; but we called a public meeting for the action of the citizens to be held at the Syracuse house, on the evening of December 26, 1838, the parlor there being then the largest public room in the city. That evening Major Burnet, Capt. Putnam and myself with our wives, took tea at the residence of the late Volney Cook on Montgomery street. While there I drew up the resolution which was adopted at the meeting and as I was to preside, handed it to Captain Putnam, with a request that he would present it, which he did and it was adopted with but one dissenting voice, that of Dr. Mather Williams.

This resolution gave to the city Vanderbilt Square, the rows of trees which still line each side of the railroad from Beach street to the heart of the city, and the first public sewer which reached the Yellow Brook and the swamp which then lying between the village and the Lodi hills. It compelled the Railroad Company to buy twenty-six feet off from the the north end of the block south of the depot, and four feet off from that north of the depot.

Previous to 1839, the Geneva Turnpike ran diagonally from northwest to southeast, through the grounds now constituting Fayette Park. In the winter of 1839, while President of the village, I drew and favored the passage of a bill, (Laws of 1839, chap. 139, p. 115,) to enable the Trustees to make a contract with said company, to discontinue that part of their road, the village providing another. The same year I negotiated the arrangement, drew up the contract, had it approved by the Board and executed by the parties, thus securing the beautiful park which is now the pride of the Seventh Ward, and of the whole city. The contract is on the city files.

In 1846-7 the Board, at my suggestion, took possession of pieces of ground, then unoccupied, now known as Warren and Ashland parks, fenced them in and set out trees about them. The title to the former was then in the late Syracuse Company, and to the latter in the State. The city has ever since kept possession of them, and has since acquired title to Ashland Park from the State, I think.

In the Spring of 1849 I was elected Mayor of the city. The city was then grading and improving the "Mill Pond Tract." Under my direction, the tract was laid out with a park in the center of it, now called Armory Park, covering with the streets about it, more than half of the entire tract owned by the State. I took the map to Albany, laid it before the Commission of the Land Office, and was able to get it approved, only conditionally —provided that upon the sale of the lots they should bring $9,000, i. e., $4,000 for the lands, $4,000 for the amount paid by the State towards the improvement, and $1,000 for interest, expenses, etc. The lands were soon after sold at auction, and brought over $16,000, far more than the whole could have been sold for without the park.

In the Fall of the same year I was elected a member of the Legislature, to represent the city district. I was Chairman of the Committee on the manufacture of salt, and a member of the Committee on railroads. I found the members violently prejudiced against Onondaga Salt, though exceedingly ignorant of its merits and disposed to remove the tolls from foreign salt when transported on the canals. This feeling had grown out of a pamphlet written and circulated over the State, by Gen. Wadsworth, of Geneseo. So great was the prejudice, that of hundreds of petitions on the subject, asking the removal of the tolls, not half a dozen in all, and not one after the first few days were referred to the committee on salt, but they were sent to the committee on agriculture. But a full and candid discussion of the subject removed every prejudice, the tolls were allowed to remain, and the committee on agriculture made a report on the subject which was entirely satisfactory to me. The Legislature willingly passed just such a bill on the subject of salt as I drew up and offered.—Laws of 1850, chap. 374, p. 794.

The general railroad law of the State, chapter 140 of the laws of 1850, was reported from the committee of which I was a member, and was violently opposed, especially with all the influence Albany could bring to bear upon it. Messrs. Nott and Pruyn, able, astute and influential members, were most ably assisted by a young man just then rising into notice—the Hon. Wm. A. Wheeler, of Franklin—and by several other members. The main support of the bill fell upon me, being the only ready debater on the committee. The Committee of the Whole had nine sittings upon the bill. It was most earnestly and ably discussed, and finally carried by a decisive majority. The clause which alarmed Albany was the provision allowing entire freedom in the construction of railroads, which it was thought might be more beneficial to Troy than to Albany.

I also carried through the Committee of the Whole, the bill to improve the navigation of the Seneca river,—chap. 153, laws of 1850—against two very elaborate speeches made by the late Gov. Raymond, the ablest debater in the House, made on two successive days. I received the warmest congratulations of a large number of the members on my triumph, not only over Mr. Raymond, but over the Canal Board also, who strongly opposed the bill, and furnished Mr. R. with the facts on which his second speech was founded. When Mr. R. closed his first speech he did not intend further to debate the question. But in the evening following, Charles Cook, Canal Commissioner, furnished him with new facts, from which he made a second and very vulnerable speech, which I attacked very successfully. After the vote was taken I walked up to Mr. R., when he, highly excited, remarked, that "he never before had made such a d——d fool of himself as that day, in undertaking to make another man's speech."

The original Select Committee appointed for that purpose, having failed to carry their bill for the preservation of Washington's Headquarters at Newburg, at the solicitation of a delegation of gentlemen from that beautiful town, I undertook to secure the object desired. On the first day of April, late in the session, I moved the reference of the bill, which was still in existence, to a new Select Committee. The resolution was adopted and a committee of my selection was appointed by the Speaker. Among the number were General Burroughs, of Medina, and Joseph B. Varnum, of New York. We remodeled the bill, striking out the objectionabie part, making some slight amendments, and I, as Chairman, reported it to the House, and it was passed without difficulty. Thus was saved for future generations one, certainly, of the most interesting relicts of our Revolutionary struggle, and it has already grown into a place of great interest and resort.

There was another bill in the House that year, which excited a very deep interest. It was called the "Mason Will Case," and grew out of a long, protracted litigation to set aside the will. The will had been sustained by the Supreme Court, and their decision was affirmed in the Court of Appeals, by a tie vote.

The bill on its face provided that the Court of Appeals should grant a re-hearing in all cases of judgments of affirmance by a tie vote, between two certain dates. But on examination it appeared there was no such case between the dates named, except the one in question. It was, therefore, a bill by which the Legislature was to grant a re-hearing in a case finally decided by the Court of Appeals.

The friends of the bill had lobbied it most thoroughly. It had passed the House without any notice, or any question being raised, and the Gov. (Fish), had sent down his veto. I had been urgently requested on both sides to take part on the veto, and declined. Daniel Lord was counsel to sustain the will. But, to my utter astonishment, when the question came before the House the veto had a *very* feeble support, and many of the best men and even the best lawyers in the House—one who afterwards became a Judge of the Supreme Court—attacked it. I sat quietly in my seat as long as it was possible. But the bill seemed to me such an outrage, such an usurpation of the province of the Court, that I could not remain silent. I entered into the debate with all the zeal of my nature, and all the powers I could command, and made speech after speech. A large audience listened to the debate; the Judges of the Court of Appeals, then in session, and every one about the Capitol came in. After a long and highly exciting debate, the friends of the bill failed to over-ride the veto by only a single vote.

Several local bills also received my attention. But whatever of reputation I obtained during the winter was received mainly from my two days' pitched battle with Gov. Raymond, from the Mason will case, and from the protracted discussion on the general railroad act, in which I stood almost alone in support of the bill, and its opponents embraced several of the ablest men and best debaters in the House. No bill that winter excited a more general interest, and few that have ever been passed have been more important in their results.

The first Presbyterian church was built in the years 1849-50. The building Committee were Moses D. Burnet, Henry Gifford Albert A. Hudson, Thomas B. Fitch and myself. The first three were in favor of a brick church in some of the Grecian styles of architecture. I took decided ground in favor of a stone church in Gothic style, and refused to serve if they built any other. Mr. Fitch was also in favor of the stone church and Gothic architecture. We prevailed, and hence our beautiful brown stone Gothic church, one of the most conspicuous ornaments of the city of Syracuse.

In the fall of 1850, Washington Hunt was nominated as a candidate for the office of Governor by the Whig State Convention and thereupon resigned the office of Comptroller. Without any solicitation on my part, Gov. Fish had selected me to fill the vacancy, when he was reminded that I was still a member of the Legislature and therefore ineligible under the seventh section of the third article of the Constitution. Gen. Amos P. Granger, late Member of Congress from this District and other friends here had, without my knowledge, seen Gov. F. on the subject as I was afterwards informed.

In the Fall of 1851 my friends ran me at the State Convention for the nomination to the office of Secretary of State. Though not "on the slate" made at Albany by Mr. Weed and his friends, I wanted but six or eight votes, as I recollect, of a nomination. Hon. Russell Sage, and the Hon. Wm. A. Sackett were very active in my behalf, not being satisfied with my opponent, who soon after left the country under a cloud. While the canvass was pending, Mr. Weed offered me the nomination for Attorney General, or Judge of the Court of Appeals. But, had I desired either of those offices, which I did not (having retired from the profession in 1850, on account of chronic bronchitis), I could not have accepted of Mr. Weed's most kind and flattering offer, in justice to the many warm personal friends who were supporting me.

In the Fall of 1853, I was nominated for the office of Secretary of State almost without opposition, and with the full concurrence and, I think, at the suggestion of Mr. Weed, who has always been one of my best and most valued friends: in some degree, perhaps, on account of his great admiration of, and friendship for, Mrs. Leavenworth's father, the late Judge Forman, in whose family he lived for some time when a boy, at Onondaga Hollow.

During my term as Secretary of State, Gen. James M. Cook and myself, as a Building Committee appointed by the Commissioners of the Land Office, took down the old State Hall, corner of State and Lodge streets, and erected the Building known as the State Agricultural Rooms and the Cabinet of Natural History. John T. Clark, the State Engineer, was a member of the committee, but, on account of other duties, gave no attention to the erection of the building. Gen. Cook and myself were also the Building Committee for the extension of the Capitol, which was carried back eighteen feet, putting up the corridor to connect it with the State Library, and refinish and refurnish the Assembly Chamber.

With the aid of Franklin B. Hough, my chief clerk in the census department, I took the census of 1855; appointing all the marshals, some 2000, drawing up the interrogatories and instructions, and all the necessary blanks, superintending their printing and distribution into every corner of the State, and giving the necessary explanations and instructions to the marshals from day to day, often replying, for weeks together, to from 150 to 200 letters daily. Dr. Hough here brought into exercise and notice that patience, and industry, and accuracy, that extensive knowledge and capacity, which have since given him a national reputation, and placed him in the first rank of the statisticians of the country. Whatever of merit there is in the census of 1855, belongs in much the largest proportion, to the untiring industry of Dr. H., and to his remarkable qualifications for the task.

The State in 1854, owned that part of the city of Syracuse lying west of Plum street, north of the Erie canal, east of Van-Rensselaer street, and south of the salt water reservoir, and a portion of the Onondaga Creek. These lands were then used for the manufacture of solar salt. The removal of the coarse salt works having been ordered by the Commissioners of the Land Office, from those portions of said tract lying on each side of West Genesee street, sixteen rods in depth, the Commissioners, at my suggestion and solicitation, resolved to survey out and map the whole tract, and appointed me to supervise and direct in regard to it. This was done under and by virtue of chap. 391 of the laws of 1854, p. 986. I caused it to be laid out substantially as it now appears on the maps, straightening West Genesee st., laying out the lots on each side, 100 feet front and 16 rods deep, making the second class streets eighty feet in width, instead of sixty-six, as they are in other parts of the city; laying out a park near the center of the tract, just as large as the Commissioners would sanction, surrounded by ample lots, and with a broad avenue 120 feet wide, leading from this park to the vacant

State lands near the Pump House. When the map of the tract was sanctioned by the Commissioners and laid before the Common Council of the city, they did me the honor to give my name both to the park and to the avenue.

When I entered upon the duties of my office on the 1st of January, 1854, the Natural History of the State was completed, except the Paleontology, and this had been put into the hands and under the care of the Secretary of the Board of Regents, Dr. T. Romeyn Beck, and of the Secretary of State. On looking into the state and condition of the work, I found that it had been settled that the Natural History of the State was never to be completed, but was to terminate abruptly with the second volume of the Paleontology. This was to me most surprising. Professor James Hall had devoted nearly twenty years to the mineralogy, geology and paleontology of the State. He had made far the largest, the most perfect, and the most valuable collection of fossils of this State, and many from beyond it, ever made in the State, or likely to be soon. He had devoted a very large portion of the best part of his life to this study, and it seemed to be but a simple act of justice to him, to his own fame, that he should be permitted to complete the great work which he had commenced, and which was so far advanced. It seemed to me that the State should feel a just pride in the fame of one of its most eminent sons, who was doing much to make it honorably known to the Scientific men and learned societies of Europe as well as of America. It seemed to be due to the cause of Science, a simple debt which the State owed, that with such a collection of fossils, and with a citizen of our own State so pre-eminently qualified to classify, arrange, name and describe them, the great opportunity should not be thrown away. And if anything more were wanting, I was deeply impressed with the conviction that the State owed it to its own good character, and to its highest honor, after having already spent $600,000 on its Natural History, to go on and complete the noble work in which Prof. Hall was engaged, and which he alone could properly perform, and which would be the final completion of the original design.

Deeply impressed with these views, in the winter of 1854-5, I conferred with the Hon. Samuel Blatchford, of New York, then Chairman of the Committee of Ways and Means in the House, and with the Hon. Henry Raymond, then Lieut.-Governor, who entered into my views, and we resolved that the work should go on to a final completion, and they promised me their assistance.

The Natural History had already cost over $600,000, and was not popular with the Legislature. The Paleontology was still less so, few appreciating its scientific value. We did not dare to trust to an independent bill, which could not have been carried. Money was not then needed for the work, as several thousand dollars were still in the treasury, of a former appropriation. But the appropriation bill seemed the only mode of proceeding which promised success. A section was therefore prepared. Mr. Blatchford inserted it in the bill, "appropriating $5000 for "the payment of any expenses growing out of the Natural His-"tory of the State, to be applied only on the certificate of the "Secretary of State and the Secretary of the Board of Regents, "who are hereby authorized and directed to take charge of all "the matters appertaining to the compilation and *completion* of "such Natural History, with power to make such contracts, *lim-"iting the number of volumes*, and fixing the compensation, and "otherwise as they may think proper."—Chap. 539 of the laws of 1855, p. 1015.

Besides Messrs. Raymond and Blatchford, there was probably not a member in either House who knew the provisions of the law as it then stood in regard to the Natural History. The words "completion," and "limiting the number of volumes," sounded very pleasantly, and the clause was passed without objection.

Various questions then arose in my mind in regard to the salary of Prof. Hall, the number of volumes, the number of years for each volume, etc., etc., and not feeling fully advised on these points, I invited the late Prof. Agassiz, Messrs. Gould and Dana, and Dr. Dewey, then of Rochester, one of the Professors when I was at Williams College, to meet me at Albany aud confer upon the subject. They came, the conference was held, they gave me their views, and I drew up the contract. I allowed Prof. H. $ yearly for his salary, and $1000 yearly to be spent in fossils, and six weeks vacation each year, and settled the rights of the Professor and of the State in the fossils when the work was completed. Dr. Beck, (Theodore Romeyn) then Secretary of the Regents, was then confined to his room and mostly to his bed, with his last sickness. After the contract was drawn and signed by Hall and myself, I took it to the Dr. for his signature. He greatly disliked Prof. H., and long refused to sign it, making many objections. But a final and strong appeal to his pride in the Natural History, in the early inception of which he took a very active part, finally won his consent and his signature, and insured the completion of the great work of Professor Hall, which forever places him in the first rank of the Paleontologists of the world.

The Professor has done ample justice to my humble efforts in the matter, on the 10th and 11th pages of the preface to the 3d volume of the work.—See upon this subject a letter from Prof. Hall, Appendix, letter H.

As Secretary of State I was also ex officio visitor of the charitable institutions of the State; and in the course of my investigations, saw the great want of some superior investigating and supervising power, which would visit them annually, look into the manner in which they were conducted, and the appropriations expended, and report each year fully to the Legislature, both in regard to their management and their wants.

With this view, I drew up a bill which was introduced into the Senate by the Hon. Mark Spencer on the 31st day of January, 1855, entitled, "An Act in relation to Charitable Institutions "supported or assisted by the State, and to City and County Poor "Houses, and to create a Board of Visitors for the same,"—See Journal of 1855, p. 174. On the 2d of February the Committee reported favorably, and it was committed to the Committee of the Whole—p. 185. The bill was not disposed of in 1855, and on coming up in Committee of the Whole on the 7th of February, 1856, (p. 165 of Journal 1856,) it was disposed of by a resolution that the President of the Senate should appoint a committee of three who should examine into the affairs of all such institutions, obtain full information, etc.

In the Legislature of 1867 this subject was again agitated, and the Hon. Chas. S. Hoyt, Chairman of the Committee on Charitable Institutions, applied to me by letter for a copy of my bill of 1855. Having retained the original, I sent him a copy, perhaps slightly amended. This is, in substance the bill passed by the Legislature of that year, and much, if not most, of it literally the same.—Laws of 1867, chap. 951. p. 2396, "An Act to "provide for the appointment of a Board of Commissioners of "Public Charities, and defining their duties and powers."

In the year 1853, the Trustees of the State Asylum for Idiots had purchased five acres of land on the Troy road, near the Patroon's Mansion, at Albany, as a site for the institution. The site was very undesirable, and the Hon. Clarkson S. Crosby, then Senator from Albany, was so much dissatisfied, that he caused a provision to be inserted in the Appropriation bill of 1854, p. 621, authorizing the said Trustees to sell or exchange the site purchased. Under this provision the Trustees appointed a Committee, consisting of Rev. Dr. Pohlman, Gen. Franklin Townsend and myself, then an ex officio member of the Board, to examine the vicinity of Albany, find a more desirable site, if possible, and report. We made the examination and reported that no better site could be found. I submitted, also, in my own behalf, a long and somewhat elaborate report against any location at Albany, and accompanied it by an offer signed by some twenty gentlemen, at Syracuse, proposing to furnish without charge, any ten acres of ground about the city, or pay the trustees seven thousand five hundred dollars in cash, provided the institution was located at Syracuse. When at home a few days previous, I had invited some twenty leading citizens to meet me at my office, unfolded to them my hopes, plans and intentions in regard to the removal of the asylum, and procured their signatures to the offer of land or money, etc. This report and offer led to a very animated discussion, in which every member, I think, expressed his views. Gov. Seymour favored the removal to Syracuse, and the Hon. John C. Spencer, President of the Board, closed the discussion with a very earnest and able argument in favor of the removal, and it was carried by the votes of every member, except Messrs. Townsend and Pohlman of Albany. Mr. Weed kindly lent me the benefit of his influence to procure the removal, and Dr. Wilbur, Superintendent of the Asylum, was well known to favor it. John C. Spencer and myself were the Building Committee to superintend the erection of the buildings, but owing to his ill health he never visited Syracuse, and died before it was completed. But his place was ably filled by Dr. Wilbur, who devoted his time and thoughts largely to the work.

On the 4th day of January 1855, I was elected a Corresponding Member of the American Historical and Geographical Society, of the city of New York, and also, the same year, of the New England Historical and Genealogical Society, Boston.

In the fall of 1856 I was again elected to the Legislature, to represent the city district. I was Chairman of the Committee on Canals, and a member of the Committee on Banks; also Chairman of the Select Committee of one from each Judicial District, on the equalization of the State Tax. This committee was appointed on my motion. Early in the session, on the 17th of January, I moved the reference of the papers on file in relation to the equalization of the State Tax to above Committee. The Committee was appointed on the 27th of January. As Chairman of that Committee I afterwards drew up and on the 31st of January reported a bill providing for the appointment of a Board of three State Assessors, to equalize the State tax. This bill was discussed four several days in Committee of the Whole, was violently opposed by the members from the counties aimed at by the bill, but was sustained by a decisive majority, and on the 3d of April, as Chairman of a Select Committee to report important bills to have preference and be acted on before the final adjournment, I reported the above bill among others, and the report was agreed to. But owing to my delicate health, impaired by excessive labor, and my consequent absence for a few days, the bill, which was in my care, was not again called up at that session. But it was again introduced the next year but one, and passed, and has been, and is now, of immense benefit to the State. It is entitled, "An Act to Equalize the State Tax among the several counties in this State."—Assembly journal of 1857, p. 120, 137, 168, 216, 313, 330, 431, 537, 1081; also Laws of 1859, chap. 312, p. 702, etc.

I also drew up and introduced the bill, (chap. 504, p. 47,) entitled, "An Act to provide for an investigation into the origin of "fires in certain cases,"—a most beneficial bill, but the public have never availed themselves of its provisions as much as they should. Also the bill, chap. 804, p. 774, to remove an evil from which some of the country banks were then grievously suffering.

Also a large number of bills in the ordinary course of legislation, relating to the canals and banks, besides several local bills for the city.

In the Winter of 1858, Governor John A. King nominated me to the Senate for the office of Auditor of the State. The Democrats and Know-Nothings having a majority, combined, and politely laid over the nomination till the then next 4th of July, when they would not be in session. When Governor Morgan came into office the following January, at my request he withdrew my name, and nominated the late incumbent, the Hon. Nathaniel S. Benton. The Republicans had in the meantime obtained a majority in the Senate, and my nomination would have been confirmed; but I did not desire the office, and originally consented to accept the nomination to oblige the Governor and some friends, he being embarrassed by the urgent importuuity of some candidates he was not willing to nominate.

In 1852 our citizens held various meetings for the purpose of establishing a Rural Cemetery. No grounds were found to compare with the hundred acres which we purchased in 1859. But the effort finally failed, mainly because there was no one who would put himself at the head of the enterprise, and assume the necessary labors and responsibilities. In 1857 meetings were again held in relation to it, but in consequence of the financial troubles of that year, all efforts were again abandoned. In 1858 Hamilton White and myself, having fixed upon a part of our present grounds, consisting of about one hundred acres, as the most desirable lands for a cemetery, began negotiations with Messrs. Charles A. Baker, who owned twenty acres in front and Henry Raynor, who owned seventy-five acres in the rear, for their purchase.

The Syracuse and Jamesville Plank Road ran through them, and we also negotiated with the directors and stockholders of said road, and the Commissioners of Highways of the town of Onondaga, for its removal, and with the late Dr. David S. Colvin for a new route through his land for the plank road. At the end of a year, after many annoyances, and the expenditure of much time, patience and labor, the preliminaries were all finally settled, and terms agreed upon. It was only necessray now to raise $25,000, or something less to accomplish the object. Mr. A. C. Powell now stepped forward to our aid, and was efficient and successful. We soon raised the necessary funds, ($24,500,) and on the 15th of August, 1859, the Association of Oakwood was organized, and Trustees elected, and on the day following the Trustees assembled at my office for the election of officers.

E. W. Leavenworth was elected President. A. C. Powell, Vice President. Hamilton White, Treasurer. Allen Munro, Secretary.

I have been elected President every year since, including the present, 1873, and the Board has left to me nearly the entire management of its affairs. We have spent annually some five or six thousand dollars in improving and keeping up the grounds, besides building a receiving vault at a cost of about $3.500, a house and barn for the Superintendent, fences, etc., and at the annual meeting in 1869 our debt was paid, and we had about $8000 cash in bank. Since then we have bought and paid for more than fifty acres of additional lands, at an expense of more than $20,000, are now out of debt, and have commenced a permanent fund, now amounting to four thousand dollars. We have now a cemetery consisting of about 150 acres, of which about 85 acres are wooded, whose natural beauties and attractions are unsurpassed, and which is kept up in a style to attract universal commendation.

In the Spring of 1859 I was again elected Mayor of the city. During this year I induced the Common Council to order the sale of all that part of Rose Hill cemetery, upon which there had been no burials, being some ten acres. The same was laid out under my direction, except a portion at the intersection of Highland, Douglass and Alvord streets, thus securing another public square, now known as Highland park.

Some ten years after this, and after Messrs. Williams & Scoville had surveyed out the fifty acres of land constituting the Prospect Hill property, and had filed their map of the same, I induced them to change the map of the land on the top of the East Hill, and to lay out there the public square which now beautifies that locality, called McBride Place. This was done at the office of Messrs. Davis & Leach, with the hearty aid of the latter gentleman, and was carried out by the making and filing of a new map of that part of the property.

In the fall of 1859 I was again nominated for the office of Secretary of State, and defeated by 1000 or 1500 majority, in a poll of 600,000 votes by David Floyd Jones, by the combined vote of the Democrats and Know-Nothings. This was brought about mainly by Erastus and James Brooks, of New York, on account of their hostility to Governor Seward, they regarding me as specially his friend. They then controlled the Know-Nothing party.

In the winter of 1860, by an act of the Legislature, I was appointed one of the Board of Quarantine Commissioners, and was, on its organization, chosen its President, and spent most of the following summer in New York and on Staten Island, in the discharge of its duties. Peter B. Sweeney, of New York, now somewhat celebrated, was one of the Board.

In the summer of the same year I was chosen President of the Republican State Convention, assembled at Syracuse to select delegates to the National Convention, then soon to assemble at Chicago. The delegates were all the friends of Governor Seward, and I was then, and before, regarded, and justly, as his warm friend, both personally and politically.

On the 5th of Feb., 1861, I was chosen by the Legislature in joint ballot, one of the Regents of the University. In the month of March in the same year, I was nominated by the President of the United States, and confirmed by the Senate, as the Commissioner on the part of the United States, under the convention with New Grenada, and I acted as such at Washington until the commission expired in 1862. To this commission was referred all claims of American citizens and corporations, from the foundation of the government of New Grenada, down to the time of the treaty, including all damages growing out of the Panama riot, and the confiscation of many vessels—several hundred claims in all, and amounting to many millions of dollars.

In the summer of 1864, I attended the commencement at Yale and was selected to preside at the annual meeting of the Alumni before which the Hon. Samuel B. Ruggles delivered his entertaining and instructive address.

In the spring of 1865 I was the President of a Board of Commissioners, appointed by the Governor, with the consent of the Senate, to locate the State Asylum for the blind, under "an act to authorize the establishment of the New York State Institution for the Blind," chap. 587, p. 1196 of the laws of 1865.

A majority of the Board first decided to locate the institution at Buffalo. I moved a reconsideration, and after a full discussion we finally decided by a majority vote, to locate at Batavia. I think the vote was finally made unanimous.

In the fall of the same year I was appointed by the Governor, a Trustee of the State Asylum for Idiots, in the place of Hamilton White, deceased, to fill the vacancy, and in January, 1866, was re-appointed with the concurrence of the Senate.

In the Summer of 1867, I was elected one of the Trustees of Hamilton College, in the place of Gen. James R. Lawrence, who resigned in consequence of age, infirmity, and total blindness; but being one of the Regents of the University, I was ineligible, and was reluctantly compelled to decline.

I was also this year appointed by the Legislature a member of a Board of Commissioners, consisting of the Adjutant General and Inspector General of the State, and myself, for the further improvement and repair of the State Armory at Syracuse. The other Commissioners left to me the performance of the duties, and among other things I constructed the iron fence which now surrounds Jefferson, or Armory, Park.

In May, 1868, I was appointed by the Legislature, a member

of a Board of Commissioners, (of which I was the President,) to establish a system of sewerage for the city of Syracuse. The Board was engaged two years in perfecting it, and filed their report with maps, plans, etc., in the city and county clerk's offices May 7th, 1870. The necessity for a system, carefully considered and co-extensive with the city, had become imperative. I suggested and urged it, drew up the bill, procured a large public meeting to be called, and submitted the bill which was unanimously approved, and became the law entitled, "An Act in relation to a system of Sewerage in and for the city of Syracuse." Chap. 780, p. 1747, laws of 1868.

As early as about 1852-3, the "Syracuse Home Association" having been previously incorporated and organized, the late Hamilton White, Thomas B. Fitch and myself raised by subscription from $12,000 to $15,000, as a partial endowment for the same. In 1868, the Board of Counselors had sold their old Home, on East Fayette Street, and Moses D. Burnet, Esq., had most generously offered the Home a most desirable site for a new building, on the corner of Hawley and Townsend streets, on condition that we should raise $25,000 for its construction. Mr. White being dead, Mr. Fitch and myself spent all the time we could spare for several weeks, and raised more than the $25,000 required. Other sums were raised by various other parties, and with the money raised by Mr. Fitch and myself, amounted to more than $32,000. The Building Committee consisted of Messrs. Cornelius T. Longstreet, Dr. Lyman Clary, David French, Thomas B. Fitch and myself, but the principal labor and responsibility fell upon Mr. Fitch and myself. The result is seen in the beautiful structure which now stands upon the ground so opportunely and kindly given to us.

In 1871 I was much occupied in the erection of the expensive Pump Works of the Syracuse City Water Works Co., (of which Co. I am the President), for the supplying the city with water.

At the Annual Commencement of Hamilton College in June, 1872, I most unexpectedly received the honorary degree of Doctor of Laws.

In the month of October 1872, I had the honor of being selected, with Governors Morgan, Patterson, etc,, as one of the bearers at the funeral of the Hon. Wm. H. Seward, which took place on Monday, the 14th day of that month. Under all the political changes of forty years, we had been unchanging friends.

On the 22d of November 1872, I was appointed by the Governor and Senate, one of the thirty-two Commissioners (four from each Judicial District) selected to amend the Constitution of the State. My colleagues from the Fifth District were, Hon. Daniel Pratt, late Judge of the Supreme Court and now Attorney General elect; Hon. Francis Kernan, late Democratic candidate for Governor and Hon. Ralph McIntosh, late member from

Oneida. We met at Albany, on the 4th day of December 1872, and adjourned March 15th 1873. The result of our labors are imbodied in the Constitution, now in process of being submitted to the people of the State for their approval.

There are two amendments adopted by the Board, which were introduced by me and for which I am mainly responsible. One applies to the statute of limitations to all claims against the State. This is the 14th section of the 7th article. The other is embraced in the 10th and 11th sections of the 8th article, which forbid the giving or loaning of the credit or money of the State, or of any city, town, county or village in a variety of cases therein specified. I also took a particular interest in section four, article eight, relating to Savings Banks, having attempted to effect the same object in the Legislature when theretofore a member; also in section nineteen of article 3d, limiting the powers of the Legislature in certain cases, a very important amendment, reported I think by Mr. Erastus Brooks.

Though in delicate health during the entire session, there were few members as regular in their attendance as myself, or who devoted more time to the business of the Commission.

I now, (1873,) hold the following positions:—

President of the Syracuse Savings Bank, having under its care about $2,000,000; was elected in January, 1862.

President of the Syracuse City Water Works Company; elected in May, 1864.

President of the Syracuse Gas Light Co.; elected in 1872, but having performed the duties for fifteen years previous to 1872. Each of these companies has an investment of about $500,000.

President of Oakwood, a rural cemetery of about one hundred and fifty acres; elected at the organization in Aug., 1859.

President of the Syracuse and Tully Plank Road Co., elected in 1856.

President of the New England Society of the city of Syracuse.

Secretary and Treasurer of Cape Cod Coarse Salt Co., from its organization in 1857-8.

A Trustee of the Onondaga County Orphan Asylum since May, 1846.

A Trustee of the Syracuse Home Association, for old ladies, etc., since 1854; also Secretary.

A Trustee of the First Presbyterian Church since Jan'y, 1837.

A Trustee of the State Asylum for Idiots since 1865, and ex-officio in 1854-5.

A Director in the Syracuse Northern Railroad, elected by the Common Council to represent the city.

A Director in the Syracuse, Phoenix and Oswego Railroad.

A Regent of the University of the State of New York, elected by the Legislature for life in 1861, and ex-officio in 1854-5.

Joshua Forman

SYRACUSE, N.Y.

I have been re-elected in each of the organizations above, in which elections are held, from the several times above stated till the present.

The following sketch of Judge Forman is taken from Clark's Onondaga, vol. 2, p. 69 to 83. The notes are by the author:—

To give anything like a perfect biographical notice of this distinguished individual, would require a person more familiar with his public acts, more intimate with occurrences whtch transpired at the period in which he was most active, and one who knew better the public worth and private excellence of his character than the author. But as he, for a period of more than a quarter of a century, was a leader in the affairs of this county, and became identified with all the majestic projects of State policy, we cannot pass him by without an attempt to do justice to his merits.

Joshua Forman was born at Pleasant Valley, in the county of Duchess, and State of New York, the 6th of September, 1777. His parents were Joseph and Hannah Forman, who previous to the Revolution, resided in the city of New York. Upon the breaking out of the war and the approach of the British to that city, Mr. Joseph Forman with his family, retired to Pleasant Valley, where the subject of this sketch was born. At an early age he evinced a strong desire for learning, in which he was encouraged by his friends. In the fall of 1793, he entered Union College at Schenectady, and in due time graduated with honor. Directly after his collegiate course was completed, he entered the law office of Peter W. Radcliffe, Esq., of Poughkeepsie, where he remained about two years. He then went to the city of New York and completed his law studies in the office of Samuel Miles Hopkins, Esq. Soon after the close of his professional course, he was married to Miss Margaret Alexander, a daughter of the Hon. Boyd Alexander, M. P. for Glasgow, Scotland. In the spring of 1800, Mr. Forman removed to Onondaga Hollow, and opened a law office on the east side of the creek, where he began early to manifest his public spirit and enterprise. At the time he settled at Onondaga Hollow, the village was mainly situated on the east side of Onondaga Creek, and he being desirous of building up the village, and of exetnding its boundaries, soon located his father on the north and south road and his brothers John, Samuel and Daniel W., near the west end of the present village, on the east and west road passing through the same, and rapidly built up the western part. This left a space in the middle, comparatively unoccupied. Here Judge Forman soon after erected a large Hotel, and afterwards a fine residence for himself, which was occupied many years after Judge Forman left the Hollow, by his brother-in-law, the late Wm. H. Sabin. He was also mainly instrumental in procuring the location of the academy, church and two or three stores in the same vicinity, before he removed from Onondaga, thereby connecting the whole into one tolerably compact settlement.

By his integrity and straight-forward course in the practice of his profession, he soon became distinguished as a lawyer, and by his talents and gentlemanly deportment became familiarly known throughout the country.

In 1803, William H. Sabin, Esq , joined him as a partner in the practice of law, and for several years they did an extensive business. The subject of the Erie canal became a theme of deep interest to several of the leading men of Onondaga, and to none more so than to Judge Forman. Conversations were held by those who were friends to the project, and measures were early taken to bring the great question before the public. Mr. Forman's talents as a public speaker, and as a man of influence and character, eminently distinguished him to be the individual who should be foremost in moving in the matter. Accordingly in 1807, a union ticket was got up, headed by John McWhorter, Democrat, and Joshua Forman, Federalist. This ticket was carried with trifling opposition. It was headed "Canal Ticket," and as such received the cordial support of a large majority of the electors of Onondaga county.

As was anticipated by the friends of Judge Forman and the great work which he was designated to advocate, be brought forward the ever memorable resolution in the House of Assembly, which alone would render his name immortal, directing a survey to be made "of the most eligible and direct route of a canal, to open communication between the tide waters of the Hudson and Lake Erie.

Mr. Forman had studied the subject of canals as constructed in foreign countries. His mind had been applied intently to their construction, utility and cost, and these labors had been brought to bear and have weight upon the subject now under investigation. He had well considered all the advantages that would accrue to the United States and the State of New York, if this important work should be completed. He had prepared an estimate of the cost of construction, based upon statistics of the Languedoc canal.

While discussing this subject in Albany, during the session, Judge Wright and General McNeill, of Oneida, became converts to the plan, through the instrumentality of Judge Forman, and Judge Wright agreed to second the resolution about to be offered whenever it should be brought up. Judge Forman had no confidence that the general government would assist New York in the construction of a canal, but the resolution framed and offered by him was so worded as to give President Jefferson an opportunity to participate in the measure if he would. Fired with the novelty and importance of this project, and somewhat piqued at the manner of its reception by the members of the House, the advocate took pains to prepare himself thoroughly upon the subject, and when the resolution was called up, he addressed the House in a forcible and eloquent speech in its favor. Fortunately the resolution was adopted, and for this he was for years called a "visionary projector," and was asked a hundred times if he ever expected to live to see his canal completed ; to which he uniformly answered, that "as surely as he lived to the ordinary age of man, he did ; that it might take ten years to prepare the public mind for the undertaking, and as many more to accomplish it, nevertheless it would be done."

Had not Joshua Forman brought forward the subject as he did, it is not easy to conceive who would have had the moral courage to meet the ridicule of proposing in earnest, what was considered so wild a measure. Had it not been for this timely movement, the subject might have lain idle for years, so far as Legislative action was concerned. But,by it the ice was broken and an impetus given to a direct canal, by the discoveries made under it, and to Joshua Forman must ever be accorded the high consideration, as the first legislative projector of the greatest improvement of the age. During all the times of darkness, discouragement and doubt, he boldly stood forth the unflinching champion of its feasibility, utility and worth, till the day of its completion.

On the occasion of the grand canal celebration, 1st of Nov., 1825, Judge Forman was selected by the citizens of Onondaga county, and as President of the village of Syracuse, to address Gov. Clinton and suite, on their first passage down the canal, accompanied by various county committees along the line. He had but three hours to prepare his address, and it thus appears in the Syracuse Gazette of Nov. 2, 1825 :—

"GENTLEMEN—The roar of cannon rolling from Lake Erie to the ocean, and reverberated from the ocean to the lakes, has announced the completion of the Erie canal, and you are this day witnesses, bearing the waters of the lakes on the unbroken bosom of the canal, to be mingled with the ocean, that the splendid hopes of our State are realized. The continued fete which has attended your boats, evinces how dear it was to the hearts of our citizens. It is truly a proud day for the State of New York. No one is present who has the interest of the State at heart, who does not exult at the completion of a work fraught with such important benefits, and no man with an American heart, that does not swell with pride that he is a citizen of the country which has accomplished the greatest work of the age, and which has filled Europe with admiration of the American character. On the 4th of July, 1817, it was begun, and it is now accomplished. Not by the labor of abject slaves and vassals, but by the energies of freemen, and in a period unprecedently short, by the *voluntary* efforts of its freemen governed by the wisdom of its statesmen. This, however, is but one of the many benefits derived from our free institutions, and which marks a new era in the history of man—the example of a nation whose whole physical power and intelligence are employed to advance the improvement, comfort and happiness of the people.

To what extent this course of improvement may be carried, it is impossible for any mere man to conjecture; but no reasonable man can doubt, that it will continue its progress, until our wide and fertile territory shall be filled with a more dense, intelligent and happy people than the sun shines upon in the wide circuit of the globe. It has long been the subject of fearful apprehension, to the patriots of the Atlantic States that the remote interior situation of our western country (for want of proper stimuli to industry and free intercourse, with the rest of the world) would be filled, with a semi-barbarous population, uncongenial with their Atlantic neighbors. But the introduction of steamboats on our lakes and running rivers, and canals to connect the waters which nature has disjoined (in both which this State has taken the lead, and its example has now become general,) have broken down the old barriers of nature, and promise the wide spread regions of the west all the blessings of a seaboard district. But while we contemplate the advantages of this work, as a source of revenue to the State, and of wealth and comfort to our citizens, let us never forget the means by which it has been accomplished; and after rendering thanks to the All-Wise Disposer of events, who has by his own means, and for his own purposes brought about this great work, we would render our thanks to all citizens and statesmen, who have in and out of the Legislature, sustained the measure from its first conception to its present final consummation. To the commissioners who superintended the work, the board of native engineers, (a native treasure unknown till called for by the occasion), and especially to his Excellency, the Governor, whose early and decided support of the measure, fearlessly throwing his character and influence into the scale, turned the poising beam and produced the first canal appropriation, and by his talents and exertions kept public opinion steady to the point. Without his efforts in that crisis, the canal project might still have been a splendid vision, gazed upon by the benevolent patriot, but left by cold calumniators to be realized by some future generation. At that time all admitted that there was a high responsibility resting on you, and had it failed you must have largely borne the blame. It has succeeded, and we will not withhold from you your due meed of praise.

Gentlemen, in behalf of the citizens of Syracuse, and the county of Onondaga, here assembled, I congratulate you on this occasion. Our village is the offspring of the canal, and with the county must partake largely of its blessings. We were most ungrateful if we did not most cordially join in this great State celebration."

Judge Forman having concluded his address, Governor Clinton replied in a very happy and appropriate manner, in the course of which he adverted to the important views presented in the address, and observed that they were such as he had expected from an individual who had introduced the first legislative measures relative to the canals, and had devoted much thought and reflection to the subject. His Excellency also adverted to the prosperous condition of Syracuse, and of the county, and concluded by expressing his congratulations on the final accomplishment of this great work.

As one of the committee from Syracuse, Judge Forman attended the ceremony of mingling the waters of Lake Erie with those of the ocean off Sandy Hook. He had now passed through all the stages in the progress of the great work, from its first announcement in the Legislature, to its final consummation in uniting the waters of Lake Erie with the Atlantic ocean. His efforts in this great undertaking will ever be an enduring monument of his wisdom, and to future generations will his fame extend.

It is not to be supposed that Judge Forman had employed all his time and talents upon this single object. As a lawyer, he became distinguished; and on account of his integrity and legal acquirements, was appointed First Judge of Onondaga County Common Pleas in 1813. He filled the station with credit and ability for ten years; in fact, he elevated the character of this tribunal to the pitch, which gained for it the high reputation which it has since enjoyed.

He took an early and active interest in the establishment of churches in this county. "The First Onondaga Religious Society," at Onondaga Hill, in 1806, and the "Onondaga Hollow Religious Society," in 1809, owe their early organization mainly to his efforts. The Onondaga Academy, founded in 1814, owes it existence to the interest he manifested in the cause of education, and to his fostering care. He was also one of the most active in promoting the organization of the first Presbyterian society in Syracuse, in 1824, and was one of its first trustees.*

In 1807, he took a lease of the Surveyor General for a term of years, of a part of the reservation lands at Oswego Falls, for the purpose of erecting a grist mill in that wilderness country, at which time not a horse was owned by an inhabitant between Salina and Oswego. This was the first mill erected on the Oswego river in modern times, and it greatly facilitated the settlement of that region.

In 1808 he founded the celebrated Plaster Company of Camillus, for the purpose of more effectually working the extensive beds in that town. In 1813, Judge Forman built the canal and excavated ground for the pond at Onondaga Hollow, where he erected a grist mill, which was then considered one of the best in the county.

In 1817, while there was yet a strong opposition to the Erie canal, and its friends were in the greatest anxiety, and even doubt as to the final result, Judge Forman furnished a series of articles, which were published in the Onondaga Register, signed X, in defense of the work. These papers were written with great ability, and are said by competent judges to be inferior to none that had been written upon that subject.

In 1821, Judge Forman obtained the passage of a law, (drawn by his own hand,) authorizing the lowering of Onondaga Lake, and subsequently the lake was lowered about two feet. The great difficulty had been caused by the high water in the Seneca river, rising to a certain hight, which obstructed the channel of the Onondaga outlet; and such was the nature of the obstructions, arising from the narrowness and crookedness of the passage, that when the Seneca

---

* NOTE.—He drew the subscription paper, obtained the great body of the subscriptions, made the contract for the building, superintended its erection, collected and paid over the money and kept the records for the years 1824-5. He was the founder of the society and at its request a marble tablet was put up in the church by the author, with the following inscription;—

"JOSHUA FORMAN,

Was born in Pleasant Valley, in the county of Duchess, on the 6th of September, 1777, Locating in Onondaga in the year 1800, he became the founder of this Church, and of the

CITY OF SYRACUSE.

For more than fifty years he spent a life of varied usefulness as a Patriot, Philanthropist, and Christian, his name untarnished, his character revered and honored.

He exchanged the responsibilities of earth for the christian's rest, at the village of Rutherfordton, N. C., on the 4th day of August, 1848,* leaving to those he loved, the testimony of a good man, whose earnest faith already realized the fulfillment of the promises.

Erected by his son-in-law, E. W. Leavenworth—1860."

*Mr. Clark is in an error in stating that Judge F. died in 1849.

river subsided to its proper limits, the water of Onondaga lake was retained, and in rainy seasons did not fall so as to make dryground around it, till late in summer, which was the cause of much inconvenience to the people living in the vicinity of the lake. To obviate this the lake was lowered, and by it the lands around Salina and Syracuse were improved, leaving bare a beach about the lake, in some places of several rods in width. For the cause of philanthropy and humanity, this was a most important measure. The country around became more healthful, and although previously infested with a fatal miasma in August and September, from that time to this, the country about Syracuse and Salina, has been considered as healthy as any other section in the State.

In 1822, Judge Forman procured the passage of a law authorizing the erection of fixtures for the purpose of manufacturing coarse salt by solar evaporation, with a three cent per bushel bounty on salt so manufactured, for a given number of years. He went to New Bedford, in company with Isaiah Townsend, Esq., to make inquiries relative to solar evaporation of salt water, from persons interested in this mode of manufacturing salt from sea water on Cape Cod. They engaged Mr. Stephen Smith. to come on to Syracuse with them, to manage the salt fields, he having had experience in this mode of manufacture. Mr. Smith was appointed agent of the Onondaga Company, and Judge Forman of the Syracuse Company, and these two proceeded to make the necessary erections for the manufacture of coarse salt.

At this time the Salina Canal terminated at the mill on the southern border of the village of Salina, and there was no water to be had, available for the purposes of carrying machinery in the immediate vicinity of the principal salt spring. With a view of accomplishing this object, Judge Forman accompanied Governor Clinton to Salina, pointed out the ground, and proposed to have the Salina Canal extended so as to communicate with Onondaga Lake. The following year this plan was carried out; the canal was continued to the lake, and arrangements were made for the erection of pump works. This grand improvement in the elevation of brine, was made at the expense of the Syracuse and Onondaga Salt Companies, under the direction of Judge Forman. Afterwards the State bought the fixtures acqueducts, etc., as they had reserved the right to do. To no individual so much as to Judge Forman, are we indebted for a modification of our salt laws, and for the substitution of water power, for hand labor, in the elevation of brine, for the reservoirs, and all the apparatus connected with those improvements, and for the introduction of the manufacture of coarse salt by solar heat. These were measures in which the public were deeply interested which particularly absorbed his attention, and which have greatly improved and increased the manufacture of salt in the town of Salina.

Judge Forman was emphatically the founder of the city of Syracuse. He came to thisplace in the year 1819, when there was but a small clearing south of the canal. and lived in a house which stood in the center of Clinton street; since removed. When he came to Syracuse, it was deemed a doubtful and hazardous enterprise. His friends earnestly desired him to withdraw. But at no time did his courage, energy or faith fail him. He foresaw and insisted, that it must eventually become a great and flourishing inland town, and in spite of much determined opposition, and amidst a variety of obstacles and almost every species of embarrassment, he persisted in his efforts, till he had laid broad and deep the foundations of this flourishing city. *

The most prominent obstacles were found in the rival villages in the vicinity, which were likely to be affected by the building up of a larger one in their

---

*NOTE.—Forman Wilson & Co., bought the Walton Tract, 250 acres, embracing the central parts of what is now the city, in 1816. Judge Forman caused it to be carefully laid out by his brother, Owen F., assisted by the late John Wilkinson, Esq., in 1818-19, and removed there with his family from Onondaga Hollow in 1819. There were then but two frame private dwelling houses at Syracuse. Thurlow Weed, Esq., says in some of his writings that Judge Forman *invented* Syracuse.

midst, and in the extensive swamps and marshes which everywhere in this region prevailed, and in the consequent unhealthiness of the locality.

His work being accomplished, circumstances required his removal from this scene of his usefulness, and the theatre of his labors. In 1826 he removed to New Jersey near New Brunswick, where he superintended the opening and working of a copper mine, which had been wrought to some extent prior to and during the revolution. Soon after his departure from Syracuse, the State of New York became sadly convulsed and deranged in its financial affairs. Our banking system was extremely defective—reform was demanded by an abused and outraged community. All saw and admitted the evil, but no one was prepared with a remedy. At this crisis Judge Forman came forward with a plan for relief, and upon the invitation of Gov. Van Buren, he visited Albany and submitted his plan to a Committee of the Legislature then in session. At the suggestion of the Governor, he drew up the bill which subsequently became a law, and is known as the Safety Fund Act, the great objects of which were on the one hand, to give currency and character to our circulation, and on the other to protect the bill holder. At the special request of Governor Van Buren Judge Forman spent most of the winter in attendance on the Legislature, in perfecting the details of this important act.

This plan operated well for many years, and the Safety Fund Banks of this State sustained themselves under some of the severest and heaviest revulsions which the monied institutions of the country have ever experienced. And it may be safely affirmed that no system in practice on this side the Atlantic, has better stood the test of experience, or secured so extensively the popular confidence as this. The Safety Fund systemn was exclusively the plan of Judge Forman, and although modifications have since been made, and others projected, in our banking laws. it may be questioned whether the system has been materially improved.

In 1829-30, Judge Forman bought of the government of the State of North Carolina an extensive tract of land, consisting of some three hundred thousand acres, in Ruthfordton County. He took up his residence at the village of Ruthfordton, greatly extended its boundaries, established a newspaper press, and was considered the most enterprising individual in that part of the State; became quite distinguished as a public man, and noted for his exertions to elevate the character, and improve the mental and moral condition of the inhabitants in that region.

In 1831, after an absence of about five years, Judge Forman visited Onondaga. He was every where received with unqualified demonstrations of joy and respect, and every voice cheered him as the founder of the city, and a benefactor of mankind. The citizens of Syracuse, through their committee appointed for that purpose, consisting of Messrs. Stephen Smith, Harvey Baldwin, Amos P. Granger, L. H. Redfield, Henry Newton, John Wilkinson, and Moses D. Burnet, availed themselves of the opportunity to present to him a valuable set of silver plate as a tribute of the high respect and esteem which was entertained for his talents and character and in consideration of his devotedness to their interests, in the early settlement of the village. The plate is in form of a pitcher, * and bears this inscription:—

A Tribute of Respect Presented by the Citizens of Syracuse, to the Honorable Joshua Forman, Founder of that Village.	SYRACUSE [clasped hands.] 1831.

At the ceremony of presenting the plate, mutual addresses were delivered; on the one hand, highly expressive of the affection and regard of a whole community, to a distinguished individual, who had toiled and exhausted his more vigorous energies for their welfare; and on the other, the acknowledgement of past favors at the hands of his fellow citizens and coadjutors, thankful that he

* NOTE.—There are also six silver goblets.

had been the humble instrument of contributing to their prosperity, hoping that the bright visions of the future importance of Syracuse, which he had so long entertained, might be realized, he bade her citizens an affectionate farewell.

On his return to his home in North Carolina, Judge Forman took with him this token of the gratitude of his fellow-citizens, and it remained with him till the year 1845, when he presented it to his daughter, the lady of Gen. E. W. Leavenworth, of Syracuse, then on a visit to her father, who was in feeble health, remarking that it constituted a part of the history of Syracuse, and that after his death there it should remain.

While his health permitted, Judge Forman's business was principally that of making sales of the lands he had purchased in North Carolina.

In 1846 this venerable man revisited his former friends and acquaintances of his earlier years, and found in each full heart an honest welcome. To all it was apparent that the advances of time had made sad inroads upon his physical and mental powers. Seventy winters had shed their snows upon his devoted head. He had heard much of the growth and prosperity of his cherished city, and of his beloved Onondaga. He had fixed his heart upon again treading the soil of his revered county. He had earnestly desired to return to the land of his fathers, before his course on earth should be closed, to witness the result of those wonderful improvements in the accomplishment of which he had taken so deep an interest, and so active a part, and to see the fulfillment of those predictions which had sometimes acquired for him the name of a visionary projector and enthusiast, and once again for the last time to behold in the body, the few surviving friends of his earlier years. He could not bid adieu to the world in peace, till this last and greatest of his earthly wishes should be gratified.

On this occasion a public dinner was tendered to him, by P. N. Rust, Esq., of the Syracuse House. A large number of the most distinguished gentlemen of the county were present, together with the few gray-headed pioneers, who still lingered in the land. Nearly all the company were the personal friends of Judge Forman, many of them having been sharers or attentive observers of his early and patriotic public efforts, for the social, mental and moral improvement of this county, Few indeed are the instances, where an individual, mantled in the hoary locks of age, after an absence of twenty years, returns to the scenes of his primitive usefulness, with so many demonstrations on the part of friends and former neighbors, of joy and thankfulness, as in the one before us. It was also a season of peculiar gratification to him. Here he beheld the results of his labors in early active manhood. Here he beheld the progress of a thriving town founded by his fostering hand. Here he received the warm greetings of the friends of his early life, and here he met with them to bid them a kind, affectionate and last adieu.

Moses D. Burnet. Esq., presided on this very interesting occasion. A formal address of congratulation, on account of the great success of his early labors, and the remarkable fulfillment of his hopes and predictions, was made by the Hon. Harvey Baldwin, which was replied to, in behalf of Judge Forman, (he being then unable to articulate distinctly, on account of a paralytic shock,) by his son-in-law, E. W. Leavenworth, Esq.

Gen. Amos P. Granger, Hon. George Geddes, Lewis H. Redfield, Esq., and several other gentlemen of note, addressed the party in a very felicitous manner. The proceedings of this very interesting meeting may be found in the Onondaga Democrat of the 3d of Oct., 1846, and other city papers of that date.

From Syracuse, Judge Forman retired to his mountain home, in the milder climes of the sunny South, carrying with him the most vivid recollections of the kindness and hospitality of his friends; looking back upon a well spent life, much of which was devoted to the service of his country, without regret; and forward, without a fear to the hour when he will be called away from the scenes of society and earth.

Judge Forman is still living, (1848,) at his home in North Carolina, having bid adieu to the cares and business occupations of life.

NOTE.—He died at the village of Rutherfordton, on the 4th of Aug., 1848. His remains were removed from Rutherfordton, at the request of his daughter Mrs. E. W. Leavenworth, and now repose beneath the shades of the beautiful Rural Cemetery at Syracuse,

The character of this distinguished man may be summed up in a very few words. His mind was of no ordinary cast, and whether we view him as a fellow-citizen, a neighbor, a legislator, a jurist, a judge, or as a man, we find nothing that we cannot respect and admire. Full of life and energy himself, he infused with uncommon facility the same spirit into others, and wherever he was found, in him was the master spirit of every plan. He possessed a mind of uncommon activity, never wearying with the multiplicity of his labors and cares ; it was stored with an unusnal variety of knowledge, extending far beyond the boundaries of his professional pursuits, and he possessed a rare felicity in the communication of this knowledge to others. This fund of solid and general information upon every variety of topic, and his forcible and happy manner of communication, joined with the most social and cheerful disposition, rendered him on all occasions a most agreeable and interesting gentleman in conversation, and the delight of every circle in which he moved. He greatly excelled in the clear perceptions of the results of proposed measures of public improvement, and in a capacity to present them forcibly to others, carrying along with him individuals, communities and public assemblies, by his easy flowing language, and a manner at once most clear, captivating and persuasive. His whole life was characterized by the most public spirited efforts for the general good, and the most disinterested benevolence—always comparatively forgetful of his own private interest, in his zeal for the accomplishment of works of public utility. Through the long period of his stirring and eventful life, he sustained a character without stain and without reproach, and now, standing on the borders of the grave, is most justly entitled to the admiration and gratitude of his conntrymen.

It was the happiness of the author in his youthful days, to spend several months in the family of Judge Forman, at Onondaga Hollow, and he takes pleasure in this opportunity of testifying to his domestic virtues and private worth.

For a brief genealogical sketch of the family of Deacon Joseph Forman, see Appendix, letter (J.)

For a fuller and more detailed account of Judge Forman's relations to the Erie Canal, see Dr. Hosack's life of DeWitt Clinton, and for his relations to the City of Syracuse, see Clark's Onondaga,—art. "Syracuse."

The Hon. James Geddes was the neighbor and friend of Judge Forman, and in all their long-continued efforts for the construction of the Erie canal, they were associates and co-laborers. I therefore take the liberty of giving a mere outline of his valuable and honorable life, for which I am also indebted to Clark's Onondaga, vol. 2, p. 45 to 50 inclusive.

I also insert in a portion of the edition, a very life-like engraving of him, furnished at my request by his son, the Hon. George Geddes, who lives four miles west of the city of Syracuse, upon the fine farm of four hundred acres, a portion of the land purchased by his father of the State in 1798 :—

BIOGRAPHICAL SKETCH OF THE HON. JAMES GEDDES.

James Geddes was born on the 22d day of July, 1763, near Carlisle, in the State of Pennsylvania. His father and mother were both descended from Scotch families, and the first accents of his infant lips were uttered in broad Scotch. His father was a farmer in very respectable circumstances, and gave

Engd by F. Halpin.

Jas Geddes. Engineer.

his children all the advantages of education that the country then afforded; and every means at the command of the subject of this memoir, was made the most of, in storing his mind with useful knowledge.

While a youth, following the plow, he carried in his pocket a book; and when his team stopped to rest, he perused its contents. In after life he frequently observed that his reading in the field was of great advantage to him, as he had full time to digest all that he read while holding the plow, and later in life could draw from these stores treasured up in his juvenile years, with pleasure and profit. He studied mathematics under charge of a Mr. Oliver, who was a thoroughly educated man. Languages he studied without masters, and he became a belle lettres scholar of the first order. In fact, few men ever acquire a knowledge of the English language that equaled his.

At an early age he visited the State of Kentucky. It was then necessary to cross the Alleghany mountains in large companies, for protection against the Indians; and unburied human bones were seen at various places along the path they followed.

In Kentucky slavery had already established itself, and having an insuperable repugnance to that institution, he determined not to locate himself where it appeared that this evil was long to exist. From the time of arriving at his majority until the age of thirty, he employed himself in teaching school, traveling and improving his mind.

In the year 1793, the fame of the salt springs induced him to visit the county of Onondaga, (then Herkimer). So well was he pleased with the prospects this region offered, that he returned home and organized a company for the manufacture of salt; and the next year, 1794, came by the way of Seneca Lake, with the necessary kettles, and early in the spring commenced the manufacture of salt, at the place now known as the village of Geddes. He lived there four years. In 1798 he moved to lands he had purchased of the State, in the present town of Camillus, where he lived the residue of his life.

In May, 1799, he married Miss Lucy Jerome, daughter of Timothy Jerome, Esq., of the town of Fabius.

Soon after becoming a citizen of this county, the public demanded his services, and he filled most if not all the important stations in his town at various times. He was appointed a Justice of the Peace in 1800, by the Council of Appointment. In 1804 he was elected a member of the Legislature.

Soon after his coming to this country, he was employed by the Surveyor-General, as one of his assistants, and he devoted himself to the profession of surveying and engineering, until age disqualified him from the fatigue of outdoor labors. His maps, plots and field books, deposited in the Surveyor-General's office, show him to be a man of great accuracy, and his accompanying remarks, the sagacity and penetration of his mind.

It was as an engineer that he became most known to the public, and it was as such that he did the State most service. The project of connecting the waters of Lake Erie with the Hudson River became an important one. Mr. Weston, a celebrated engineer from England, had examined the Oswego river, and other water courses, with a view to improving their navigation; and among men of enlarged views the scheme became an engrossing topic. Mr. Geddes, at an early period, enlisted in the matter, and commenced with ardor the gathering of facts. In 1804 the Surveyor-General said to him, that Gouverneur Morris had mentioned to him the project of "tapping Lake Erie." The Surveyor General considered this "a romantic thing," but not so the man to whom he communicated the crude, undigested thought. He knew that Mr. Weston had reported the Oswego river, from the Falls to Lake Ontario, as "hardly susceptible of improvement, by means of canaling," and if there was a way that the waters of the upper lakes could be led across the country without going down to the level of Ontario, and then rising to the summit again at Rome, that vast results must grow from it, and at once his untiring industry and energy was put in requisition. Maps were examined, surveyors were enquired of, and every means within his reach resorted to, to ascertain the topography of the country through which since has been constructed the Erie canal.

In 1807 Judge Joshua Forman was elected to the Legislature from this county, upon the express understanding that he would try to procure the appropriation of money to make examinations of the country. No man could have been better qualified than was Judge Forman to succeed. A man of eloquence, ardent, and peculiarly calculated to make men think as he himself thought upon any subject, he did succeed, and as was understood, the Surveyor-General, who had the selection of the man to make the surveys, (if he did not himself do it,) appointed Mr. Geddes. He "entered with enthusiasm upon the task assigned him by the Surveyor-General," and made surveys, not only of the Oneida and Oswego rivers, and around the Falls of Niagara, but he reported a route, which was, in the language of the Surveyor-General, in his letter to Mr. Darley, of February 25, 1822, "almost precisely in the line which, after repeated elaborate and expensive examinations, has been finally adopted."

To quote further from Mr. DeWitt's letter, "the favorable light in which the report of this year's work presented the projected enterprise, after encountering prejudices from different sources, and oppositions made for various reasons, induced the Legislature in 1810, to organize a Board of Commissioners, with powers and means to prosecute the business."

This survey furnished the necessary information to justify prudent men to commit themselves in favor of a canal; and Mr. Clinton, grasping with his powerful intellect at once the vast advantages of the scheme, embarked in it with uncompromising zeal, and by his elevated position in the State, was enabled to render such assistance as ensured success.

After the war with England was ended, the Canal Commissioners sent to that country to secure the services of Mr. Weston, or some other engineer of reputation, to take charge of and lay out the canals, but they failed entirely, and it became necessary to rely upon their own inexperienced countrymen. In 1816, they appointed five principal engineers, placing Mr. Geddes at the head of the list, who throughout the progress of the work, maintained a high standing as a civil engineer, and whose labors and opinions were most favorably estimated by the Canal Commissioners, as their reports in various instances will show.

In 1822 the State authorities of Ohio applied to Governor Clinton to select a proper person to make the necessary explorations for their canal from the Ohio river to Lake Erie; and he, in the most flattering manner, recommended Mr. Geddes as the most competent man in the service of the State. Mr. Geddes accepted proposals from Ohio, and assumed the responsibility of Chief Engineer of the Ohio Canal. This duty he discharged to the perfect satisfaction of the authorities of the State of Ohio.

In 1827 Mr. Geddes was employed by the general government, (associated with Mr. Roberts), in the location of the Chesapeake and Ohio canal. In 1828 he was engaged in locating the Pennsylvania canals, and in the same year he was appointed by the general government to examine the country in reference to the connection of the waters of the Tennesee and Altamaha rivers, in the States of Tennesee, Alabama and Georgia. This appointment he declined, on account of distance from home, and his advanced age.

In 1809 Mr. Geddes was appointed an Associate Justice, and in 1812, a Judge of Onondaga County Common Pleas. In 1813, he was elected a member of the 13th Congress, and in 1821 he was again elected a member of the Legislature of this State. He was elected to Congress by the Federal party, but belonged to that branch of the party who favored the vigorous prosecution of the then existing war, and it is proper to say, that he voted for every appropriation that was made during his term, for carrying on the war with vigor.

The infirmities of age crept upon him apace, and during the last year of his life, his constitution gave way rapidly, and he closed his earthly career at his residence, in the town of Camillus, on the 19th of August, 1838, being a little more than seventy-five years of age. He was the father of seven children, only one of them surviving him—all the rest having died without issue. The Hon. George Geddes, of Fairmount, now a member of the Senate of this State, is the survivor.

Perhaps it is safe to say that no man who had been as much in public service and who had come in contact with so great and conflicting interests, represented by men so different in capacity and character, ever died, leaving fewer enemies. His reputation for integrity, probably was never questioned, even by those whose opinions differed from his own. To be just in all his ways, was apparently a part of his nature, and the least lack of moral integrity, once detected by him in a man, destroyed his confidence in that man forever. It was his good fortune to live to great age, and enjoy almost uninterrupted good health. All his time was most diligently improved ; and such was the extent of his knowledge, that he was greatest in the estimation of those who saw him most, and who had the best means of observing him critically. Integrity, industry, perseverance and sound judgment, were prominent traits of his character.

Although a self-educated man, relying entirely on his own resources, without the aid of artificial helps, he became eminent in the profession of his adoption, and by his talents and zeal for the public welfare, secured for himself a reputation that might well be envied.

He early stood forth among the hardy and honorable pioneers of our county, as one of the main pillars of its support, and by his acts has largely contributed to its advancement and prosperity. His name will ever be associated with the noblest works of the age, and his fame will descend with admiration to those who shall succeed.

355. Hiram Leavenworth.[6]—John,[5] Asa,[4] Thomas,[3] Thomas[2], Thomas.[1]

Born August 28, 1797, at New Canaan, N. Y.

Married, first, Lavinia Holden, of Lansing, (then Tompkins Co,,) N. Y., July 4, 1819. She was born November 4, 1800, at Milton, (now Genoa,) Cayuga Co., N. Y., November 4, 1800, and died May 14, 1832, at St. Catharines, C. W.

Married, second, Lucy Emmerson, of Ridgeway, N. Y., October 20, 1834. She was from Vermont. He died at St. Catherines, C. W., February 7, 1857. By trade he was a printer. She and the children she had, still reside there.

CHILDREN.

614. Matilda, b. June 11, 1820.
615. Clarinda, b.September 10, 1821.
616. Edwin S. b. September 21, 1823.
617. John Holden, b. March 4, 1826, d. March, 1847, at sea.
618. Hiram F., b. March 19, 1828.
619. Lavinia, b. December 26, 1829, d. October 29, 1864, in California.
620. Gilbert, b. December 28, 1831, d. April ? 1849,at Auburn.
621. Elizabeth, b. October 24, 1835, d. August 26, 1836, at St. Catherins, C. W.

622. LUCY, b. June 26, 1839, m. Thomas Smith, of St. Catherines, C. W., and has one child.
623. CLARA, b. February 20, 1841, unmarried and is a teacher at St. Catherines.
624. FANNY, b. April 8, 1844, d. November 2, 1846, at St. Catherines, C. W.
625. MARY, b. March 17, 1846, m. James McEdwards, of St. Catherines.

He edited and published the Waterloo Gazette, at Waterloo, Seneca Co., for several years after 1817. In 1822, he in connection with William Ray, published at Geneva, the Miscellaneous Register. In 1823 he moved to Queenstown, C. W., and published a paper in the interest of the celebrated Wm. L. McKenzie, which was soon removed to Little York, but in 1825, he removed to St. Catherines, and established the Farmers' Journal and Welland Canal Intelligencer, which name was changed to the St. Catherines Journal. He sold it out in 1843 and left the editorial chair and thereafter devoted himself simply to printing.

356. POLLY LEAVENWORTH.[6]—JOHN,[5] ASA,[4] THOMAS,[3] THOMAS[2], THOMAS[1]

Born December 26, 1799, at Canaan, Columbia Co., N. Y.

Married Heman Holden October 5, 1819. He was a farmer and resided in Reading, N. Y., but soon removed to East Genoa and died there. She died June 19, 1866. He bought a portion of his father-in-law's farm, and lived and died across the street from him.

CHILDREN.

1. OSCAR, b. October 30, 1820, at Reading, N. Y. He is now in Kansas; m Sally Wilson about 1843, has two sons, Wilson and Winfield. Wilson Holden is married and lives in Nebraska.
2. MARY, b. July 9, 1829, at Reading, N. Y.; m. Norman Devine, had one son, Walter, and d. January 17, 1870.
3. HOBART, b. February 15, 1834, at Reading, N. Y., unmarried.

357. FANNY LEAVENWORTH.[6]—JOHN,[5] ASA,[4] THOMAS,[3] THOMAS,[2] THOMAS.[1]

Born August 1, 1803, at Milton, (then Cayuga Co.,) now Lansing, Tompkins Co., N. Y.

Married William W. Manchester, November 10, 1830. He was a farmer and resided in Venice, Cayuga Co., N. Y. She died June 13. 1842.

CHILDREN.

1. CHARLES W., b, November 16, 1832, m. Sarah Henderson, at Starkey, Yates Co., and has no children.
2. JOHN L., b. March 16, 1834, m. Martha Billings at Macedon, Wayne Co., and has a son William.
3. JULIA W., } Twins } b. May 25, 1842. Are
4. FANNY L., } } unmarried—1870.

358. CLARA LEAVENWORTH.[6]—JOHN,[5] ASA,[4] THOMAS,[3] THOMAS,[2] THOMAS.[1]

Born June 28, 1808, at Milton, then Cayuga Co., (now Lansing, Tompkins Co.,) N. Y.

Married William P. Thornton January 10, 1827, at East Genoa. He was at the time of marriage, a merchant at East Genoa, N. Y. She died October 27, 1844, at Fleming, Cayuga Co., her death being hastened by the melancholy death of her eldest son. She was a lady of great refinement, cultivation and worth. He died at Auburn, May 20, 1865.

CHILDREN.

1. STEPHEN, b. February 22, 1828. Perished in the flames that consumed his father's dwelling, at Fleming, Cayuga Co., N. Y., June 25, 1844.
2. EDWIN L., b. March 30, 1837, at Fleming, N. Y., m. Martha Knox, daughter of Manasseh and Margaret (Johnson) Knox, February 22, 1860, at Scipio. She was born August 29, 1838. Her father was a farmer.

Children.

1. CARRIE L., b. at Auburn December, 1861.
2. WILLIAM P., b. " August 17, 1863.
3. MARTHA K., b. " October 2, 1865.
4. WINIFRED, b. at Oswego, September 1, 1869. Edwin L.'s family resided at Auburn, now at Oswego. He is an extensive lumber dealer.

359. OLIVIA LEAVENWORTH.[6]—JOHN,[5] ASA,[4] THOMAS,[3] THOMAS,[2] THOMAS.[1]

Born May 9, 1810, at Milton, (now Genoa,) Cayuga Co., N. Y.

Married Alanson Ferris March 4, 1840. He was a farmer, then of Genoa, N. Y., now resides at Springport, Mich., to whioh place he removed Oct. 5, 1842.

CHILDREN.

1. HENRY, b. August 17, 1841, at Genoa, N. Y., d. July 30, 1847.
2. ADELINE, b. May 30, 1845, at Springport, Jackson Co., Mich., m. Oscar F. Smith, of Springport, Mich., and has two children—Henry and Clara.
3. HIRAM, b. February 9, 1849.
4. JOHN L., b. February 1, 1852.

360. Horace Leavenworth.[6]—JOHN,[5] ASA,[4] THOMAS,[3] THOMAS,[2] THOMAS.[1]

Born July 8, 1817, at Milton, (now Genoa,) Cayuga Co., N. Y.

Married ELIZA J. HENDERSON, October 23, 1844, daughter of Horace Henderson, farmer, Starkey, Yates Co. Resides at East Genoa, N. Y. Married at Rock Stream, Town of Starkey. He now (1874) occupies the homestead of his father, a farm which his father bought and cleared when the country was new, early in this century.

CHILDREN.

626. ALETHE, b. November 9, 1849, d, November 21, 1849.
627. ELMINA JOSEPHINE, b. July 3, 1851, m. Oscar Tifft, of the town of Venice, Cayuga Co., March 22, 1871. They now, 1874, reside with her father at East Genoa,

628. SON, (not named) b. September 21, 1851, d. Septembr 24, 1851.

361. EVELINE THEODOSIA LEAVENWORTH.[6]—TRUMAN,[5] ASA,[4] THOMAS,[3] THOMAS,[2] THOMAS.[1]

Born August 25, 1818, at Canaan, Columbia Co., N. Y.

Married June 23, 1869, C. B. Crofut, of Canaan Four Corners, son of Comfort Crofut and Mehitable Kellogg, of Canaan Center. Mr. Crofut is a hardware merchant, end resides at East Chatham, Columbia Co., N. Y. No children.

362. Edwin Waldo Leavenworth.[6]—TRUMAN,[5] ASA,[4] THOMAS,[3] THOMAS[2], THOMAS.[1]

Born April 3, 1822, at Canaan, Columbia Co., N. Y.

Married LUCINDA VANDERBURG, daughter of Martin and Mary V., of Canaan, December 20, 1849. She was born November 19, 1831, at Canaan. Resides at Canaan, N. Y. He is a stage proprietor and farmer. He still owns and occupies the home where he was born, which was built by his father, and where he resided fifty years or thereabouts.

CHILDREN.

629. MARY THEODOSIA, b. March 19, 1851, at Canaan, m. Wm. H. Palmer.

363. CAROLINE EMILY LEAVENWORTH.[6] — ISAAC[5], ASA[4], THOMAS,[3] THOMAS,[2] THOMAS.[1]

Born August 27, 1812, at Great Barrington, Mass.

Married, first, Julius Page, September 25, 1831, at Binghamton, N· Y. He was born September 2e, 1799, and died February 19, 1840, at Binghamton. He was a merchant.

Married, second, George Salmon, June 19, 1862, at Brooklyn, N. Y. He resides at Fulton, Oswego Co., and is an extensive leather merchant and manufacturer. He is the son of George Salmon and Jerusha Lyman. Born at Goshen, Mass., August 6, 1801.

364. Elisha Lee Leavenworth.[6]— ISAAC,[5] ASA,[4] THOMAS,[3] THOMAS,[2] THOMAS.[1]

Born September 20, 1814, at Great Barrington, Mass.

Married, first, MARY THERESSA BROWN, September 10, 1840. She was born at Waterloo, N. Y., August 2, 1821, and died at Wolcott, N. Y., November 3, 1841; daughter of Chester Brown and Elizabeth Force.

Married, second, JANE ELIZABETH WILDER, March 13, 1843, at

Wolcott, N. Y. She was born at Wolcott, N. Y., March 13, 1824; daughter of Jedediah Wilder and Prudence Wells. He died at Wolcott, November 16, 1860.

CHILDREN.

630. MARY ELIZABETH, b. February 16, 1844.
631. CAROLINE PAGE, b. September 14, 1845.
632. CORNELIA WILDER, b. October 12, 1851, d. at Fulton, N. Y., May 14, 1862.
633. FREDERICK AUGUSTUS, b. January 26, 1855, now, 1874, at Yale College. All born at Wolcott.

He was an iron manufacturer and merchant at Wolcott, in the county of Wayne, N. Y. He was a highly valuable citizen—active, enterprising, public spirited, and of the highest character. The primary cause of his death—though he survived for a number of years—was a very severe injury which he received from the upsetting of his carriage near Canadaigua and from being dragged quite a distance upon the highway. It greatly impaired his activity and usefulness and finally resulted in his death.

His father was a merchant at Great Barrington at the time of his birth, but within a year or two removed to Sheffield, Mass., where he remained until about 1825, when he removed to Binghamton, N. Y., still continuing in the same business, though largely interested in iron works, at Wolcott, N. Y. This led him to close his business at Binghamton, and remove to Wolcott, about 1835. Elisha remained with his father and early became a partner with his father in the business at Wolcott, which was largely carried on and with success until near the close of their lives. The family still reside at Wolcott.

366. Lucius Leavenworth.[6] — JOHN,[5] GIDEON,[4] THOMAS,[3] THOMAS[2] THOMAS.[1]

Born May 1st, 1802, at New Haven, Conn. His sister Betsey says, 1803.

Married, first, HANNAH GATES, in 1828.

Married, second, AZUBAH GRIGGS, daughter of Solomon and Elizabeth Griggs, of Plymouth, Litchfield Co., Conn. Married at Windsor, Broome Co., N. Y. He died December 25, 1864, at Trumansburg, N. Y., of consumption. He resided some years at Colesville, Broome Co., and went there in 1828.

He owned a pail and tub factory there. Removed to Ithaca about 1835, and a few years after to Trumansburg. Had no children. His second wife died at Great Bend, Pa., July 26, 1873, aged eighty years.

367. CAROLINE LEAVENWORTH.[6]— JOHN,[5] GIDEON,[4] THOMAS,[3], THOMAS,[2] THOMAS.[1]

Born February 19, 1806.

Married James Savage January 10, 1827, of Auburn, N. Y. Removed to Albany in May of the same year, and they still reside there.

CHILDREN.

1. EDMUND, b. December 14, 1827. Is unmarried—1870.
2. EMMA JONES, b. November 9, 1850.

James Savage, d. at Albany in 1873.

369. BETSEY LEAVENWORTH.[6]—JOHN,[5] GIDEON,[4] THOMAS,[3] THOMAS,[2] THOMAS.[1]

Born November 28, 1808.

Married John Savage, of Albany, at Albany, May, 1841. Removed to Brooklyn, in 1848.

CHILDREN.

1. ISABELLA, b. March 12, 1842, at Albany, m. Dr. John Stanton Grove, and lives in Brooklyn, N. Y. Married February 17, 1864. They have had four children :—
   1. IDA MAY, b, May 27, 1865. 2. ELIZABETH MAUD, b. Sept. 21, 1867.
   3. LILLIAN, b. March 9, 1869, d. July 29, 1869. Above all born in Brooklyn
   4. EDMUND STANTON, b. July 26, 1870, in Parkville, L. I.
2. WILLIAM L., b. December 22, 1843, at Albany.
3. ELIZABETH L., b. December 14, 1845, at Albany.
4. JOHN EDMOND, b. 1847, d. within first year, at Brooklyn.
5. ROBERT JOHN, b. Angust 27, 1850, at Brooklyn.

370. MARY ELIZA LEAVENWORTH[6] —JOHN,[5] GIDEON[4], THOMAS,[3] THOMAS[2], THOMAS.[1]

Born February 12, 1812.

Married Rufus Loomis, June 12, 1838, son of Lyman Loomis, Esq., of Fleming. Resides at Rushville, N. Y. Married at Genoa. He was born at Fleming, Cayuga Co., in 1812. He is a carriage maker, as is Elbert, his son.

CHILDREN.

1. ELBERT, b. at Genoa, Cayuga Co., July 22, 1839.
2. CAROLINE, b. at Throopsville, May 6, 1841.
3. EDGAR, b. at Goodwin's Point, March 8, 1847. He is a harness maker.

371. RACHEL LEAVENWORTH.[6]—JOHN,[5] GIDEON,[4] THOMAS,[3] THOMAS[2], THOMAS.[1]

Born September 17, 1815.

Married, first, George Avery, of Genoa, son of the Hon. Daniel and Abigail Avery, February 25, 1840. He was a merchant and removed to Meadville,

Va., where he died April 30, 1849, leaving two children. He was born at Aurora, Cayuga Co., April 2, 1815.

Married, second, March 18, 1854, Rev. Joseph Strickland, and had no children by him. Resides at Danville, Va.

CHILDREN.

1. MARION FRANCES, b. March 29, 1841, at Meadville, Halifax Co., Va. Unmarried in 1870.
2. AMELIA SOPHIA, b. May 20, 1844, at Meadville. Unmarried in 1870.

373. SUSANNA LEAVENWORTH.[6] — JARED,[5] GIDEON,[4] THOMAS,[3] THOMAS,[2] THOMAS.[1]

Born March 16, 1801, at Hamden, Conn.

Went with her father to Towanda, and after his second marriage returned to her friends at or near New Haven, Conn.

Married Aeneas Sperry at New Haven, Conn. She had a number of children, lost some, and one or more in the rebellion. Did live at New Haven and probably still does—perhaps at Hotchkisstown.

374. HENRIETTA LEAVENWORTH.[6]—JARED[5], GIDEON,[4] THOMAS,[3] THOMAS[2], THOMAS.[1]

Born October 18, 1804, at New Haven, Conn.

Went with her father to Towanda, and after his second marriage returned to her friends, at New Haven.

Married, first, —— Hotchkiss, at or near New Haven.

" second, Philo Bradley, of Woodbridge. She lives, or lived, in New Haven, Conn., or at Hotchkisstown.

377. Franklin James Leavenworth.[6]— JARED,[5] GIDEON[4], THOMAS,[3] THOMAS,[2] THOMAS.[1]

Born January 24, 1827, at Delaware City, Del.

Married, first, June 1, 1848, HARRIET C. STEELE, of Wilkesbarre, Penn. Only daughter of George P. Steele, sheriff of Luzerne Co., State Senator etc., and of Mary Chrisman. She was b. in Hanover, Penn., March 27, 1827. She died July 25, 1849, at Wilkesbarre, Penn., without issue.

Married, second, November 6, 1852, ANNIE, daughter of Rev. Enos Woodward, an Episcopal clergyman and the rector of St. Andrews and St. Marys churches, Chester Co., Penn., formerly of Washington, Ky. Her mother was Sarah Murphy, of Maryland. She was born in Washington Ky., August 5, 1829.

CHILDREN.

634. WOODWARD, b. November 22, 1853, at Scranton, Penn.
635. JANE, b. May 6, 1855, at Scranton, Penn.
636. ENOS, b. April, 24, 1859, at Scranton, Penn.
637. FRANKLIN, b. March 2, 1862, at Brooklyn, N. Y.
638. ANNIE, b. April 19, 1865, at Phildelphia, Penn.

Frankiln J. was educated at the Towanda Academy, studied law with Luther Kidder, Esq., of Wilkesbarre, for four years, practiced there for three years. In 1853, removed to Scranton, and for some years was paymaster of the Delaware, Lackawanna and Western Railroad Co., and Superintendent of the Lackawanna and Bloomsburg Railroad Co. In 1859, removed to New York and was in the office of the Comptroller and City Chamberlain until 1863, when he engaged in Banking and was unsuccessful. Removed then to Philadelphia, and in 1865 to Wilkesbarre, and has since been engaged in the coal trade.

378. HARRIET LEAVENWORTH.[6]—JOSEPH,[5] SAMUEL,[4] THOMAS,[3] THOMAS,[2] THOMAS.[1]

Born November 19, 1798, at Waterbury.
Married December 25, 1815, William Lockwood, of Watertown, Conn., a farmer. He died October 6, 1863. She died July 17, 1870.

CHILDREN.

1. SON, b. July 22, 1819, d. in infancy without name.
2. MARY REBECCA, b. May 1, 1823, unmarried, lives in New Britain.
3. THOMAS COLE, b. July 29, 1825, farmer, unmarried, resides in Waterbury.
4. WILLIAM NEWTON, b. June 7, 1832, m. October 1, 1860, in New Britain, Jane Louisa Alfred, of Harwinton, Conn. Resides at Harwinton, (Campville.)

Children.

1. HERBERT NEWTON, b. December 10, 1863.
2. WILLIAM ALFRED, b. August 29, 1867.
3. SON, b. May 10, 1869, d. June 13, 1869.
4. TWIN SONS, b. June 16, 1870, one d. July 31, 1870.

379. HANNAH P. LEAVENWORTH.[6]—JOSEPH,[5] SAMUEL,[4] THOMAS,[3] THOMAS,[2] THOMAS.[1]

Born September 16, 1800.
Married January 20, 1820, Lyman Bradley, carpenter, afterwards manufacturer of pocket cutlery at Waterbury. She died February 25, 1864. He has since married the widow of Rev. Joseph Scott, of Naugatuck.

CHILDREN.

1. SAMUEL ELI, b. August 30, 1823, m. Sarah D. Beach, November 15, 1843, d. February 14, 1867, leaving one child, name Clarissa Hannah Leavenworth, b. February 12, 1864.
2. FRANKLIN ELLIOT, b. June 26, 1830, d. October 25, 1840.

380. Joseph Stanley Leavenworth.[6]— JOSEPH,[5] SAMUEL,[4] THOMAS,[3] THOMAS,[2] THOMAS[1].

Born December 2, 1802, at Waterbury, died Dec. 28, 1841.
Married April 28 or '9, 1824, MINERVA NEWTON, of Waterbury.

CHILDREN.

639. JOSEPH N., b. March 4, 1828.

640. MARTHA J., b. May 27, 1830, m. May 9, 1851, Edmund B. Fairchild.

641. FREDERICK ELI, b. July 21, 1833, d. Sept. 8, 1834.

642. FREDERICK C., b. July 14, 1835, lives (1870) at Hamden, (Centreville P. O.)

382. REBECCA LEAVENWORTH.[6]—JOSEPH,[5] SAMUEL,[4] THOMAS,[3] THOMAS[2], THOMAS.[1]

Born February 9, 1811.
Married William R. Hotchkiss, of Watertown. Died April 11, 1838.

CHILDREN.

1. CATHARINE A., b. February 14, 1836, m. November 16, 1856, George W. Bristol, farmer of Thomaston, Plymouth, Conn.

Children.
1. MARION ELIZABETH, b. November 29, 1857.
2. NELLIE JANE, b. July 17, 1861. 3. GEORGE ALBERT, b. March 16, 1863.
3, EDWARD THOMAS, } Twins, b. Feb. 23, 1868.
4. EDSON LEWIS, }

383. MARY G. LEAVENWORTH.[6]—JOSEPH[5], SAMUEL,,[4] THOMAS,[3] THOMAS,[2] THOMAS.[1]

Born September 6, 1814.
Married William Newton, merchant, Plainville, Conn.

CHILDREN.

1. ANTHONY, b. July, 1, 1836.
2. CATHARINE, b. December 18, 1840.
3. GEORGE L., b. July 22, 1843.
4. FRANKLIN B., b. June 8, 1846.

384. SARAH ANN LEAVENWORTH.[6]—JOSEPH,[5] SAMUEL[4], THOMAS,[3] THOMAS,[2] THOMAS.[1]

Born August 9, 1817, at Waterbury.
Married October 26, 1834, Joseph Wheeler, of Watertown, farmer.

CHILDREN.

1. AUGUSTA, b. February —, 1836, m. Anson Hard, March 4, 1867.

Children—
1. HELEN AMELIA. b. January 9, 1868.
2. CALVIN, b. April 25, 1837, m. October 10, 1858, Annie Conover.

Children.
1. MARY E., b. June 17, 1861.
2. JOSEPH D., b., March 26, 1865. Calvin d. November 30, 1867.
3. MARY, b. December 14, 1840, d. February 19, 1844.
4. JOHN, b. April 22, 1842, d, May 3, 1866, unmarried.
5. ELI, b. April 30, 1844, m. November 11, 1868, Estella Saxton, no children.
6. ANSON, b. October 2, 1847, d. August 19, 1848.
7. MYRON, b. July 22, 1849, d. September 29, 1870, unmarried.

385. Lyman Leavenworth.[6]—SAMUEL,[5] SAMUEL,[4] THOMAS,[3] THOMAS,[2] THOMAS.[1]

Born February 5, 1805, in Waterbury, Conn.

Married NANCY CHURCH, ——, 1830. She was the widow of ——— Church, and daughter of ——— Scott, a farmer of Pepperell, Mass. Lyman L. is a wagon maker at Lockport, N. Y. He worked several years as a carpenter. Now (1870) lives in Canandaigua. Died January 26, 1871, at Canandaigua? and on the same day with his brother Joseph. No children.

386. BETSEY LEAVENWORTH[6] — SAMUEL,[5] SAMUEL,[4] THOMAS,[3] THOMAS,[2] THOMAS.[1]

Born February 8, 1808, in Waterbury, Conn.

Married Philip Baker, November 22, 1830, in Pike, now Wyoming Co., N. Y. He was born in Whiting, Addison Co., Vt., in 1795, and is a farmer at Eagle Wyoming Co., N. Y., where their children were all born.

CHILDREN.

1. ESTHER L., b. April 9, 1832, d. September 3, 1850.
2. LEVERET S., b. June 26, 1834, m. Wealthy S. Howes, September 11, 1859. He is a farmer.
3. BURTON P., b. March 3, 1836, d. February 27, 1858.
4. EMILY P., b. July 19, 1836, m. James W. Flint October 31, 1858. He is a farmer.
5. MARY F., b. June 9, 1842, m. Albert P. Gage, April 27, 1865. He is a farmer. She taught school eight years.
6. SARAH F., b. August 24, 1849, d. February 24, 1853.

387. Davis Leavenworth.[6] — SAMUEL,[5] SAMUEL,[4] THOMAS,[3] THOMAS.[2] THOMAS.[1]

Born April 23, 1810, at Genoa, Cayuga Co., N. Y.

Married LYDIA ANN MCCALLUM, July 25, 1839, at Clinton, Mich. Her father had resided in Rochester, N. Y., and was a fancy dyer. He lives at Grand Rapids, Mich., has done so since 1856, and is a miller. They have no children. Removed to Prattsburgh about 1811, then Pike, in Allegany Co., and about 1823 to Batavia, Genesee Co., and to Michigan in the Spring of 1838.

388. Joseph Leavenworth.[6] —SAMUEL,[5] SAMUEL,[4] THOMAS,[3] THOMAS,[2] THOMAS.[1]

Born July 7, 1822, at Prattsburg, Steuben Co., N. Y.

Married ELIZABETH A. DURFEE, (daughter of A. C. Durfee, of Jackson, Mich.) February 16, 1851. He was a miller at Allegan, Mich. He died at Allegan, January 26, 1871, (on the same day with his brother Lyman) respected and beloved.

CHILDREN.

643. EDMUND CHARLES, b. January 21, 1852, at Detroit, Mich.

Is an operator in the telegraph office at the R. R. depot.

644. MARY E. b. Jannary 15, 1854, at Jackson Mich., d. February 21, 1854.

645. BEN. C. b. Feb. 1, 1855, at Manchester, Mich. Is now a clerk in a store in Allegan.

646. ANNIE LUELLA, b· August 31, 1857, at Manchester, Mich. d. April 20, 1869, at Allegan, Mich.

He was well known at Allegan and in the vicinity, for his fine social qualities, his humane and generous instincts and his many virtues.

390. Edmund Leavenworth.[6]—SAMUEL,[5] SAMUEL,[4] THOMAS[3], THOMAS,[2] THOMAS.[1]

Born November 5, 1820, at Prattsburg, Steuben, Co., N. Y.

Married HARRIET W. CORNING, December 26, 1853, at Manchester, Washtenaw Co., Mich. She was daughter of Alexander B. Corning, a clergyman, who died at Scio, Washtenaw Co., Mich. Edmund L. is a miller, and has been a trader and merchant. Resides at Ann Arbor, Mich. He moved first to Allegan, from Manchester, then to Scio, staying a brief time at each place and then to Ann Arbor. Is in the post office there. Now, 1874, at Leslie, Mich., in the lumber business.

CHILDREN.

647. EDMUND C., b. January 4, 1855, in Manchester.

648. HARRIET E., b. September 12, 1856, d. March 19, 1860.

649. MARY E., b. January 14, 1859, in Scio.

650. CLARA E., b. January 2, 1864, in Ann Arbor, Mich.

651. MARK ELIAS, b. January 18, 1866 " " "

652. THOMAS HENRY, b. Dec. 11, 1868 " " " d. June 14, 1871, at Ann Arbor.

653. A. PHILIP DAVIS, b. August 12, 1871, at Ann Arbor.

653½ PAUL JOSEPH, b. January 11, 1874, at Leslie, Mich.

I am greatly indebted to Mr. L. for his prompt attention to all my requests for information, and for the time and care he has expended in procuring the same.

395. Abel Edgar Leavenworth.[6]—ABEL,[5] ABEL,[4] THOMAS[3], THOMAS[2], THOMAS.[1]

Born September 3, 1828, at Charlotte, Vt.

Married MARY EVELINA GRIGGS, of Corning, N. Y., September 14, 1853.

CHILDREN.

653¾ ANNA MARIA, b. August 7, 1854, d. at Hinesburgh February 6th, 1859, b. at Bolivar, Mo.

654. FRANCIS ABEL, b. May 20, 1856, at Hinesburgh.

655. SAMUEL EDGAR, b. March 7, 1858. "

656. CLARENCE GREENMAN, b. February 28, 1860, at Hinesb'h.

657. WILLIAM STOWELL, b. July 28, 1862, at Brattleboro, Vt.

658. EMILY REYNOLDS, b. May 31, 1865, at Hinesburgh, d. Nov. 11, 1866, at Hinesburgh.

659. PHILIP REYNOLDS, b. February 18, 1867, at Hinesburgh.

Resided with his father till he was twenty-one, working on the farm summers, studying or teaching winters.

Entered Hinesburg Academy at seventeen. Taught school five winters from his eighteenth year. Entered the University of Vermont, at twenty-one. Was one of the founders of the Delta Psi Fraternity and a member of the Society for Religious Inquiry, and of the Phi Sigma Nu Society.

Having received a severe injury in his head he was advised to leave college and go south. He received a highly complimentary letter from the President, Worthington Smith, D. D., which was fully endorsed by Ex-Gov. William Slade.

He left in April 1852, near the close of his junior year and about the twentieth entered upon the duties of Principal of Bolivar Male and Female Academy, at Bolivar, Polk Co., Mo., in connection with Miss Mary E. Griggs, as Preceptress, who was previously in charge of the school. The institution was very prosperous. He remained there till 1855.

He was unable to conform his views to those of the majority of the trustees and patrons, in regard to affairs in Kansas. They had several of them voted at the election in Kansas, though living sixty miles from the border, and had actually elected one of the trustees to the Kansas Legislature. He therefore concluded to return east, although every inducement was held out to him to remain.

The institution ran rapidly down after he left and the town was badly wasted by the rebellion.

On his return, he was invited to take charge of the Hinesburg

Academy, which he did, just ten years after entering it as a student, in September 1855. At the end of his first year there, he unexpectedly received the degree of A. B. in course, from the trustees of the University of Vermont, and four years after, that of A. M.

At the end of five years he resigned against the wishes of the Trustees, and became Principal and proprietor of the Brattleboro Academy, at West Brattleboro, Vt., in 1860.

In 1859 he became one of the proprietors and editors of the Vermont School Journal and Family Visitor, and in 1860 he became sole proprietor and editor, the name having been abridged to the Vermont School Journal, with which he was connected until he entered the army in 1862. In the Spring of 1862, he was prostrated by an attack of erysipelas, and was obliged to disband his school, which he had changed to a select school of thirty scholars, young men and boys, whom he was fitting for business or for college. The whole were organized into a well-disciplined military company, from whose ranks several entered the army of the Union.

When partially recovered, he heard and responded to the call of Father Abraham, "for three hundred thousand more," and with one of his students, was the first to enlist under that call from Vermont, having yielded to a desire long felt. On May 24th, 1862, he became a private in the Ninth Vermont Volunteers, to serve as a soldier for the Union, at eleven dollars per month, in lieu of one hundred dollars per month as a teacher. He became First Sergeant of Co. K, July 5th, 1862; First Lieutenant Nov. 17, 1862, and Captain December 4, 1864.

He was appointed by Major-Gen. Dix, commanding department of Virginia and North Carolina, A. A. Inspector-Gen. of Wistar's Brigade, at Suffook, Va. June 10, 1863, of the U. S. Forces at Yorktown, Gloucester, Fort Magruder and vicinity, July 9, 1863, to May 3, 1864, was confirmed by Maj. J. G. Foster, October 14, 1863, and reappointed by Maj. Gen. B. F. Butler, February 22, 1864, of Sec. Brig., Sec. Division, 18th A. C., May 3d, to June 10th 1864. Was in Officer's General Hospital, and on sick leave of absence till September, 1864. Provisional Brigade Defences of Bermuda Hundred, September 21, to December 4, 1864. Also A. A. Adjt. General of the same command, from October

13, 1864, which held the line between the James and Appomattox rivers, three miles and covered the base of supplies for the armies of the Potomac and of the James. December 4, 1853, was transferred to the 2d Brig., 3d Div., 24th Army Corps of which he was made A. A. Adjt. General. This command held the line fronting Richmond, eight miles distant, but in sight of the State House, during the winter of 1864-5. April 3d, 1865, he commanded the skirmish line of Vermonters, which led the advance into that city. April 5th, he was appointed by Maj. Gen. Weitzel, Ast. Provost Marshall and assigned by the P. M. Gen'l Departm3nt of Virginia, to the head office at Richmond. On the restoration of order to that city, he was assigned to duty April 30th as A. A. Adj't General of the Department of the Appotomáx embracing the five counties between the James and the Appotomax rivers, with headquarters at first at Manchester, then at Petersburg. This position he held till his discharge at Richmond, June 13th, 1865.

Returned home in June, 1865, the rebellion being closed, with thirty-two men of his company who left with him in 1862, the largest number of any company in the regiment, though his company entered the smallest by some twenty men.

From 1865 to 1868 he was principal of the Hinesburgh Academy; from then till 1870, of New Haven Academy. In 1869 the latter institution was re-chartered as Beeman Academy, and in 1870 it was reorganized, and a fund of eleven thousand dollars secured towards support of instruction. The charter provides for a classical, a scientific, and a normal course, of three years. The chief work of the school is to prepare young men and women for higher institutions, and for teaching. Hr continues in charge of this school at the present time.

He was a member of Chitten Co. Teacher's Association from its organization in 1847, most of the time one of its active officers, and President from 1868 to 1870. Also, delegate from the same to the National Teacher's Association, at Trenton, N. J., in August, 1869. He has been a member of the State Teacher's Association since 1857, and is now Treasurer and Vice-President of the same. He is also a leading member of Otter Creek Valley Teacher's Association, and Chairman of the Executive Committee of the Vermont Teacher's Club. In 1872 he was a

Abel Edgar Leavenworth.

NEW HAVEN, VERMONT.

member of the General Convention of Vermoat Congregational body. He is also an active member of the Re-union Society of Vermont officers of the late war.

In the winter of 1871-2, he was one of the six prominent teachers selected by the Vermont Board of Education, to examine text books for the use in the Vermont schools, five years from November, 1873.

396. LYDIA ANN LEAVENWORTH.[6]— Abel,[5] Abel,[4] Thomas,[3] Thomas,[2] Thomas.[1]

Born June 28, 1830, at Charlotte, Vt.

Married Alfred William Sherman, October 29, 1851, born October 7, 1825, at Charlotte, Vt., a farmer.

CHILDREN.

1. Mary Anna, b. September 9, 1853, at Charlotte. Teaching or at school.
2. Lillie Louisa, b. June 1, 1855. " " "
3. Harriet Orilla, b. May 8, 1857, d. January 23, 1867, at Charlotte, Vt.
4. Leveret Abel, b. Nouember 2, 1862, d. Jan. 16, 1867, at Charlotte, both of Diphtheria.
5. Alfred Leavenworth, b. April 23, 1870. All born at Charlotte.

398. LUCY JANE LEAVENWORTH.[6] — Abel,[5] Abel,[4] Thomas,[3] Thomas,[2] Thomas.[1]

Born August 26, 1834, at Madrid, N. Y. Was for several years a teacher of painting, drawing and French, in Virginia, Missouri, etc.

Married June 22, 1860, John Nichols Alvord, of Trenton, Ill., at Waukegan, Ill., who was born at Chateaugay, Franklin Co., N. Y., August 19, 1823. He was early a telegraph operator and manager, now a farmer.

CHILDREN.

1. Frank Edgar, b. September 27, 1861, at Trenton. Ill.
2. Frederick Leavenworth, b. January 5, 1864, at Trenton, Ill.
3. Jennie Louisa, b. November 12, 1865, at Noble, Ill., d. November 15, 1865, at Noble.

The first four years they lived on a farm near Trenton, Ill. They then moved to Decker, Richland Co., Ill., where Mrs. A. died November 19, 1865, where she and her daughter were buried in the same grave. She fell a prey to the miasmatic influence of the climate. She was a lady of rare attainments and many virtues.

399. CHARLOTTE LAURA LEAVENWORTH.[6]—Abel[5], Abel,[4] Thomas,[3] Thomas[2], Thomas.[1]

Born August 17, 1837, at Madrid, N. Y.

Married January 15, 1861, Joshua C. Russell, who was born January 2, 1837. He was for several years a farmer at Charlotte. In 1866 they removed to Illinois, living first at Decker, then at Carlisle, where they now reside, and he follows the business of a carpenter.

CHILDREN,

1. Florence Louisa, b. October 18, 1861, at Charlotte.
2. Burton Leavenworth, b. October 4, 1863, at Charlotte.
3. Harry Miller, b. October 2, 1869, at Noble, Ill.

400. SARAH SABRINA LEAVENWORTH[6]—ABEL,[5] ABEL[4], THOMAS,[3] THOMAS,[2] THOMAS.[1]

Born February 17, 1840, at Madrid, N. Y.

Married December 3, 1864, Sylvester Smith Tuttle, b. April 5, 1831, in Lyon Co., Kentucky, son of Ezra Tuttle and Rebecca Allison Fairchild. Married at Trenton, Ill. They reside at Pleasant Ridge, five miles from Carlisle, Ill. Mr. T. is a horticulturist. Have no children, but have adopted George William Townshend, b. at Carlyle, November 8, 1869. Mrs. T. was educated at Hinesburgh, at Mrs. Worcester's school at Burlington, Vt., and at Glenwood Ladies Seminary at West Brattleboro, and taught music at Trenton before her marriage.

405. Henry Arza Leavenworth.[6]—ARZA,[5] ABEL,[4] THOMAS[3], THOMAS[2], THOMAS.[1]

Born October 19, 1835, at Madrid, N. Y.

Married ADALINE O'FARRELL, May 4, 1856, at Norfolk, N. Y. Is a blacksmith, and resides, 1873, at Sandy Creek, Oswego Co., N. Y. Adaline O'Farrell is the daughter of a Methodist clergyman, Francis Asbury O'Farrell, and was born in Spafford Hollow, Onondaga Co.. June 28, 1837.

CHILDREN.

661. JENNIE M., b. May 7, 1858, in Norfolk, N. Y.
662. EDWIN ARZA, b. June 24, 1859, " "
663. FRANCIS HENRY, b. January 27, 1864, at Sandy Creek, Oswego Co., N. Y., d. there October 6, 1872.

406. Sidney Brook Leavenworth.[6]—ARZA,[5] ABEL,[4] THOMAS,[3] THOMAS,[2] THOMAS.[1]

Born August 5, 1841, in Norfolk, N. Y.

Married February 28, 1870, CLEMENTINE O'FARRELL, at Sandy Creek, Oswego Co., N. Y. Is a blacksmith and resides at Sandy Creek, 1873. Clementine O'Farrell is the sister of Mrs. Henry A. Leavenworth, and was born at Hannibal Center, Oswego, Co. N. Y., May 12, 1850. She is the daughter of the Rev. Francis Asbury O'Farrell, a Methodist clergyman, and Ann Jane Van Buckhouse, who died in 1869, at Hannibal.

CHILDREN.

664. LILLIAN BELLE, b. January 28, 1872, at Sandy Creek.

408. Edmund S. Leavenworth.[6]—ISAAC,[5] THOMAS,[4] THOMAS[3], THOMAS,[2] THOMAS.[1]

Born October 1, 1815.

Married February 25, 1841, ELLEN M. THOMAS. Auger-maker, by trade, at West Haven, Conn.

CHILDREN.

665. EDSON HOBERT, b. August 14, 1843, and d. September 1, 1843.
666. MARY ELLEN, b. December 19, 1846, m. William Fuller.
667. EDDIE SMITH, b. September 8, 1851, d. Sept. 14, 1854.
668. ISAAC STANLY, b. October 31, 1855.
669. ETTA HELENA, b. April 29, 1865.

410. John Leavenworth.[6] — ISAAC,[5] THOMAS,[4] THOMAS,[3] THOMAS[2], THOMAS.[1]

Born December 15, 1821.

Married October 20, 1844, MARY A. WOLLESTON. By trade was an auger-maker, near New Haven, Conn. Died February 24, 1859.

CHILDREN.

670. ANN ELIZA, b. September 27, 1845.
671. SARAH JANE, b. February 28, 1849, d. March 3, 1849.
672. MARY JANE, b. August 29, 1850.
673. FRANCES LOUISA, b. September 26, 1856.
674. EMMA JEANETTE, b. April 12, 1859.

411. Clark Leavenworth.[6] — ISAAC,[5] THOMAS,[4] THOMAS[3], THOMAS,[2] THOMAS.[1]

Born May 12, 1827.

Married July 5, 1848, MARY C. BRADT. Lives in Chester; by trade an auger-maker.

CHILDREN.

675. ARMINDA CAROLINE, b. April 18, 1854.
676. ESLI, b. August 16, 1858.
677. CHARLES, b. January 13, 1859.

412. David Johnson Leavenworth.[6]—CALVIN,[5] THOMAS[4], THOMAS,[3] THOMAS[2], THOMAS.[1]

Born November 24, 1813, at Oxford Conn. Is a shoemaker by trade, and resided at Chesaning, Saginaw Co. Mich., in 1870.

Married October 7, 1840, MARIA LOUISA JAY, at New Haven, Conn., at the house of the Rev. Mr. Merwin. She was the daughter of William Jay, and the grand-daughter of John Jay, a French Huguenot, who came over before the American Revolution; was in our army, fought at Bunker Hill, and died in Canada in 1822. William Jay was born in Albany in 1786, and died in Otsego, near Cooperstown, in 1838, aged 52. Her mother was Susan Henrietta Cviatt, and was born in Watertown, Conn., and her grandmother in Oxford, Conn. They were married at Hartwick, Otsego Co., December 3, 1820. Maria Louisa Jay was born January 14, 1822, at Hartwick, and was the granddaughter of Amos A. Oviatt, and Susan Henrietta (Bartholomew) O. Amos A. was born in Derby.

CHILDREN.

677¼ Ellen Albertine, b. July 11, 1841, at Naugatuck, Conn. Married July 6, 1860, John Connor, b. in the county of Meath, Ireland, June 29, 1840, and d. April 4, 1872. He was the son of Patrick C., b. in 1782, in the county of Meath, and d. in Newark, N. J., September 3, 1872, and of Ann Sheridan, b. in the county of Cavan, Ireland, in 1790, d. in New Brunswick, N. J., November 2, 1850.

Children.—1. Mary Ellen, b. June 15, 1861, at New Brunswick.
2. Emma Theresa, b. Oct. 1, 1863, " "
3. Lizzie, b. October 11, 1867, " "

677½ Vernon Jay, b. October 6, 1845, at Southbury, Conn., drowned at Penn Haven, Pa., on the night of Oct. 9, 1856.

677¾ Blanche Amelia, b. March 2, 1860, at New York.

Mrs. L. now resides in the city of New York, and her youngest daughter with her.

413. ELIZA A. LEAVENWORTH.[6]— Calvin,[5] Thomas,[4] Thomas,[3] Thomas[2], Thomas[1]

Born February 29, 1816, at Oxford, Conn.

Married Elisha Wheeler, of Southbury, Conn., April 10, 1838. He is a farmer and was formerly a State Senator, and son of Moses W.; Southford is her post office, and the children were all born there.

CHILDREN.

1 Frances E., b. October 17, 1840, m. October 17, 1865, to Truman E. Hurd, Southbury, Conn. Paper manufacturer; has a daughter, Mary Frances, b. May 26, 1866, and two more children, named Katy May and Henry B. Harrison. All born in Southford.

2. Martha E., b. August 12, 1842.

3. Ralph E., b. May 17, 1844, d. June 7, 1858.

4. Mary S., b. April 26, 1846, m. June 9, 1870, Charles E. Webster, engineer

on Chesapeake and Ohio Railroad, now at White Sulphur Springs, in Va.
5. HENRY S., b. August 5, 1848.
6. ALFRED N., b. January 2, 1855.

414. Thomas Burr Leavenworth.[6] — CALVIN,[5] THOMAS,[4] THOMAS,[3] THOMAS,[2] THOMAS.[1]

Born December 14, 1821, in Bethany, Conn. Left that State in 1842, from Woodbury, where he had learned the trade of silver spoon maker. Went to Newbern, N. C., and in June 1843, to Buffalo, N. Y., where he married and lived until May 1, 1851, when he removed to Detroit. He is now carrying on his business at that place.

Married ELLEN DOYLE, October 26, 1845, at Buffalo. She was born at Drumsno, Ireland, July 16, 1823.

CHILDREN.

678. GEORGE CALVIN, b. July 6, 1846, d. July 27, 1846.
679. THOMAS BURR Jr., b. September 14, 1847, d. at Detroit, in 1869.
680. ELLEN, b.
681. SOPHIA, (adopted daughter).

415. MARIA LEAVENWORTH.[6] — CALVIN,[5] THOMAS,[4] THOMAS,[3] THOMAS,[2] THOMAS.[1]

Born November 23, 1822, at Oxford, Conn.

Married Harris Bishop Munson, July 23, 1843, at Humphreyville, Conn. He was born at Middlebury January 31, 1821; was formerly a teacher, is now a lawyer, and represented Seymour in the Legislature in 1854, 1864-5-6, and '7.

CHILDREN.

1. ELEANOR J., b. July 22, 1844, at Middlebury, d. March 31, 1867, at Seymour, Conn.
2. BYRON WOOSTER, b. December 3, 1845, at Oxford, Conn.
3. SOPHIA L., b. April 30, 1849, at Humphreyville, Conn.
4. IRIS E., b. April 4, 1852, at Seymour, Conn.
5. HARRIS BENNET, b. February 23, 1854, at Seymour, Conn.
6. MARY SOMERS, b. March 21, 1861, " "

416. George Leavenworth.[6]—CALVIN,[5] THOMAS,[4] THOMAS,[3] THOMAS,[2] THOMAS.[1]

Born January 30, 1826.

Married MABEL H. STEVENS, May 28, 1848, in Naugatuc, Ct. Is an auger maker and resides at Seymour, New Haven Co., Ct.

CHILDREN.

682. IDA A., b. June 20, 1851.
683. GEORGE B., b. May 12, 1854.

684. ALICE S., b. October 26, 1856.
685. FRANK R., b. April 18, 1859.
686. SARAH J., b. January 6, 1861.

417. Calvin B. Leavenworth.[6]—CALVIN,[5] THOMAS,[4] THOMAS,[3] THOMAS[2], THOMAS.[1]

Born September 11, 1829, at Oxford, Conn.

Married December 31, 1854, SARAH JANE HILL, daughter of Thomas and Mary Hill, of Medina, O., by Rev. Mr. Granville. Reside at Montrose, Lee Co., Iowa. He is a farmer and teacher.

CHILDREN.

687. MARIETTA, b. June 26, 1856, at Medina, d. at Montrose, Iowa, October 3, 1856.
688. ETTIE MAY, b. February 18, 1869.

He removed from Medina to Montrose in August 1856.

418. JULIA S. LEAVENWORTH.[6]— CALVIN,[5] THOMAS,[4] THOMAS,[3] THOMAS,[2] THOMAS.[1]

Born August 1, 1846, at Oxford, Conn.

Married March 23, 1869, at Montrose, Iowa, Corliss A. Burton, and now resides at Lewis, Cass Co., Iowa. Her husband is a farmer, and she was a teacher for a number of years.

419. SARAH LEAVENWORTH.[6] — CALVIN,[5] THOMAS,[4] THOMAS,[3] THOMAS,[2] THOMAS.[1]

Born October, 1849, at Oxford, Conn.

She is now, 1872, a teacher at Edna, Iowa, but her home is with her sister Julia.

421. BETSEY LEAVENWORTH.[6]—MARK,[5] THOMAS,[4] THOMAS,[3] THOMAS[2], THOMAS.[1]

Born November 4, 1837, at Huntington, Vt.

Married November 25, 1861, William McIntosh, at Stockholm, St. Lawrence Co. He was the son of William McIntosh, and was born at Albany April 12, 1808. He is a farmer, laborer and nurse.

CHILDREN.

1. GEORGE, b. January 7, 1864.
2. ALICE, b. November 14, 1866.
3. VIOLA, b. February 3, 1868—all at Stockholm.

422. James Leavenworth.[6] — MARK,[5] THOMAS,[4] THOMAS,[4] THOMAS[2] THOMAS.[1]

Born February 30, 1845, at Bangor, Franklin county, N. Y.

Married MARY CAZA, October 21, 1869, at Westville, N. Y., and lives at Bangor. He is a farmer. She was born July 27, 1846, at St. Anicet, Lower Canada; was daughter of Baptiste Caza and Ausele Adete; a farmer. He was born at St. Anicet, she at Montreal.

424. Henry Clay Leavenworth.[6]—BURK,[5] DORMAN,[4] THOMAS,[3] THOMAS,[2] THOMAS.[1]

Born July 28, 1827, at Charlotte, Vt.

Married, JULIANA LANE, at Jericho, Vt., January 1, 1857. She was born July 8, 1829, and was a daughter of Stevens Lane, of Jericho; farmer. He resides in Charlotte, and his children were all born there. He is a farmer.

CHILDREN.

689. GEORGE STEVENS, b. August 17, 1858.
690. EMMA CHARLOTTE, b. November 21, 1860.
691. BURK, b. October 20, 1862.
692. DORA, b. August 24, 1864.
693. LUCY, b. August 17, 1866.
693¼ HENRY, b. December 10, 1868.
693½ EDGAR LAW, b. February 4, 1874.

425. FANNY MARIA LEAVENWORTH[6]—ABIJAH,[5] GIDEON[4], EDMUND,[3] THOMAS[2], THOMAS.[1]

Born October 15, 1808, at Huntington.

Married May 30, 1827, Bennet Bray, of Southbury; a blacksmith, She now lives with her daughter Eliza A., at New Haven, Conn., who married Thomas F. Hamilton.

CHILDREN.

1. THADDEUS GOULD, b. September 5, 1828, d. in California.
2. ELIZA A., b. November 15, 1829, m. Thos. F. Hamilton, artist of New Haven, December, 1868.
3. JANE E., b. October 24, 1831, m. Joshua Keeney Oct., 1862. No children.
4. DELIA M., b. June 24, 1833, m. Thos. F. Hamilton January 13, 1856, d. January 30, 1858, leaving Delia Jane, b. Nov. 22, 1856.
5. STEPHEN B., b. January 2, 1837, d. April 17, 1838.

426. EMELINE ELIZA LEAVENWORTH.[6]— ABIJAH,[5] GIDEON,[4] EDMUND,[3] THOMAS,[2] THOMAS.[1]

Born January 11, 1812, at Huntington, Ct.

Married Truman Percy, of Woodbury, at Huntington, May 22, 1833; a blacksmith. She died January 19, 1834, leaving no child, in Huntington, and was buried at the White Hills.

427. Eli Leavenworth.[6]—MARK ELI,[5] GIDEON,[4] EDMUND,[3] THOMAS[2], THOMAS.[1]

Born August 19, 1824, at Huntington, Conn.

Married Lucy A. Mason, June 6, 1852, daughter of John Mason, of Rochester. She was born June 21, 1830. Resides in Rochester, N. Y., and is foreman of a large manufactory.

CHILDREN.

694. Frank Henry, b. February 6, 1854, at Newtown, Conn.
695. Cora Elizabeth, b. June 2, 1858, at Rochester, N. Y.
696. Lilian Louisa, b. November 25, 1863, " "
697. Dexter M. F., b. February 18, 1866, " "

428. ABIGAIL LEAVENWORTH.[6]—Mark Eli,[5] Gideon,[4] Edmund,[3] Thomas,[2] Thomas.[1]

Born April 25, 1826. Died May 21, 1854, unmarried.

429. ELIZABETH LEAVENWORTH.[6]—Mark Eli,[5] Gideon,[4] Edmund,[3] Thomas,[2] Thomas.[1]

Born December 31, 1827. Unmarried, lives with her father, at Newtown.

430. George Gideon Leavenworth.[6]— Gideon,[5] Gideon[4], Edmund,[3] Thomas,[2] Thomas.[1]

Born December 2, 1841, at Rochester.

The 14th regiment of heavy artillery was organized at Rochester in 1863. Col. Elisha G. Marshall, now of Rochester, commanded it through the war. George Gideon was First Lieutenant of Company H, Capt. Jones. He entered the service December 9, 1863, being mustered in by H. C. Cook, of Rochester, mustering officer U. S. A. He served till August 12, 1864, when he was honorably discharged.

431. Charles Frederick Leavenworth.[6]—Gideon,[5] Gideon,[4] Edmund,[3] Thomas,[2] Thomas[1].

Born October 2, 1845, at Rochester.

Married March 29, 1873, Kate M. Mead, of Warren, Penn.; married in California, at the home of Dr. C. Leavenworth—probably Rev. Chauncey L.

436. George Leavenworth.[7]—Daniel,[6] Andrew,[5] Daniel,[4] James,[3] Thomas,[2] Thomas.[1]

Born October 15, 1828, at Monroe.

Married June 25, 1851, Anna M. Barnum, at Danbury, now

Bethel, Conn. He died November 3, 1859, aged thirty-one, in Danbury, Conn. He was a hatter.

CHILDREN.

698. GEORGE E., b. December 26, 1858, at Bethel.

The widow married in 1869, Capt. —— Hale, of Norwalk, Conn.

437. ABBEY JANE LEAVENWORTH.[7] — DANIEL,[6] ANDREW,[5] DANIEL,[4] JAMES,[3] THOMAS,[2] THOMAS.[1]

Born October 15, 1832, at Monroe.

Married Peter Parmely, of Newtown, a joiner. She died December 16, 1863, in Monroe, Conn., aged thirty-one.

CHILDREN.

1. FLORA, b. ——
2. GEORGE, b.

438. MARY LEAVENWORTH.[7]—ELI,[6] ANDREW,[5] DANIEL[4], JAMES,[3] THOMAS,[2] THOMAS.[1]

Born May 1, 1838, in Monroe, Conn.

Married February 3, 1869, Beach Hill. (Yale College 1868.)

439. Andrew Leavenworth.[7] — ELI,[6] ANDREW,[5] DANIEL,[4] JAMES,[3] THOMAS,[2] THOMAS.[1]

Born August 12, 1840, in Monroe, Conn.

Went to Ohio surveying for a map. Married December 12, 1865, AMELIA A. KANE, of Newark, Licking Co., Ohio. Was prepared for college, but the rebellion occurring, he enlisted in the 17th Conn. Vols., was taken prisoner at Chancellorsville, was exchanged and then discharged for disability. He is a farmer and lives in Monroe, Conn.

CHILDREN.

699. NELLIE GRACE, b. November 9, 1866, at Monroe.

443. LOUISA JANE LEAVENWORTH.[7] — TREAT MILLS[6], EBENEZER,[5] JAMES,[4] JAMES,[3] THOMAS,[2] THOMAS.[1]

Born August 20, 1823, in Johnstown, N. Y., at Kingsboro.

Married James Davis November 27, 1844. Resides in New York city; b. at Burtonville, Montgomery Co., N. Y., November 19, 1821. Son of Benjamin and Anna Davis. Is a merchant.

CHILDREN.

1. CATHARINE LOUISA, b. October 22, 1845.
2. ALBERT DUDLEY, b. September 27, 1847, at West Galway, Fulton Co., N. Y., hardware merchant.
3. JAMES HENRY, b. May 14, 1850, at same place, d. August 27, 1851.

447. Edwin T. Leavenworth.[7]—TREAT MILLS,[6] EBENEZER,[5] JAMES,[4] JAMES,[3] THOMAS[2], THOMAS.[1]

Born Eebruary 14, 1831, in Johnstown, N. Y.

Married LIZZIE C. JACOBS, July 24, 1862. She was a daughter of Charles Jacobs, and was born in Delaware Co., N. Y., February 15, 1843. Resides at Amsterdam, N. Y., and is a hardware merchant.

CHILDREN.

700. LOUISA JANE, b. May 16, 1863.
701. CATHARINE, b. June 16, 1865.
702. EDWIN TREAT, b. June 26, 1867.
703. LILLIAN M., b. October 27, 1869.
——— ———, d. February 26, 1871.

All born at Amsterdam, N. Y.

448. SOPHIA JENNETT LEAVENWORTH.[7]— TREAT MILLS,[6] EBENEZER,[5] JAMES,[4] JAMES,[3] THOMAS,[2] THOMAS.[1]

Born April 16, 1833, in Johnstown, Fulton Co., N. Y.

Married Alexander M. Hageman June20 , 1865. He is a farmer, and resides in Amsterdam, and is the son of Nicholas and Isabella Hageman.

CHILDREN.

1. CATHARINE ROBERTSON, b. June 6, 1866.

450. ELEANOR LEAVENWORTH.[7]— ELI,[6] EBENEZER[5], JAMES,[4] JAMES,[3] THOMAS[2], THOMAS.[1]

Born September 23, 1818, at Kingsboro, N. Y.

Married Peter McLaren January 7, 1855. He was a son of Archibald McLaren, who emigrated from Scotland, and settled one mile east of Kingsboro soon after his marriage. Peter M. was a farmer, and died January 22, 1855, leaving no children.

451. Ebenezer Leavenworth.[7] — ELI,[6] EBENEZER,[5] JAMES,[4] JAMES,[3] THOMAS,[2] THOMAS.[1]

Born March 9, 1820, near Kingsboro, N. Y.

Married MARY L. HEACOCK, January 23, 1843, daughter of Philander Heacock, glove manufacturer. She was born December 31, 1822. He died November 11, 1869, at Gloversville, Fulton Co., N. Y.

CHILDREN.

705. MILLARD H., b. June 30, 1844, d. August 17, 1845.
706. HERBERT CLIFTON, b. May 24, 1846, m. Miriam Potter.
707. CELIA ELLEN, b. October 23, 1848, d. May 14, 1865.

708. Sarah Margaret, b. July 6, 1854.

709. Mary Heacock, b. June 17, 1858.

710. Eli, b. ——— 1868. All b. at Kingsboro or Gloversv'lle.

He died in the prime of his life and of his usefulness and was one of the most active, enterprising and valued citizens of Gloversville, where he had long resided. His life was a perfect and harmonious whole, and the one great trait underlying his whole character and to which all others were subservient, was his deep and unobtrusive piety.

In an editorial of one of the papers of Gloversville, published soon after his death, he is thus spoken of,

"In common with our readers, we are called upon to mourn the loss of one of our best citizens. We feel ourselves unable to approach a just tribute to his memory. It needs a pen more eloquent then ours, to perform the task. When young he united with the Presbyterian church at Kingsboro, and at the death of his father was chosen a ruling elder. After his removal here he was soon elected one of the trustees of the Presbyterian society in this village and soon after was chosen a ruling elder in the church.

In the duties and activities of christian life, he was one of the foremost in work but never pushing himself forward as "a man in authority."

As a citizen he was ever ready to foster and care for every improvement which would tend to enhance the charms, increase the value or augment the population of our village.

As a man he was honored and loved by all who knew him, and those who knew him best, loved him most and they feel most his loss. His death is a serious loss to the church, the community and the town.

One who had been his pastor for nine years, and for many more his friend and his correspondent, wrote as follows;

"Of all the men whom I have known intimately, I think Mr. Leavevworth the most perfect. I am grateful to God for having known him, and for the delightful hours of intercourse with him; thankful that I have known a character so symmetrical, in which was united so remarkably manly vigor, with delicacy and tenderness, and as the crown of all, religion in its noblest form."

453. MARY DOWNS LEAVENWORTH[7]—WHITMAN,[6] DAVID,[5] EBENEZER,[4] DAVID,[3] THOMAS,[2] THOMAS.[1]

Born August 24, 1801, at Nassau, N. Y., or Stephentown.

Married Truman Tucker, of Sandgate, in 1820, at Sandgate. Removed to Minnesota, where he died.

CHILDREN.

1. LYDIA MARIA, b. ——, m. Martin Botsford, and lives at Decotah, Iowa.
2. HARVEY SAUNDERSON, b. ——

454. JUDA LEAVENWORTH.[7]—WHITMAN,[6] DAVID[5], EBENEZER,[4] DAVID,[3] THOMAS,[2] THOMAS.[1]

Born October 27, 1803, at Nassau, N. Y.

Married May 31, 1821, Joseph Snow, of Sandgate, at Sandgate, Vt., son of Joseph Snow, and Persis Balch. She died there in February, 1831, leaving three children. He was born at Townsend, Vt., July 9, 1798; boot and shoe manufacturer, and after marriage a farmer, and engaged in navigation on Lake Champlain, and still resides at Sandgate.

CHILDREN.

1. JOHN WILSON, b. February 16, 1824. In Van Benthuysen's printing office, Albany.
2. JOSEPH WHITMAN, b. June 11, 1827. First clerk in N. Y. Central R. R. Office, Albany.
3. SARAH JANE, b. July 5, 1829, m. Joseph Smith, of Sandgate, son of Anson S., about 1852-3, and died at Aurora, Ill., February 16, 1864, leaving two childen, Julia, b. 1853, Jessie, b. 1862. One b. at Sandgate, and one at Aurora. Nos. 1, 2, and 3 born at Sandgate.

Joseph W. m. October 1, 1856, Helen M. Livingston, of Albany, daughter of John D. L., counsellor at law at Albany.

Children.

1. JOHN LIVINGSTON, b. August 25, 1857.
2. JESSIE LEAVENWORTH, b. March 9, 1862. Both born at Albany.

HELEN M. L., was born March 17, 1832.

455. LYDIA S. LEAVENWORTH.[7]—WHITMAN,[6] DAVID,[5] EBENEZER,[4] DAVID,[3] THOMAS[2], THOMAS.[1]

Born December 27, 1806, in Nassau, N, Y., or Stephentown.

Married Hiram Boughton, of Nassau, Rens., Co., (her cousin) a farmer, March 29, 1835, and died December 1865, in Clifton Park, Saratoga Co., N. Y. where the family then lived.

CHILDREN.

1. GEORGE, b. August 4, 1836, at Nassau, m. Maria Ostrander, of Clifton Park, November 12, 1862. Has one child. A farmer.
3. SARAH, b. December 20, 1840, at Nassau, m. Whitmore Turner and lives at Clifton Park, N. Y. He is a farmer.
2. JOHN, b. February 1842, at Nassau, m. Caroline House, of Clifton Park, about 1864, a farmer.

456. Russell Leavenworth.[7]—WHITMAN,[6] DAVID,[5] EBENEZER,[4] DAVID,[3] THOMAS.[2] THOMAS.[1]

Born December 19, 1809, in Nassau, N. Y., or Stephentown.

Married SARAH MAURY, daughter of Abiah M., of Schaghticoke,

September 21, 1831, at Schaghticoke, N. Y., and now lives at Millport, Chemung Co., N. Y. He is a sash, blind and door manufacturer. She was born at Windham, Greene Co. They now, 1870, live at Croton, Schuyler Co., N. Y. He was married at Schaghticoke, Rensselaer Co., N. Y.

CHILDREN.

711. SARAH PHILENA, b. March 6, 1835, m. Err Stone at her fathers, February 4, 1857. He is a car builder at Elmira, for the Erie Railroad Company.

Children.

1. WYATT C., STONE, b. February 13, 1859, at Elmira, N. Y.
2. MINNIE STONE, b. July 28, 1861, at Elmira, N.Y.

457. John S. Leavenworth.[7]—DAVID DOWNS,[6] DAVID,[5] EBENEZER,[4] DAVID,[3] THOMAS[2], THOMAS.[1]

Born July 25, 1807, at Nassau, Rensselaer Co., N. Y.

Married SAMANTHA WHITE, daughter of Timothy White, of Rupert, Vt., in the fall of 1847. She was 18. He was a carpenter, farmer and millwright. Lived in Rupert until about 1860, when he went to Iowa. Lives at Canoe, Winneshick Co., Iowa, where he is a farmer and millwright. Now, 1871, at Prophetstown, Whiteside Co., Ill. Now married again.

CHILDREN.

711½ ANNA, b. in 1848, at Sandlake, m. Mr. —— Drain, about 1866, and has sundry children.

712. LESTER B., b. at Rupert, has been married twice, lives near his father.

713. GILBERT, b. at Rupert, d. about 1860.

714. WILLIAM HENRY, b. at Rupert, d. about 1860.

715. IRA, b. at Rupert, d. about 1860.

They and their mother all died about the same time, within a few days, at Canoe, Winneschick Co.

459. MARY ANNA LEAVENWORTH.[7]—DAVID DOWNS,[6] DAVID,[5] EBENEZER,[4] DAVID,[3] THOMAS,[2] THOMAS.[1]

Born August 11, 1810, at Nassau, N. Y.

Married William G. Vandenburg, farmer, of North Greenbush, May 5, 1833, and lived there till about 1847, when they moved to Johnstown Center, Rock Co., Wis. Married at Sandlake, Rensselaer Co., by John S. Sawyer. Wm. G. V. was born at Greenbush, N. Y., March 1, 1807.

CHILDREN.

1. CAROLINE, b. February 22, 1835, d. February 24, 1853, at Bradford, Rock Co., Wis.

2. Sarah Anna, b. February 8, 1837, at Greenbush, d. December 19, 1840, at Greenbush.
3. Elizabeth C., b. November 12, 1838, m. March 12, 1861, Stanly H. Joiner, in Bradford, Wis. Child—Mary Estelle, b. there March 4, 1862.
4. Minard A. b. January 12, 1841, at Greenbush, N. Y., m. August 24, 1864, Maggie Holland, in Bradford, Wis.

Children.

1. William G.V., b. Feb. 12, 1868. 2. Stanly H., V. b. Aug. 6, 1869, both at Johnstown.

5. Rebecca A., b. April 14, 1843, at Schodack, m. George H. Hawthorn September 1, 1862, at Allen's Hill, Wis.

Children.

1. Oscar Duane, b. March 7, 1864, at Bradford.
2. Orlando, b. July 8, 1869, at Johnstown Center.

6. Burzinah, b. May 28, 1845, at Schodack, m. November 15, 1870, Hiram L. O'Mealy, in Bradford, Rock Co., Wis., by the Rev. C. S. Shattuck. Mr. O'M. lives at Boas, Richland Co., Wis.
7. Jonah B., b. December 17, 1847, in Bradford, Wis., m. December 17, 1868, Mrs. Mary G. File, in Rockford, Ill.
8. Adelriga, b. April 7, 1850, in Bradford, Wis., m. May 14, 1870, James A. Kipp, of Bradford.
9. David L., b. May 3, 1852, at Bradford, Wis.

460. Rev. David Waterbury Leavenworth.[7]—David Downs[6], David,[5] Ebenezer,[4] David,[3] Thomas[2], Thomas.[1]

Born September 30, 1812, in Nassau, N. Y.

Married Achsah Lawton, at Sandlake, N. Y., September 7, 1836, and lived there several years. About 1846 went West and now lives in Milwaukee, Wis. Is a Methodist minister and millwright. No children.

461. William Leavenworth.[7]—David Downs,[6] David,[5] Ebenezer,[4] David,[4] Thomas[2] Thomas.[1]

Born April 3, 1815, at Nassau, N. Y.

Married Maria Town, February 27, 1839. Lives at Nassau, N. Y., and is a carpenter and millwright.

CHILDREN.

716. John Henry, b. March 3, 1840.
717. Sylvester B., b. September 3, 1841.
718. Charlotte A., b. August 1, 1847.
719. Calvin J., b. January 2, 1852.
720. Albert H., b. February 4, 1857.
721. Grace A., b. November 8, 1858.
722. Charles R., b. August 8, 1860.

462. BURZINAH LEAVENWORTH.[7] — David Downs,[6] David,[5] Ebenezer,[4] David,[3] Thomas,[2] Thomas.[1]

Born July 3, 1817, at Sandgate. Vt.

Married Hezekiah DeGolyer December 9, 1846, in East Troy, Walworth Co., Wis.. by the Rev. James Delano. Reside in Milwaukee.

CHILDREN,

1. ORLANDO, b. May 18, 1849, at Milwaukee.

463. Josiah Burton Leavenworth.[7]—DAVID DOWNS,[6] DAVID,[5] EBENEZER,[4] DAVID,[3] THOMAS,[2] THOMAS[1].

Born June 5, 1820, in Sandgate, Vt.

Married, first, DIANA HAZARD, May 11, 1844, in Hancock, Mass.. daughter of Rodman Hazard. She died without issue, July 5, 1850' at Novi, Mich.

Married, second, CATHARINE FLINT, October 2, 1850, at Novi, Mich. She was daughter of Loren Flint, farmer. Children all born at Novi, Mich.,where the family reside. He is a millwright and farmer.

CHILDREN.

723. SARAH, b. July 13, 1851.
724. JOHN, b. July 9, 1854.
725. MARY, b. February 10, 1857.
726. JAY, b. August 9, 1860.
727. JOB, b. November 22, 1861.
728. DELOS, b. June 29, 1863.

464. Ira H. Leavenworth.[7]— DAVID DOWNS,[6] DAVID,[5] EBENEZER,[4] DAVID,[3] THOMAS,[2] THOMAS.[1]

Born September 1, 1822, in Sandgate Vt.

Married ELIZABETH S. HASKINS, of Pardeeville, Columbia Co., Wis., March 4, 1849. Was a carpenter and farmer. Removed to Johnstown, Wis., many years ago. Now his address is Janesville, Wis.

CHILDREN.

729. WILLIS W., b. January 30, 1855, at Bradford, Rock Co., Wis., d. at Madison, Wis., October 8, 1861.

466. Reuben Leavenworth.[7]—ISAAC,[6] DAVID,[5] EBENEZER,[4] DAVID,[3] THOMAS,[2] THOMAS.[1]

Born July 22, 1817, at Nassau, Rensselaer Co., N. Y.

Married, JANE E. LEROY, of Albany, May 2, 1838. She was born November 26, 1824. Resided in Troy, (1865) and was baggage master on steamer "C. Vanderbilt." Had been a boatman from boyhood, d. about 1867, at Troy. She died at Lansingburg, October 1, 1870.

CHILDREN.

730. Mary Jane, b. March 31, 1839.
731. Charles R., b. July 18, 1842, is at Troy.
732. Seaman, b. October 22, 1844, U. S. army, 1870.
733. Adeliza, b. December 7, 1846, d. August 13, 1864.
734. Adelia, b. April 26, 1849, m. Wm. Goodspeed, of Troy.

467. ADELINE LEAVENWORTH.[7]—Isaac,[6] David,[5] Ebenezer,[4] David,[3] Thomas,[2] Thomas.[1]

Born ———
Married John K. Grace, of Troy.
Had one child and died ———. Her sister married Mr. Grace and they removed to Brooklyn. Mr. G. is a pilot on one of the Fulton ferry boats, or was.

468. SARAH LEAVENWORTH[7]—Isaac,[6] David,[5] Ebenezer[4], David,[3] Thomas[2], Thomas.[1]

Born ———
Married ———
Resides in Brooklyn, a widow.

469. EMMA LEAVENWORTH.[7]—Isaac,[6] David,[5] Ebenezer,[4] David,[3] Thomas,[2] Thomas.[1]

Born ———
Married John K. Grace. Resides in Brooklyn. He is a pilot on a Fulton ferry boat, or formerly was.

470. MARIETTE LEAVENWORTH.[7] — Isaac,[6] David,[5] Ebenezer,[4] David,[3] Thomas,[2] Thomas.[1]

Born ——
Married James Fuller a Troy boatmau. He died there 18—.
She is a widow without chilnren.

474. Philo Curtiss Leavenworth.[7]—Ebenezer,[6] David,[5] Ebenezer,[4] David,[3] Thomas,[2] Thomas.[1]

Born November 8, 1814.

Married Abiah D. Maury, April 9, 1837. She was born March 13, 1816. Resides at the Agrlcultural College farm, Lansing, Mich. He is a farmer.

CHILDREN.

735. Matilda Jane, b. February 4, 1838, at Hornby, N. Y., d. November 6, 1840.

736. Philo Conniff, b. December 1, 1839.
737. Jonas Curtiss, b. December 22, 1841, d. July 3, 1842.
738. Eliza J. P., b. August 4, 1858, d. August 18, 1858.

477. MITTEE ANN LEAVENWORTH.[7]—Ebenezer,[6] David,[5] Ebenezer,[4] David,[3] Thomas[2], Thomas.[1]

Born August 13, 1819.

Married Jonas C. Maury, January 3, 1841. He was born November 13, 1813. She died November 2, 1848. He subsequently married and had other children. Before his first wife's death he lived in various places in Chemung and Steuben counties, N. Y. About 1847 ? moved to Wheatfield, Ingham Co., Mich., where she died. He died February 7, 1873. He was a miller.

CHILDREN.

1. Silvan J., b. April 7, 1844, near Millport, N. Y., and is a miller.
2. Jane Elizabeth, b. July 17, 1845, " " m. ———

479. Silvan Ebenezer Leavenworth.[7]—Ebenezer,[6] David,[5] Ebenezer,[4] David,[3] Thomas[2], Thomas.[1]

Born June 28, 1824.

Married Anna Maria Switzer, of Orange, Schuyler Co., N. Y., September 16, 1846. She was born March 15, 1822. They were married at Bradford, Steuben Co., N. Y. Resides at Risingville, town of Thurston, N. Y., where he is, or was, post master, lumberman and farmer.

CHILDREN.

739. Stephen S., b. January 17, 1848. He is a farmer.
740. Eugene L., b. July 2, 1849. He is a sawyer.
741. Peter L., b. July 29, 1853, d. September 13, 1854.
742. Almon C., b. Novemper 13, 1857.
743. Henry L., b. February 21, 1860.

482. John Robbins Leavenworth.[7] — Ebenezer,[6] David,[5] Ebenezer,[4] David,[3] Thomas,[2] Thomas.[1]

Born January 22, 1837, in Campbell, Steuben Co., N. Y.

Married, Kate Rebecca Stevens, November 7, 1860, at Hornby, N. Y. She was born March 10, 1839, and died at Risingville N. Y., June 26, 1862.

Married second, Jerusha Knickerbocker, August 30, 1865. She was b. January 21, 1837, and died June 5, 1866, at Risingville. In 1862 he enlisted in Co. K, 107th N. Y. Vols., and served until discharged in 1865. Lives at Wellsboro, Pa., and is a sawyer. Married Artemitia Bixby in July, 1867.

CHILDREN.

744. Betsey Julia, b. June 19, 1862, d. September 17, 1862.

483. Isaac Hill Leavenworth.[7] — EBENEZER,[6] DAVID,[5] EBENEZER,[4] DAVID,[3] THOMAS,[2] THOMAS.[1]

Born September 22, 1838, in Campbell, N. Y.

Married MINNIE MAY KING, at Bridgeport, Mich., March 19, 1867. She was born September 23, 1843. He went to Michigan October, 1860. Came to St. Charles, Mich., August, 1861, and began surveying. In June, 1863, having been sick a year of ague, he returned to New York, and enlisted as a private, Aug. 3, 1863, in Co. B., 1st N. Y. Veteran Cav., and served two years, Was discharged August 1, 1865, returned to Michigan, was elected County Surveyor, and one of County Drainage Commissioners. Resides at East Saginaw Mich.

CHILDREN.

745. ELLA MAY, b. April 20, 1868.

484. MATILDA ELIZABETH LEAVENWORTH.[7]—EBENEZER,[6] DAVID,[5] EBENEZER,[4] DAVID,[3] THOMAS,[2] THOMAS.[1]

Born May 1, 1841, at Campbell, Steuben Co., N. Y.

Married Jonathan K. Sprague, of Savonia, N. Y., December 14, 1861. He was born September 4, 1825. By a former wife he had a daughter Clarrissa Ann, born July 26, 1852; John S., born Jan. 16, 1854; George H., born June 24, 1855, and Daniel A., born Nov. 4, 1856. Lives now at Bath, Steuben Co.

CHILDREN.

1. ROBERT E. LEAVENWORTH, b. March 3, 1862?

485. David Downs Leavenworth.[7]—EBENEZER,[6] DAVID,[5] EBENEZER,[4] DAVID,[3] THOMAS[2], THOMAS.[1]

Born January 21, 1844, Campbell, Steuben Co., N. Y.

Married SARAH THORP, September 17, 1865.

Left his wife and went roving. Spent most of his time on the canals. Served in six different regiments in the late war viz., in Co. E, 86th N. Y.; Co. C, 107th N. Y.; 16th Cav.; Co. B, 1st Vet. Cav.; Co. A. 73d N. Y. (as Henry Smith) and Co. D 120th N. Y. Was discharged three times, deserted twice, and was transfered once. Died September 18, 1869.

486. Lyman Bixby Leavenworth.[7]—EBENEZER,[6] DAVID,[5] EBENEZER,[4] DAVID,[3] THOMAS,[2] THOMAS.[1]

Born November 1, 1846, at Campbell, Steuben Co., N. Y.

Married ELIZABETH ROGERS, March 28, 1866. She was born September 21, 1838. Her parents were John M. and Betsey Lewis Rogers, of this State. Resides at Savonia, N. Y.

Enlisted in Company B., 9th N. Y., Heavy Artillery. Was wounded by a minnie ball through the tibia at Cedar Creek, October 19, 1864. Was discharged in the spring of 1865.

495. George J. Leavenworth.[7] —CHARLES,[6] EBENEZER ISAAC,[5] EBENEZER,[4] DAVID,[3] THOMAS,[2] THOMAS.[1]

Born at St. Johns, Perry Co., Illinois, September 7, 1855. Died at the same place March 18, 1874 unmarried.

696. Edwin E. Leavenworth.[7] — HEMAN E.,[6] EBENEZER ISAAC,[5] EBENEZER,[4] DAVID,[3] THOMAS[2], THOMAS.[1]

Born in Wisconsin. He now, March, 1874, lives at Amity, Jewell Co., Kansas; has taken up 160 acres of Government land. Not named on page 196.

497. Oscar B. Leavenworth.[7]— RUSSELL,[6] GIDEON,[5] DAVID,[4] JOHN,[3] THOMAS,[2] THOMAS.[1]

Born November 27, 1818 in Woodbury.

Married ELIZABETH DOWD, of Northford, April 29, 1849. He resided in New Haven and was a druggist. Died at New Haven, June 28, 1871, of apoplexy.

CHILDREN.

746. IDA E., b, April 15, 1852.
747. JOSEPHINE, b. July 6, 1857.
748. JESSIE C., b. July 6, 1860.

498. REBECCA LEAVENWORTH.[7]—RUSSELL,[6] GIDEON,[5] DAVID,[4] JOHN,[3] THOMAS,[2] THOMAS.[1]

Born December 9, 1820, in Woodbury.

Married Jerome B. Jackson February 1, 1843; a farmer. She resided in Brooklyn, N. Y., now in New Haven. He died about 1860, in Woodbury.

CHILDREN.

1. ELLA, b. about 1851, m. Benjamin Day, Springfield, Mass., and lives there and has one child, Amy L. Day, b. in October, 1868.

499. Boardman H. Leavenworth.[7]—RUSSELL,[6] GIDEON,[5] DAVID,[4] JOHN,[3] THOMAS,[2] THOMAS[1].

Born January 16, 1826, in Woodbury.

Married, first, ANTOINETTE MERRIAM, of Waterbury, Conn., September 23, 1846. She died April 20, 1854.

Married, second, CAROLINE Todd, at Plainville, Conn., October 9, 1856. He is a druggist and resides in Chicago, Ill., now, formerly at New Haven, Conn. Lost all his property in the great fire October 12, 1871. Now, (1873-4) in business again and doing well.

CHILDREN.

749. ELLA A., b. June 26, 1849, m. Charles Rathay, of St. Charles, Mo., and has one child.
750. FRANK L. b. March 6, 1858.
751. ESTHER J., b.February 11, 1862.

500. Dr. Daniel Carlos Leavenworth.[7]—RUSSELL,[6] GIDEON,[5] DAVID,[4] JOHN,[3] THOMAS,[2] THOMAS.[1]

Born April 29, 1828, at Woodbury, Conn.

Married JULIA A. HILL, daughter of Rev. Aaron S. Hill, of New Haven, May 13, 1869. Resides in New Haven and is a physician. Graduate of Medical College, Yale, 1865.

501. Clinton Leavenworth.[7]—RUSSELL,[6] GIDEON,[5] DAVID,[4] JOHN,[3] THOMAS,[2] THOMAS.[1]

Born November 6, 1830, in Woodbury.

Went to sea in 1854, and has never since been heard from.

502. JULIA A. LEAVENWORTH.[7]—SHELDON,[6] GIDEON[5], DAVID,[4] JOHN,[3] THOMAS[2], THOMAS.[1]

Born June 2, 1831, at Roxbury,

Married Henry A. Warner, of Roxbury, Conn., June 2, 1850. He is a hatter, and was born March 25, 1829.

CHILDREN.

1. EMMA DORA, b. October 5, 1857, at Roxbury.

503. CHARLOTTE S. LEAVENWORTH.[7]—SHELDON,[6] GIDEON,[5] DAVID,[4] JOHN,[3] THOMAS,[2] THOMAS.[1]

Born August 27, 1833, at Roxbury.

Married Henry Burton Beach, September 5, 1851. He was born March 17, 1832. Resided in Roxbury, now, 1870, at Meriden.

CHILDREN.

1. JOSEPH BROWN, b. May 4, 1852.
2. JULIA LOUISA, b. July 6, 1853, m. George Byron Paddock May 21, 1873.
3. HENRY BURROWS, b. August 17, 1862.
4. SHELDON BURTON, b. April 13, 1866.
5. FREDDIE, b. August 17, 1871, d. January 15, 1872.

504. LOUISA MARRIE LEAVENWORTH.[7]— SHELDON,[6] GIDEON,[5] DAVID,[4] JOHN,[3] THOMAS,[2] THOMAS.[1]

Born August 27, 1835, at Roxbury.

Married William Henry Cooper, December 23, 1856, at Roxbury, Conn. Resides in New Haven, Conn., and is a coach maker. He was b. May 26, 1833, in Hanover, Morris Co., N. J.

CHILDREN.

1. FRANK WOOSTER, b. August 10, 1861.
2. WM. HENRY, JR., b. August 19, 1864.
3. JENNIE LOUISA, b. April 4, 1870—all born at New Haven.

504½. George F. Leavenworth.[7] — SHELDON,[6] GIDEON,[5] DAVID,[4] JOHN,[3] THOMAS[2], THOMAS.[1]

Born June 14, 1839, at Roxbury.

Married July 5, 1861, Rrs. HARRIET MAYNARD, of Southbury, Conn. She had been twice married and is the sister of the Hon. Truman Wheeler.

He resides in Roxbury, and is by profession a teacher. No children.

505. JEANETTE LEAVENWORTH.[7]—MARTIN,[6] MORSE,[5] DAVID,[4] JOHN,[3] THOMAS[2], THOMAS[1]

Born September 30, 1809, at Woodbury.
Married Harvey Lambert, October 23, 1829, son of Jesse Peck Lambert.

CHILDREN.

1. FRANCES, b. August 6, 1830, d. August 11, 1854.
2. JULIA, b. July 9, 1832, m. David W. Mead, September 6, 1853, and d. January 9, 1855, leaving a son, Frank G., b. June 30, 1854.
3. DANIEL WEBSTER, b. October 16, 1838, m. Laura King, September, 1865.
4. HARVEY CLARK, b. July —, 1849, d. January 6, 1850.

They live at Mt. Vernon, Ohio.

506. ELIZABETH LEAVENWORTH[7]—MARTIN,[6] MORSE,[5] DAVID,[4] JOHN,[3] THOMAS,[2] THOMAS.[1]

Born August 7, 1812, at Woodbury, Conn.
Married Columbus Delano, July 14, 1834. November 6, 1831, she joined the First Congregational church, Woodbury. Lives at Mt. Vernon, O.

CHILDREN.

1. ANTOINETTE, b. September 30, 1835, d, January 8, 1838.
2. ELIZABETH C., b. April 1. 1839, m. Rev. John J. Ames.

Children.

   1. THEODORA, b. December —, 1866, d. December, 1866.
   2. DELANO, b. February 25, 1868.

3. JOHN SHERMAN, b. August 7, 1841, m. April 22, 1862, Ella E. Hurd, has two sons.

   1. HARMON BONTA DELANO, b. January 22, 1863.
   2. GEORGE BATEMAN DELANO, b. March 14, 1865.

Hon. Columbus Delano was born at Shoreham, Vt,, in the year 1810. At ten years of age he removed to Ohio, in the care of immediate relatives, who settled in the county of Knox. His boyhood was there passed in the lighter occupations of the farm, joined to habits of persistent devotion to study. He pursued his elementary education at such schools as were then available, learning the latin language with but little aid from classical teachers. His historical reading at the age of eighteen was extensive. With a seriousness becoming his disposition rather than his years, he began thus early to consider how he should make his way in the world, and what pathway was to lead him up from obscurity to a useful position in life. Without the aid of influential friends, but cheered by the encouraging advice of those who knew and loved him, and with such assistance as they could render, he determined to undertake the study of law.

In 1830 he entered the office of Hosmer Curtis, Esq., then a noted special pleader, practicing at Mt. Vernon, as a student. After three years of the most diligent preparation, he was admitted to the Bar of the Supreme Court of Ohio in 1833, and commenced practice at Mt. Vernon at the age of twenty-two.

Though no extraordinary display of precocious talent had been exhibited, to justify the expectation that he would triumph suddenly over the formidable obstacles in the way of the young attorney, his success was immediate. He had the unusual fortune in the first year of his practice, to be employed as junior counsel in a local suit, involving important legal questions, and the title to a considerable estate. Having been left by an accident to the sole management of the case through the trial, or the alternative of seeking a continuance, which was denied him, he was forced to enter alone upon the argument and trial against able and experienced opponents, and was triumphantly successful. He thus gained a reputation the immediate effect of which was his election to the office of prosecuting attorney for the State, in a county adverse to his political associations and views. He had, from the first, been a supporter of Mr. Adams's administration. After three years service as prosecuting attorney, he was re-elected, but within a few months, resigned the trust, which interfered with his more extensive civil practice. His constant attention upon the courts, from this time for a period of fifteen years, his thoroughness and integrity as a lawyer, and his uniform success as an advocate, met with ample reward. And, although more indifferent than many others to the gains of his profession, his reputation grew, *pari passu*, with his estate. The germs of a modest and prudent avarice had not been foreign to his breast. But his aims were not less to do some good, to make society and posterity his debtors, to be a benefactor in his place and sphere, than to cultivate and improve his own mind, to acquire a just relish for excellence, and to become independent and possess himself of those accomplishments which become a lofty and amiable character. His professional business, however important, was not allowed to exclude him from society, nor to cause him to neglect the christain duties of his position. As a member of the Episcopal church he has ever taken an active interest in its prosperity, zealously endeavoring to promote its welfare and elucidate its faith. For many years he was the careful and beneficent superintendent of its sabbath schools.

In the political issues of the past, he was actively opposed to slavery and to the democratic policy. Seeking no office for himself, he was still the frequent exponent of the whigs in the local contests of his vicinity. Surrounded by a cordon of democratic constituencies, largely in the minority in his congressional district, there seemed to be but little hope for his popular preferment. But having unexpectedly been placed in nomination for congress in 1844, he was elected by a majority of twelve votes over his competitor, Hon. Caleb J. McNulty, a democratic politician of extensive popularity, resources and power. To illustrate the significance of this triumph, it is only necessary to state that the democratic candidate for governor carried the district, at the same election by a majority of more than six hundred votes.

On the first of December 1845, Mr. Delano took his seat as a member of the 39th congress. This may be termed one of the epochs in the congressional history of the country. Contemporaneous with Mr. Polk's administration of the Presidency, it comprised statesmen of great experience and great ability. The disputed policy of war and conquest of Oregon and Mexico, and the extension of slavery, were the unsettled questions of that day, which darkened the door of the future, and lengthened their evil shadows into the coming years. On the Oregon question Mr. Delano spoke at length, advocating the claims of the United States to the farthest northern boundary, departing from the views of many of his colleagues, and opposed to the policy which eventually prevailed.

On the 11th of May, 1846, he voted with John Quincy Adams and twelve others, against the famous and long-controverted declaration that "war exists by the act of Mexico," and subsequently he defended his vote, and *the twelve*, in his speech in the House, on the thirteenth of May following.

Chosen as the exponent of this Spartan band of dissenters, who alone had the courage to vote against the false declaration, he rose to the full majesty of the occasion, answering the hopes and expectations of his colleagues, not only in their vindication, but in a most striking and aggressive attack on the administration. Of this speech much was said and written at the time, both in favor and against it. Its truths were not gainsaid, but it proved to be a subject of general attack, and may be considered in the politician's view, as impolitic. It served, however, the purpose of reinforcing the anti-slavery and free-soil parties and damaged both the whigs and democrats. The occasion was one which seemed to call forth the devices of the *dodger*, if such arts can be justified in legislation, but to these devices Mr. Delano scorned to resort. The speech was reckoned of such great significance, that Mr. Douglass of Illinois, Mr. Thurman, of Ohio, Mr. Chipman, of Missouri, and Mr. Tibballs, of Kentucky, continued the debate, and gave themselves serious concern to reply to it. Mr. Adams was seated near to the Speaker throughout its delivery, and at the conclusion, in admiration of its completeness, declared that, "There shouldn't be a 't' crossed, nor an 'i' dotted!"

Mr. Delano retired at the close of this Congress. His district having been changed by adverse party legislation, he was not a candidate for re-election. His name was brought before the Whig State Convention, at Columbus, on the 22d of February, 1848, for nomination as Governor of Ohio, and though he had voted in Congress to supply the army, and to reinforce the army in Mexico, his speech against the *declaration* contributed to place him, in the minds of some, with the opposition to the war. He was defeated in the convention by two votes. In the following national campaign he supported Gen. Taylor for the presidency.

Having retired wholly from the Bar, he removed with his family in 1850, to New York City, and became a member of the commercial firm of Delano, Dunlevy & Co. with a branch at Cincinnati, Ohio. After five years of successful business in New York, he withdrew from the firm and in 1857, returned to his home in Ohio, and engaged in general business and agriculture, as *farmer*.

His extensive lands were placed under a higher state of cultivation and were supplied with valuable and profitable breeds of stock. Exempt from onerous public duties, his leisure for a time was given to his family, to society and to his library.

Unlike many lawyers, he had not found it difficult to withdraw from the practice of law. How much virtuous earnestness is intended in the assurance that they are attached to the profession *for its own sake*? And to what purpose? Special pleading, wrangling at courts, quibbling, supressing scorn for villainous attornies, temporizing with convenient vices, mingling with the administration of justice! To what end? For some thousands yearly, and the vanities and accomodations of upper life. With better views and a better taste than to follow this irksome occupation, he chose a position of more consequence; one involving the destination to which he was entitled, as well as the devotion of his zeal for liberty and his liberal and just sentiments of the real interests of mankind to the public service.

In 1860, he was chosen a delegate to the Chicago Convention which nominated Mr. Lincoln to the presidency. In 1861, he was appointed commissary general of the State of Ohio, doing active service until the general government made full provision for the volunteers. In 1862, the republicans of the Ohio

Legislature, ballotted in conference, for United States Senator and he again wanted but two votes of a nomination. In 1863, he was elected to the Ohio house of representatives, at Columbus, serving as chairman of the judiciary committee. His defense of the act providing for soldiers voting in the field and which secured that measure, was one of the most important of the session. In 1864, he was again chosen to the national convention, at Baltimore, and was chairman of the Ohio delegation which voted for the renomination of Mr. Lincoln.

In the same year he was elected to the 39th congress and was appointed chairman of the committee of claims. His conduct on this important committee, met with universal approval. Sufficient evidence of this is found in the fact that every congressional report made from his committee, was adopted by the house. He was reelected to the 40th congress, and served on the committee of foreign affairs, but declined to be a candidate for reelection in his district.

As a legislator, he took a frequent part in the debates of the house. He was opposed to the policy of free trade and advocated a tariff for revenue with incidental protection. He was strongly opposed to the extravagant claims of rail road companies for land grants and government subsidies. From the committee of foreign relations, he opposed in debate the appropriation for the purchase of the Russian territory of Alaska. His views were regarded as most important on questions of the tariff, of excise taxes and the public debt. To his speech of the 24th of July, 1866, was given the credit of carrying the tariff bill of that session, against what had been considered to be the sense of the house.

It is no exaggeration to say that the solid matter of his speech, the earnestness of his manner and the judicious use of the ear of the house "not abusing it" made him more certain of attention, and surer to carry his views than more frequent debaters. But his command over his audience was not from any wit that sparkled, nor lively sallies of the imagination, nor by impassioned or pathetic appeals, nor even by rare powers of vehement declamation, though that was a characteristic, but it was from a combination of most lucid statement, aptness of argument and of familiar illustration, frequently a forcible exposure of the adversary, mingled with a sparing use of sarcasm, in the tones of a voice rich, full and unhesitating.

At the close of his third term in congress Mr. Delano was appointed commissioner of internal revenue and continued to discharge the duties of that most exacting and laborious office till November, 1870, when he was appointed secretary of the interior, in the cabinet of the present adinistration of the government.

Of his more recent public acts and those of to-day, it is only proper that the public voice, not the partial chronicler should speak.

As commissioner of internal revenue it is sufficient to his credit, as a public officer, that he collected the taxes, paid the revenue into the treasury, destroyed the whiskey ring and silenced public complaint. This achievement alone, ought to be deemed enough to establish the fame and character of a public man. It is what others equally honest in their purposes, had failed to do and indeed, it is all that Alexander Hamilton did to send down his great name to be praised by posterity.

The present sketch of Mr. Delano's services may be closed with the remark that he has been found ever equal to the largest questions, and not impatient of the most ordinary; that he never was deficient in political knowledge required by the occasion, whether the subject was that of foreign or domestic policy, indian civilization and wars, economical and financial science, the bearing of constitutional law, or claims against the treasury, for he possesses in a large degree, the lawyers' faculty of gaining information for every emergency and of using it with the authority and confidence of a master.

There is no perceptible line of manners dividing his public and private life. The same courteous and thoughtful attention given to the councils of great men, is accorded as promptly by him to the interests of the humblest person. In his own family circle, a peculiarly gifted and happy one, there are vases but no jars. It is a Mansion of rest without the probationary state.

C Delano

MOUNT VERNON, OHIO
(NOW WASHINGTON, D.C.)

507. SALLY LEAVENWORTH.[7]—TRUMAN,[6] MORSE,[5] DAVID,[4] JOHN,[3] THOMAS[2], THOMAS.[1]

Born October 9, 1809, at Roxbury.
Married January 17, 1829, William Hartwell, a farmer at Roxbury, no doubt.

CHILDREN.

1. OLIVER S.
2. RACHEL M.
3. FREDERICK W.
4. HENRY H.
5. MINOT L.
6. ROGER T.

509. NANCY A. LEAVENWORTH[7]—TRUMAN,[6] MORSE,[5] DAVID,[4] JOHN,[3] THOMAS,[2] THOMAS.[1]

Born April 23, 1813, at Roxbury.
Married November 23, 1836, Harvey P. Smith, a farmer.
They lived fourteen years in Washington Ct., and fourteen years in Monroe.

CHILDREN.

1. CATHARINE A.
2. DANIEL A.
3. JULIA M.

513. Edward Benedict Leavenworth.[7]—PHILO,[6] MORSE,[5] DAVID,[4] JOHN,[3] THOMAS,[2] THOMAS.[1]

Born August 13, 1816, in Roxbury. Is a carpenter and builder.

Married, first, CANDACE BROWN, daughter of Abner Brown, of Waterbury, October 28, 1840. Was divorced from her in 1862, on his application.

Married, second, SUSAN A. ROWLAND, April 5, 1866, daughter of Moses Mills, of Bridgeport. He lives in Bridgeport.

CHILDREN.

752. MARY, b. July 26, 1846, in Waterbury, m. Elias Stanton of Stafford, Conn., September 28, 1868, has a boy, Edward, b. September 15, 1869.
753. SON, b. June, 1847, d. September, 1848.
754. EDWARD B., b. March 26, 1850, in Waterbury.
755. CAROLINE, b. September 22. 1852, "

514. Charles John Leavenworth.[7]—PHILO,[6] MORSE,[5] DAVID,[4] JOHN,[3] THOMAS,[2] THOMAS.[1]

Born September 22, 1818, at Roxbury, Conn.

Married December 25, 1841, SARAH J. JENKS, daughter of John Jenks, wool-carder of Amenia, N. Y., and of Mary White daughter of John White, of Seymour, Conn. She was born at Amenia, June 3, 1821. He resides at Norfolk, Conn., and is a woolen manufacturer.

CHILDREN.

756. CHARLES B., b. November 13, 1842, at Norfolk, Conn.
757. GEORGE H., b. March 5, 1859, at Norfolk.

515. Theodore Leavenworth.[7]— PHILO,[6] MORSE,[5] DAVID,[4] JOHN,[3] THOMAS[2] THOMAS.[1]

Born July 10, 1821, at Roxbury, Conn. Is a builder.

Married January 26, 1842, CHESTINE P. ALDERMAN, daughter of Truman Alderman and Julia Hadsell, of Burlington, Hart. county, Conn. She died November 18, 1855, at Burlington. Lived five years in Roxbury; moved to Goshen in 1826; became a carpenter and joiner; removed to Waterbury, and in 1850 to New York city, remained till 1860, then moved to New Jersey, and in Spring of 1870, to Montgomery, N. Y.

Married, second, July 6, 1856, CHARITY ANN HUEY, of Montgomery, Orange Co., N. Y., daughter of Stephen Huey and Hannah Swalm, born at Montgomery March 1, 1829, married at Newburg by the Rev. D. Buck.

CHILDREN.

758. ELLEN J., b. June 3, 1844, m. Marcus Conant, of Mass., June 20, 1869, has a daughter, Ida M., b. at Bricksburg, Ocean Co., N. J., May 25, 1869.
759. EMMA, b. July 29, 1862.
760. ALICE, b. February 22, 1867.

516 Noble Leavenworth.[7]—PHILO,[6] MORSE,[5] DAVID,[4] JOHN[3], THOMAS[2], THOMAS.[1]

Born May 5, 1824, at Roxbury.

Married August 15, 1842, LOUISA ELIZABETH, daughter of Edward E. Davis, of Watertown, born November 12, 1824.

He removed to Goshen, with his mother in 1826, and remained there till 1841, then to Watertown, and remained there till 1856, then to Herrick, Bradford Co., Penn. He is a carpenter, joiner, and builder.

Married second, May 1, 1853, SABRINA ALLEN, of Herrick, Bradford Co.

CHILDREN.

760½ FREDERICK THEODORE, b. September 29, 1846, at Watertown.
761. ANNA SABRINA, b. June 16, 1854.
762. CHARLES NOBLE, b. August 12, 1856, d. September 28, 1860.
763. FLORA ADELAIDE, b. May 13, 1861.
764. MARTHA JANE, b. April 7, 1863.
765. JOHN PHILO, b. May 26, 1866. All born at Herrick.

518. James Martin Leavenworth.[7]—WAIT,[6] MORSE,[5] DAVID,[4] JOHN,[3] THOMAS,[2] THOMAS.[1]

Born at Roxbury September 28, 1815.

Married JULIA HURD, daughter of Jehiel and Deborah Hurd, of Roxbury, on the 7th of February, 1844. Is a carpenter and joiner.

CHILDREN.

766. WALTER JAMES, b. in Roxbury, February 20, 1845.
767. JULIA ISABEL, b. in Roxbury, October 8, 1848, d. in Wallingford, May 29, 1858.
768. D. MARGARET PERCY, b. in Wallingford, May 21, 1859.

James M. removed to Wallingford in 1852, and has since resided there.

519. William Leavenworth.[7]—WAIT,[6] MORSE,[5] DAVID,[4] JOHN,[3] THOMAS.[2] THOMAS.[1]

Born July 23, 1816, at Roxbury.

Married SARAH ANN HUBBELL, daughter of Hezekiah and Anna Maria Hubbell, September 24, 1840, of Huntington. He is a farmer, in Roxbury.

CHILDREN.

769. THEODORE WARREN, b. January 23, 1843, is unmarried.
770. MARY ANTONETTE, b. October 7, 1848.
771. MARTHA JANE, b. January 3, 1855. All born at Roxbury.

520. George Leavenworth.[7]—WAIT,[6] MORSE,[5] DAVID,[4] JOHN,[3] THOMAS[2], THOMAS.[1]

Born September 15, 1820, at Roxbury.

Married CAROLINE COLLINS, daughter of Levi C. and Abigail Frisbie, of Litchfield, in October, 1845. He died May 12, 1847, and was buried in the new cemetery at Roxbury. Was a joiner.

CHILDREN.

772. CHARLES SPENCER, b. October 1, 1846, d. March 20, 1847.

521. Wait Leavenworth.[7]—WAIT,[6] MORSE,[5] DAVID,[4] JOHN,[3] THOMAS,[2] THOMAS[1].

Born May 9, 1827, at Roxbury.

Married SARAH ELIZA MINOR, of and at Woodbury, daughter of Horace and Emeline Minor, and grand daughter of Wait's great uncle David L., on the 25th of December 1847. Wait is a carpenter and joiner, lives in Ansonia.

CHILDREN.

774. Margaret Josephine, b. in Roxbury June 23, 1850.
775. George Wesley, b. in Waterbury September 23, 1852.
776. Spencer Colby, b. in Woodbury, July 1, 1854.
777. Horace Minor, b. in Woodbury August 23, 1859.
778. Cornelia Emily, b. " " April 25, 1861.

522. Edwin Leavenworth.[7]—Wait,[6] Morse,[5] David,[4] John, Thomas[2], Thomas.[1]

Born April 21, 1831, at Roxbury.

Married January 17, 1858, Jane Maria Weeks, daughter of Samuel B. and Lydia W., of Litchfield. Edwin is a farmer in Roxbury.

CHILDREN.

779. Charles Royal b. October 30, 1858.
780. Arthur Douglas, b. October 25, 1860.
781. Frederick Hartwell, b. May 20, 1862.
782. Carrie Weeks, } b. Oct. 11, 1866.
783. Hattie Percy, }
784. Willard Morse, b. April 10, 1868. All born at Roxbury.

523. Charles Royal Leavenworth.[7] — Wait,[6] Morse,[5] David,[4] John,[3] Thomas,[2] Thomas.[1]

Born December 14, 1834, at Roxbury.

Married October 21, 1868, to Floretta, daughter of Nelson and Hannah Buckingham, of Woodbury. He is a farmer.

526. John H. Leavenworth.[7]— Morse,[6] Morse,[5] David,[4] John,[3] Thomas,[2] Thomas.[1]

Born at Roxbury, Conn., August 13, 1830.

Married Mary Ann Peck, daughter of Marquis D. Peck Esq., of Morris, Conn., April 13, 1852.

He is a farmer and teacher and lives in Roxbury, on the old homestead of his father and his grandfather.

CHILDREN.

785. George Washington Peck, b. April 12, 1855.

786. FLORENCE ELIZA, b. July 22, 1859. Both born at Roxbury.

Mr L., has been indefatigable in his efforts to aid me in my labors, particularly in Woodbury and Roxbury, the original home of the family and still its principal seat.

527. Jerome B. Leavenworth.[7]—MORSE,[6] MORSE,[5] DAVID,[4] JOHN,[3] THOMAS,[2] THOMAS.[1]

Born at Roxbury, October 9, 1832.

Married LOUISA PECK, daughter of Dr. Peck, of Bridgewater, Conn., July 21, 1859. He is a merchant in Chalyles (Roxbury) Conn.

CHILDREN.

787. MORSE JEROME, b. November 22, 1863, at Vineland, N. J., where his father lived from 1862 to 1864.

528. Burnet Morse Leavenworth.[7]—MORSE,[6] MORSE,[5] DAVID,[4] JOHN,[3] THOMAS[2], THOMAS.[1]

Born at Roxbury, February 13, 1838.

Married EROZABETH BARBER, October 7, 1862, daughter of Wm. B. Barber Esq. of Harwinton, Conn.

CHILDREN.

788. ANNIE BELL, b. May 15, 1864, in New Milford.

789. WALTER BURNET, b. July 26, 1867, in New Milford.

Burnet M. is a farmer and lives in New Milford, Conn. on the homestead of his grandfather, Deacon John Beecher.

531. Alonzo D. Leavenworth.[7]—WOLCOTT,[6] DAVID,[5] DAVID,[4] JOHN,[3] THOMAS[2], THOMAS.[1]

Born at Earlville, Madison Co., N. Y., August 2, 1846.

Married April 13, 1868, to SUSAN E. HOWARD, of South Edmeston, Otsego Co., N. Y. Resides near Rockford, Kent Co., Mich., and is a farmer.

535. MARY LEAVENWORTH.[7]—WILLIAM CURTISS,[6] JOHN PECK[5], JOHN,[4] JOHN,[3] THOMAS,[2] THOMAS.[1]

Born September 24, 1827, in Reading, Penn.

Married Henry A. Dreer, of Philadelphia, seedsman and florist, June 22, 1847, son of Frederick and Frederika Dreer, from Germany, a cabinet maker. Henry A. born at Philadelphia, August 24, 1818, and died there, December 22, 1873, in the 56th year of his age.

CHILDREN.

1. MARY LEAVENWORTH, b. at Reading, April 3, 1848.

2. WILLIAM FREDERICK, b. at Philadelphia, November 11, 1849, seedsman and florist.
3. SUE ADELE, b. at Philadelphia, February 15, 1852.
4. AUGUSTA NOTHENIUS, b. at Philadelphia, January 4, 1855.
5. HARRY, b. at Philadelphia, August 18, 1856, d. there September 14, 1857.
6. LOUISA GREBLE, b. at Philadelphia July 28, 1858.

1. Mary Leavenworth Dreer, b. at Reading, Pa., April 3, 1848, m. Edwin Greble, Jr., October 6, 1869, son of Edwin and Susan Greble, b. January 24, 1846, and brother of Lieut. John T. Greble, U. S. A., killed at Great Bethel, June 10, 1861. He is a manufacturer of marble mantles and monumental work at Philadelphia.

536. CAROLINEE CRAIG LEAVENWORTH.[7]—CHAUNCEY,[6] JOHN PECK,[5] JOHN,[4] JOHN,[3] THOMAS,[2] THOMAS.[1]

Born at Mount Vernon, Ohio, June 3, 1842.
Married Henry Chase, of Macomb, Ill., Jan. 3, 1865, d. May 5, 1869, childless.

537. MARY LEAVENWORTH.[7]—CHAUNCEY,[6] JOHN PECK[5], JOHN,[4] JOHN,[3] THOMAS,[2] THOMAS.[1]

Born in Madison, Ind., December 4, 1844. Married John McFarland at Galesburg, Ill., October 6, 1869.

CHILDREN.

1. CHAUNCEY LEAVENWORTH, b.

541. FRANCES LEAVENWORTH.[7]—HOBART[6], JOHN PECK,[5] JOHN,[4] JOHN,[3] THOMAS,[2] THOMAS.[1]

Born May 25, 1840, at Rush.
Married June 21, 1871, at her father's in Rush, Benjamin Westfall Bonnell. He was born at Forrestburg, Tioga Co., N. Y., August 31, 1837. He is a merchant and miller, and resides at Waverly, Tioga Co., N. Y. He is the son of Jonathan and Rosilla Bonnell, formerly of New Jersey, now of Waverly.

542. Henry H. Leavenworth.[7]—HOBART,[6] JOHN PECK,[5] JOHN,[4] JOHN,[3] THOMAS,[2] THOMAS.[1]

Born at Honeoeye Falls, Monroe Co., N. Y., November 6, 1845. Is a farmer at Avon, Livingston Co.,

Married SARAH M. CLARK, of Livonia, Livingston Co., December 30, 1868.

CHILDREN.

790. HENRY CLARK, b. March 20, 1870, at Avon.

545. CORNELIA HENRIETTA LEAVENWORTH.[7]—BENJAMIN J.,[6] JOHN PECK,[5] JOHN,[4] JOHN,[3] THOMAS,[2] THOMAS.[1]

Born August 18, 1849, at Rush, N. Y.
Married January 25, 1872, Charles Hamilton Stanton, of Sheridan, Montcalm Co., Mich., merchant and lumber dealer, and Supervisor of the town of Sheridan. He was born in Green Co., N. Y., May 29, 1843. They were mar-

ried at the residence of David H. Albertson, at Marengo, Calhoun Co., Mich., by the Rev. G. E. Peters.

546. SARAH M. LEAVENWORTH.[7]—JOHN D.,[6] RUSSELL[5], JOHN,[4] JOHN,[3] THOMAS[2], THOMAS.[1]

Born June 10, 1826. Married Samuel Wakeley, September 10, 1845, of Monroe, Conn., then an engineer on the Housatonic Railroad. She died June 14, 1849, at Stepney, town of Monroe, Conn. He died December 2, 1866.

CHILDREN.

1. SARAH M., b. June 1, 1848, at Monroe, Conn. She was adopted by her grandmother, after her mother's death; m. December 13, 1867, Wm. H. Wheaton.

547. Charles D. Leavenworth.[7]—JOHN D.,[6] RUSSELL,[5] JOHN,[4] JOHN,[3] THOMAS,[2] THOMAS.[1]

Born June 2, 1839.

Married May 31, 1848, URSULA J. MORGAN, at Bethel, Conn.

Resides in New Milford, Conn., in grocery business.

CHILDREN.

791. CHARLES DELANCY, b. March 2, 1850, killed on the Housatonic R. R,, June 7, 1870.
792. FLORENCE IDELIA, b. November 12, 1853.
793. HOWARD MORGAN, b. August 11, 1859.
794. EDGAR JOHNSON, b. June 6, 1864.

548. John Merritt Leavenworth.[7] — JOHN D.,[6] RUSSELL,[5] JOHN,[4] JOHN,[3] THOMAS,[2] THOMAS.[1]

Born June 2, 1839.

Married SARAH SOMERS in 1861, by Rev. Mr. Ackley, of New Milford, and lived in Bridgewater, Conn. Died March 11, 1867, at Danbury, Conn.

555. John Randolph Leavenworth.[7]–MARK,[6] RUSSELL,[5] JOHN,[4] JOHN,[3] THOMAS,[2] THOMAS.[1]

Born at Monroe, Conn., September 6, 1836.

Married ELIZA GREFFOZ, of San Francisco, December 25, 1868.

CHILDREN.

795. RANDOLPH JULIEN, b. June 6, 1871, at San Francisco.

551. Royal Ralph Leavenworth.[7] — MARK,[6] RUSSELL,[5] JOHN,[4] JOHN,[3] THOMAS[2], THOMAS.[1]

Born in Monroe, Conn., September 6, 1836.

Married MARY E. CASTLES, at San Jose, Cal., August 3, 1859.

CHILDREN.

796. FANNIE LEONORA, b. October 8, 1860.
797. RANDOLPH, b. October 8, 1861.
798. EDWARD, b. March 9, 1863, d, June 28, 1863.
799. GRACE M., b. February 11, 1867. All b. at San Jose, Cal.

554. Mark R. Leavenworth[7]—LORENZO W.,[6] RUSSELL,[5] JOHN,[4] JOHN,[3] THOMAS,[2] THOMAS.[1]

Born January 19, 1846, in Monroe, Conn.

Married, January 19, 1872, MARY E. PERRY, only daughter of W. H. Perry, of Bridgeport, Conn. Engaged in the tin and stove business, with A. D. Barlow, at New Milford, Conn.

1872. Now in the same business at Bridgeport Conn.

555. Teeodore D. Leavenworth[7]—LORENZO W.,[6] RUSSELL,[5] JOHN,[4] JOHN[3] THOMAS,[2] THOMAS.[1]

Born March 19, 1850, in New Milford, Conn.

Clerk in a store at New Boston, Conn. Now, 1872, bookkeeper at Bridgeport, Conn.

570. John Jehiel Leavenworth.[7]—ELIHU,[6] JEHIEL,[5] ELIHU,[4] JOHN,[3] THOMAS[2], THOMAS.[1]

Born in Spring of 1824, in Hillsdale, Columbia Co., N. Y.

Enlisted in the army for the Mexican war, and died in Mexico.

571. MARIA LEAVENWORTH.[7]—ELIHU,[6] JEHIEL,[5] ELIHU,[4] JOHN,[3] THOMAS,[2] THOMAS.[1]

Born in Spring of 1827, at Hillsdale, Columbia Co., N. Y. Married ——. Died at Binghamton, Broome Co., N. Y., in 1858, leaving one child.

572. William H. Leavenworth.[7]—ELIHU,[6] JEHIEL,[5] ELIHU,[4] JOHN,[3] THOMAS,[2] THOMAS.[1]

Born March 7, 1832, at Canandaigua, N. Y. He is a miller and clothier.

Married, November 16, 1853, Melissa Briggs, daughter of John and Catharine Maria B., born at Orion, Oakland Co., Mich. October 29, 1835. Resides at Imley, Lapeer Co., Mich., and has no children.

573. William Leavenworth.[7]—LEGRAND,[6] JEHIEL,[5] ELIHU,[4] JOHN,[3] THOMAS,[2] THOMAS.[1]

Born March 27, 1835, at Johnsonville, Trumbull Co., Ohio. Died June 2, 1857. He lived in Canaan, Conn. Unmarried.

574. Phineas Leavenworth.[7]—LEGRAND,[6] JEHIEL,[5] ELIHU,[4] JOHN,[3] THOMAS,[2] THOMAS.[1]

Born March 10, 1837, at Johnsonville, Trumbull Co., Ohio.

Married MARION JUDD, November 8, 1861. She was born December 26, 1841, in Canaan, Conn. He died January 1, 1866. Was a miller.

CHILDREN.

800. WILLIAM, b. September 15, 1862. Lives in Canaan, Ct.
801. SETH, b. August 16, 1864. Lives in Sharon, Conn.

575. LAURA A. LEAVENWORTH.[7]—LEGRAND,[6] JEHIEL,[5] ELIHU,[4] JOHN,[3] THOMAS,[2] THOMAS.[1]

Born July 13, 1839, at Johnsonville, Trumbull Co., O.

Married George G. Lawrence, January 20, 1857, of East Canaan; flour merchant. He was born November 16, 1835.

CHILDREN.

1. EDWARD P., b. November 8, 1861.
2. CHLOE, b. June 2, 1870. Both b. at East Canaan.

576. CARRIE LEAVENWORTH[7]—LEGRAND,[6] JEHIEL,[5] ELIHU[4], JOHN,[3] THOMAS[2], THOMAS.[1]

Born July 13, 1843, at Salisbury, Conn.

Married Pierre Mundry, November 8, 1861. He was born September 1, 1838, in Balfort, France; came to America in 1848; lived in Canaan till 1854; went to New York and in three years returned to Canaan, Conn. He is an artist. They, (1870,) lived at Bridgeport, Conn. She died of consumption at Bridgeport on the 16th day of July, 1872, without leaving children. She was in delicate health for some years before her death. She was refined, cultivated, and possessed of a character of great beauty and excellence. She was buried in the family ground, at Falls Village, Canaan, Conn.

577. MARY LEAVENWORTH.[7]—LEGRAND,[6] JEHIEL,[5] ELIHU,[4] JOHN,[3] THOMAS,[2] THOMAS.[1]

Born May 12, 1844, at Canaan, Conn., and resides now, 1871, with her mother at Bridgeport, Conn.

593. Frederick P. Leavenworth.[7]—ABNER JOHNSON,[6] FREDERICK,[5] JESSE,[4] MARK,[3] THOMAS,[2] THOMAS.[1]

Born June 13, 1833, at Charlotte, N. C.

Married, first, CAROLINE PORTER, October 16, 1858. She died September 1, 1863.

Married, second, ELIZA C. LAWRENCE, of Shreveport, La.,

December 6, 1864. Resides in Shreveport, La., and is a railroad engineer.

CHILDREN.

802. HESTER, b. October 28, 1865.
803. ELIZA HELEN, b. October 4, 1868, d. October 9, 1869.
804. MARY PEABODY, b. March 8, 1870.

594. HELEN ELIZABETH LEAVENWORTH.[7]—ABNER J.,[6] FREDERICK,[5] JESSE,[4] MARK,[3] THOMAS,[2] THOMAS.[1]

Born June 11, 1836, at Charlotte, N. C. Married John McGill, December 1, 1857, at Petersburg, Va., where they reside.

CHILDREN.

1. HELEN LESLIE, b. September 19, 1858.
2. JOHN PEABODY, b. January 21, 1861, d. September 24, 1868.
3. FREDERICK LEAVENWORTH, b. May 24, 1863, d. September 19, 1868.
4. FANNY PAGE, b. March 20, 1866.
5. WILLIAM McGILL, b. February 25, 1869.
6. DORA STUART, b. August 29, 1870.
7. MARIANNA PEABODY, b. November 30, 1873. All b. at Petersburg, Va.

598. CYNTHIA MARIA LEAVENWORTH.[7]—FREDERICK[6], JESSE,[5] JESSE,[4] MARK,[3] THOMAS,[2] THOMAS.[1]

Born January 8, 1819, at Wheelock, Vt.

Married, first, Oren Young, ——, 1843. of Vt., then resident at Stanstead, C. E., a machinist. Removed to Massachusetts in 1845-6, and was there, and in Michigan, (where he resided one year,) engaged in the construction and operation of steam engines for railroads. Some years before his death he had made a permanent settlement in Springfield, Mass., where he died Jan. 2, 1859.

Married, second, George C. Cahoon, April 12, 1864, of Lyndon, Vt., a lawyer by profession and also a farmer. He had lost a first wife six years before, having a son George W., also a lawyer, in partnership with him, and a daughter Mrs. Henry S. Bartell, widow of a lawyer who was settled and died at Providence, R. I.,both having families and now residing in Lyndon, Vt.

CHILDREN.

1. CYNTHIA AURILLA, b. about 1851.

599. MELINA LEAVENWORTH.[7]— FREDERICK,[6] JESSE,[5] JESSEE,[4] MARK,[3] THOMAS[2], THOMAS.[1]

Born June 29, 1822, at Wheelock, Vt.

Married MANOAH LEAVITT, of Sheffield, Vt., November 18, 1840, but at the time of her fathers removal to Dochester, Mass., in 1845,or soon after, they removed to the same place. He was at one time depot master at Neponset, at other times in trade, and engaged as a dealer in real estate, building, and as a broker. Has now retired from business and lives (1870) at Wrentham, Mass.

CHILDREN.

1. FREDERICK LEAVENWORTH, b. July 12, 1843, d. December 6, 1850.
2. MELINA AUGUSTA, b. June 7, 1851.
3. ADELINE M., b. January 18, 1853, d. September 2, 1853.
4. IDA MAY, b. May 27, 1855.
5. ALONZO M., b. April 20, 1858, d. May 20, 1860.

600. HARRIET FRANCES LEAVENWORTH.[7]—FREDERICK,[6] JESSE,[5] JESSE,[4] MARK,[3] THOMAS,[2] THOMAS.[1]

Born August 3, 1830, at Wheelock, Vt.

Married, first, Barzillai Paine, August 30, 1851, a wholesale fish dealer, at Dorchester, Mass., who died November 13, 1856.

Married, second, George W. Berry of Neponset, Mass , a blacksmith, May 13, 1859.

CHILDREN.

1. FREDERICK LEAVENWORTH, b. July 3, 1852.
2. GEORGE W., b. May 11, 1862.
3. HARRIET F., b. August 25, 1863, d. August 25, 1864.
4. ERNEST Y. b. November 25, 1869.

604. Henry Clark Leavenworth.[7]—JESSE HENRY,[6] HENRY[5], JESSE,[4] MARK,[3] THOMAS[2], THOMAS.[1]

Born August 1, 1833, on the Island of Mackinac, Mich.

Died November 2, 1856, at Peshtigo, on the north shore of Green Bay, Wis., in consequence of a carbuncle on the back of his neck, which affected his spine and brain.

605. MARY ELIZABETH LEAVENWORTH.[7] — JESSE HENRY,[6] HENRY,[5] JESSE,[4] MARK,[3] THOMAS,[2] THOMAS.[1]

Born May 21, 1836, on the Island of Mackinac, Mich., where her father, then in the army, was stationed.

Married December 24, 1856, to Charles T. Kershaw, produce and commisson merchant, and insurance agent. Resides in Milwaukie. Son of John and Margaret Kershaw, of Montreal, but originally of Bernly, Lancashire, Co., England, a gentleman farmer.

CHILDREN.

1. PHILLIP HENRY, b. November 17, 1857 at Chicago.
2. JOHN, b. June 19, 1860, at Chicago, d. April 28, 1863.
3. ALICE, b. February 13, 1863.
4. CHARLES JAMES, b. November 14, 1864.
5. HENRY BALDWIN, b. September 4, 1866.
6. THOMAS, b. March 5, 1868.
7. LEAVENWORTH, b. September 10, 1869.
8. RALPH JOHNSON, Feburary 27, 1872.
9. JESSIE, b. November 19, 1873. All at Milwaukie, except the first.

606. ALIDA CAROLINE LEAVENWORTH.[7]—JESSE HENRY,[6] HENRY,[5] JESSE,[4] MARK,[3] THOMAS,[2] THOMAS.[1]

Born April 2, 1841, at Chicago, Ill.

Resides with her father, at Milwaukie.

607. JESSIE ELVIRA LEAVENWORTH.[7] —JESSE HENRY[6], HENRY,[5] JESSE,[4] MARK,[3] THOMAS,[2] THOMAS.[1]

Born November 16, 1843, at Milwaukie, Wis.

Married August 17, 1864, to James Mitchell, formerly of Scotland, now a produce merchant at Chicago, Ill.

Procured a divorce about 1867.

1870. Is now studying German and music in Paris; was in 1868 and 1869, studying German and music in Berlin.

September 2, 1870, arrived at New York from Paris, and is at Milwaukie, with her father.

1872, Fall—Returned to Europe with nine young ladies under her care, to spend a year—the winter in Italy, and the residue traveling. Returned in the fall of 1873.

608. Franklin Leavenworth.[7]—JESSE HENRY,[6] HENRY,[5] JESSE,[4] MARK,[3] THOMAS,[2] THOMAS.[1]

Born July 28, 1846, at Milwaukie, Wis. Died there August 18, 1846.

609. Festus Akerly Leavenworth.[7]—JESSE HENRY,[6] HENRY,[5] JESSE,[4] MARK,[3] THOMAS[2], THOMAS.[1]

Born January 6, 1848, at Milwaukie, Wis. Died there September 6, 1849.

610. HARRIET MAY LEAVENWORTH.[7]—JESSE HENRY,[6] HENRY,[5] JESSE,[4] MARK,[3] THOMAS,[2] THOMAS.[1]

Born March 9, 1851, at Milwaukie.

Married January 13, 1874, Averry Melvin Ingersoll, of Milwaukee, at her home there. He is a son of Allen J. and Augusta Ingersoll, of Winneconne, Wis. Averry M. is ticket agent at Milwaukie, of the M. and St. Paul Railroad Co. His father is a lumber merchant.

611. KATE LEAVENWORTH.[7]—JESSE HENRY,[6] HENRY,[5] JESSE,[4] MARK,[3] THOMAS[2], THOMAS.[1]

Born September 17, 1853, at Milwaukie, Wis., d. June 17, 1868, at Milwaukie.

612. Henry Charles Leavenworth.[7]— CHARLES,[6] DAVID,[5] ASA,[4] THOMAS,[3] THOMAS[2], THOMAS.[1]

Born August 6, 1826, at Egremont, Mass.

Married MARY E. TRUESDELL, October 18, 1854. She was born February 27, 1835, at Onondaga, Onondaga Co., N. Y., and was fourth child of Wheeler and Lucy (Jerome) Truesdell, now of Syracuse.

He entered Yale College as a Freshman, in the Class of 1845, but was compelled by the failure of his health to leave College early in the following year. In the fall of 1848 he entered the Law School at Yale, and remained one year. He studied his profession with Noxon & Leavenworth, at Syracuse, andin 1850 succeeded his uncle in the firm. He resides at Syracuse, N. Y., and is an attorney and counselor at law, and Secretary and Treasurer of Oakwood Cemetery.

CHILDREN.

805. MARY ELIZABETH, b. November 15, 1861, at Syracuse—

97 James street. Named after her great-aunt, Mary E. (Forman) Leavenworth.

613. James DeBow Leavenworth.[7]—WILLIAM,[6] DAVID,[5] ASA,[4] THOMAS,[3] THOMAS.[2] THOMAS.[1]

Born July 5, 1831, at Allentown, N. J.

Died, unmarried, April 1, 1856, at the ranche of Thaddeus M. Leavenworth, in Sonoma, Cal. He was a young man of unblemished character, and of much promise. At the age of 15-16, he spent two years with his uncle, E. W. Leavenworth, attending school at Syracuse, and went to California at or before becoming of age. He had a fine constitution, and was prosperous in his business. He died from some sudden and violent attack of disease.

614. MATILDA LEAVENWORTH[7]—HIRAM,[6] JOHN,[5] ASA,[4] THOMAS,[3] THOMAS,[2] THOMAS.[1]

Born June 11, 1820, at Waterloo, N. Y.

Married, first, Charles Roberts, October 15, 1837. He was a farmer, and resided at Reading, Schuyler Co., N. Y.

Married, second, George DeMun, March 15, 1852. He is a farmer, resides at Reading, Schuyler Co., N. Y.,—P. O., Rock Stream. She died Nov. 11, 1871, at Reading.

CHILDREN.

1. HIRAM LEAVENWORTH, (Roberts,) b. August 11, 1838; farmer; m. Elvira Harvey, March 9, 1855. No children. Resides at Reading, N. Y.
2. FRANK CHARLES, (Roberts,) b. December 10, 1840, m. Minerva Harvey, October 13, 1863, d. February 15, 1865. He was a farmer, then a petroleum refiner, at Oil Springs, Canada. The place of his birth and permanent residence was Reading, N. Y. He left no children.

615. CLARINDA LEAVENWORTH.[7] — HIRAM,[6] JOHN,[5] ASA,[4] THOMAS,[3] THOMAS,[2] THOMAS.[1]

Born September 10, 1821, at Waterloo, N. Y.

Married Smith D. Elliott, October 10, 1847. He was of Auburn, N. Y., formerly of Mass.; a mechanic, and resides near Eddytown, (Starkey,) Yates Co., N. Y.

CHILDREN.

1. CLARA LAVINIA, b. October 25, 1848, at Auburn, N. Y., m. Anson M. Sutton, June 5, 1872, of Reading Center, Schuyler Co., farmer.
2. LAURA AMELIA, b. November 2, 1850, at Auburn, N. Y.
3. EMILY ADA, b. March 15, 1852, " "
4. EDWIN LEAVENWORTH, b. Feb. 22, 1855, " "
5. HIRAM LINCOLN, b. September 19, 1857, at Starkey, Yates Co., N. Y.
6. ELIAS LEAVENWORTH, b. March 19, 1863, " " "

616. Edwin S. Leavenworth.[7]—HIRAM,[6] JOHN,[5] ASA,[4] THOMAS,[3] THOMAS,[2] THOMAS[1].

Born September 1, 1823, at Geneva, N. Y.

Married, first, ELIZABETH HESTER GOULD, of St. Catharines, C. W., November 18, 1852. She died a year after marriage.

Married, second, CINDERELLA GOULD, of St. Catharines, C. W., May 1, 1855. Resides at St. Catharines, and is a printer.

CHILDREN.

806. HESTER ELIZABETH, b. October 5, 1853, d. at St. Catharines, October 1, 1870.
807. EMMA LAVINIA, b. August 15, 1856.
808. JOHN EDWIN, b. March 27, 1859.
809. ALICE CLARINDA, b. June 6, 1861.
810. JESSIE, b. July 1, 1865.

617. John Holden Leavenworth.[7]—HIRAM,[6] JOHN,[5] ASA,[4] THOMAS,[3] THOMAS[2], THOMAS.[1]

Born March 4, 1826, at St. Catharines, C. W.

Died March —, 1847, on board a vessel, near the Island of St. Helena, and was buried at sea.

618. Hiram F. Leavenworth.[7]—HIRAM,[6] JOHN,[5] ASA,[4] THOMAS,[3] THOMAS,[2] THOMAS.[1]

Born March 19, 1828, at St. Catharines, C. W.

Married MARY ELIZA ALWARD, of Venice, Cayuga Co., N. Y. January 8, 1857. She was a daughter of Jairus Alward, farmer. He is a speculator; has no children. She died at Venice, June 29, 1873. He resides at St. Catharines, C. W.

619. LAVINIA LEAVENWORTH.[7]—HIRAM,[6] JOHN,[5] ASA[4], THOMAS,[3] THOMAS,[2] THOMAS.[1]

Born December 26, 1829, at St. Catharines, C. W.

Married Harrison Roberts, of Reading, a farmer, in 1849, at Reading, N. Y. They removed to Massachusetts Flats, Eldorado Co., California, in February 1851, where she died October 29, 1864.

CHILDREN.

1. FRANCES MATILDA, b. December 1, 1850, at Fort Wayne, Ind , m. Joseph Francis Schottler May 21, 1871, at San Francisco, and had a son born February 1, 1872.
2. EUREKA, b. November 9, 1852, d. December 6, 1853.
3. JOSEPH, b. March 16, 1854, d. July 24, 1859.
4. FREDERICK, b. February 7, 1856, d. —— 1858.
5. OLIVER M., b. February 2, 1858.
6. EMMA, b. August 1, 1845. Last five children born in California.

620. Gilbert Leavenworth.[7]—HIRAM,[6] JOHN,[5] ASA,[4] THOMAS,[3] THOMAS,[2] THOMAS.[1]

Born December 28, 1831, at St. Catharines, C. W. Died March 15, 1849, in Auburn, N. Y.

622. LUCY LEAVENWORTH.[7] — HIRAM,[6] JOHN,[5] ASA,[4] THOMAS,[3] THOMAS,[2] THOMAS.[1]

Born June 26, 1839, at St. Catharines, Canada. Married June 5, 1867, Thomas P. Smith, of St. Catharines.

CHILDREN.

1. BLANCHE ELLEN, b. June 17, 1869, at St. Catharines.

625. MARY LEAVENWORTH.[7] — HIRAM,[6] JOHN,[5] ASA,[4] THOMAS,[3] THOMAS,[2] THOMAS.[1]

Born March 17, 1846, at St. Catharines, C. W.
Married September 29, 1869, James McEdwards, of St. Catherines.

CHILDREN,

1. JESSIE LEIGHTON, b. November 22, 1870, at St. Catharines.

627. ELMINA JOSEPHINE LEAVENWORTH.[7]–HORACE,[6] JOHN[5], ASA,[4] THOMAS,[3] THOMAS[2], THOMAS.[1]

Born July 3, 1851, at East Genoa.
Married March 22, 1871, at East Genoa, to Oscar Tifft, of the town of Venice, Cayuga Co. They now (1873) live with her father at East Genoa. No children.

629. MARY THEODOSIA LEAVENWORTH.[7] — EDWIN W.,[6] TRUMAN,[5] ASA,[4] THOMAS,[3] THOMAS,[2] THOMAS.[1]

Born at Canaan, Col. Co., N. Y., March 19, 1851.
Married William H. Palmer, of Canaan, September 27, 1870, at Canaan. He is the son of Obadiah Palmer, of East Chatham, Col. Co., and is a merchant at Canaan, now (1871) at Schenectady.

CHILDREN.

1. EDWIN OBADIAH, b. June 17, 1872.

630. MARY ELIZABETH LEAVENWORTH.[7] — ELISHA LEE,[6] ISAAC,[5] ASA,[4] THOMAS,[3] THOMAS,[2] THOMAS.[1]

Born February 16, 1844, at Wolcott, Wayne Co., N. Y.
Married Benjamin Wilson, May 15, 1866. He was born at Wolcott, N. Y., July 25, 1840, and was the son of the Hon. James M. Wilson, a physician at that place, and Cordelia Benjamin, and is himself a physician practicing there.

CHILDREN.

1. ANNA LEE, b. at Wolcott November 17, 1869.

631. CAROLINE PAGE LEAVENWORTH.[7]—ELISHA LEE[6], ISAAC,[5] ASA,[4] THOMAS,[3] THOMAS,[2] THOMAS.[1]

Born September 14, 1845, at Wolcott, Wayne Co., N. Y., and resides there with her mother.

639. Joseph N. Leavenworth.[7]—JOSEPH S,[6] JOSEPH,[5] SAMUEL,[4] THOMAS,[3] THOMAS,[2] THOMAS.[1]

Born March 4, 1828, at Waterbury.
Married June 3, 1851, FANNY MANN.

CHILDREN.

811. MARTHA, b. June 10, 1855.
812. IDELLA, } Twins, b. June 17, 1860.
813. ESTELLA, }

640. MARTHA J. LEAVENWORTH.[7]—JOSEPH S.,[6] JOSEPH,[5] SAMUEL,[4] THOMAS,[3] THOMAS,[2] THOMAS.[1]

Born May 27, 1830.
Married Edmund B. Fairchild May 9, 1851.

CHILDREN.

1, EDWARD, b. February 12, 1855.
2. SARAH b. September, 1857.

666. MARY ELLEN LEAVFNWORTH.[7]—EDMUND,[6] ISAAC[5] THOMAS,[4] THOMAS,[3] THOMAS,[2] THOMAS.[1]

Born December 19, 1846. Married March 8, 1863, Wm. Fuller.

CHILDREN.

1. ELLEN MARIA, b. April 7, 1868.

706. Herbert Clifton Leavenworth.[8]— EBENEZER,[7] ELI,[6] EBENEZER,[5] JAMES,[4] JAMES,[3] THOMAS[2] THOMAS.[1]

Born May 24, 1846, at Kingsboro, N. Y.

Married MIRIAM POTTER, January 24, 1867, at Kingsboro, daughter of William and Ann Eliza Potter, and resides at Gloversville. He is a manufacturer and wholesale dealer in gloves mittens, etc.

CHILDREN.

814. ERNIE, b. July 23, 1871, d. Sept. 23, 1871, at Gloversville.

711. SARAH PHILENA LEAVENWORTH.[8]—RUSSELL,[7] WHITMAN,[6] DAVID,[5] EBENEZER,[4] DAVID,[3] THOMAS,[2] THOMAS.[1]

Born March 6, 1836, in Chemung Co. Married E. Stone.

716. John Henry Leavenworth.[8] — WILLIAM,[7] DAVID D.,[6] DAVID,[5] EBENEZER[4], DAVID,[3] THOMAS,[2] THOMAS.[1]

Born March 3, 1840.

Married EMILY MARTIN, June 30, 1866, of Sandlake, N. Y.

CHILDREN.

815. WILLIAM, b. May, 1868.
816. CHILD, b. ——, 1870.

717. Sylvester B. Leavenworth[8] —WILLIAM,[7] DAVID D.,[6] DAVID,[5] EBENEZER,[4] DAVID,[3] THOMAS,[2] THOMAS.[1]

Born September 3, 1841.

Married, September 1, 1863, HARRIET MARTIN, of Sandlake, N. Y. He is a teamster and lives in Chatham, N. Y.

CHILDREN.

817. JOSIAH B., b. about 1865, at East Nassau.
818. LEMUEL, b. about 1868, " "

718. CHARLOTTE A. LEAVENWORTH[8]—WILLIAM[7], DAVID D.,[6] DAVID,[5] EBENEZER,[4] DAVID,[3] THOMAS,[2] THOMAS.[1]

Born August 1, 1847, at E, Nassau. Married June, 1868, at E. Nassau, Lorenzo Strait.

CHILDREN.

1. JESSIE L., b.——

723. SARAH LEAVENWORTH.[8]— JOSIAH BURTON,[7] DAVID DOWNS,[6] DAVID,[5] EBENEZER,[4] DAVID,[3] THOMAS[2], THOMAS.[1]

Born July 13, 1851, at Novi, Oakland Co., Mich.

Married William Risner, March 6, 1868, at Novi. He is a farmer and resides in Oxford, Mich.

730. MARY JANE LEAVENWORTH.[8]—REUBEN,[7] ISAAC[6], DAVID,[5] EBENEZER,[4] DAVID,[3] THOMAS,[2] THOMAS[1].

Born March 31, 1839, at Troy. Married August Shaw, express agent, St. Louis, Mo.

731. Charles R. Leavenworth.[8]—REUBEN,[7] ISAAC,[6] DAVID,[5] EBENEZER,[4] DAVID,[3] THOMAS,[2] THOMAS.[1]

Born July 18, 1842, at Troy.

736. Philo Conniff Leavenworth.[8]—PHILO CURTIS,[7] EBENEZER,[6] DAVID,[5] EBENEZER,[4] DAVID,[3] THOMAS,[2] THOMAS.[1]

Born December 1, 1839.

Married SARAH ANN PLACE, April 14, 1859, at Woodhull, Mich. She was born April 14, 1840, and died November 5, 1864. Resides at the Agricultural College, Lansing, Mich.

CHILDREN.

819. MARY FIDELIA, b. April 16, 1860.
820. MARTHA, b. October 6, 1864, d. October 29, 1864.

756. Charles B. Leavenworth.[8] — CHARLES J.,[7] PHILO,[6] MORSE,[5] DAVID,[4] JOHN,[3] THOMAS,[2] THOMAS.[1]

Born November 13, 1842, at Norfolk, Conn.

Married September 11, 1867, SARAH ELIZABETH TRASK, at Waterbury, Conn. She was born at Worcester, Mass., April 29, 1845, daughter of Henry Trask and Roxana Quimby. Her father is section-master on the Hartford, Prov. and Fishkill railroad.

Charles B. resides now at Camden, N. J.

766. Walter James Leavenworth.[8]—JAMES MARTIN,[7] WAIT,[6] MORSE,[5] DAVID,[4] JOHN,[3] THOMAS[2], THOMAS.[1]

Born in Roxbury, February 20, 1845. He is an accountant.

Married ANNETTIE A. WALLACE, of Wallingford, Oct. 23,1867.

CHILDREN.

821. WALTER CLIFFORD, b. in Wallingford May 16, 1869.

770. MARY ANTOINETTE LEAVENWORTH.[8]—WILLIAM,[7] WAIT,[6] MORSE,[5] DAVID,[4] JOHN,[3] THOMAS[2], THOMAS.[1]

Born October 7, 1848, in Roxbury.
Married Wallace D. Beers, of New Milford, Nov. 26, 1866, and resides there.

CHILDREN.

1. MERRITT W., b. July 10, 1870, at New Milford.

774. MARGARET JOSEPHINE LEAVENWORTH.[8]—WAIT,[7] WAIT,[6] MORSE,[5] DAVID,[4] JOHN,[3] THOMAS,[2] THOMAS[1].

Born in Roxbury June 23, 1850.
Married, October 15, 1866, James T. Ladd, of Waterbury, who d. there October 26, 1869. He was a machinist.

CHILDREN.

1. FREDERICK T., b. May 1, 1869.

APPENDIX.

APPENDIX.

FIRST CIRCULAR.

"A."

SYRACUSE, N. Y., 1865.

DEAR SIR:—About twenty-five years since I made a Genealogical Tree of the Leavenworths, which was lithographed, and to some extent distributed to the different branches of the family.

That Tree was made without as full reference to authentic data as should have been had, and there are in it a number of important inaccuracies and some omissions. Further investigations will no doubt reveal still more.

I now propose to revise that work, to supply its omissions, correct its errors, bring the different families down to the present time, and enlarge its plan. I desire the aid of every member of the family who can furnish any information. I wish to include in the work, every person of the name of Leavenworth, both male and female, living or dead, the residence and profession of every person who has married into that family, male or female. And I intend. as far as may be, to note the date and place of the birth, marriage and death of each one, their occupation or profession, and their residence or residences at different periods.

I would also include brief notices of any of the more prominent members of the family, and hope their descendants and friends will furnish me with such incidents, remarks and suggestions, as they may think proper. Entire accuracy is most desirable, and where it *can* be had *should* be. Town, County, Church and Probate records furnish many facts with accuracy, and grave stones and family Bibles may often be consulted with great benefit. When a person cannot furnish information HIMSELF, a reference to the place where, or the person from whom it can be obtained is very desirable.

I hope and believe that every person who receives a copy of this circular will, without unnecessary delay, give me all the information above requested, tracing back his ancestors as far as may be possible, and all collateral branches, and all descendants—giving me in regard to each individual, the date and place of his or her birth, death, marriage and to whom, with residence and profession, and any interesting facts. To each person contributing information I shall be happy to present one or more copies of the Genealogy, when finished. I hope to complete the work during the present year, which makes it very desirable that information should be furnished as early as possible.

I am, most Respectfully Yours,

E. W. LEAVENWORTH.

SECOND CIRCULAR.

"B."

SYRACUSE, N. Y., 187 .

DEAR SIR:—I have been engaged for the past five years in issuing the circular on the next page "A." I have prosecuted my inquiries with all the diligence which multiplied public and private duties would permit.

1st. I have clearly ascertained our first common ancestor in this country.

2d. I have been easily able to trace all the families back to our common source—Thomas Leavenworth, of Woodbury, who died in 1683.

3d. I find no person of the name, who is not descended from the said Thomas L.

4th. I have obtained from abroad the Coat of Arms of the family, no doubt that of Sir Lewis Leavenworth, who lived in the time of Cromwell, and who is mentioned in Russell's Lives of Eccentric Characters. Vol. 1, p. 96, Note B.

5th. I have traced out nearly every family in the Union,—from the Atlantic to the Pacific,—and in most cases with a large portion of the facts sought for.

6th. I hope to have all the facts attainable, gathered in the course of the coming year, and then put them into form and publish them at once in a book.

7th. I hope every person who may receive a copy of these circulars, will give them early attention, and furnish all the facts within their reach.

The labor of searching out all the families, and collecting all the desirable statistics, is immense, and in many cases the facts are unattainable. But the work will be as perfect as it is possible for me to make it, without an expenditure of time and an amount of travel which it is impossible for me to bestow upon the subject. But I shall accomplish all within my reach, and bring the work to an early close.

E. W. LEAVENWORTH.

"A." Meaning the preceding page.

NOTE B.—There is an error of a century in the time when Sir Lewis lived in London, which was about 1750. This error arose from writing from my recollection, instead of referring to to the work. Having subsequently found the Coat of Arms of the family in this country, I omit that obtained from abroad.

"C."

DISCONNECTED NAMES.

A small number of persons have been found whose relation to the family I have been unable to ascertain. There is no doubt of their connection with it, and yet the most diligent enquiries which I have been able to make have not enabled me to attach them to any family of the name. They are as follows:

First. Lemira Leavenworth, of Woodbury, was married in September, 1793, to Truman Stiles, the son of Isaac Stiles, and had the following children: Sherman, Robert, Erastus, Hancey, Harriet L. and Ann S. Hancey d. unm. Harriet m. Abraham Bassett, and Ann S. m. Joel Loch, who was born at Falmouth, Maine.—Cothren's Woodbury, p. 701, of Vol. 1st.

Second. John Leavenworth was the father of the said Lemira. His granddaughter, Mrs. Joel Loch, is now (1871) living at Watertown, Ct. He came from Stratford. He was a miller by occupation, and during the Revolution lived at White Oak, in the town of Southbury, Ct. When the French troops passed through, he furnished them with wheat and corn, butter and pork, gratuitously. He was well acquainted with Gideon and Ebenezer Leavenworth, who were his near relations. He had five children, Sherman, Grace, Lemira, Damie and Levina. Grace m. Enoch Johnson in 1794, and had two children, Seymour and Marshall. Sherman m. Esther Gunn and had a son, William. Truman Stiles m. Lemira, and had the first five children above mentioned, (No 1.) When she died, he married her sister, Damie, by whom he had one child, Ann Sennitt, now Mrs. Loch. Sherman, or his son William, or both, removed to Monticello, N. Y., and were back at Southbury, in 1823, on a visit. All of Lemira's children are dead. Lemira died in 1857. The above facts in regard to the said John and his family, were obtained from Mrs. Loch. It will be observed that Mrs. Loch and Mr. Cothren do not agree in one point. Cothren says that Truman Stiles

m. Levina, such is probably the record. Mrs. Loch says he married Lemira, and it would seem that she ought to know.

Third. Upon the Town Records of the town of Huntington, on page 139, is an entry that on the 22d day of May, 1833, Munson Pearce, of Newtown, and Cornelia Leavenworth, of Huntington, were legally joined in marriage. The said Cornelia does not appear in any of the families which I have been able to find, nor does any one at Huntington seem to be able to call her to mind.

Fourth. At page 806, of the 1st vol. of Cothren's Woodbury, appear the names of David and Alma Leavenworth. David, sometimes called Marcus, was the illegitimate son of Ada Nettleton, of Woodbury, and had no claim to the name of Leavenworth. Alma is his widow. They had one child, Arvesta, who is also dead.

Fifth. The following is taken from the Genealogy of the Peck family: Henry Peck, the son of Ephraim P., first of Milford, then of Newtown, was b. Ap. 14, 1719, and died at Newtown, July 23, 1760. His will is recorded at Danbury, Book 7, page 1. He was twice married. He m. (1st) Ann Smith, Dec. 23, 1755. (2d.) Hannah Leavenworth, Aug. 6, 1765. Children: 1. Zalmon, b. May 10th, 1758; 2. Lemuel b April 30th, 1766. He was twice married. His first wife was Amy Peck, daughter of Jabez Peck. His second wife was Mary Griffin. He lived in Newtown, where he died in 1839, leaving no issue. 3. Mercy, b. August 10th, 1767, m. Levi Peck; 4. Hannah, b. April 6, 1770, m. Daniel Peck; 5. Andrew, b. May 21, 1773; 6. Samuel, b. July 2, 1775. This Hannah L. m. in 1765, could not have been the d. of John of Stratford, for several reasons, and Hannah, the d. of his brother, Dr. Thomas, m. Nicholas Moss. She could have been the d. of no person but of one of the eight sons of Dr. Thomas. She does not appear in any one of the families. But there is no other known person of whom she could have been the daughter, unless it can be supposed that John of Stratford—the brother of Dr. Thomas actually had a son, Ebenezer, who lived to man's estate—married and had children, which does not seem probable. Hannah L., the d. of Dr. Thomas, who m. Nicholas Moss, was a widow before 1765, but *she* married (2d) the Rev. Mr. Dickerman. In 1765 her name was Moss or Dickerman. Vide No. 14, Hannah L.

LETTER OF JOHN WARD DEAN, SECRETARY, &c.

"D."

[L.S.]

NEW ENGLAND HISTORIC GENEALOGICAL SOCIETY,
SOCIETY HOUSE, 18 Somerset Street, BOSTON, Sept. 23, 1873.

DEAR SIR:—*Lawrence Hammond*, was of Charlestown, freeman, 1666, was Captain in the Militia and a representative to the General Court. He was admitted to the *Ancient and Hon. Artillery Company* in 1666, and died at Boston, July 29th, 1699. *Francis Burroughs* was a bookseller, in Boston, in 1685, Adm. to the Art Co. in 1686. His will was proved Dec. 11, 1713. *Benjamin Bullivant*, was a physician in Boston, in 1685. He was Gov. Andros' Attorney General. He returned to England, and was living in Northampton in 1711. Both Burroughs and Bullivant are mentioned in John Dunton's letters from New England. In 1685, Governor Bradstreet resided in Boston, and James Russell, the assistant, lived in Charlestown.

We should be very happy to receive any communication from you for the *Register*, even if it be to correct our mistakes, or, rather I should say, we are very anxious to have our errors corrected. I enclose one of our blanks which we are sending to members, of which you are one, whose personal record is not full in our archives. Please fill it up at your convenience, and return it.

Respectfully Yours,

JOHN WARD DEAN.

Hon. E. W. LEAVENWORTH, Syracuse, N. Y.

LETTER OF CHARLES J. HOADLEY, STATE LIBRARIAN.

(Great Seal of the State.)

STATE LIBRARY OF CONNECTICUT,
HARTFORD, August 17th, 1864.

Hon. E. W. LEAVENWORTH:

Dear Sir,—I am very little of a Genealogist, and can add nothing to the account given of the family by Cothren and Bronson. I have the custody of a mass of the old Colonial documents, and one volume of early Probate records of Connecticut. Among the former, are two bonds of Grace Leavenworth, of Woodbury, widow, dated the same day, *i. e.* June 11, 1684, one to George Musgrave, of London, Skinner,—the other to Mary Gawthorne, of London, widow. There was a seal attached to her name on both bonds, with a coat of arms, but both these seals were stolen from the documents since 1842, and before 1856. Upon one of the bonds (both of which seem to have been executed in Boston,) the name of John Leavenworth appears as a witness. I send you a *fac simile* of both the autographs.

Cothren and Bronson are both living—the former in Woodbury—the latter in New Haven. Mr. P. M. Trowbridge compiled the genealogical part of both their histories, I believe, but I do not know his residence, and have never seen him to my knowledge. With both the other gentlemen I am acquainted.

Yours, Respectfully,

CHARLES J. HOADLEY.

"E."

COPY OF WILL OF THOMAS LEAVENSWORTH.

In the name of God, Amen,—I, Thomas Levensworth, of Stratford, being weak in body, but through ye goodness of God, being of sound mind and memory, think it best at this time to make this my Last Will and Testament.—And first of all, I commend & give my soul into the hands of God who gave it, hoping in & through the mediation & intercession of Jesus Christ my only Saviour and Redeemer, to find Pardon & acceptance & a blessed Resurrection to Immortal Glory & Felicity, and my body to return to the dust from whence it was taken, to be decently entered at ye Discretion of my Executors, hereafter named, and as to what worldly goods & estate it hath plea ed the Lord to bless me with I freely give and bequeath as followeth. My Will is that all my just debts and funeral expences be first paid & satisfied out of my moveable *estate*.

Item.—I freely give and bequeath unto my loving wife Mary Leavensworth, all ye rest & remaining part of my moveable Estate to be her own forever, and also three small pieces of land. One lying Southwardly from my farm where I now live, near ye Clench of Rocks so called adjoining Northerly on ye land of Zacheriah Tomlinson, & Southerly on ye land of Ebenr. Curtis, & one lyeth on ye lower white Hill, bounded westerly on Wilcockson's land, and Southerly on Jos. Wells' land: and the other lying on ye Southerly Side of the highway or road running from ye great River to ye white hill road; also I give to my said wife ye use & improvement of one half of my house, and all my other buildings on ye farm where I now dwell & ye use and improvement of all ye plain from ye river to ye hill on which my house stands, during her natural life & one quarter part of the apples in ye Orchard upon the hill on my said farm, & ye privilege of cutting of Timber on ye said farm, what she shall have occasion for, for firewood & fencing & repairing said fences, & buildings if need be, and the privilege of pasturing on my said farm, if she desires it, three cows & one horse during her natural life.

Item.—As to my loveing son James Leavensworth I having already given him his full portion, I give to him my said son five shillings old tenor.

Item.—I freely give & bequeath unto my two grandsons, Nathan and Ebenr. Leavensworth, (sons to my son David dec'd) twenty pounds, each of them to have ten pounds, old tenor.

Item.—I freely give unto my loving son John Leavenworth and to his heirs forever, the equal half of all my land in Woodbury, already laid out and not disposed of and also one third part of all my right in Comonage in said Woodbury after my son Thomas hath had one whole right.

Item.—I freely give unto my loving son Zebulon Leavensworth and unto his heirs forever ye equal half of all my land in Woodbury, already laid out and not disposed of, and also one third part to all my right in Comonage, in Woodbury after my son Thomas hath had one whole right.

Item.—I freely give unto my loving son Thomes Leavensworth and to his heirs forever, one whole right in Comonage at Woodbury, and also one third part of ye remainder of my said right in Comonage in said Woodbury, & also one hundred pounds to be paid him by my Executors, old tenor.

Item.—I freely give and bequeath unto my loving son Mark Leavenworth and to his heirs forever two hundred pounds old tenor to be paid by my Executors, and also my great mare.

Item.—I freely give to my loving daughter Mary Perry, wife to Joseph Perry, (A) one hundred pounds besides what she hath already had, to be paid by my Executors: to be paid in old tenor.

Item.—I freely give unto my loving daughter Hannah Moss, wife to Nichols (B) Moss, besides what she hath already had one hundred pounds old tenor, to be paid by my Executors.

Item.—I freely give unto my loving daughter Sarah Perry, wife to Abner Perry besides what she hath already had, one hundred pounds old tenor, to be paid by my Executors.

Item.—I freely give and bequeath unto my loving son Edmund Leavenworth and to his heirs forever, the whole of my farm House & buildings on said farm where I now live in Stratford, to enjoy ye same immediately after my decease save only ye privilege to my said wife, and also all my right in comonage in Stratford.

Item.—And my will is, and it is to be understood that after all debts, charges & legacies are paid, that my said wife is to have all ye rest and remainder of my Estate both real & personal what is not given away in this my will.

And I do hereby appoint my loving wife Mary Leavensworth and my loving son Edmund Leavensworth to be Executors, ot this my last Will and Testament hereby disallowing & making null & void all other, and former wills by me heretofore made, allowing rattifying, & confirming this & only this to be my last will and testament. In witness whereof I have hereunto set my hand and seal in Stratford, this 6th day of July A. D. 1748.

THOS. LEAVENWORTH. [SEAL.]

(A.) This should read *Joshua* Perry, as in the will. The Recording Clerk made the error.
E. W. L.

(B.) This should have been *Nicholas Moss*. I follow the spelling of the Will.

Signed sealed, published, pronounced and declared by ye said Thos. Leavensworth to be his last will and Testament ye day & date above in presence of us witnesses

Ebenr. Basit
Abram Basit
Saml. Adams

New Haven County St. Derby July ye 15th day 1754.

then personally appeared Messrs. Saml. Adams & Ebenr. Basit two ye witnesses to ye within will & made solemn oath that they see Doctr. Thomas Leavensworth ye within Testator sign & seal ye within written will & heard him declare ye same to be his last will and testament, & yt they signed as witnesses at the same time with Abram Bassit the other witness and that they see the other witness sign, and that they all signed in ye presence of ye testator, and that they judged the testator to be of a sound disposing mind. Sworn before me. Saml. Basit, Justice of the Peace.

From Book dated 1754 *to* 1757—*Page* 41 *to* 44.

Know all Men by these presence yt I Thomas Leavensworth of Stratford, do hereby make & annex this writing as a codicil to ye within will which is my last will & testament, and I do hereby ratify and confirm ye within will to be my last will and testament in every part and paragraph thereof excepting only the Executorship of my son Edmund Leavensworth which part thereof I do hereby disallow & make utterly Null and Void.

In Witness, whereof I have hereunto set my hand and Seal in Stratford this 25th day of July A. D. 1749.

Signed Sealed &c. in presence of
James Shilton THOS. LEAVENWORTH. [l. s.]
Saml. Adams

New Haven County St. Derby July ye 15th day 1754.

Then Personally appeared Messrs. Saml. Adams & James Shilton witnesses to ye above instrument & made solemn Oath that they see Doctr Thos. Leavenworth now dec'd Sign and Seal ye foregoing writing and heard him declare ye same to be a Codicil to ye foregoing Will & that they signed at the same time as witnesses, & that they see each other sign & that they signed in ye presence of ye said Thomas Leavensworth & that they judged the said Leavens' to be of Sound disposing mind.

Sworn before me.—Saml. Basit—Justice of Peace.

A true copy of ye original recorded by David Burr—Clerk.

AT A COURT OF PROBATE HELD IN FAIRFIELD, JUNE 11TH, 1754.

Personally appeared Mary Leavensworth Executrix of the last will and testament of Thos. Leavensworth Late of Stratford dec'd & Exhibited the foregoing will to said Court in order for probation & accepted ye trust Committed to her by ye testator. Said will being proved is by said Court approved and ordered to be recorded.

Test. David Burr, Clerk.

STATE OF CONNECTICUT, }
County of Fairfield. } ss. FAIRFIELD, June 27th, 1870.

[L. S.] I, Rufus Turney, Sole and Presiding Judge of the Court of Probate, within and for the District of Fairfield, in said County of Fairfield, and keeper of the records and seal thereof, hereby certify that the within and foregoing is a true copy of the records.

RUFUS TURNEY, Judge.

The original Will is now (1873) on file in the Probate office of the Fairfield District.

"F."

COPY OF WILL OF JAMES LEAVENWORTH.

In the name of God Amen,—I James Leavensworth of Stratford, being weak of body but through ye goodness of God, of sound mind and memory, thanks be to God therefor, think it best at this time to make this my last will and testament. And first of all I recommend my soul into ye hands of God who gave it hoping yt thro' the merits and intercession of Jesus Christ, to find pardon and acceptance and my body to return to the dust from whence it was taken, to be decently buried at the discretion of my Execr hereafter named and as touching what worldey goods it hath pleased ye Lord to bless me with in this life, I freely give and dispose of the same as followeth.

Impr.—My will is yt all my just debts & funeral expenses shall be first paid out of my moveable Estate.

Item.—I freely give to my loving wife Easter Leavensworth the one half of my moveable Estate, Excepting my Negro boy—after my debts & funeral charges are paid, to be at her own disposal forever and also the use and improvement of all my dwelling house—Except what I, have given to my son by deed with liberty of using ye well & one third part of my barn, and also one third part of my Orchard and all my other lands, ye use of my of ye said Real estate as aforesaid, to remain so long as she shall remain my widow, and at all times in her widowhood state during her natural life.

Item.—I freely give and bequeath unto my loving daughter Mehetible Wetmore and to her heirs forever besides what she hath already had: twelve acres of land lying southward of blanket meadow, which I purchased of Yelverton Perry the southeast corner, bounds of s'd piece land is a white Oak pole marked 4. P. being the whole of yt piece—and also ten acres off, at the southeasterly end of a sixteen acre piece of land in Burritts Rocks, and also forty pounds, old tenor—which I have a bond for of her husband.

Item.—I give and bequeath unto my loving daughter Tamar Hurd & to her heirs forever, besides what she hath already had—Thirty acres of land south of Blanket Meadow to be taken off at the south end of a piece of land containing forty seven acres and to run across Wolf swamp brook.

Item.—I freely give and bequeath unto my two loving sons Saml. & Daniel Leavensworth, and to their heirs forever besides what I have already given them by deed ye whole of my land at Blanket Meadow, which I purchased of Yelverton Perry Except what I have, and shall otherwise particularly dispose of by this will, and also seventy acres and half of land which is bounded easterly on ye said Saml. & Daniels land where they now dwell, to be equally divided between them, and also a six acre Right, in Commons in Stratford, to be divided as aforesaid between them.

Item.—I freely give and bequeath unto my loving daughter Ann Lake, and unto her heirs & forever—five acres be it more or less adjoining to the land I sold to Jabez Lake, and also five acres more of leand at blanket Meadow, bounded Easterly on land I Bought of Yelverton Perry and also six acres of land in Burretts Rocks at the North end of a piece of sixteen acres adjoining Southward on land given to Mehetible.

Item.—I freely give & bequeath unto my two loving daughters, Mary & Easter Leavensworth and to their heirs forever, to be equally divided between them my lot of land Northward from my dwelling house containing about fifty-three acres & is my Northermost piece of land, and also ten acres of land adjoining Westerly on the said fifty-three ac.es, and also Seventeen acres of land South of the blanket meadow at the Northward End of a forty-seven acre piece—and bounded Southwardly on part of the same Lot given Tamar, and also one other piece of land being about sixteen acres Lying southward of the brushy-hill so called, all ye sd pieces to be equally divided between them.

Item.—I freely give and bequeath unto my loving son James Leavensworth, and unto his heirs forever all my old farm where I now live, and all the buildings thereon, after ye use of my wife ends—and also all the several parcels of land yt I have laid out adjoining to said old farm—not herein disposed of,—and also my negro boy called Jeffery—and also my long gun & sword, and also six sheep, and also one Mare, and one Cow which he has already received, and the increase which has been raised from them since they was his, and also a pr of Steers three years old past, called his, and also a three acre right in Commons in sd Stratford.

Item.—I freely give and bequeath unto my three daughters, viz: Ann, Mary and Easter, ye remaining part of my moveable estate not yet disposed of to be equally divided between them, reckoning & computing what my daughter Ann hath already had towards her part being things towards set out her house.

Item.—I give and bequeath unto my three sons viz: Sam'l Daniel and James Leavensworth,—and also my five viz: Mehetable—Tamar—Ann—Mary & Easter—& to her heirs to be equally divided between all my children—sons & daughters, all my lands rights of land yt I have or hereafter shall have or yt shall come to me or after my decease at or near the susquehannah, by virtue of a purchase I have already made Each of them to bear their equal proportion of future charge yt shall arise about the same.

And I do hereby constitute & appoint my loving wife Easter Leavensworth —and my son Saml Leavensworth to be Executors of this my last will and testament—hereby disallowing & making null & void all former wills by me heretofore made, ratifying & confirming this and this only to be my last will and testament. In witness whereof I have hereunto set my hand & seal this 1st day August A. D. 1759.

Signed sealed published and declared by the sd James Leavensworth to be his last will and testament—

JAMES LEAVENWORTH. [L. S.]

DANIEL SHELTON
ESTHER SHELTON
SAMUEL ADAMS

From Book Dated 1761 *to* 1763—*Page* 465 *to* 468.

FAIRFIELD COUNTY—SS. STRATFORD April 25th 1763.

Then personally appeared Daniel Shelton one of the witnesses to the foregoing will and made solemn Oath yt according to the best of his remembrance he saw Mr. James Leavensworth ye testator, Sign & Seal ye foregoing will and heard him declare ye same to be his last will and testament, & yt he signed as witness at ye same time with the other witnesses and that he see the other witnesses sign as witnesses and yt they all signed in the presence of the testator and yt he judged ye testator to be of sound disposing mind.

Sworn before me—SAML. ADAMS—Justice of Peace.

FAIRFIELD COUNTY—SS. STRATFORD June 17th A. D. 1763.

Then personally appeared Samuel Adams one of the witnesses to ye foregoing Will and made Solemn Oath yt he see James Leavensworth ye testator sign and seal ye foregoing Will and heard him declare ye same to be his last will and testament and yt he signed as witness to said will at ye same time and yt he see ye other witnesses sign as witness and yt they all signed in the presence of ye testator and yt he judged ye testator to be of sound disposing mind.

Sworn before me ICHABOD LEWIS, Judge.

Copy by Rufus Turney, Judge of Probate for District of Fairfield, June 27, 1870.

"G."

TITLES OF BOOKS EXAMINED FOR NAME OF LEAVENWORTH.

FAMILY GENEALOGIES CONSULTED.

Abbott Family, by Revs. Abiel & Ephraim Abbott
Adams, (of Kingston, Mass.) by George Adams
Adam, by William Adam
Alden, by Ebenezer Alden
Allen, by Joseph Allen
Angell, by Avery H. Angell
Bellows, by Henry W. Bellows
Benedict,
Bergen, by Tunis G. Bergen
Bill, by Ledyard Bill
Bird,
Bissell,
Blake, by Samuel Blake
Bolling, by Robert Bolling
Brainerd, by Dudley D. Field
Bradford, by William Merwin and Guy M. Fessenden
Brattle, by Edward D. Harris
Bright, by J. B. Bright
Burgess,
Brown, I.
Buckingham, by Rev. H. W. Chapman.
Burke and Alvord Memorial
Burke, by John Alonzo Boutelle
Burnham, by Roderick H. Burnham
Capron Family, by Fred. A. Holden
Chapin, by Orange Chapin
Chapman, by F. W. Chapman
Chase, by George B. Chase
Chauncey, by W. C. Fowler
Checkley,
Clarke, Thomas, by Samuel C. Clarke
Clark, Hugh, by John Clark
Coe.
Coffin,
Cole, by James Edward Cole
Coleman,
Comberbach, by George W. Marshall
Cushman, by Henry W. Cushman
Cutter, by Abner Morse
Davenport, by A. D. Davenport
Day Family, by Robt. A. Day
Dinsmore,
Drake.
Dudley, by Dean Dudley
Dunnell and Dwinnell,
Dumaresq,
Eliot, by Wm. H. Eliot and Wm. S. Porter
Fairfax, by E. D. Neill
Fiske, by Albert A. Fiske
Fiske, by Wm. Fiske, (sen.)
Flint, by John Flint and John H. Stone
Foote, by Nathaniel Goodman
Gale, by George Gale
Gilman, by John Gilman
Gilman, by Arthur Gilman
Glover,
Goddard, by William A. Goddard
Grant, by E. C. Marshall
Greenleaf, by Jonathan Greenleaf
Guild, Calvin Guild
Halleck,
Haven,
Harris, by Luther M. Harris
Hastings,
Hayden,
Herrick, by Jedediah Herrick
Hodge, by Almon D. Hodge
Holt, by Daniel S. Durrie
Hotchkiss Ancestry, by L. Chester
Hoyt Family, by David W. Hoyt
Hull, R. descendants, 1869
Hunt, by F. B. Wyman
Huntington, by Rev. E. B. Huntington
Hyde, by Reuben H. Walworth
Janes, by Frederick Janes
Judd, by Sylvester Judd
Kellogg,
Kilbourn, by Payne K. Kilbourn

FAMILY GENEALOGIES CONSULTED.

Lane, Regner and Whipple, by W. H. Whitmon
Lathrop Family,
Lawrence,
Lawrence, by Thomas Lawrence
Lawrence, John,
Lee, of Virginia, by Edward C. Mead
Leland, by Sherman Leland
Leonard, by William R. Deane
Leverett,
Loch, William, by John G. Loch
McKinstry, by William Willis
Macy, by S. J. Macy
Mather, contained facts relating to immediate family of E. W. L.
Marvin, by T. R. Marvin
Messinger, by George W. Messinger
Minshall,
Montgomery, by T. H Montgomery
Moody, by C. C. P. Moody
Morgan, N. H. Morgan
Mudge, by Alfred Mudge
Nash, by Sylvester Nash
Olcott, by Nathaniel Goodwin
O mstead, by E. L. Thomas
Otis, by Horatio N. Otis
Oxnard, by N. Preble
Peabody, by B. P. Peabody
Peck, 1868
Phelps, by D. S. Phelps
Pope, by William Pope
Pratt, by V. W. Rhapman
Pratt, Zadock,
Prentiss, by C. J. F. Binney
Preston, by Orlando Brown
Quincy,
Rawson, by S. S. Rawson
Redfield, by J. H. Redfield
Redfield, (of U. S.) by W. C. Redfield
Reed, by J. W. Reed
Rice, by A. H. Ward
Richards, by Abner Morse
Ripley, by H. W. Ripley
Rockwood, by E. L Rockwood
Salkeld,
Sanborn, by Nathan Sanborn
Sawin, by T. E. Sawin
Sevanton, by Rev. E. Sevanton
Sigourney, by H. W. H. Sigourney
Shattuck, by Lemuel Shattuck
Sill,
Slafter, E. F. Slafter
Smith, Nathaniel, H. D. Smith
Spotswood, by Charles Campbell
Sprague, by Richard Soule, Jr
Steele, by Daniel S. Durrie
Stetson, by J. S. Barry
Stickney, by Mathew H. Stickney
Stiles, by H. R. Stiles
Stoddard,
Stranahan, Josslyn, Fitch and Dow
Sumner, by H. H Sumner
Sutton,
Toynter, by D. W. Toynter
Thurston, by Charles M. Thurston
Todd, by R. H. Greene
Townsend,
Turner, by Jacob Turner
Van Brunt, by G. Bergen Tnuis
Vassalls, by E. D. Harris
Vinton, by J. A. Vinton
Waldo,
Walker, by J. B. R. Walker
Ward, by A. H. Ward
Wetmore, by J. C. Wetmore
White, by A. S. Kellogg
Wright, by D. P. White
Willard, by Joseph Willard
Williams, by S. W. Williams
Worcester, by J. F. Worcester
Wynkoop, by Richard Wynkoop
Yale, by Elihu Yale.

COLLECTIONS OF MORE GENERAL NATURE, AND THOSE EMBRACING SEVERAL FAMILIES.

Abbott's General Register
Acta Dominorum Concilii, 1 vol
Acta Dominorum Auditorium
Andrews' Genealogical and Ecclesiastical History
Andrews' New Britain
Arthur on Family Names
Bettz's Order of the Garter
Bond's Genealogies of Watertown, Mass.
Bowdich's Suffolk Surnames
Bridges' Index to Printed Pedigrees in County and Town Histories
Bright's [The] of Suffolk, England
Broussant, [Henry] History of Waterbury, Conn., 1 vol
Burke's History of Commoners
" Dict. of the Landed Gentry, 2 vols., with Supplement and 3 Indexes
" Peerage and Baronetage
" General Armory
Calendar of Proceedings in Chancery
Calendarium Rotulorum Patentium, 1 vol
Catalogue of Lownbourne Mss. in Brilst's Museum, 2 vols
Collertanea Typographica a Genealogica, 8 vols
Collins' Peerage, 9 vols
Coleman's General Index to Printed Genealogies
Coleman's Catalogue of Pedigrees, hitherto unindexed
Connecticut Colonial Reviews—1636, 1665, 1678, 1689, 1689, 1705.
Connecticut Public Records, 1665, 1671
" Hist. Soc. Collections, vol 1
Cothren's (Wm.) History of Ancient Woodbury, 1854, 1872, 2 vols.
Davies' Index to American Pedigrees
Delmet's Peerage
Dixon on Surnames
Dodds' (S.) East Haven Register, 1647, 1823
Drake's Founders of New England
Durfees' Biographical Annals of Williams' College
Farmer' Genealogical Register
Ferguson's English Surnames
Flint's (T.) General Register, 1860
Giles' Memorial—Families of Giles, Gould, Holmes, Jennison, Leonard, Lindall, Carmen, Marshall, Robinson, Sampson and Webb, by John Adams Vinton
Goodwin's Genealogical Notes of Connecticut Settlers, 1856
Guild's History of Brown University
Hadley's Families
Hall's (B. H.) Eastern Vermont
Hall's (William) History of Vermont
Heraldic Journal, Boston, vols. 1, 2, 3, 4,—1865, 1864
Hinman's First Settlers of Connecticut
Hinman's Catalogue of First Puritan Settlers of Connecticut
Holgate's American Genealogies, 1848
Hollister's History of Pawlett
Index to Gentleman's Magazine, 2 vols —names
Lodge's Peerage of the British Empire
Lowe's English Surnames, 1842
Lowe's Patronymica Britannica
Merrimack Valley Hist. and General Register
Moore's Genealogical Register of Several Eminent Families, vols. 1, 2
New Haven Hist. Soc. Papers, vol. 1
New England Hist. and Gen. Register, 21 vols
Nichols' Historic Peerage of England
Nichols' "What's in a Name."
Notitia Anglicana, 2 vols
O'Reilly's Rochester
Savage's (J) General Dict. 1860–2, 4 vols
Shirley's Noble Gentlemen of England
Sims' Index to Pedigrees in Herald's Veritativery, British Museum
Sims' Genealogists Manual, 1856
Southold, N. Y.—Index to Town Record of
Stickney's Family Genealogy
Stiles' Ancient Windsor, supplement
Topographic Genealogist, 3 vols
Thayer's Family Memorial of fourteen families
Townsend's Calendar of Knights
Weaver's Ancient Windham, part 1
Whitmore's Handbook of American Genealogy
Whitmore's American Genealogist.

VOLUMES OF THE ENGLISH RECORDS COMMISSION.

Rotulorum Originalium in Curia Scaccarii, Abbreviatio, 3 vols, folio
Documents Illstrative of English History, 13 and 14 contain 1 vol
Taxatio Ecclesiastica Angliæ et Walliæ
Rotuli Scotiæ in Turris Londonensis et in domo Capitulari Westmonasteriensis Asservati, 2 vols
Rotuli Literarum Patentium in Turri Londonensi Asservati, 1 vol
Testa de Nevili Cive Liber Feodarum in Curia Scaccarii, 1 vol
Rotuli Hundredorum (Henry 3 and Edward 1st) 2 vols
Rotuli Literarum Clausarum—in Turri Londonensi Asservati, 2 vols
Registrum Magni Sigilln Regum Scotorum, 1 vol
Record of Caernarvon, 1 vol
Placitorum in domo capitulari Westmonasterense Abbreviatio, 1 vol
Parliamentary Writs, 4 vols
Novarum Inquisitiones in Curia Scaccarii, Cir. 1341—in
Inquisitionum in Capellam Domini Reis Retornatorum Abbreviatio, 2 vols
Foedera, 6 vols
Ducatus Lancastriæ Calendarium Inquisitionum, 3 vols
Catalogue of Harleian Mss., 4 vols
Catalogue of Mss. in Cottonian Library 2 xols
Calendarium Inquisitionum post mortem, &c., 4 vols

TRIENNIAL COLLEGE CATALOGUES.

Amherst, 18 3.
Bowdoin, 1867.
Brown, 1866.
College of Pharmacy & Surgery, N. Y. 1865.
Columbia, 1864.
Dartmouth, 1864.
Hamilton, 1862.
Harvard, 1866.
Hobart Free, 1856.
Union, 1868.
University of Vermont, 1861.
Williams, 1865.
Yale, 1865.

DIRECTORIES.

Albany, 1870, &c., &c.
Bailtimore, 1867-8.
Beverly,
Boston, various years.
Buffalo, 1865.
Fall River,
Hartford, 1863.
Hudson, 1862-3.
Indianapolis, 1855-60.
Jersey City, 1859.
Kingston and Rondout, 1858.
Nashville, 1860-1.
Newbury, 1856-7.
Newburyport, 1860.
New York, many years.
Louisville, 1855-6.
Lynn,
Madison, 1855.
Marblehead,
Middletown, 1857-8.
Montreal, 1852-3.
New Albany, 1856-7.
Newport, 1858.
Norwich, 1857.
New Orleans, 1855.
Oswego, 1866.
Patterson, 1857.
Philadelphia
Pawtucket and Woonsocket, 1857-8.
Poughkeepsie, 1856-62-3.
Providence. 1867.
Quebec, 1852-3.
Richmond, 1856.
Roxbury, 1864.
Rutland, 1867.
Salem, 1859.
Schenectady, 1867-8.
Trenton, 1857.

"H."

PROFESSOR JAMES HALL'S LETTER.

ALBANY, Feb. 24th, 1874.

HON. E. W. LEAVENWORTH:

My Dear Sir :—I have received your favor of the 23d. I can readily give you the information you desire. When you were elected Secretary of State, or at least, when I became acquainted with you, I had already given five years of my life to the work for which I had received no compensation from the State. My services were coming to a close, because I had spent nearly everything I possessed in carrying on the work, previously and during these five years I had gone on, making my collections of fossils throughout the State and beyond its limits, paying assistants and draughtsmen, and incurring other expenses. I had sold nearly everything in the shape of property, and I had before been possessed of a considerable amount, and I had mortgaged the last, the place on which I was then and still am living. Under these circumstances, it seemed about time that my services to New York should come to a close.

I had accepted the offer of a position in the Geological Survey of Canada, and had returned to Albany to close my affairs here before removing to Montreal, where I had left directions that a house should be rented for me.

You can readily find this statement to be true, I think, so far as data can be had from Legislative documents, but it will be seen that money due me in 1850 for services of 1849, was not paid till 1851, or something of this kind. I know it remained due for more than a year before being paid.

Had your action in 1855 been deferred for two or three months longer, the New York Palæontology would have been ended with Vol. II, and I should long since have been a subject of Queen Victoria, and would have lived in much more peace than I have done since, and woutd now have been the Government Geologist of the Dominion, extending from the Atlantic to the Pacific.

Your action extended the time, and was the means of completing Vols. III and IV, and the MS. for Vol. V, which was deposited with Dr. Woolworth, in 1866.

The old contract for engraving became profitless from increase of prices during the war, and owing to this fact no progress was made for several years. In fact, it was only in December, 1871, that the contract was modified so that Mr. Van Benthuysen was willing to go on at all.

I have to-day lettered plates 77 and 78 of Lithographed plates for Vol. V, and have drawings ready for more than 100 plates beyond.

The Appropriation bill has come from the House with everything relating to the Palæontology left out, and to-morrow I go before the Finance Committee of the Senate, to learn what they will do.

My health is not good, my nervous energies are prostrated. I am sleepless and wretched, and I do not think I shall contend very hard against closing the work at an early day. I have been working hard for forty years, and the nervous force expended on my scientific investigations has been less than half what I have wasted in contending for the privilege of working.

I am indebted to you for a few quiet years, but some one more wise than his generation was generally found to raise his voice in the Legislature and propose stopping the work, and then I must see Committees and *lobby* with the Legislature. I have wasted in this way much time and energy. I have made some pleasant acquaintances, and have learned a little of human nature.

My duties at the Museum these last years have been a severe tax upon me in every way, and have caused too much neglect of my scientific investigations. In trying to do both, I have broken down my strength, and after all this, a few years of neglect or bad administration of the affairs of the Museum may undo all I have done, while had I made and published the results of scientific investigation, *that* would have been a permanent contribution to knowledge which nothing could undo.

I am now at that time of life, and in a condition of health, to need quiet and relief from petty duties while I finish the work, for I am sure no one will take it up if I leave it unfinished. I have every reason to believe that Mr. Wood* is favorably disposed towards the work, but the tendency is to reduce appropriations, and this work is a luxury appreciated by fewer persons than are some other things for which the State makes appropriations.

Should I not have the pleasure of seeing you here soon, I shall send you for examination, a set of the plates that are finished, which I have had set up to show the Committee the progress of the work.

I am, very sincerely, your obedient servant,

JAMES HALL.

"J."

GENEALOGY OF DEACON JOSEPH FORMAN, OF ONONDAGA.

Deacon Joseph Forman, born in New Jersey, (?) July 27, 1752, died at Onondaga Hollow, January 15, 1824. Hannah Ward, born January 19th, 1755, died at Onondaga Hollow, May 24th, 1816. They were married October 24th, 1772, probably in New York. He married (2) Anna Thompson, of New York, about 1820.

Joseph F. was from New Jersey, probably from Monmouth County; of the same family with Major-General Forman, of Revolutionary fame.

He was a merchant of New York at the breaking out of the Revolutionary war—retired to Pleasant Valley, Duchess County; remained there till near the close of the last century: then removed to Troy, where he was a merchant many years; the firm was Forman & Tracy; early in this century, to Onondaga Hollow, Onondaga County, where both he and his wife died and were buried. His second wife survived him some years. He was many years a Deacon in the First Presbyterian Church, at Troy.

CHILDREN.

1. Joshua, born September 6, 1777, at Pleasant Valley, married Margaret Alexander, daughter of Boyd Alexander, Member of Parliament for Glasgow, Scotland, in 1800, at New York.

Children :—

1. Caroline, born in 1802, married Dr. Mather Williams, at Syracuse, lived there many years; died at Norwalk, Ohio, leaving two daughters, 1st. Margaret, who married Dr. John M. Craton, of Rutherfordton, N. C., lives now at Spartanburgh, S. C., and has eight children. 2d. Mary, who married Oscar Kellogg, a lawyer, at Norwalk, Ohio, where they live. She has one child.

---

*The Hon. Daniel P. Wood, Senator from Onondaga and Chairman of the Committee on Finance.

2. Boyd Alexander, born in May, 1805, was an engineer, went with his father to North Carolina, married there, moved to Texas, was engaged in the survey of Government lands, and died early, leaving one daughter, who has married a Mr. Fox.

3. Mary Elizabeth, born May 27th, 1807, married (1st.) in 1824, Hiram Hyde, a forwarder, at Syracuse, who died in 1828; married (2d.) June 21st, 1833, Elias W. Leavenworth, both marriages at Syracuse, where she still lives. No children.

4. Margaret Ann, born in March, 1809, married in 1825, Matthew W. Davis, at Syracuse, son of Matthew L. Davis, of New York, and died at Columbia, S. C., and was buried at Rutherfordton, N. C., about January, 1855, leaving—1, Matthew, who was educated at West Point,—an officer in the Rebel army, and died at Lynchburg, Va., in or about 1862, unmarried; 2, Sarah, who married Edward H. Lane, of the firm of Lane, Boyce & Co., of New York, at Rutherfordton, N. C., lived first at Charleston, then New York. On the breaking out of the Rebellion, went south with her husband and family, and she and her husband died at Orville, near Selma, Ala., in a few months, leaving four children: Matthew D., Mary Jessie, Annie Laurie, and an infant, which soon followed his mother; 3, Forman, who died at Charleston, early in life, while a clerk in the store of the Lane's; 4, Mary, who married in 1861, William V. R. Watson, an officer in the Rebel army, lived many years at Selma, Ala., and is now at Galveston, Texas, and has one daughter, Margaret; 5, John, an engineer, now at the south, unm. The first three born at Syracuse, the rest at Rutherfordton, N. C. Matthew W. Davis died at Rutherfordton some years before his wife.

5. Helen, born in March, 1813, married Elisha Whitney, a merchant at Poughkeepsie, about 1830, where they now live. Children: 1, Forman, a lawyer, in New York, married; 2, James, a carriage maker; 3. Mary, married, and died childless soon after; 4, Henry, who died young; 5, Margaret, who married Ross Leslie, of Syracuse, April 22d, 1868, resides there, and has a daughter, Gracie Whitney, born Jan. 12th, 1871. He is a son of John Leslie, of Syracuse, born there October 30th, 1841.

6. Joseph, the sixth and last child of Joshua Forman and Margaret Alexander, was born in September, 1815,—went to North Carolina with his father, studied medicine at the Medical School, New York, married Martha Breeding, of South Carolina, in or about 1854, had one son, Joshua, born Oct. 10th, 1855, in Transylvana county, N. C., formerly a part of Henderson county. He settled in Hendrson county, was loyal during the Rebellion, was harrassed, imprisoned and driven out of the State, and fled with his wife and child to East Tennessee, and settled in Sweetwater, Cock county, where he now resides. The son is now living at Syracuse, with his uncle, E. W. Leavenworth, and perfecting his education.

The children of Judge Forman were all born at Onondaga Hollow. His wife died at Ten-mile Run, near New Brunswick, New Jersey, in July, 1828. He died at Rutherfordton, N. C., August 4th, 1848. Mr. Clark, in his sketch of Judge Forman, errs in stating that his death was in 1849.

His remains were removed by the author from Rutherfordton, through the kind offices of Dr. John W. Craton, in the spring of 1872, and buried in Oakwood Cemetery, at Syracuse.

2. Elizabeth Forman, second child of Joseph F., born March 2d, 1780, married Oct. 19, 1805, at Onondaga Hollow, Dr. John Devotion Bissell, and she died at Alton, Ill., September, 23, 1838. He was born January 13th, 1782, and died at Chicago, Ill., September 10, 1856. He practiced many years at Geddes, Onondaga county; followed Judge Forman to North Carolina, and moved from there to Illinois.

Children:—

1. Gordon Needham, born Sept. 17, 1806, married Luthera Ward, February 3, 1829, and has children—Mary Luthera, Margaret Ann, Charles Forman, John Gordon, William Ward, Laura Jane, Frances (deceased).

2. Charles Forman, born April 29, 1808, married Annie Beckwith, Oct. 5th, 1840, and has children—Gordon Charles, Ann Eliza.

3. Margaret Ann, born February 3, 1810, married Richard Church in 1832, and has children—Montgomery, Charles, (killed at the siege of Richmond,) William, Elizabeth.

4. Hannah Matilda, born November 16, 1812, married Orrin Cowles in 1843, and died without issue, at Rockford, Ill., March 10, 1857.

5. Jane Elizabeth, born September 3, 1814. married Benjamin Woodworth, November 27, 1839, and has children—Jane Elizabeth, John, Edward.

6. Lucy Jeannette, born June 29, 1816.

7. John Ward, born September, 1818, married Edith H. Jackman, February 19th, 1848; children: Ella, Jeannette.

8. Joseph Ebenezer, born June 7, 1821, married Margaret E. Pearson, in 1850; children: Eva, Edgar, John.

3. Mary Forman, born February 28, 1782, died September 4, 1831, married about 1805, (?) Dr. Gordon Needham, at Onondaga Hollow. He was born in Conn., April 29, 1776. They both lived and died at that place, and without children; he died February 1, 1864, aged 88 years. He first came to Onondaga Hollow in 1795, permanently in 1797.

4. Sally Forman, born June 3d, 1784, married May 17, 1806, William H. Sabine, at Onondaga Hollow, died at the same place, July 11, 1832. William H. S. was born at Pomfret, Conn., January 21, 1779, died Sept. 4th or 11th, 1842, at Syracuse.

Children:—

1. Sarah, born January 17, 1807, married Royal Stewart, July 19 1825, died at Cleveland, Ohio, March 17, 1843, leaving a son and daughter, Ellen and William. Ellen married (1) Henry Pike, had two children, Henry and William; 2, married William H. Dickinson, a lawyer, in New York. William married a daughter of Seth Hutchinson, of Syracuse, and lives at St. Louis, Mo.; has no children.

2. Elizabeth, born September 4, 1808, married John W. Smith, May 10th, 1831, lives at Dubuque, Iowa. They had three children, of whom two are living.

3. William, born Aug. 18, 1810, died Dec. 18, 1812.

4. William, born May 20, 1814, married Anzonette Cotton, Nov. 9, 1840. She was born March 24th, 1819, living at Onondaga Hollow, and has two daughters and one son; 1, Eva, born January 8, 1844; 2, Jessie, born Aug. 7, 1851; 3, Joseph F., born May 1, 1853. Eva married Gen. Clinton D. McDougall, of Auburn, and has three children.

5. Joseph Forman, born May 20, 1814, married Margaret Lawrence, daughter of Gen. James R. Lawrence, February 6, 1840, living at Syracuse, has one daughter, Alice, who married John Magee, (deceased). She was born November 3, 1840.

6. Joshua R., born January 19, 1816, married Lucy Moseley, May 2, 1838, died Aug. 24, 1839. No children.

7. James Harvey, born September 17. 1822, died April 30, 1843. Unmarried.

5. John Forman, born March 26, 1786, married Eliza Sisson, October 19th, 1806, born February 11, 1789. He died September 17, 1852; she died November 4, 1862, both at Onondaga Hollow.

Children :—

1. Delia A. Forman, born December, 16, 1807.
2. Joshua Forman, born January 29th, 1809, died January 1st, 1810.
3. Caroline Amelia, born September 10th, 1811, died September 10th, 1811.
4. Julia Elizabeth, born October 16th, 1812, died September 28th, 1814.
5. William, born May 22d, 1815, died June 15th, 1815.
6. Hannah Maria, born July 13th, 1816.
7. Harriet Elizabeth, born May 22d, 1819.
8. Sarah Caroline, born February 19th, 1822, } died November 16th, 1838.
9. Sophia Catherine, born " " " } twins.
10. Julia Adeline, born Feb. 4th, 1824, died March 18th, 1825.
11. John Joseph, born Sept. 13th, 1827, died February 15th, 1831.
12. James Sisson, born February 15th, 1830, died February 17th, 1831.
13. John Edward, born October 23d, 1832.
14. Charles Henry, b. April 26th, 1835, married and died a few years since.

Married :—

Delia A. with Richard Woolworth, October 23, 1831; children, Mary E., Frances J., Louisa.

Hannah M., with Lemuel Clift, October 12th, 1840; children, Joseph F., Eliza, Frank Dains.

Harriett E., with Norman Rude, October 12th, 1840; child, Sarah H.

Sophia C., with Wm. P. Forman, January 18th, 1847; no children.

Charles H., to Harret Lyman, April 9th, 1856; no children.

John E., to Laura C. Wells, June 13th, 1866; children, Mary S.

6. Samuel Forman, born April 27th, 1788, married Dec. 27, 1812, Sophia Hooker, died at Onondaga Hollow, some 30 years since; she died before her husband.

Children :—

1. Eugene, born September 25th, 1813, married Mrs. Elizabeth W. Turner, daughter of Hon. Daniel Moseley, January 20, 1858.

2. William Pitt, born May 27, 1816, married his cousin, Sophia Forman. Father and sons, lawyers; Samuel and William P., at Onondaga Hollow, and Eugene at Syracuse.

7. Nancy Forman, born November 3, 1790, died early.

8. Catharine Forman, born September 18, 1792, died January 8, 1795.

9. Ann Forman, born November 6, 1794, married April 25, 1811, James Lyon, at Onondaga Hollow. James Lyon, born April 12, 1787, at Northumberland, Penn. Lived some years at Oswego Falls, as a forwarder, before the Oswego Canal was built, and about the time of its construction removed to Oswego, and was many years engaged in the forwarding business with the late Henry Fitzhugh. He died August 28, 1851. He was one of nature's noblemen.

Children :—

1. Joseph Benjamin; born March 3, 1812, at Onondaga Furnace, married Miss Terry, of Geddes, N. Y., no children, and died at Cleveland, O., a few years since, and his wife some years earlier.

2. John Edward, born June 18, 1813, at Onondaga, married Catharine M. Tracy, at Utica. September 6, 1836. Resides at Oswego, is a miller. firm, Penfield, Lyon & Co. Has a large family of children.

3. Mary Elizabeth Lyon, born December 24, 1314, married (1) September 12, 1838, at Oswego, Col. Theophilus Morgan; married (2) Col. Whittlesy. They reside at Cleveland, Ohio. Had one son, James, by Col. M., who was an officer under General Sherman, and killed between Atlanta and Savannah.

4. James Henry, born April 6, 1817, married February 23, 1846, Mary Ann Mahoney, at Oswego. Live at Chicago, and have three daughters.

5. Margaret Ann, born August 29, 1822, married September 21, 1843, Geo. M. Noxon, of Syracuse, at Oswego. He was a lawyer, resided at Syracuse, and died there some 25 years since, leaving three children, George W., Margaret and Mary.

6. Sophia Forman, born November 11, 1826, died July 15, 1827.

7. Joshua Forman, born June 6, 1830, died April 12, 1856, unmarried.

The last five children of James Lyon were born at Oswego Falls. Mrs. Lyon is still alive, living with her daughter, Mary,—Mrs. Col. Whittlesey, at Cleveland, Ohio.

10. Daniel W. Forman, born April 26, 1796, married February 15, 1820, Elizabeth Bliss, of Springfield, Mass., born July 27, 1799.

Children :—

1. Catharine Elizabeth, born October 30, 1820, married Charles E. Woolsey, January 5th, 1843. Resides at Winona, Wis.; no children. He died there in 1873.

2. Ann Williams, born May 22d, 1823, married Samuel M. Robinson, of Watertown, January 1, 1846, died August 21, 1849; Children: Anna Elizabeth, born August 20th, 1849, married Samuel B. Bliss, November 10, 1870.

3. Margaret Bliss, born May 21, 1825.

4 Frances Adams, born March 5, 1827, married October 12, 1847, Coles Bashford, of Clyde, N. Y., who was born January 24, 1816; children: 1, Lizzie Frances, born Dec. 28, 1848; 2, Maggie Forman, born June 8, 1851; 3, Wm. Coles, born April 5th, 1853; 4, Helen Louise, born Jan. 28, 1855; 5, Mary Isabella, born July 10, 1857, died May 31, 1868: 6, Lillian Estelle, born July 13, 1862; 7, Edward Levi, born May 15, 1869.

5. Alexander Henry, born February 24, 1832

6. Mary Ward, born March 13, 1835, died May 26, 1839,

7. Lucy Myrtis, born April 23, 1838, died June 11, 1839.

8. Edward Bayard, born March 24, 1842.

Daniel W. Forman died by a razor in his own hand, at Watertown, N. Y., August 1, 1850, while suffering from religious insanity. He was an able lawyer, and a most worthy and excellent citizen. He lived at Onondaga Hollow till after 1830, then removed to Seneca Falls, and near the close of his life to Watertown, N. Y.

11. Owen Forman, born Nov. 13, 1797, married (1) Nancy Giddings, of Springport, Cayuga county, She was a niece of Solomon Southwick; and on her death he married (2) Maria Canfield, of Syracuse, by whom he had one son. Owen F. died in July or August, 1831, while engaged in surveying, engineering, &c., at Rutherfordton. The son died unmarried, some years later.

Index to Subjects.

Index to Leavenworths.

Index to Other Names.

NOTE.—The number of times any name is repeated on any one of the foregoing pages, (whether it be a repetition of the name of one person or of different persons bearing the same name,) is designated in the following index by a figure immediately following every name so repeated. Where a person's name occurs on different pages, each page is given.

ERRATA AND ADDENDA.

I confess myself greatly surprised and mortified by the number of errata which a very careful review of my whole work has brought to light. Some have arisen from errors in the original manuscript, far more from carelessness in correcting proofs and not a few from the neglect of the printers.

My mortification would be greater than it is, had I not discovered—greatly to my surprise—many more errors per page in the only two Genealogies which I have critically examined, and that none of them are referred to in the errata of the respective works. And yet these works were compiled with unusual labor and care.

Its length too has been materially increased by additions and explanations, and also by correction of errors not very material.

I hope the great body of errors are embraced below, and that all persons who take an interest in the work, will, pen in hand, proceed to correct them before giving it a farther examination. With all its errors and imperfections I now commit it to the hands of the family, most sincerely thankful and happy that its slow and tedious length has finally been drawn to a close this first day of May, 1874.

E. W. LEAVENWORTH.

7th page, 6th line from the bottom, for Mills read Hills.

8th page, 15th line from the top, for Edwin read Edgar.

13th page, 7th line from the top, for containing read contain.

16th page, 13th line from the bottom, the exact words were lost, but the substance was found.

17th page, 17th line from the bottom, for of read or.

18th page, 11th line from the top, insert Asa before another.

18th page, 13th line from the top, for this read his.

19th page, 1st line, for Edwin read Edgar.

19th page, 2d line from the top, for Melinus read Melines.

20th page, 11th line from the top, for 1629 read 1729.

20th page, 29th line from the top, for 1629 read 1664.

21st page, 10th line from the top, fill the blank with (C.)

22d page, 21st line from the top, after unmarried add "and Col. Jesse H., of Milwaukie."

42d page, 12th line from the bottom, for 1755 read 1735.

46th page, first line, for 4 read 14.

47th page, last line, for 1784-5 read 1783.

48th page, 3d line from the top, for 1821 read 1802.

49th page, 7th line from the bottom, for 1802 read 1812.

50th page, 16th line from the top, for £100 read £150.

52d page, 6th line from the bottom, for b read bap.

52d page, 7th line from the bottom, for 1849 read 1850.

52d page, 11th line from the bottom, for David read Jared.

54th page, 23d line from the bottom, put 4 before David.

55th page, 26th line from the top, for Mass., read Conn.

56th page, 21st line from the bottom, for 1 before Catharine read 2.
57th page, first line, put 7 before Jerusha.
66th page, 26th line from the top, for Thomas B. read Horace B.
68th page, last line, add, "they were examined in 1874."
69th page, after children, 15th line add, Eunice died in 1865.
69th page, 19th line from the bottom, for Jonah read Josiah,
72d page, 27th line from the bottom, for June read January.
77th page, 17th line from the top, for 28th read 17th.
79th page, 7th line from the bottom, for Alvah read Abiah.
80th page, bottom line, for 1764 read 1765. This is the date given by his daughter, Mrs. Wilson.
80th page, 6th line from the bottom, for 1809 read 1804.
81st page, 11th line from the top, for 19 read 14.
81st page, 15th line from the top, for Azulah read Azubah.
81st page, 18th line from the top, for 1638 read 1738.
81st page, 11th line from the bottom, for bap, read b.
82d page, 22d line from the top, for 1684 read 1784.
84th page. The sketch of the Hon. Truman Smith was kindly furnished by C. F. Sedgwick, Esq., of Sharon, Conn.
89th page, 6th line from the top, for 1840 read 1845.
89th page, 20th line from the top, strike out "d. unmarried."
90th page, 11th line from the top, for 1800 read 1801.
90th page, 25th line from the top, for 1847 read 1747.
91st page, 3d line from the top, strike out "d. at Leavenworth, Ind., in 1832."
91st page, 12th line from the top, add "m. Israel Beach, July 3, 1783."
91st page, 18th line from the top, for 1766 read 1761.
91st page, 20th line from the top, for 1740 read 1741.
91st page, 21st line from the top, for 1784 read 1759.
91st page, 30th line from the top, after "family" add:—This is the date of death of his first wife.
96th page, 8th line from the top, for 187 read 153.
96th page, 19th line from the bottom, put 1 before Henry. B. F.
96th page, 18th line from the bottom, for 2836 read 1836.
97th page, 12th line from the top, for 1815 read 1814.
99th page, 6th line from the top, for April 6 read April 30.
99th page, 7th line from the top, for Nov. 19, 1862, read Dec. 19, 1861.
99th page, 9 lines from the top, for 1780 read 1781.
101st page, top line, for 27 read 28.
105th page, 17th line from the top, for 27, 1821, read 21, 1827.
107th page, 11th line from the top, for 1868-9 read 1768-9.
108th page, Nos. 3, 4, 5, 6, 7 and 8, from Nicholas W. to John, inclusive, are the children of Annie Maria Hubbell, No. 6.
113th page, 12th line from the top, for quiet read quick.
118th page, after married, 9th line from the top, add d. at Hinesburgh, Feb. 21, 1873.
120th page, 2d line from the bottom, for March 17, 1780, read March 16, 1781.
121st page, 4th line from the top. His children differ on date of death.
122d page, bottom line, for 1830 read 1826.
123d page, bottom line, for Feb. 25, 1869, read June 17, 1868.
124th page, 2d line from the top, for Feb. 25, 1869, read June 17, 1868.
124th page, 4th line from the bottom, for 15 read 16,
124th page, 13th line from the bottom, for born read bap.
124th page, 11th line from the bottom, for Whitmore read Whitman.
125th page, 8th line from the top, for April 7 read Sept. 15.
127th page, No. 281. I received a letter from her Jan. 10, 1867. The date of her death is from her sister Emeline.
128th page, 5th line from the top, for Jaques read Jaggers.
128th page, 6th line from the top, for Feb. 22, 1853, read Feb. 22, 1854?
128th page, 7th line from the top, for 1855 read 1859.
128th page, 26th and 27th lines from the top, for Jan. 11, 1872, read Dec, 12, 1872.

128th page, 27th line from the top, after daughter insert Mary Leavenworth.
128th page, 3d line from the bottom, for 1869 read 1849.
128th page, 4th line from the bottom, for 1857 read 1851.
128th page, 8th line from the bottom, for 1835 read 1838.
128th page, 12th line from the bottom, insert 4 before George and 5 before Amarillis.
129th page, 14th line from the top, for 1827 read 1829.
132d page, 10th line from the bottom, for 1825 read 1865.
137th page, 20th line from the top, for 1865 read 1866.
141st page, 2d line from the top, for country read county.
142d page, 1st line, for 25 read 27.
142d page, 7th line from the top, for Nov. 7 read Nov. 5.
142d page, 13th line from the top, for 18 4 read 1854.
143d page, 7th line from the top, for 1855 read 1825.
144th page, 4th line from the top, for 1864 read 1865.
148th page, 15th line from the top, for Nov. 18 read Nov. 20.
154th page, 2d line from the bottom, for Cockran read Cochran.
155th page, 14th line from the top, for d. read b.
159th page, 16th line from the top, for April 39 read April 30.
159th page, 15th line from the bottom, for April 25 read April 28.
163d page, 16th line from the bottom, for 1863 read 1864.
164th page, 20th line from the top. This date of birth is given by her son Jared L.
173d page, 6th line from the top, add Dec. 9, 1856.
181st page, 8th line from the top, for 3 read 23.
183d page, 28th line from the top, for 19 read 12.
184th page, 16th line from the top, for 21 read 14.
184th page, bottom line, for 25 read 24.
185th page, 23d line from the top, for 1833 read 1835.
189th page, 4th line from the bottom, for Popham read Nassau.
190th page, 11th line from the bottom, for Lucinda read Lucenia.
190th page, 6th line from the top, for 1780 read 1781.
190th page, 11th line from the top, for 1825 read 1823.
190th page, 26th line from the top, for 1856 read 1866.
191st page, 5th line from the bottom, for 1783 read 1782.
191st page, 24th line from the bottom, for July 8 read July 9.
192d page, 5th line from the top, for 1810 read 1816.
196th page, 9th line from the bottom, for 28 read 12.
196th page, 16th line from the bottom, for 248 read 249.
198th page, 2d line from the bottom, for 15 read 14.
198th page, 6th line from the bottom, for March 17, 1851, read Sept. 5, 1850.
198th page, 7th line from the bottom, for Henry M. read Henry B.
200th page, 9th line from the bottom, omit A. before James M.
202d page, 10th line from the top, for Morse read David.
204th page, 14th line from the top, after 1825 insert, at Woodbury.
207th page, 22d line from the top, for April 18, 1840, read Aug. 7. 1839.
210th page, 12th line from the bottom, for 1854 read 1824.
213th page, 13th line from the bottom, for 1824 read 1825.
214th page, 12th line from the bottom, for June read January.
216th page, 12th line from the top. 1840 is an error, but I cannot explain it.
217th page, 14th line from the top. 308 was bap. as Martha Ann Helen, but early in life dropped "Martha Ann."
217th page, 5th line from the bottom, for 1852 read 1862.
226th page, 6th line from the top, for Jan. 57 read Jan. 5,
226th page, 13th line from the bottom, for 22 read 29.
229th page. The following should have followed the 17th line from the top;

DEATH OF DOCTOR M. C. LEAVENWORTH.

It is with no ordinary emotions of sadness that we record the death of this worthy man and physician, which took place in the hospital at New Orleans, on the 20th of November last, in the 67th year of his age. The Doctor was attached to the Twelfth Regiment C. V., Col. Deming, as First Assistant Surgeon, and accompanied that regiment first to Ship Island, then to New Orleans, in Gen. Butler's expedition, where he was stationed at the time of his death. Up to a few days before his death his health had been uncommonly good, having never lost a day while attending to his professional duties. He often communicated with his relatives and friends at home, seemed in the best of spirits and having been used to the climate in early life, entertained few fears that stood in the way of his ultimate return. He was not, it seems, in Gen. Weitzel's expedition, having been appointed Superintendent of the Hospital for Contrabands, recently established, where he met his death.

231st page, 21st line from the bottom, for 1858 read 1848.
236th page, 11th line from the bottom, for June 6 read Jan. 6.
237th page, 6th line from the bottom, for 1757 read 1857.
239th page, 7th line from the top, for Jan. 19 read Jan. 15.
239th page, 9th line from the top, for brother read father.
240th page, 9th line from the bottom, for Mr. read Daniel.
241st page, 15th line from the bottom, for Northram read Northam.
243d page, 15th line from the top, strike out which.
243d page, 19th line from the top, for Geneva read Seneca.
243d page, 22d line from the top, for favored read procured.
243d page, 6th line from the bottom, for Commission read Commissioners.
249th page, 28th line from the top, fill blank with $2,000.
250th page, 17th line from the top add: For the report of the Committee see Senate Doc., 1857, vol. 1, No. 8.
256th page, 7th line from the top, strike out the first "to."
264th page, first line, for 1849 read 1848. This note ends with the 4th line.
267th page, 8th line from the bottom, for 21 read 1.
268th page, 13th line from the bottom, for Hobart read Hobart J.
269th page, 4th line from the bottom, for Nov. 9 read Nov. 13.
269th page, 18th line from the bottom, for 1847 read 1846.
270th page, first line, for 1851 read 1857.
273d page, 10th line from the top, for March 16, 1801, at Hamden, read Oct. 18, 1804, at New Haven.
273d page, 18th line from the top, for Oct. 18, 1804, read Jan. 12, 1806.
276th page, 8th line from the bottom, for 388 read 391.
276th page, 19th line from the bottom, for 1853 read 1858.
276th page, 23d line from the bottom, for 1836 read 1839.
277th page, 8th line from the bottom, strike out A. before Philip.
280th page, 3d line from the top, for 1853 read 1864.
282d page, 14th line from the bottom, for Brook read Burk.
283d page, 7th line from the bottom, for January read June.
286th page, last line, for 30 read 3.
294th page, 13th line from the bottom, for 3 read 23.
297th page, 6th line from the top, for Aug. 13 read Aug. 20.
298th page, 3d line from the bottom, insert J. after Elizabeth.
298th page, 20th line from the bottom, for Sept. 4. read Sept. 1.
298th page, 21st line from the bottom, for December read February.
299th page, 8th line from the top, for 696 read 496.
303d page, 11th line from the bottom, for mingling read mingled.
307th page, 9th line from the top, omit D. before Margaret.
310th page, 23d line from the top, for 25 read 23,
311th page, 7th line from the top, for 1849 read 1848.
311th page, 12th line from the top, for June 2, 1839 read May 18, 1828.
311th page, 8th line from the bottom, for 555 read 550.
318th page, 5th line from the bottom, for 1845 read 1859.
320th page, 14th line from the bottom, for 1836 read 1835.
347th page, last line, for son of Asa read son of Ebenezer.
347th page, last line but one, for son of Ebenezer read son of Asa.
351st page, 3d line from the top, for page 295, No. 447, read page 290, No. 702.
351st page, 9th line from the bottom, for Frederick, read Edwin S.

www.ingramcontent.com/pod-product-compliance
Lightning Source LLC
LaVergne TN
LVHW020057110826
845151LV00001B/1

* 9 7 8 1 4 2 5 5 4 5 3 0 7 *